David Feehan, MSW
Marvin D. Feit, PhD
Editors

Making Business Districts Work
Leadership and Management of Downtown, Main Street, Business District, and Community Development Organizations

Pre-publication
REVIEWS,
COMMENTARIES,
EVALUATIONS . . .

"This is a great book for anyone who wants to know what's going on downtown. New business district models are helping make downtowns that had been written off in the 1970s and 1980s into lively places where people want to live, work, and play. This book is full of practical ideas on how to make downtowns work."

Lee W. Munnich, Jr.
Senior Fellow and Director,
State and Local Policy Program,
Humphrey Institute of Public Affairs,
University of Minnesota

"A must-read for anyone interested in grasping current issues, concerns, and nuances in downtown and business management. This sorely needed text fills a distinct void in the literature in an area which many disciplines 'assume' and stake claim to. The book's simplicity, coupled with its comprehensiveness, is indeed impressive. It reads as 'everything you wanted to know about downtown and business management.' I was fascinated by the range of chapters and the appeal to a variety of stakeholder groups. The author threads the central concept of leadership through downtown trends, issues, and realities; their context; implementation concerns; case studies; and an analysis of where this field is going in the future."

Michael J. Holosko, PhD, MSW
Pauline M. Berger Chair,
School of Social Work,
University of Georgia

The Haworth Press®
New York • London • Oxford

Making Business Districts Work

Leadership and Management of Downtown, Main Street, Business District, and Community Development Organizations

HAWORTH Health and Social Policy
Marvin D. Feit, PhD

Maltreatment and the School-Age Child: Developmental Outcomes and Systems Issues by Phyllis T. Howing, John S. Wodarski, P. David Kurtz, and James Martin Gaudin Jr.

Health and Social Policy by Marvin D. Feit and Stanley F. Battle

Adolescent Substance Abuse: An Empirical-Based Group Preventive Health Paradigm by John S. Wodarski and Marvin D. Feit

Long-Term Care: Federal, State, and Private Options for the Future by Raymond O'Brien and Michael Flannery

Health and Poverty by Michael J. Holosko and Marvin D. Feit

Financial Management in Human Services by Marvin Feit and Peter Li

Policy, Program Evaluation, and Research in Disability: Community Support for All by Julie Ann Racino

The Politics of Youth, Sex, and Health Care in American Schools by James W. Button and Barbara A. Rienzo

Race, Politics, and Community Development Funding: The Discolor of Money by Michael Bonds

Changing Welfare Services: Case Studies of Local Welfare Reform Programs edited by Michael J. Austin

Accountability in Social Services: The Culture of the Paper Program by Jill Florence Lackey

Voices of African-American Teen Fathers: "I'm Doing What I Got to Do" by Angelia Paschal

Making Business Districts Work: Leadership and Management of Downtown, Main Street, Business District, and Community Development Organizations edited by David Feehan and Marvin D. Feit

Making Business Districts Work

Leadership and Management of Downtown, Main Street, Business District, and Community Development Organizations

David Feehan, MSW
Marvin D. Feit, PhD
Editors

The Haworth Press®
New York • London • Oxford

For more information on this book or to order, visit
http://www.haworthpress.com/store/product.asp?sku=5137

or call 1-800-HAWORTH (800-429-6784) in the United States and Canada
or (607) 722-5857 outside the United States and Canada

or contact orders@HaworthPress.com

The Haworth Press, Inc., 10 Alice Street, Binghamton, NY 13904-1580.

PUBLISHER'S NOTE
The development, preparation, and publication of this work has been undertaken with great care. However, the Publisher, employees, editors, and agents of The Haworth Press are not responsible for any errors contained herein or for consequences that may ensue from use of materials or information contained in this work. The Haworth Press is committed to the dissemination of ideas and information according to the highest standards of intellectual freedom and the free exchange of ideas. Statements made and opinions expressed in this publication do not necessarily reflect the views of the Publisher, Directors, management, or staff of The Haworth Press, Inc., or an endorsement by them.

Cover design by Jennifer M. Gaska.

Library of Congress Cataloging-in-Publication Data

Making business districts work : leadership and management of downtown, main street, business district, and community development organizations / David Feehan, Marvin D. Feit, editors.
    p. cm.
Includes bibliographical references and index.
ISBN-13: 978-0-7890-2390-2 (hard : alk. paper)
ISBN-10: 0-7890-2390-3 (hard : alk. paper)
ISBN-13: 978-0-7890-2391-9 (soft : alk. paper)
ISBN-10: 0-7890-2391-1 (soft : alk. paper)
    1. Central business districts. 2. Urban renewal. 3. Community development. I. Feehan, David. II. Feit, Marvin D.

HT170.M325 2006
307.76—dc22

                                                                        2005024740

CONTENTS

About the Editors   xvii

Contributors   xix

Introduction   1

**PART I: THE FIELD OF DOWNTOWN AND BUSINESS
DISTRICT MANAGEMENT**   5

Chapter 1. The State of Business District Revitalization   7
   Brad Segal

Chapter 2. Leading the Downtown   11
   Richard Bradley

   A Long History of Leadership   12
   Continuous Demands for Leadership   12
   Leadership As a Collective and Cooperative Undertaking   13
   Leadership As Initiating and Managing Change   13

Chapter 3. The New Role of Downtown Leaders   15
   Richard T. Reinhard

   Comparing Past and Present   15
   Some Specific Causes of Change   15
   Reality of Today   16
   Spectrum of Changes   17
   Conclusion   20

Chapter 4. The Vision-Driven Downtown Organization   23
   David Feehan

   Creating a Shared Vision   23
   The Vision Statement   25
   Past Experience, Future Vision   27

**PART II: ORGANIZING THE DOWNTOWN
CORPORATION**   **33**

Chapter 5. Complex Organizational Structures   **35**
James A. Cloar

Background   35
Simple Structures   36
Evolving Responses   36
Expanded Missions   37
Complex Structure Models   38
Case Study: Downtown St. Louis   38
Points to Consider   41

Chapter 6. Boards and Committees—Governance   **45**
Kate Joncas

Introduction   45
Conflicts of Interest   46
Achieving Consensus   47
Successful Relationships with Organizations   49
Too Many Issues, Too Little Time   51
The New Reality: Local Business Leadership
    Is No Longer Local   53

Chapter 7. Making the Most of Human Resources   **57**
Catherine Coleman

Introduction   57
Who's the Boss?   58
Good Management Begins with Good Employees   58
Motivating Employees and Building the Team   61
Know the Law and Follow the Rules   61
A Bad Apple Can Spoil the Bunch   62
No Need to Reinvent the Wheel   62

**Chapter 8. Financial Management—Keeping
the Numbers Straight**   **65**
Michael Weiss

Getting Started   65
Assessments and Revenue   66
Preparing a Budget   67

Revenue   68
Cash Flow   68
Expenses   68
Financial Records and Reports   69
Expense Monitoring   69
Internal Controls   70
Audits   71
Reporting to Your Board and Others   72
Staffing and Skills Required   72
Conclusion   73

**Chapter 9. Staffing Structure and Compensation
Management   75**
   Dong Soo Kim
   David Feehan
   Sarah Rose

Introduction   75
About the Survey   75
CEO Characteristics   76
Downtown Organizations   76
Compensation   77
Staffing   78
Funding   79
Conclusion   79

**Chapter 10. Resource Raising As a Downtown
Management and Revitalization Strategy   81**
   Tom Verploegen

Quality, Quality, Quality   81
Defining Resource Raising   81
Three Resource-Raising Categories   82
Resource Raising: General Examples   83
Resource Raising: Specific Examples   84
The 5 Ws and H   86
How to Close the Deal   89

PART III: OPERATING IN A COMPLEX ENVIRONMENT   **93**

Chapter 11. Strategic Planning—Charting the Course   **95**
    Sandra Goldstein

Introduction   95
What Is Strategic Planning?   96
What Are the Benefits of Strategic Planning?   96
What Are the Steps in the Strategic Planning Process?   96
How Is a Work Plan Created Through the Strategic
    Planning Process?   98
Where Do You Start?   100
What Is the SWOT Analysis?   100
Outcomes   102
How Is the Work Plan Reinforced?   103
Conclusion   103
Appendix A: Stamford Downtown Special Services
    District   104

**Chapter 12. Diversity: Incorporating and Benefiting
from Differences**   **109**
    Barbara Askins

Introduction   109
What Does Diversity Mean for Downtown Organizations?   110
Benefits of Inclusion   111
Tools and Strategies   112
Goals and Objectives   112
Actions of the Board of Directors   113
Moving into the Future   114

Chapter 13. Attracting and Keeping Members   **115**
    Polly McMullen

Background and History   115
Downtowns Today: Membership Organizations and BIDs   117
Downtown Membership Programs and Services   118
Attracting and Retaining Members: Best Practices
    from Cities Large and Small   120
Trends in Downtown Membership Programs   121

Chapter 14. The Advocacy Role of a Downtown Organization   **123**
    Richard T. Reinhard

Organizational Structure   124
Consensus   124
The Downtown Plan   125

PART IV: MARKETING AND COMMUNICATING   **127**

Chapter 15. Creating the Downtown Experience: The New Fundamentals for Downtown Programming   **129**
    Stephen J. Moore

Making Shopping Fun Again   129
New Fundamentals   130
Seven Areas of Programming   131
Conclusion   137

Chapter 16. Marketing the Shopping Experience   **139**
    Maureen Atkinson

Introduction   139
Downtown's Shopping Image   140
The Retail Marketing Planning Process   140

Chapter 17. Electronic Marketing   **151**
    Andrew M. Taft

Active Electronic Marketing   151
Passive Electronic Marketing   154
Updating   155
Maximizing the Potential of Your Site   156
Feedback—Sustaining the Information Search   157
Guerilla Marketing   158

PART V: MANAGING DOWNTOWN'S MANY ELEMENTS   **161**

Chapter 18. Clean and Safe—Basic Requirements   **163**
    Rob DeGraff

Clean Programs   163
Safe Programs   165
Special Programs Enhancing Safe Programs   166

Ordinances   169
Accountability   170

Chapter 19. The Public Realm and Urban Design   **171**
Jill M. Frick

Introduction   171
The Importance of Good Urban Design   172
Guidelines and Principles of Urban Design   173
Design and Planning Process: Internal versus External
    Strategic Planning   175
How Downtowns Use Design to Create a Sense of Place   176
Conclusion   178

Chapter 20. Managing Hospitality   **179**
James E. Peters

Perspective   180
Trends   180
2020 Vision   181
Hospitality, Safety, and Development   182
Learning by Example   185
Conclusion   189
Recommendations   190

**Chapter 21. Transportation Management
and Downtown Revitalization**   **193**
Elizabeth Jackson

Downtown As a Historic Transportation Hub   193
Transportation and Downtowns of the Future   194
Urban Transportation Basics   194
Managing Transportation—Role of the Downtown
    Organization   198
The Bottom Line: Creating Transportation Choice   204

Chapter 22. Parking: Finding Solutions   **207**
E. Larry Fonts

Proven Options   207
Improve the Appearance   208
Improve Public Safety   208
Proactive Strategies   209

Pegasus Parking   210
Business Issues   212
Expansion Opportunities   213
Summary   214

Chapter 23. "Best in Class" Parking Operations   **215**
Dennis Burns

Introduction   215
Parking 101: Choose Any Two   215
Characteristics of Effective Parking Programs   217
Case Examples: Exceptional Parking Programs   241
Summary   243

Chapter 24. Managing Downtown's Social Behavior   **245**
Elizabeth Jackson

Introduction: Furthering the Social Environment
    of Downtown   245
Understanding the Problem   246
Tools of Response   246
Communication   251
Picking Your Partners   252
Building Partnerships   254
Measuring Success   256
Conclusion   258
Useful Resources   259

Chapter 25. Getting the Right Consultant
for the Right Job   **261**
Richard Marshall

Setting Goals for the Project   261
Issuing the Request for Proposal   262
Reviewing the Submissions and Interviewing
    the Consultants   263
Making the Decision   264
Doing the Work   264
Conclusion   264

**PART VI: DISCOVERING DOWNTOWN'S
DEVELOPMENT SECRETS**   **267**

Chapter 26. Economic Development for BIDS   **269**
Gary Ferguson

A Definition of Economic Development   269
Downtowns and Economic Development Policy   270
Points of Divergence and Convergence   270
The Role of BIDS in Economic Development   272
Economic Development Intervention   272
The BID As Data Manager   273
The BID As a Business Facilitator   274
Managing Prospects   275
Start-Up and Expansion Businesses   276
Business Retention Strategies   278
Making Projects Happen   280
Intervention Options: Concluding Remarks   281

**Chapter 27. Residential Development: Creating
a Living Downtown**   **283**
Dan Carmody

Historical Trends   283
Housing's Link to Economic Development   285
Residential Development Prerequisites   286
Housing Market by Sector   287
Affordable Housing   288
Urban Housing Is Different   289
Conclusion   292

Chapter 28. Retail Revitalization and Recruitment   **293**
Maureen Atkinson
John Archer

Understanding Retailing   293
Creative Planning   294
The Process   296
Revitalization and Recruitment Action-Plan Schedule   297
Step 1: Get the Facts   298
Step 2: Retail Recruitment Strategy   304

Chapter 29. A Guide to Developing a Retail Base   **311**
    H. Blount Hunter

Background   311
Step 1: Create an "Inventory" of Downtown Attributes   312
Step 2: Define the Nature of Downtown's Retail
    Challenge   312
Step 3: Evaluate Prevailing Usage and Customer
    Perceptions of Downtown   313
Step 4: Document Downtown's Trade-Area Drawing
    Power and Its Mercantile and Dining Successes   314
Step 5: Identify Downtown's Most Sustainable
    Competitive Retail Niche   315
Step 6: Pinpoint the Retail "Bulls-eye" and Acknowledge
    the Need for a Critical Mass   315
Step 7: Target the Most Appropriate Retailers for Success   316
Step 8: Groom Downtown for Long-Term Retail
    Evolution   317
A Practical Model of Downtown Retail Evolution   318

Chapter 30. "One-of-a-Kind" Regional Attractions   **321**
    Donald E. Hunter

Cycles of Change   321
Revitalization in Downtown   322

Chapter 31. Managing the Politics of Downtown
Redevelopment Projects   **325**
    N. David Milder

Introduction   325
Redevelopment Projects Are Prone to Generating
    Conflicts   326
Some Do's and Don'ts   327

PART VII: INTERNATIONAL PERSPECTIVES   **331**

Chapter 32. Canada As an Urban Country   **333**
    Douglas B. Clark

Introduction   333
Economic Development, Tax Policy, and the New
    Economy   334

Canadian Cities Today 337
Housing 340
Homelessness 341
Transportation 342

Chapter 33. Case Studies from Around the World **345**
Sarah Rose

South Africa 345
Serbia 348
United Kingdom 350
Ireland 353
A Common Goal 355

Chapter 34. Commercial Urbanism in Portugal:
Evolution and Future Perspectives **357**
Carlos J. L. Balsas

Introduction 357
Evolution of Commercial Urbanism in Portugal 358
PROCOM and URBCOM Programs 359
Case Studies: Aveiro, Coimbra, and Porto 362
Conclusion and Recommendations 363

PART VIII: CASE STUDIES **371**

Chapter 35. The Kalamazoo Prism: Downtown Michigan
Metamorphosis **373**
John E. Hopkins
Kenneth A. Nacci

Authors' Perspective 373
Introduction 373
Kalamazoo 374
Key Elements of Project Downtown 380
Stakeholders and Their Roles 383
Cutting-Edge Collaboration 386
Lessons Learned 386
The Challenges That Lie Ahead 388

Chapter 36. Incredible Crisis and Downtown Response: Alliance for Downtown New York   **391**
    Carl Weisbrod
    Jennifer Hensley

Chapter 37. The Homeless Situation in Los Angeles and the BID Response   **403**
    Kent Smith

The Role of Business Improvement Districts   404
The Class Action Lawsuit   405
The Personal Possession Check-In Facility   405
Outreach Teams   406
Addressing Disorderly Behavior   407
The Positive Effect of Residential Development   407
Steps to Address the Situation   408
An Optimistic Outlook   409

PART IX: REEVALUATING THE PAST AND ANTICIPATING FUTURE ADVENTURES   **411**

Chapter 38. Looking Backward, Looking Forward: The Future of Downtowns and Business Districts   **413**
    Paul Levy

Looking Backward   413
Looking at Today   415
Looking Forward   415

Index   **423**

ABOUT THE EDITORS

David M. Feehan, MSW, is President of the International Downtown Association (IDA) in Washington, DC. He has been active in IDA for over 15 years, serving as a board member and officer as well as Chairman before being appointed to serve as President and Chief Executive Officer in 2001. The programs he has directed have won several awards from IDA, the International Parking Institute, and the US Department of Housing and Urban Development. Mr. Feehan has devoted more than three decades to rebuilding and revitalizing cities. He has directed downtown programs in Des Moines, Detroit, and Kalamazoo, and neighborhood development programs in Pittsburgh and Minneapolis. In addition, he maintained an active consulting practice for several years, assisting a number of cities, including New York, Chicago, Las Vegas, and Miami Beach, and has served as an adjunct professor at the University of Iowa and at Metropolitan State University in St. Paul, Minnesota.

Marvin D. Feit, PhD, is Dean and Professor in the Norfolk State University Ethelyn R. Strong School of Social Work in Norfolk, Virginia. He is the author or co-author of several books and has written many articles and chapters in the areas of group work, substance abuse, health, and practice. Dr. Feit has made numerous presentations at national, state, and local conferences and has served as a consultant to for-profit and nonprofit organizations, federal and state agencies, and numerous community-based agencies. He is the founding editor of the *Journal of Health and Social Policy* (Haworth) and of the *Journal of Evidence-Based Social Work* (Haworth). In addition, he is a co-founding editor of the *Journal of Human Behavior in the Social Environment* (Haworth).

doi:10.1300/5137_a

CONTRIBUTORS

John Archer, BCommH, MPL, is a consultant with Urban Marketing Collaborative, a subsidiary of J.C Williams Group, Chicago and Toronto. He has been active in creating results-oriented strategic retail plans for downtowns and business districts throughout North America. In addition, he has worked on retail operations, site location, and target—customer segmentation for retailers and shopping centers. John holds a bachelor's degree with honors as well as a master's degree in urban and regional planning from Queen's University at Kingston.

Barbara Askins is President and CEO of the 125th Street Business Improvement District in Upper Manhattan (Harlem) in New York City. She has done extensive work in the field of improving cities as a public involvement specialist on transportation, environmental and facility planning projects, working on major projects in several cities that included reconstruction of highways and city streets, upgrading rail and bus systems, improving sewage-treatment facilities, creative public spaces, and sports and conventions centers. In 1993, she successfully created the first and only business improvement district in the Harlem community. Under her leadership, the 125th Street BID has received local, state, national, and international recognition. She is vice president of the International Downtown Association and chaired the Diversity Committee. She has served as Vice Chair and Treasurer of New York City's BID Manager's Association. She was an adjunct professor at New York University teaching urban tourism development and served as chairperson for Manhattan Community Board #10 in Central Harlem. She holds a BFA with a minor in business from North Texas State University.

Maureen Atkinson is senior partner of the Urban Marketing Collaborative. From 1972 to 1982, she was with T. Eaton Company, a national department store chain, in sales management, marketing research, and merchandising management. She was involved in such projects as the opening of Eaton's flagship store in the Toronto Eaton Centre; assessment of consumer-research studies to determine the marketing direction for the company's Pacific Division; and merchandise-assortment planning for new

doi:10.1300/5137_b

stores. Ms. Atkinson joined J.C. Williams Group Limited in 1982 as a marketing and research associate; in 1987 she founded Urban Marketing Collaborative. She has consulted with many governments, business associations, and individual retailers in her consulting career. She has also co-authored *Mainstreet Marketing,* a workbook on the marketing issues of downtown revitalization for Heritage Canada, and has written articles for the National Trust for Historic Preservation, the International Downtown Association, and the Urban Land Institute. She is a frequent speaker on public markets and retailing in downtowns, and is on the Board of Directors for the International Downtown Association, Inc. Ms. Atkinson holds a degree in administrative studies from York University, Toronto, Ontario, and is a member of the Professional Marketing Research Society (PMRS).

Carlos J. L. Balsas, PhD, AICP, is an assistant professor in the School of Planning at Arizona State University, and is a senior researcher at the Phoenix Urban Research Laboratory (PURL). He holds an MRP and a doctorate in regional planning from the University of Massachusetts at Amherst, and a bachelor's degree in urban and regional planning from the University of Aveiro in Portugal. He worked as a transportation planner in California and Massachusetts. He has published two books and many papers on urban and sustainable transportation planning.

Richard Bradley has been serving as the executive director of the Downtown BID Corporation, and its predecessor, the Downtown BID Committee, since January 1997. He is guiding the implementation planning of a proposed $7.6 million program of special services to help regenerate the economy of downtown Washington, DC. Prior to this, he was president of the International Downtown Association in April 1984; its mission is to be an advocate and champion for vital and livable urban and community centers throughout the world. Prior to assuming the position of president in 1984, Mr. Bradley was the executive director of the Downtown Hartford Council of Hartford, Connecticut. This organization played a leadership role in the continuing revitalization of that city with a particular emphasis on addressing the zoning and design ordinances, and downtown and neighborhood linkages. Mr. Bradley is a graduate of Cornell University where he received bachelor's degree in 1964 and a master's of education in 1965.

Dennis Burns is Vice President of the Studies and Operations Consulting Group for Carl Walker, Inc., a national parking design and consulting firm. Dennis has over twenty-five years of parking operations, management, and consulting experience. His particular areas of expertise include: parking master planning, municipal parking strategic planning, feasibility studies, supply/demand analysis, shared parking analysis, parking revenue control and operational audits, and organizational analysis. He is the author of over 100 parking studies and has published extensively in several professional journals and books including the International Parking Institutes' *Parking Management—The Next Level*. Dennis is a member of the exclusive Parking Consultants Council of the National Parking Association and a board member of the International Downtown Association.

Dan Carmody led Renaissance Rock Island (RRI), a consortium of non-profits, from 1988 until late 2005 helping to revive a community in north-western Illinois. From a budget of $70,000 and a staff of one, RRI grew its budget to $4 million and its staff to fourteen. Carmody recently became president of the Downtown Improvement District in Fort Wayne, Indiana, where he is seeking to build another organization. He is a frequent presenter at state and national conferences. He has served as a consultant to a number of downtown programs and is a member of the board of directors of the International Downtown Association. Carmody has a degree in urban planning from the University of Illinois

Douglas B. Clark, FCSLA, MCIP, is a principal in the landscape architecture and urban design firm of Scatliff, Miller & Murray. He was the former executive director of the Downtown Winnipeg BIZ, and a past urban design coordinator with the City of Winnipeg. Doug has been a strong advocate for the promotion of innovation that would strengthen urban redevelopment policy initiatives. He holds a master's degree in landscape architecture and has been involved in teaching graduate-level planning and design programs at the University of Saskatchewan and University of Manitoba throughout his career.

James A. Cloar is President and CEO of the Downtown St. Louis Partnership and the Downtown St. Louis Community Improvement District. Previously, he was president of the Tampa Downtown Partnership, a partner with LDR International, executive vice president of the Urban Land Institute, and president of the Central Dallas Association. Cloar has been a consultant or advisor to more than forty cities throughout the United States and abroad. He is a past chair of IDA, and currently on its board. He is the assistant chair of ULI's Public-Private Partnership Council. Among his St. Louis activities, he is on the Board of Directors of Downtown Now! and the St. Louis Regional Chamber and Growth Association.

Catherine Coleman is President and CEO of the Downtown Norfolk Council in Norfolk, Virginia. She has more than twenty-five years of experience in nonprofit management, much of that time spent as CEO of Norfolk's award-winning downtown organization. Since 1999, she has also managed the Downtown Norfolk BID and oversees a thirty-member staff.

She is a past board member and past chair of the International Downtown Association and has served as a panelist and speaker at numerous conferences and meetings addressing the topics of urban revitalization and downtown management. She has also been called upon to serve as a facilitator for many nonprofit organizations and currently serves on a number of nonprofits' boards. She received her bachelor's degree from the University of California and she is also a graduate of Hampton Roads CIVIC Leadership Institute.

Rob DeGraff is currently the project director for the Oregon Department of Transportation's billion dollar I-5 Columbia River Crossing Project. Prior to joining ODOT, Rob was vice president for Policy with Portland, Oregon's, successful business improvement district (BID)—Downtown Clean & Safe. One of the oldest BIDs in the United States, Downtown Clean & Safe is well known in the field for its creative problem solving around a host of "clean and safe" issues. He was instrumental in Clean & Safe's support for the Portland Police Bureau's "Cops on Bikes" program; the creation of the Multnomah County District Attorney's "Downtown DA" position; and the BID's support for Project Respond, which is an innovative outreach program for the chronically mentally ill homeless run by a downtown social service agency. He holds a law degree from Northwestern School of Law at Lewis and Clark College.

Gary Ferguson is Executive Director of the Ithaca Downtown Partnership, a comprehensive downtown revitalization and management organization based in Ithaca, New York. Ferguson has worked in downtown development for over twenty-five years in Dayton, Ohio, Grand Junction, Colorado, Haverhill, Massachusetts, and Lewiston, Maine. In his years of downtown development practice, he has been involved with the retention and attraction of hundreds of retail, office, service, and entertainment businesses of all sizes. He is a frequent speaker, workshop leader, and consultant on issues of downtown economic development.

E. Larry Fonts, AICP, retired after a forty-five-year career in city planning that spanned the public, private, and nonprofit sectors. While president of the Central Dallas Association, he created a wholly owned for-profit subsidiary called Pegasus Parking Ventures, Inc. Its mission was to foster Tolltag use in downtown parking garages that interfaced with similar installations at the two Dallas airports and the region's toll roads. The result was a seamless transaction for the user and improved throughput fort he garage operator. It was the first such application in the country.

Jill M. Frick is Vice President of education, certification and communications for the International Economic Development Council. She has previously served as executive director of the Georgetown Partnership and a member of the staff of the International Downtown Association. She holds a bachelor's degree in journalism from the E. W. Scripps School of Journalism at Ohio University.

Sandra Goldstein, MS, is President of the Stamford Downtown Special Services District, a not-for-profit organization responsible for the revitalization of the downtown in Stamford, Connecticut. She is a past elected member of the Stamford Board of Representatives (city council) where she served as president for ten years. She currently serves on numerous boards of directors including the Chamber of Commerce, the Stamford Partnership, Stamford Center for the Arts, the Mill River Collaborative, and the International Downtown Association. In addition, she is chairperson of Keep Stamford Beautiful. She is the author of numerous articles on economic development and a guest speaker and lecturer on development throughout the region. She has an MS in management from the Wagner School at New York University. She is the recipient of the 2006 Stamford Citizen of the Year Award.

Jennifer Hensley is currently Assistant Vice President of Corporate and Intergovernmental Affairs at the Alliance for Downtown New York. She previously served as its marketing manager and then director of community affairs. Prior to joining the Alliance, Ms. Hensley was marketing assistant at the City of San Diego's Office of Small Business where she managed projects for the city's business improvement districts. Recently, Ms. Hensley acted as a consultant to the New Orleans Downtown Development District and performed a study on the status of small-business post-disaster recovery efforts. She received her BA from Barnard College and will receive her MBA and MPA from New York University in 2008.

John E. Hopkins, MA, PhD, is President/CEO of the Kalamazoo Community Foundation. Dr. Hopkins joined the Kalamazoo Community Foundation in 1983 and was named its president/CEO in 1994. Under Dr. Hopkins' leadership, the Foundation's assets have grown from $61 million in 1983 to $262 million at the end of 2004. Dr. Hopkins has served on more than thirty boards of nonprofits and foundations in twenty years. Recently, he has devoted his time to organizations dedicated to enhancing the economic vitality of the Kalamazoo area, serving on the boards of the Kalamazoo County LISC Housing Partnership, Downtown Tomorrow, Inc., and Southwest Michigan Innovation Center (an incubator for emerging life sciences and biotech companies). Dr. Hopkins received a BA from Marietta College, Marietta, Ohio, and an MA and PhD in communications from Ohio University, Athens.

H. Blount Hunter began his retail research career in 1977 and founded his advisory firm in 1996 after twelve years as a senior analyst specializing in urban properties at The Rouse Company. Over his twenty-eight-year career in real estate analysis, Hunter has performed feasibility studies, assessed sales potential and supportable retail square footage, created downtown trade area delineations and patron profiles, and provided leasing support for shopping centers and urban districts in more than forty states, Canada, and Puerto Rico. Hunter was a juror for IDA's 2000 Achievement Awards and has participated in several Urban Land Institute Advisory Panels. He authored a chapter titled "Main Street Retail Market Analysis" in a ULI textbook published in June, 2001, as well as a chapter on retail fundamentals for downtown managers in an upcoming text to be published by the IDA. He is a 1977 graduate of the University of Virginia with concentrations in economics and sociology.

Donald E. Hunter is President of Hunter Interests Inc., a twenty-year-old real estate investment, development, and consulting firm headquartered in Annapolis, Maryland, with offices in New York City and Clearwater, Florida. Consulting assignments in which the firm's services caused development to occur total $3.8 billion in value. Mr. Hunter is a member of the board of IEDC and is active in ULI, APA, and ICSC. He hold's a master's degree from the University of California at Berkeley.

Elizabeth Jackson is President of The Urban Agenda, Inc., in Ann Arbor, Michigan. She was the president of the International Downtown Association from 1997-2001, during which time she helped to create IDA's "Addressing Homelessness" initiatives. She holds a master's degree in urban planning from the University of Michigan.

Kate Joncas has been President of the Downtown Seattle Association since 1994. She has over twenty-seven years of experience in downtown revitalization in the private, public, and nonprofit sectors in communities around the world. She has written workbooks on downtown revitalization and won awards in national urban design competitions. Ms Joncas is the past chair of the International Downtown Association. She is very active in her community serving on SEAFAIR, Seattle Police Foundation, United Way Seattle Community Council, Interagency Council to End Homelessness, Nightlife Task Force, and Advisory Councils for the Seattle Art Museum and the Museum of History and Industry.

Dong Soo Kim, MSW, PhD, at the time of this writing, is Professor of social work at Norfolk State University and upon his recent retirement he is a visiting professor at Presbyterian College and Theological Seminary in Seoul, Korea. He has done research and publications in areas of international

adoption, child welfare services, drug prevention training, program evaluation, and ethnic minority issues. He received his master's degree in social
work from the University of Pittsburgh and his doctorate from the University of Chicago.

Paul R. Levy is President of both the Center City District (CCD) and Central Philadelphia Development Corp. (CPDC). The CCD is a private-sector
funded, $14 million business improvement district, providing security,
crime prevention, hospitality, cleaning, marketing, promotion, capital improvement, and planning for the central business district of Philadelphia.
CPDC is a membership organization supported by the downtown business
community to conduct research, advocacy, and planning to make Center
City Philadelphia a more competitive location. Paul R. Levy lives in Center
City. He has a BA from Lafayette College, a PhD from Columbia University, and teaches as an adjunct professor of city planning at the University of
Pennsylvania. He serves on the boards of the Greater Philadelphia Chamber
of Commerce and the Philadelphia Convention and Visitors Bureau.

Richard Marshall, RAIA, is a principal and regional director of urban design (Asia) with EDAW Inc., an international design and planning firm. He
is responsible for directing EDAW's urban design practice in China and
throughout Asia. He has worked as an urban designer and architect for fifteen years conducting architectural and urban design projects in Australia,
the United States, Singapore, Thailand, Malaysia, China, as well as other
parts Asia. Prior to joining EDAW, he was Associate Professor and Director of Urban Design Programs at the Harvard Design School. He has
authored three books: *Emerging Urbanity—Global Urban Projects in the
Asia Pacific Rim* (2003), *Waterfronts in Post Industrial Cities* (2001), and
Designing the American City (2003). Marshall is a member of the Royal
Australian Institute of Architects. He holds a master's degree in architecture and urban design from Harvard University. Michael Grisso, senior
planner at the San Francisco Redevelopment Agency, was interviewed for
Marshall's chapter.

Polly McMullen has served as President of the Downtown Lincoln Association (DLA) since 1997. She oversees the activities of a sixteen-member
staff and three business improvement districts (BIDs) serving a sixty-six-
block downtown area. Prior to joining DLA, McMullen served as an aide to
former mayor of Lincoln and U.S. Secretary of Agriculture, Mike Johanns.
She currently serves on numerous city task forces and advisory boards and
is an officer and director of United Way of Lincoln/Lancaster County.
McMullen has served as a board member and officer of the International
Downtown Association. She has a master's degree from the University of
Wisconsin and a bachelor's degree from San Francisco College for
Women.

N. David Milder is Founder and President of DANTH, a leading urban planning consulting firm. A nationally recognized authority on downtown revitalization and a leading proponent of developing market niches, he has more than twenty-five years of experience utilizing marketing research and management skills to help revitalize business centers. Mr. Midler has been widely quoted in the media, written for numerous publications, and authored books and more than fifty technical reports and articles in urban land, comparative political studies, and comparative public administration. He received a PhD from Cornell University and taught at Cornell and Ohio State University. He also served as the director of the Urban Institute at the University of North Carolina at Charlotte, executive director of the Ohio Cities Consortium, and vice president for sales and marketing at the Man-Data Corp. in Columbus, Ohio.

Stephen J. Moore is Deputy Executive Director for the Downtown DC Business Improvement District where he oversees the leasing, marketing, and special-event planning for the 130-block downtown of the nation's capital. Prior to joining the Downtown DC BID, Steve founded The Moore Group in 1998 to advise towns, downtowns, BIDs, and developers on branding, smart growth, tourism strategies, merchandising, communications, market and consumer research, event planning, and sponsorship development. During his fifteen-year tenure at The Rouse Company, a Maryland-based shopping center developer, Steve oversaw the marketing pro-grams for many of the country's most high-profile urban redevelopment projects including Faneuil Hall Marketplace in Boston, South Street Seaport in New York City, Westlake Center in Seattle, The Tabor Center in Denver, Pioneer Place in Portland, The Gallery at Market Street East in Philadelphia, and The Arizona Center in Phoenix. As the senior vice president for marketing and communication at Horizon Properties, Steve was responsible for directing the marketing of the largest outlet center developer in the United States, as well as overseeing the corporate public affairs, marketing, investor relations, operating properties marketing, and the research departments. Steve and his staff at the Downtown DC BID direct all aspects of the marketing of the downtown including merchandising strategy, community, media and government relations, special event programming, the street-vending pilot program, research, and the newly proposed downtown circulator. Steve holds memberships in the International Downtown Association, the Urban Land Institute, and the International Council of Shopping Centers. He is on the boards of the National Cherry Blossom Festival and the Downtown Public Space Management Corporation.

Kenneth A. Nacci, MS, has been President of Downtown Kalamazoo Incorporated since 1998. He directs all aspects of downtown management including real estate acquisitions, economic development strategies, and the downtown parking system. Ken is a twenty-five-year veteran in the urban planning and development industry. He was a principal at STS Consultants from 1994-1998 and served as vice president of Downtown Kalamazoo Incorporated from 1987-1994, during which time he managed the development of the $120 million Arcadia Creek project. Prior to that, Ken worked for the City of Kalamazoo and the City of Jackson. He is a 1981 graduate of Michigan State University with a master's degree in community development, and he earned a bachelor's degree in geography and urban planning from Western Michigan University in 1977.

James E. Peters is the Founder and President of the Responsible Hospitality Institute (RHI). Peters has been researching issues and trends in cities throughout the United States and is considered a leading authority on legal and social trends impacting the hospitality industry. As RHI's founder, Peters has organized and administered numerous conferences, symposia, and forums involving national and international experts on a variety of topics relating to planning, managing, and policing dining and entertainment districts. He is a graduate of the University of Massachusetts Department of Hotel, Restaurant and Travel Administration.

Richard T. Reinhard is managing director of urban development and infrastructure finance at the Urban Land Institute, where he advances strategies to improve America's urban public infrastructure. He has spent more than two decades working on the revitalization of cities, having managed urban revitalization organizations in Richmond, Virginia, Buffalo, New York, Atlanta, Georgia, and Londonderry, Northern Ireland, and served as chief of staff to the Mayor of Buffalo. He has a bachelor's degree from the College of William and Mary and a master's degree from Rice University. He was a Loeb Fellow in Advanced Environmental Studies at the Harvard University Graduate School of Design.

Sarah Rose is a 2006 master's of public policy candidate at Georgetown University, studying international policy and development. Her research includes empirical work on the impact of property titling on labor force participation in urban informal areas in Ecuador. She spent four years at the International Downtown Association as a staff member, conducting research and serving as policy liaison to the board of directors. She has a bachelor's degree in foreign service from Georgetown University.

Brad Segal is President of Progressive Urban Management Associates (PUMA), a Denver-based consulting firm providing management, marketing, and economic development services to advance downtown and community development. Prior to establishing PUMA, Brad served as the senior director of the Downtown Denver Partnership where he managed its economic development and marketing programs. He currently serves on the board of directors of the Colorado Community Revitalization Association and is a past board member of the International Downtown Association. He is the author of many articles and publications, including *ABCs for Creating BIDs* and *Ten Keys for Creating a Competitive Downtown.* Brad holds an MBA degree from Columbia University and a BA from the University of California at Berkeley.

Kent Smith is Executive Director of the Los Angeles Fashion District, the creative heart of the California apparel industry. The ninety-block business improvement district in downtown Los Angeles has added over 500 new stores and 800 new residences since 2000 and has one of the most vibrant street scenes in the country. He has worked extensively in downtown revitalization, transportation planning, and waterfront development. He is currently on the boards of the Santa Monica Pier Restoration Corporation and the International Downtown Association. He holds a master's degree in environmental design from the University of Calgary.

Andrew M. Taft is President of Downtown Fort Worth, Inc. He was formerly the marketing director for the Florida Commercial Development Association, the director of Marketing and Business Development at the Tampa Downtown Partnership, and the executive director of Shreveport's Downtown Development Authority. Andy serves on the boards of the Fort Worth Chamber of Commerce, Sister Cities, and Convention and Visitor's Bureau, and is an International Downtown Association board member. A native of Tampa, Florida, Andy is a graduate of the University of South Florida.

Tom Verploegen has thirty years of downtown management, business, economic development, and city planning experience in Pittsburgh, Pennsylvania, his hometown of Pensacola, Florida, and Mesa, Arizona. Tom has been president of the Downtown Mesa Association (DMA) since 1984 and guided the establishment of the first downtown improvement district in Arizona in 1985. Tom received a bachelor's degree in political science from the University of Florida, and a master's degree in urban and regional planning from the University of Pittsburgh. Tom is also a past chairman of the board of the International Downtown Association.

Michael Weiss is Executive Director of two business improvement districts in downtown Brooklyn, New York, the MetroTech BID and the Fulton Mall Improvement Association. Together, they cover a thirty-six-square-block area consisting of the third largest retail business district in New York City, including 350 retail stores, over 7 million square feet of office space, a government center, and four colleges serving over 30,000 students. MetroTech BID has won numerous awards including the 2001 International Downtown Association's Achievement Award for Downtown Management and the New York City Department of Small Business Services Neighborhood Development ShopABLE Award. Prior to assuming his current position, Mike served for ten years as chief of staff and deputy commissioner for administration at the New York City Department of Transportation. He was elected to the position of chairman of the International Downtown Association for the year 2005-2006.

Carl Weisbrod is currently President of the executive vice president of Real Estate Division for Trinity Church and executive vice president of Trinity Church—St. Paul's Chapel, an Episcopal parish chartered in 1697. He manages and develops Trinity's real estate holdings in Manhattan, which total approximately 6 million square feet over twenty-eight sites. Weisbrod has had a distinguished career focused on revitalizing and developing New York City neighborhoods. Beginning in the 1970s, he led the successful city and state efforts to revive the Times Square area. During this period he was the executive director of the New York City Planning Commission, then president of the 42nd Street Development Project, Inc., a subsidiary of the New York State Urban Development Corporation, and from 1990 to 1994 was founding president of the New York City Economic Development Corporation. Prior to joining Trinity, he was the founding president of the Alliance for Downtown New York, a business improvement district established in 1995 charged with revitalizing lower Manhattan. Weisbrod serves as an adjunct associate professor at Columbia University's Graduate School of Architecture, Planning and Preservation. He is a director of the Lower Manhattan Development Corporation, the Convention Center Development Corporation, and the Tarragon Corporation, a publicly traded national homebuilding company, and is a trustee of the Ford Foundation and NYU Downtown Hospital, among other organizations. In 2002, Crain's New York Business named him one of the "100 Most Influential Leaders in Business." He is a graduate of Cornell University and New York University's School of Law.

Introduction

This is a book for practitioners of business district management and for those who hope to be practitioners. It is both a pragmatic, how-to guide to effective downtown leadership and a group of essays on more theoretical and conceptual aspects of downtown and community development. It will serve as an always-handy desk reference for the downtown or business district CEO or executive director; it will be an important compendium for board members of these organizations as they seek to understand in more depth and in context what downtown organizations, business improvement districts (BIDs), downtown development authorities, and community development corporations are trying to achieve; and finally, it will provide a thorough introduction for students in planning, economic development, public and business administration, architecture, social work, marketing, and other academic programs who see a potential future in downtown management and leadership.

As far as we know, no college or university currently offers an entire degree program in downtown management. As a result, downtown organization staff members come from virtually every undergraduate discipline. The ranks of downtown executives and staff are peopled with former bankers, lawyers, planners, journalists, social workers, accountants, artists, engineers, and architects, to name a few. This mixture certainly has contributed to the richness and texture of thought and practice among downtown managers; however, the absence of an academic "road map" into the field means that many people find their way into this profession almost by accident.

What those entering the profession of downtown management find in terms of roles and responsibilities, skill sets and practices, can be confusing and daunting. At any given time, a downtown manager may be called upon as an expert in real estate development, civil engineering, transportation, marketing, finance, retail management, office leasing, human resources, workforce development, social work, architecture, planning, urban design, and any number of other professions. It often seems as if this is not one job but ten, and there is no predicting on any given day which hats the downtown professional may be called upon to wear.

doi:10.1300/5137_01

1

Imagine what a typical day might be like. On her way into the office, the CEO of a downtown organization notices that several lights are out in the public parking garage and makes a mental note to call the director of the parking authority so replacement lighting gets ordered and installed. Walking from the garage to her office, she encounters a homeless panhandler and directs him to a drop-in center where he can begin the "continuum of care." Her first meeting of the day is with the mayor and a couple of city council members to decide on a strategy for funding streetscape improvements on the downtown's main shopping street.

After the meeting, she gathers her marketing and events staff to review final implementation plans for the upcoming arts festival that her organization sponsors and manages. By midmorning, she's out with a local developer who wants to convert an empty warehouse into loft condominiums and wants the backing of her of her organization. After touring the building, she meets the police chief for lunch to secure a commitment for more beat officers on downtown streets.

Her first appointment of the afternoon is with her board chairman, who wants to review the agenda for the next board meeting and work out a strategy for expanding the business improvement district. Midafternoon finds her taking a few minutes to return calls and e-mails, and toward the end of the day she participates as a member of a panel reviewing designs for a new downtown library. Finally, after a quick dinner with colleagues, she heads over to the office of a nearby neighborhood association where she is the featured speaker for the monthly meeting.

During the course of one day, she's engaged top-level public and private officials, helped make decisions that will shape the course of the downtown and the city for years to come, and forged positive relationships with neighborhood residents as well.

The question is not how does one person wear so many hats, but how does one person do so effectively and successfully? In the world of downtown management, with boards of directors made up of bottom-line-oriented businesspeople, one has to be able to perform and produce results.

This book will not provide all of the answers. What it will do is provide students and practitioners with a guide to how some of the best professionals in the downtown management and leadership field think and act. It will be useful for anyone who wants to understand and work for a downtown, business district, or community development organization; but it will be especially so for anyone who has management aspirations.

Although we know of no university degree programs in downtown management and leadership, we are aware that several universities are beginning to offer courses in this subject. We hope that faculty members teaching courses in this area, whether in business administration, public administration, planning, social work, or other areas of study will find this book to be a great resource. *Making Business Districts Work* represents the work of more than thirty professionals who are respected for their work and their knowledge, not only in their profession but in their communities.

When the International Downtown Organization (IDA) decided to undertake the creation of this book, it was with the realization that while there were many experts within the association, no one person was an expert in everything related to downtown management and leadership. Thus as a reader, you'll benefit from the collective wisdom of each chapter's authors.

The book is organized in nine sections. Part I introduces the field of downtown leadership and management, and offers some perspectives on how the profession has changed and continues to change.

Part II focuses on the downtown organization itself. It addresses some of the most important issues: its structure, governance, resources, and accountability. Without downtown organizations it is further doubtful that the remarkable renaissance of older business districts would have occurred.

Part III examines the environment in which downtown leaders and the organizations they command operate. In the context of systems theory, downtown and business district organizations are part of large and complex systems that include public entities, private companies, individuals and groups, all of which influence and are influenced by these downtown organizations.

Parts IV through VI discuss what downtown and business districts do. For example, what problems are they trying to solve? What are some of the more important programs and activities that these organizations undertake? How do they communicate with downtown users and constituents? What kinds of experiences are they seeking to create for downtown users? What resources, both human and financial, do they seek to secure, and toward what ends are these resources committed?

Part VII explores the growing trend toward town center organizations and business improvement districts outside of North America. Although the United States and Canada still boast the largest concentration of such organizations, regions such as the United Kingdom have seen explosive growth in the past five years, and many other areas of the world are experiencing the birth of similar organizations.

Three case studies are presented in Part VIII. Two of these represent examples of leadership and management in North America's two largest cities—New York City and Los Angeles—and they tell the tales of how downtown organizations responded to crises of major proportions. New York City, the Alliance for Downtown New York was at the center of the disaster when terrorists attacked the World Trade Center Towers on September 11,

2001. The response of this organization and its leaders is one of courage, intelligence, and coolness under fire.

In Los Angeles, a crisis of a different sort has been brewing for many years, but became nearly unmanageable about five years ago when homeless individuals became so numerous on the streets of downtown's various districts, that businesses, customers, residents, and visitors reacted first with alarm and then with thoughtful determination. Their actions not only alleviated undesirable conditions for businesses, but brought renewed focus and increased help for the area's thousands of homeless persons.

The final case study looks at a much smaller town—Kalamazoo, Michigan—and its persistent efforts over more than twenty years to rebuild and remake a downtown that suffered from being in a floodplain. This not only caused physical damage to buildings, but meant that development in the north half of downtown was impossible due to restrictions on financing and insurance. Kalamazoo's success in overcoming these challenges has won it a number of awards and national recognition.

Part IX is devoted to a look backward and a look forward. Downtowns and business districts have grown, declined, revived, and blossomed during the past fifty years. New forms have emerged, in new towns and suburbs. However, as population characteristics, working patterns, and consumer desires change, what does the future hold? This section examines some of the many possibilities we might see.

The co-editors and IDA are deeply indebted to the authors of the many chapters that make up this unique book. Some authors have spent all or most of their careers in one community; others have had more nomadic existences, serving downtowns in many places. Some are downtown CEOs, some are consultants, some are academicians. Together, they represent knowledge, wisdom, and experience. IDA and our readers around the world can be thankful that they have given us their time and effort to create this unique collection of perspectives.

Part I:
The Field of Downtown and Business District Management

What does it take to be a successful downtown leader and manager? What makes this profession different from related professions, such as city manager and chamber of commerce manager? Why is the downtown manager's role so vital in the revitalization of cities and towns? In this section, you'll explore the roles and responsibilities of downtown leaders and the context in which they operate.

Chapter 1

The State of Business District Revitalization

Brad Segal

What a difference a decade makes.

Following the relative prosperity and unfettered optimism of the 1990s, the new millennium has delivered a new reality with economic malaise, political instability, and overall uncertainty. Unlike the gradual change of past cycles, our new world outlook has been heavily influenced by the national trauma suffered on one crystal clear morning on September 11, 2001. America's business districts, mirroring the resiliency of their citizenry, have done their best to adapt.

Despite the radical changes and challenges of the past several years, the underlying convergence of demographics and technology that led to the recent renaissance in many downtowns, main streets, and neighborhood business districts still apply. Long-term trends creating an older, yet healthier and wealthier population, will continue to supply an expanding market for the urban experience. The economy will continue to evolve in response to information technologies, allowing for more professional choices and independence. These trends, and the hope for business district revitalization, are reinforced by the most respected trend watchers of today, ranging from Richard Florida's *The Rise of the Creative Class* to Storm Cunningham's *The Restoration Economy*.

Although the contextual forces supporting the revival of business districts are still intact, the tools are not. Both the private and public sectors are either shrinking or redirecting investment. Many of the traditional sources of support for business district revitalization, particularly financial assistance from local government, are rapidly eroding and unlikely to completely re-emerge throughout the remainder of the decade.

To remain competitive in an uncertain and volatile world, business districts must diversify on all levels, including leadership, management, development, and financial support. This approach requires business districts to: build upon the practices that worked best in the 1990s, adapt, and then *sustain* them

doi:10.1300/5137_02

in the new realities of the post-9/11 world. Imperatives for diversification include:

- *Leadership:* Business districts must cast a wide net in engaging both visionary and pragmatic leaders. To be most responsive and nimble, district leadership must not only include traditional stakeholders such as property owners and businesses, but also representatives of their consumer and investor markets. To stay accountable to increasingly diverse constituents and their respective interests, business districts will explore more complex organizational structures. Moving beyond traditional membership organizations and/or assessment districts, new business district holding companies will add community development corporations, events production companies, and transportation management associations.
- *Management:* Beginning with a keen understanding of their markets, business districts must continue to guide their emergence as niche destinations. The "complete" business district experience, including a rich combination of retail, entertainment, culture, education, office, and housing, will differentiate to be more distinctive and competitive. Management of the business district experience is a holistic and sophisticated endeavor, incorporating marketing, planning, development, and mobility in addition to the basics of "clean and safe."
- *Development:* Perhaps more than any time in the past fifty years, incrementalism is the mantra that will best guide business district development. Worldwide instability will continue to challenge capital markets making big project solutions less feasible. Perhaps the most important lesson of the recent wave of business district successes is that most great places are the sum of many small interesting parts. Details, ranging from a unique mix of locally owned, independent businesses to the subtleties of street furniture, distinguish authentic and desirable destinations.
- *Financing:* Business districts must get more creative and diversify the financial support needed to advance revitalization. Broadening participation and "ownership" in both the public and private financing arenas is key. Building upon the business improvement district model, business districts must seek diverse sources of support that distribute financial burden to public and private benefactors, engage and empower investors, and can be sustained for long periods of time.

Challenging times? Sure, but by responding with diverse entrepreneurial and innovative approaches, business districts will thrive during these times of uncertainty and be far better positioned to benefit from future stability and growth.

REFERENCES

Cunningham, S. (2002). *The Restoration Economy: The Greatest New Growth Frontier: Immediate & Emerging Opportunities for Businesses, Communities & Investors.* San Francisco: Kerrett-Koehler Publishers.

Florida, R. (2002). *The Rise of the Creative Class: And How It's Transforming Work, Leisure, Community and Everyday Life.* New York: Perseus Books Group.

Chapter 2

Leading the Downtown

Richard Bradley

Leading is still the most important activity of any downtown organization.

Over the past decade, with the growth of business improvement districts (BIDs), the focus in many communities has been directed to the management of downtown. Making downtown clean, safe, and friendly has become the mantra and with it a host of administrative and management responsibilities which are necessary to achieve the desired end. Typical programmatic responsibilities include:

- hiring, training, and supervising ambassadors, hosts, or guides;
- organizing security coalitions;
- planting and maintaining flowers and other landscape elements;
- designing new streetscape standards;
- creating new Web sites;
- organizing outreach programs for the homeless; and
- installing pedestrian countdown signals.

Beyond these are many other types of programs operated by downtown organizations, especially within business improvement districts, which require high degrees of management control and investing huge amounts of energy in attending to details. Running festivals, promoting holiday events, operating parking programs, and staging farmer's markets are only a few examples. Without a doubt, these efforts have had a transforming effect and have played a key role in the renewed appreciation of both the importance and vitality of downtowns.

Yet leadership still remains the primary responsibility of downtown organizations.

Business improvement districts require vast amounts of leadership energy in order to be created in the first place. As each community explores the necessary steps to create a BID, a major leadership effort is required and needs to be sustained over a lengthy period of time. The initial idea of

doi:10.1300/5137_03

11

establishing a BID has to be proposed and tested. A process of engaging key stakeholders has to be launched. Preliminary resources need to be raised to fund the development of business plans. Coalitions of interests need to be nurtured and developed. Trusted emissaries need to be engaged in mediation and persuasion. Individuals must take formal positions in newly created organizational efforts. Communication and public relations outreach efforts must be organized. Ultimately, someone or some group needs to shepherd a decision-making process through the city council and some kind of formal decision must be made through the use of some type of election. All of these represent leadership tasks that are different from management and administrative tasks.

A LONG HISTORY OF LEADERSHIP

Since the beginning of the movement to renew North American downtowns, which began over fifty years ago with the start of suburbanization, most organizations that were created to address downtown renewal had or have a leadership agenda. Sometimes, this leadership is extended through advocacy, which was the basic style in the 1950s and 1960s. However, beginning in the 1970s, many organizations responded to the changing political environment, adopted a catalytic style, and the term public/private partnership was defined by organizations such as Central Atlanta Progress. Today, downtown organizations use a variety of approaches to carry out their leadership agenda with most choosing to use informal power-sharing strategies and techniques.

CONTINUOUS DEMANDS FOR LEADERSHIP

Downtowns that established BIDs and exercised leadership have focused on one of numerous challenges. A business improvement district is not an end to itself, but rather a means to an end—attracting more users and expanding more businesses in a downtown area. Achieving a diverse set of goals for downtown, which include but also go beyond economic goals, requires a continuous dance of leadership energies. Improving the nature and mix of retail, residential, cultural, entertainment, or commercial entities requires, in most instances, the same kind of leadership required to establish a BID. Someone or some group needs to be continuously monitoring the health and well-being of the downtown, determining the next critical issues, and establishing priorities and compelling collective action.

LEADERSHIP AS A COLLECTIVE
AND COOPERATIVE UNDERTAKING

Although there still may be individuals leading institutions of substantial resources and authority who have the power and influence to compel action, by and large, the period of heroic leadership has ended. In the past, a group of bank presidents and corporate CEOs could chart the course of action for a downtown and drive change through their own investments. Baltimore in the 1970s is a representative model. Power and influence have been lateralized in most communications, and mass communication requires open processes that are relatively transparent. Yet "partnership building," the name associated with leadership activities, clearly implies joint decision making and action. Much falls on the shoulders of individuals and requires individual responsibility, and downtown organizations need to provide these individuals. Someone has to be the steward of a process: initiating, convening, cajoling, following up, closing, confirming, and communicating. The value orientation, however, is almost always about "we" rather than "me." Today, effective leadership requires vast amounts of communication, interaction, negotiation, and mediation to bring along a large number of stakeholders with diverse interests and resources.

LEADERSHIP AS INITIATING AND MANAGING CHANGE

Change must often be initiated, and this comes from individuals or groups. Downtown organizations always face an adaptive challenge. Competing forces in the form of technology alter how and where people shop and/or are entertained. Forces in transportation or infrastructure development alter the ease with which people have access to new areas; forces of the marketplace, in which new products and offerings, whether they be in the form of a new shopping center on the edge of downtown or new office parks in the suburbs, create a competitor to the downtown. Each challenge requires continuous focus on the emerging adaptive challenge. At least one organization should have the responsibility to monitor change and, where necessary, initiate change.

Leading is still the most important activity of a downtown organization.

Chapter 3

The New Role of Downtown Leaders

Richard T. Reinhard

COMPARING PAST AND PRESENT

Leading America's downtowns is more challenging today than ever. Why? Change. Competition. And failure to keep up with change and competition.

It used to be that the downtown was the "big dog"—the center of a region's economic power. Today, that's not likely to be so.

It used to be that downtown's business leaders were born, reared, and, perhaps, educated in the region. Not any more.

It used to be that a city's and a region's elected officials either came from or came with the backing and blessing of the downtown business community. Not any longer.

It used to be that city hall paid unique attention to the city center—police patrolled it, planners planned it, public works dug it. Now, that's less likely to be so.

Downtowns, which used to be privileged, now find themselves in the middle of an ultracompetitive marketplace—for capital, for business leadership, for political leadership, for services. Yet often, the boards and staffs of our downtown organizations find themselves harking back to another time and place, almost disconnected from the present.

SOME SPECIFIC CAUSES OF CHANGE

Loss of Economic Preeminence

There was a time (up until the 1960s or 1970s in most places) when most of the economic power of a region—the jobs, the office space, the economic activity—was located downtown. Today, downtown is at best one of several economic activity centers in a region; in Atlanta, there's Buckhead, Midtown,

doi:10.1300/5137_04

15

Perimeter, Cumberland, Aiport, Alpharetta, Gwinnett County, just to name a few.

Lack of Homegrown Leaders

There was a time (again, up until the 1960s or 1970s) when not only were corporations headquartered in the downtown of a region, but their CEOs grew up with one another. Now, this is not so. Multinationals control each region's biggest employers, the corporations are often headquartered in another state or country, and the division heads who control the major employers are, likely as not, "passing through" our communities for a few years, on their way up the career ladder.

"Nonfamily" Mayors

There was a time when, in many cities, the chief local elected officials came from the downtown business community. (Harry Truman, the downtown haberdasher, was elected Jackson, Missouri as a county judge.) Now, he or she is more likely to be elected based upon support from minority church groups or neighborhood associations. Running apart from—if not against—the downtown business community often gets more votes than being tied to it.

Overwhelmed Local Governments

There was a time when, in local governments, police policed, planners planned, and parks' workers cut grass and planted flowers. Now, with the downshifting of responsibilities from federal to state government, and state to local governments, the latter often deliver only elemental public services, relying on nonprofits, neighborhood groups, and individuals to pick up the slack.

REALITY OF TODAY

Unfortunately, many downtown organizations seem less than cognizant of these changes. They remain stuck in the 1960s or 1970s. They expect that constituents will naturally line up behind downtown—whether by fear of power, respect of money, or dint of old logic. They're not dealing with today's ultracompetitive dynamics.

Downtown leadership is changing, moving—sometimes ever so slowly—away from an old model and toward a new model. It is not a comfortable change, but no substantive change ever is.

SPECTRUM OF CHANGES

Following are some of the elements of change with regard to downtown organizations, what they are moving away from and what they are moving toward:

Boards

> *Away from:* Only chief executive officers of major businesses.
> *Toward:* Amalgams of business leaders, institutional leaders, public officials, and residents.

The major economic engines in today's downtown are often universities, hospitals, convention centers, stadiums and arenas, and other nonbusiness groups. Downtown's "CEOs" often either aren't CEOs (they're regional vice presidents of a larger corporation, with little leeway to make decisions) or, if they are CEOs, they're more concerned with New York or London (or Singapore or China) than they are with the city within which they reside. Leadership today often emerges from what one or two decades ago would be considered unlikely places.

Staff

> *Away from:* Executive directors who are "just like" the CEOs on the board and echo their community views.
> *Toward:* Executive directors who are "translators" between the business community and the city's various publics.

The "languages" of business and the community are often quite different. The former wants profitability, efficiency, and quarterly results. The latter wants popularity, participation and sometimes, immediate and permanent results. They speak different languages, e.g., Greek and Chinese. Someone who speaks one language and not the other will do no one much good. Someone who speaks a little of both languages will get the conversation flowing.

Revenues

> *Away from:* Reliance on annually raised private-sector dues and contributions.
> *Toward:* Multiple sources, including dues, special assessments, government contracts, foundation grants, and earned income.

The days of corporate largesse, if not over, certainly are waning. Boards of directors want returns on investment, not feathers and plaques. The days of big-government spending seem be over, too. The best way for a downtown organization to support itself is through a diversity of revenue sources, including many that require contracts for specific goods and services.

Work Plans

> *Away from:* Only development projects on the agenda, or, on the other hand, only "clean and safe" programs.
> *Toward:* A work plan of goods and services that need to be provided to make the downtown excellent, including partnerships with other public, private, and nonprofit entities.

Many downtown organizations remain what Otis White, President of Civic Strategies, Inc., calls "power" organizations ("Let us tell government what it should be doing"), when what they need to be are "goods-and-services delivery" organizations ("Let us deliver to you our part of what we all agree needs to be done") (personal communication). Other organizations have picked up the "clean and safe" mantra and end their aspirations there. Today's downtown organization must determine what needs to be done to make its area excellent and figure out ways to get the job done.

Organizational Structure

> *Away from:* Overly simple structures that are unlikely to accomplish complex tasks; on the other hand, overly complex structures that confuse everyone.
> *Toward:* A "right-sized" structure, with clear lines of accountability between and among entities.

It used to be that the downtown organization was part of the local chamber of commerce, or part of the city planning department. After that, a separate downtown organization was formed. Sometimes, a business improvement district (BID) was formed; or a real estate development corporation; or a transportation management organization; or a festival and event production company. Some downtown organizations still resemble a one-room school-house. Others are more like "The House That Jack Built." The best ones think through how these organizations relate to one another in a strategic way.

Relationship with City Hall

Away from: Using the power and influence of business interests to pressure the city.
Toward: Using arguments about mutual interests to partner with the city.

Although the business community still has economic power, its political power in most American cities is quite limited. Mayors and city council members often are elected by neighborhood associations, church groups, or by "good government" groups. Often, business leaders don't even reside in the city. Sometimes, a lavish endorsement from the business community can backfire, resulting in electing his or her opponent. The political power of the downtown business community isn't what it used to be. Roger Fisher's *Getting to Yes* may be a more instructive text than Machiavelli's *The Prince*.

Relationship with Center-City Neighborhoods

Away from: Thinking that every dollar that goes to a neighborhood is a dollar that doesn't go downtown.
Toward: Helping neighborhoods get support, understanding that "as go center-city neighborhoods, so goes downtown."

When a citizen of a region says "downtown," chances are that he or she is referring to a relatively large swath of the center city. (Chances are infinites-imal that he or she knows the city's boundaries for the central business dis-trict.) A crime in an inner-city neighborhood is a crime "downtown." A ramshackle center-city public housing project is bad "downtown" housing. An underperforming inner-city school is "downtown." That's just the way it is. Fighting with a neighborhood over Community Development Block Grant money makes little sense—either politically or image wise.

Credit

> *Away from:* Hogging it.
> *Toward:* Sharing it.

Make no mistake: a downtown organization needs a record of accomplishment if it is to continue to earn its constituents' support. Yet there is a difference between hogging credit and sharing credit. Local mayors or city council members face election every two to four years. Local city managers are up for recall at every city council meeting. The currency of their jobs is getting credit. The currency of the downtown organizations is getting respect. All too often, downtown organizations seem to "compete" with city hall. Public graciousness makes sense.

Media Relations

> *Away from:* Secrecy and opacity.
> *Toward:* Openness and transparency.

Many downtown organizations' board chairs and executive directors take a legalistic view of open meetings and sunshine laws. "We're *not required*" to have board meetings open or budgets reviewed, downtown leaders sometimes say after cursory legal research. That may or may not be the point. Downtown organizations, now more than ever, are public trusts. A public trust requires openness and transparency.

Flexibility

> *Away from:* Less.
> *Toward:* More.

A vacant building, in a key location, needs to be adaptively reused. The mayor needs help restructuring his city parking authority. The Oscar Mayer Wienermobile is coming to town. "That's not our job; it's not in our strategic plan," say some downtown organizations. "We'd better find out a way to make things happen," say others.

CONCLUSION

The old ways of doing things are comfortable, like an old pair of shoes. The boundaries of the downtown organization are clearly delineated. We know who to blame if things go wrong, and it's not us.

The new ways are a little confusing, like a high-tech pair of cross-trainer shoes. Where our responsibility stops and the next entity's starts is anyone's guess. We are constantly trying to solve problems, constantly adjusting.

That's what makes today's downtown organizations so challenging—and so interesting.

REFERENCES

Fisher, R. (1983). *Getting to Yes: Negotiating Agreement without Giving In.* New York: Penguin.
Machiavelli, N. (1998). *The Prince.* Oxford: Oxford University Press.

Chapter 4

The Vision-Driven Downtown Organization

David Feehan

At some point, many downtown organizations engage in what is commonly called "visioning." The point of this exercise is often to provide an opening paragraph for the organization's strategic plan. After suitable reflection, debate, and discussion, the "vision statement" usually ends up as something like this: "Our vision is a clean, safe, attractive, and friendly downtown, a great place to work, shop, live, and play."

All of these attributes—clean and safe, attractive and friendly—are important, but they hardly constitute a "vision." They describe basic attributes that should apply to any downtown or business district. It is akin to an auto manufacturer saying, "Our vision is to build a car with four wheels, an engine, and seating for five." This might describe any vehicle from an economy sedan to a Rolls-Royce.

The purpose of this chapter is to help practitioners and students understand the importance of creating a vision for the business district or downtown that they help to manage and lead; to differentiate between a "place" vision and an "organizational" vision; and to suggest some practical ways to build a vision statement that provides a beacon guiding the organization to a shared destination.

CREATING A SHARED VISION

Imagine that you have decided to take a vacation. The basics are in place—you have the time and resources to get away for a while and enjoy yourself. It is unlikely that you would plan your vacation by saying to yourself, "I am going to go to a place other than home, a place that is clean and safe, friendly and attractive." More likely, you would envision a place with a beautiful beach with sand as pure as granulated sugar, with palm trees and gentle surf. Or perhaps you would dream of a Rocky Mountain cabin surrounded by evergreen forests, with every breath of air perfumed by the

doi:10.1300/5137_05

wind-caressed pines and spruces. If you want something less laid back, maybe your vision is a pulsing place such as Times Square, surrounded by Broadway musicals, great restaurants, street musicians, nightclubs, and the unmistakable sounds of Midtown Manhattan.

However you envision your ideal vacation spot, you can see, smell, hear, feel, and taste the sensations each mental picture conveys. It's a much different experience than "clean, safe, attractive, and friendly" which has about as much sensory appeal as a cardboard sandwich.

Think of the following cities: Las Vegas, Nashville, Orlando, Hollywood, Miami Beach. Even if you've never visited these cities, you probably have a mental picture of Las Vegas as a brilliantly lit, never-asleep place with casinos at every intersection. Nashville conjures up images of the Grand Ole Opry and country music joints; Orlando has Disney World; Hollywood has handprints of stars imbedded in the sidewalks; and Miami Beach has incredible art deco hotels and condos, and, of course, a great beach.

Unfortunately, most cities and business districts aren't nearly as well known and don't have the unmistakable identity, for better or worse, that these cities have.

Vision versus Brand

It is important to distinguish between vision and brand. Much has been written about brands in general; many "branding" consultants have attempted to give relatively unknown cities, downtowns, and business districts clever branding treatments—catchy slogans about whatever the business district is or wants to be. Brands seek to place in the prospective visitor's head a belief that "this is the place to go for (fill in the blank)." For example, some places want to be known as 24/7 downtowns—always alive, always ready to party. Others may choose to be known as family-friendly business districts—good libraries and bookstores, schools and day care facilities, moderate-priced restaurants. But the key distinction between a brand and a vision is that a brand describes the image you want people to have of your downtown right now, while a vision describes what the business district or downtown will look like at some point in the future, provided you are successful as a downtown manager and leader in achieving your goals.

Most downtowns and business districts have a long history, but not all do. Some are evolving in new communities such as the Woodlands near Houston, Reston, the new community in Northern Virginia, or Southlake near Dallas. Some have evolved from relatively minor, first-ring suburban business districts into true downtowns, such as Bethesda, and Silver Spring, Maryland. These are becoming authentic downtowns, different from the "lifestyle centers" that have largely taken center stage from regional malls as the preferred shopping center design.

History can help shape the identity, character, and personality that in turn can bring a vision to life. From the Alamo in San Antonio to Philadelphia's Independence Hall, from Beale Street in Memphis to Newberry Street in Boston, from the numerous old city halls and warehouse districts to wharfs and boardwalks, history can be the context that makes the vision authentic.

Whether your district is new or old, a real vision implies change—and change for the better. If you could wave a magic wand, what would be different in your downtown? Lots of people on the street? Sidewalk cafes? Tree-lined boulevards? Ethnic restaurants and coffeehouses? A vision for Clematis Street in West Palm Beach is going to be different from a vision for the Nicollet Mall in Minneapolis.

To summarize, a vision is a description of a desired condition at some point in the future. If you could somehow climb into a time machine and transport yourself into your downtown five or ten years hence, what would you see, hear, feel, touch, and taste? That description, artfully crafted, should guide your mission, goals, objectives, strategies, and actions.

Creating the vision for your downtown or business district is the central focus of this chapter. One organization executive said that his vision was to create "the organization I always wanted to work for" (Robert Kellar, CEO of Detroit Renaissance, personal communication, 1994). Although this is certainly vague, he had in his mind a vision—an organization (in his case) that was very horizontal in structure, informal in style, based on trust and shared information.

A powerful vision for a downtown or business district conveys a sense of personality, character, and identity—what Pittsburgh-based organizational consultant Denys Candy calls "community DNA" (Candy, 2002). Many elements make up the strands of community DNA—history, architecture, geography, topography, local economy, and of course, most important, people. The social fabric of a community, the connections that exist between people, the ethnic character and diversity that make up a complex urban society, all of these and more contribute to community DNA.

THE VISION STATEMENT

As a downtown manager, how would you go about discovering and articulating a community vision that is authentic and energizing?

Reaching Agreement

The first step, of course, is convincing the downtown organization board of directors that such an exercise is warranted. You may find that several board members, who consider themselves hardheaded, clear-thinking businesspeople, are resistant to any "touchy-feely" exercises. This resistance seems to be waning, however. Perhaps this is because over the past decade many respected business publications have urged businesses to be more vision driven. Many companies, especially bigger corporations, have found vision statements valuable for employees and shareholders.

If there is resistance, a good exercise is to bring the issue up at a board meeting. Ask the chairperson to have everyone, without prior discussion, write what they perceive to be the downtown vision on a piece of paper. Read the results aloud and list them on a flip chart. Certainly, there will be significant variation among the individual vision statements. This alone should allow the chairperson to convince any dissidents that the organization needs a unified vision for downtown. Without it, the executive director will certainly be guaranteed to fail in the eyes of at least some board members, because their personal visions will remain unfulfilled.

Once agreement is reached on the need for a unified vision, the board should agree to spend sufficient time to produce a quality product. It is possible, but unlikely, that board members will produce a quality vision statement at a regular board meeting. Time is short, and there will probably be too many other agenda items to think about. This suggests that the board should schedule a special retreat or visioning session. Holding such an event on a Saturday morning is often a good idea, because board members will not be as distracted by concerns at their own business or organization. If the vision session is held during the week, ask board members to block out either a morning or an afternoon.

An outside facilitator should at least be considered. Any "insider," including the chief executive or board chairperson, may be suspected of having an axe to grind, and, perceived bias could sour the process. Most towns of any size have process facilitators who are capable of managing a visioning session. Sometimes local corporations, especially if the headquarters are in town, have a professional facilitator on staff. The International Downtown Association (IDA) sometimes facilitates vision sessions or arranges for experienced downtown leaders from other cities to do so.

The visioning session should occur in comfortable surroundings with no distractions. The main goal is to get participants to be able to dream—to envision what downtown will look like five or ten years hence.

Five or ten years is a good "vision horizon." Any shorter time period does not allow enough time for change to be accomplished—thereby almost guaranteeing failure in terms of achieving the vision. Anything more than ten years may seem too far in the future to foresee, and will be beyond at least the working life of many of the participants.

Participation should be as inclusive as possible. At a minimum, it should include all board members of the downtown or business district organization. If there is a separate board or advisory committee for a BID, those members should also be included. If there are constituencies that are not represented on the board (residents, social service or religious organizations, government agencies), it is advisable to have those perspectives represented.

PAST EXPERIENCE, FUTURE VISION

All information comes to the human brain through a person's senses. Experiences become memories, and memories remind us of things we found to be either pleasant or unpleasant. So one of the ways to begin a visioning workshop is to ask people to recall experiences they have had, even as children, that evoke positive memories of downtowns. Someone may recall an early experience of going to a downtown movie house—the smell of popcorn, the taste of chocolate candy, the power of the cinema's sound system. Another participant may recall a day in a downtown park with a grandparent, learning to play chess on a board that was part of the park furniture. Perhaps the child was surrounded by other chess players and observers, a common scene in some big-city parks. Recollections of summer breezes, birds chirping, and hot dogs from a nearby stand may have cemented that experience in memory. Or another participant may remember a downtown parade or festival, with lots of music, colorful costumes, riders on horseback, and cotton candy.

What is the downtown experience like today? Participants may be asked to describe something they experienced in the past month. A great meal at a new bistro? A street musician singing the blues? An aggressive panhandler thrusting out a plastic cup? The sounds of construction as a new office tower is erected? The early morning smells of a European bakery?

Once the participants have explored early and recent recollections, and described things in terms of sensory experiences ("it smelled like . . . tasted like . . . was a brilliant blue . . .") they will be ready to peer into the future and describe what the downtown or business district will look like five or ten years hence.

A good technique to use at this point is to ask participants to close their eyes and spend a few minutes dreaming about downtown in five years. After perhaps two to three minutes have passed, ask each participant to describe one thing he or she sees, hears, smells, feels, or even tastes: Colorful, flower-filled parks? Sidewalk cafes? Exotic new retail shops? Two-way streets? Pedestrian-oriented intersections? Bike racks in parking garages? Music played by a street musician? A new restaurant featuring South American cuisine? The smell of ground-roasted coffee coming from a new deli and coffee house? The feel of a marble statue?

As these suggestions are listed on the flip chart, patterns start to form. What kind of downtown do they suggest? Highly energized or laid back? Cutting edge or more conservative? Focused on work, play, or living? By the time the session is over, a shared vision should emerge.

Either the downtown executive or the facilitator, or possibly another person who is a talented copywriter, should craft a powerful, well-written vision statement. That statement then should become the beacon for the organization. The mission statement should be a statement of commitment by the organization to achieving the vision. Broad goals should support the mission statement; specific objectives with time limitations and measurement of results should support each goal. Strategies and actions will follow from each objective.

Without a vision, an organization can successfully manage downtown "clean-and-safe" programs; it can create and market events, produce brochures, and carry on other activities typical of downtown and business district management organizations. There is a reasonably good chance that these activities, if implemented effectively, will improve the business district. However, there is very little chance that the downtown or business district will ever achieve its full potential. In fact, without a vision, it is nearly impossible to determine what that full potential might be.

Ken Blanchard and Jesse Stoner (2004) propose three critical factors essential to world-class organizations:

1. Clear vision championed by top management.
2. Trained and equipped people focused on the implementation of the agreed-upon vision and direction.
3. Established recognition and positive consequence systems that sustain the behaviors and performance that the vision and direction require.

Clearly, according to Blanchard and Stoner (2004), it all starts with vision. Neither of the other two critical factors is possible if the vision does not exist. A compelling vision is not a formulaic document that gathers dust in a file. Blanchard and Stoner contend that a compelling vision must:

1. State a significant purpose—answering the question, "What business are you in?"

2. Paint a picture of the future—what will the future look like if you live according to your purpose?
3. Articulate clear values—how do you want people to behave when they are working according to your purpose and on your picture of the future?

The following statement articulates a vision for Downtown Albany, New York, that can be utilized by both the Albany community and the Downtown Albany BID (Coleman and Feehan, 2003).

The board and staff defined the following elements to possibly be included in a vision statement:

- The nation's premier state capital
- The region's best choice for culture, arts, and recreation
- Albany's most exciting residential opportunities
- The best dining choices, from simple to gourmet, within a hundred miles
- Three hundred and fifty years of history, captured in the region's architectural jewels
- An extraordinary collection of one-of-a-kind shops
- Sparkling clean—family friendly
- Music on every corner
- Local residents mix with tourists from all over the world
- A dynamic spirit, a passion for excellence
- Unforgettable experience, treasured memories
- Big-city energy, small-town charm
- A downtown where ethnicity is a cause for celebration
- The stage on which we celebrate our community
- Major center for technological innovation and implementation

Based on these vision elements, the board and staff composed the following vision statement:

> Downtown Albany is the nation's premier state capital. The sparkling-clean, family-friendly center of the region's arts, architecture, culture, education and entertainment, downtown Albany is big-city energy and small-town charm. Blessed with the most exciting and unique residential opportunities, an extraordinary collection of one-of-a-kind shops, dining that ranges from simple to elegant, and a major international center for technological innovation and implementation, downtown Albany pulses with a dynamic spirit and a passion for

excellence. The heart of a region of more than a million people at the crossroads of great mountains, rivers, and cities, downtown Albany is an unforgettable experience, a theater stage known worldwide for its celebrations of past, present, and future.

Although it may not be perfect, this vision statement gives the board, staff, and stakeholders of the Downtown Albany BID—a clear picture of what they envision for downtown Albany in the future.

What is the business of the Downtown Albany BID? Clean and safe—yes, but that's a small part of the description of this capital city as it grows over the next several years. The organization has a vision of a downtown that sparkles. This is a downtown that "pulses with a dynamic spirit and a passion for excellence." Does this description make you want to be a part of this community's future?

Downtowns are vital to the future of every city. Research has shown repeatedly that regions with strong central cities fare much better economically than those with weak central cities. Downtown is the economic engine that pulls the city train. Downtowns provide many dollars in tax revenues for each dollar of service consumed.

Great downtowns and great business districts are built on potent, well-crafted, broadly understood and supported visions. It is incumbent on every member of a downtown organization to know and understand the vision, and act consistently to achieve that vision.

Recommended Reading

Blanchard, Ken and Jesse Stoner. "The Vision Thing: Without It, You'll Never Be a World Class Organization." Leader to Leader Institute, Winter 2004.

Civic Strategies, Inc. *From Vision to Reality: How City Administrations Succeed in the Long Haul.* Available online at www.civic-strategies.com.

Florida, Richard. *The Rise of the Creative Class.* New York: Basic Books, 2002.

Garreau, Joel. *Edge City—Life on the New Frontier.* New York: Anchor Books, 1991.

Gilmore, James and Joseph Pine. *The Experience Economy.* Cambridge: Harvard Business School Press, 1999.

Gratz, Roberta with Norman Mintz. *Cities Back from the Edge—New Life for Downtown.* New York: John Wiley and Sons, 1998.

Hudnut, William H. *Cities on the Rebound—A Vision for Urban America.* Washington, DC: Urban Land Institute, 1998.

Morgan, Gareth. *Imaginization—The Art of Creative Management.* Sage Books, 1993.

Palma, Delores P. and Doyle G. Hyett. *America's Downtown Renaissance.* Washington: National League of Cities, 2001.
Rybczyniski, Withold. *City Life.* New York: Scribner, 1995.
White, William H. *The Social Life of Small Urban Spaces.* Washington, DC: The Conservation Foundation, 1980.

REFERENCES

Blanchard, Ken and Jesse Stoner. "The Vision Thing: Without It, You'll Never be a World Class Organization." Leader to Leader Institute, Winter, 2004. Available online at www.leadertoleader.org.
Coleman, Morton and Feehan, David. Advisory Panel Report, Downtown Albany BID (unpublished) 2003.
IDA Annual Conference. Boston, 2002.

Part II:
Organizing the Downtown Corporation

Any journey requires an appropriate vehicle—and the vehicle that the private and public sectors have found works best is a nonprofit corporation focused on a specific place—a downtown or business district. Designing and building that vehicle takes a whole set of tools and skills. Driving that vehicle to the desired destination takes another set of skills. Organizational vehicles, like other vehicles, need a means of propulsion. They need guidance systems and they need fuel. This section shows you how some of the best downtown leaders have built and driven their organizational vehicles to success.

Chapter 5

Complex Organizational Structures

James A. Cloar

Typically, downtown organizations are formed in response to a specific threat or opportunity. Accordingly, their structures in the first years of operation are likely to be simple in nature, reflecting a distinct mission and solitary funding source.

Over time, corporate mergers may prompt membership-based associations to look for a more stable funding source; a business improvement district may feel the need to address issues "beyond clean and safe"; or, quasi-public development authorities may look to establish a broader constituent base. For these and other reasons, management structures typically have become more complex, with a common staff serving several allied but separately incorporated entities.

BACKGROUND

When the International Downtown Association (then the International Downtown Executives Association [IDEA]) was formed in 1954, it was prompted by the mutual discovery by the directors of four downtown organizations that there were "others like them" out there in the world. In fact, there were many more already in existence or soon to follow. Primarily located in the United States, they could be found in every geographic region and included cities such as Chicago, Dallas, San Antonio, Atlanta, Oakland, and Seattle. Even smaller cities such as Richmond, Virginia, Syracuse, New York, and Flint, Michigan, had formed downtown associations.

This period in time was marked by emerging challenges to central business districts. These challenges were clearly of concern to the business community, where the traditional forum for collective private sector activity had been the chamber of commerce. Some had organized downtown committees but often, especially in cities undergoing rapid suburbanization, the

doi:10.1300/5137_06

ability of chambers to give downtown issues needed focus or action was compromised.

Understandably, the newly forming downtown associations usually had chamber of commerce characteristics, including management structure. Some even referred to themselves as the downtown chamber.

SIMPLE STRUCTURES

By the late 1970s, membership in IDEA had grown to about 200. Although the members were varied in focus (such as retail revitalization, development, traffic and parking, etc.) and in strategy (marketing, general promotion, planning, and/or advocacy), a common characteristic was clarity, and almost single-mindedness of mission.

The typical result was a simplified management structure with a small staff comprised of an executive director, an administrative assistant/bookkeeper, and sometimes a special project manager or two. Predominantly, they were nonprofit organizations that relied on funding from dues or other forms of member support.

The word "executive" had particular significance in IDA's original name, beyond forming the clever acronym IDEA. Its annual meeting agenda devoted ample time for discussions on board makeup, dues structure, membership recruitment, and the business of running an association.

EVOLVING RESPONSES

A small but growing number of downtown organizations did not neatly fit this mold, however. By the early 1980s, enabling legislation for tax increment financing in Florida fostered the organization of downtown development authorities (DDAs) in cities and towns throughout that state. In Memphis, Tennessee, the Center City Commission (CCC) led the downtown revitalization effort.

Although the DDAs in Florida and the CCC in Memphis were intended to play a direct role in fostering development, the new Downtown Development District in New Orleans was organized to provide enhanced security, maintenance, and streetscape improvements. Funded by a special assessment to provide and emphasize services rather than projects, it was possibly the first "business improvement district."

These entities had several things in common. They were not associations as such; they had no members and were not funded by dues. Instead, they were "quasi-public," with the boards comprised of business and community leaders appointed by the mayor and/or city councils.

Another common trait was their involvement with IDA (in fact, the first IDA chair from a nontraditional downtown organization was the executive director of the Miami DDA in 1986). Their interest was in downtowns rather than organizational management, leading to the name change for the organization.

EXPANDED MISSIONS

For decades, community leaders threw their energies behind "magic potion" projects, or strategies such as pedestrian malls, convention centers, high-powered marketing campaigns, or elaborate festivals and events. All too often, these valiant and well-intended efforts fell short of lasting transformation.

It became clear that to be successful, downtown organizations needed to take multipronged approaches. For many, this meant moving past being a cheerleader/advocate/convener, though these remained significant roles. Downtown organizations also saw the need to take on a more direct catalytic character. To do so meant creating additional organizational arrangements.

Being a meaningful partner in specific development projects likely means being party to confidential negotiations and transactions. For the traditional membership organization or the business improvement district partner, that role may risk premature disclosure or conflicts of interest with those who pay significant dues or assessments. The size of dollar commitment would likely require special funding beyond the capacity of a typical budget income line item.

Managing a BID also requires isolating operations funded by assessment income. Whether received directly or through a government entity, these assessments, being mandatory and authorized by law, implies that they are essentially public dollars. This imposes obligations, with respect to media and public interest group scrutiny, that could jeopardize development deals and/or bring discomfort to potential private-sector funders. It may also constrain lobbying or other advocacy activities.

The sources of funding also play a role in determining structure. No longer able to count on dues from local, downtown-based corporations to support the level and consistency of budget needed, downtown organizations have increasingly turned to foundations, grants, and (as noted earlier) structures such as BIDs.

In a reverse trend, newly created BIDs, originally more quasi-public in character, have begun to move "beyond clean and safe" and have found that creating companion entities best fits their new mission. An independent parallel group can offer more freedom to assume a leadership role on more controversial issues, including some at variance with the elected bodies which may influence the assessment district's budget or board appointments.

During the 2004 IDA Leadership Forum, many discussions related to the sometimes conflicting roles of management versus leadership. In their 1992 book *Reinventing Government,* co-authors David Osborne and Ted Gabler (1992) wrote of the importance of separating "rowing" from "steering," noting that the former applies to activities that focus "intently on one mission and perform it well" while the latter involves shaping communities, states, and nations (p. 35).

COMPLEX STRUCTURE MODELS

Possibly the best-known of these complex structures, and often considered a model, was The Denver Partnership (now the Downtown Denver Partnership). The Partnership essentially was comprised of the existing membership organization, along with the new Mall Management District (focusing on the recently developed 16th Street Mall) and Denver Civic Ventures, an organization geared toward broader community development goals (see Figure 5.1). Though separate legal entities, they share a common staff and the leadership of each of the boards meets monthly.

Similar types of organizations were in place or soon followed in cities such as Atlanta, Syracuse, Seattle, Orlando, and Kalamazoo. By 1985, the Central Dallas Association housed seven entities within in its offices.

CASE STUDY: DOWNTOWN ST. LOUIS

In 1997, Downtown St. Louis, Inc., a long-standing membership organization formed under section 501(c)(6) of the Internal Revenue Service Code (2003), adopted a structure similar to that of the Downtown Denver Partnership. Its motivation, in part, was to prepare for undertaking responsibilities for managing a planned Community Improvement District (CID).

Three new entities under the St. Louis Inc. organization were created to oversee activities related to (1) housing and economic development, (2) special events, and (3) traditional assessment district roles of managing security,

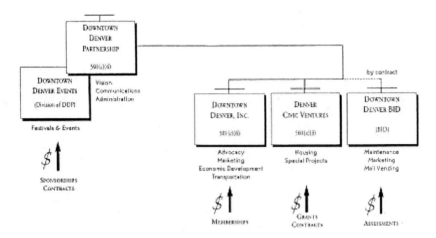

FIGURE 5.1. Downtown Denver, Colorado. *Source:* Prepared by Progressive Urban Management Associates 8/99. Reprinted with permission.

maintenance, and beautification, and marketing/promotion. Each was organized under IRS Section 501(c)(3).

A fourth new organization was the Downtown Saint Louis Partnership, a 501(c)(4) formed to provide overall private sector leadership along with broad management direction for CID programs (see Figure 5.2). The Partnership was the recipient of assessment district funds and employed all staff.

Via annually renewed agreements, the Partnership then contracted with its three subsidiaries ("Development," "Presents" and "Management") to carry out the various programs authorized by the overall CID budget, effectively reimbursing them for nonpersonnel costs (responsibility for funding personnel and associated overhead expenses remained with the parent organization). The Partnership also managed the affairs of the existing Downtown St. Louis Inc. and was in turn reimbursed for associated personnel and overhead costs, again by annual contract.

The chair and vice chair of each of the "subsidiary" organizations were ex-officio members of the Partnership Board. In addition, the president and CEO of the Partnership also served in the same capacity on the other four Boards.

The emerging structure was dictated in part as a response to explicit requirements of state enabling legislation for CID-funded entities. It also provided a large number of additional board positions and thereby provided a direct link to a broader stakeholder base, critical to winning support for the

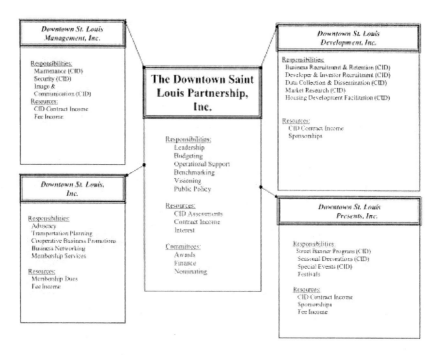

FIGURE 5.2. The Downtown Saint Louis Partnership, Inc. structure (prior to June 30, 2003). Reprinted with permission.

new assessment district. In addition, it offered the opportunity to cast a new image, reconnecting to the kind of upper-level corporate leadership that had once been the backbone of the organization but had drifted away over the years.

Despite these advantages, over time, the structure proved cumbersome. The boards—and their committees—began to meet with increased regularity and became more assertive about presumed prerogatives. Turf questions arose as to budget control, direction of various staff, and the authority of various entities to take positions supporting or opposing different issues. There was external confusion as well, since the organization actively operated under five different names.

Administrative procedures also became unwieldy. Preparing for five board meetings monthly with five separate bank accounts and sets of financial statements and five separate sets of officers required inordinate amounts of time for administrative duties and resulted in unproductive redundancies. Regularly, at least two checks would be written for the same product or service, one to pay the vendor and another to reimburse the contracting entity. In addition, since the four operating entities were only responsible for nonstaff expenses while the Partnership paid for staff and overhead, it was difficult to define the true cost of various programs.

A combined strategic planning retreat of the boards in late 2001 placed a high priority on corporate reorganization, with the goal of achieving simplification and clarification of roles while maintaining accountability. The result was a two-board format, one to focus on management of the downtown environment (funded primarily though assessment district revenues) and the other to provide private-sector advocacy and leadership (supported by dues and other "non-dues" income).

Although simple in concept, the legal details of the transition were fairly complex and dealt with matters of incorporation, recognition of not-for-profit status, and absorption of funds and liabilities. In essence, however, the resultant format involved merging the three assessment district operating corporations ("Management," Development" and "Presents") into the newly named "Downtown St. Louis Community Improvement District," thus clarifying its unique role and responsibilities within the overall structure (see Figure 5.3).

In a concurrent action, the "Partnership" and "Inc." also effectively merged, consolidating their leadership, advocacy, and "vision" functions and operating under the locally more recognizable name "Downtown St. Louis Partnership." For ease of benefits and payroll, the Partnership employs all staff.

Assessment district funds and related revenues go directly to Downtown St. Louis CID, which reimburses the Partnership for relevant salary and overhead expenses per an annual contract agreement. The Partnership funds its own operations from dues, sponsorships and other similar sources.

The chairs and vice chairs of each organization are ex-officio directors of the companion entity; the president/CEO serves in the same capacity on both boards. In addition, there are joint committees for finance and for nominations. Senior staff attends both monthly meetings.

POINTS TO CONSIDER

Although the St. Louis example may be instructive in that it compares two different formats in basically the same setting, there are numerous other models of complex structures from which to draw. Following are some considerations to keep in mind in developing the corporate structure:

1. *Segregate and clarify functions* among the entities, making an unambiguous distinction as to the role and purview of each.

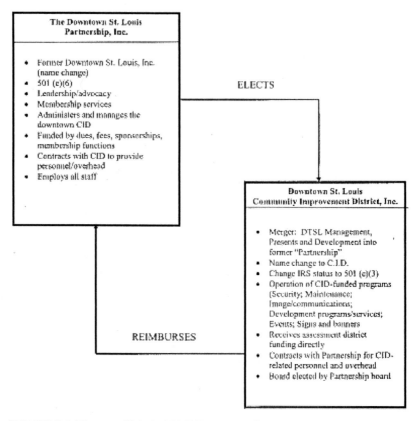

FIGURE 5.3. The new (July 1, 2003) Downtown St. Louis Partnership structure. (*Source:* Cloar, J. *New Downtown St. Louis Partnership Structure* [unpublished] 2003.)

2. A companion organization can facilitate the *ability to take controversial positions* or protect confidences without jeopardizing other funding sources.
3. Subsidiary can *distinguish leadership roles from management activities.*
4. Subsidiary can open up *new sources of funding.* (Organizations recognized under section 501(c)(3) of the IRS Code may more likely be eligible for certain grants, sponsorships, or other forms of financial support.)

5. Depending on the IRS status and Article of Incorporation, there *may be restrictions on certain types of activities.*

6. There may be potential sales or other tax exemptions that can be achieved through one entity and not the other.

7. *Special project funds can be isolated,* giving assurance to sponsors or underwriters that their support for specific projects or programs will not be redirected.

8. Creating one or more companion organizations can provide an opportunity to *rebrand the organization,* particularly in cases in which the involvement of business leaders has gradually trickled down from CEOs to second- or third-tier officers.

9. If restructuring, have a *clear understanding of what is to be accomplished.* Do not add another entity just for the sake of doing it.

10. *Be prepared to modify the structure over time* as conditions change. The 1997 restructuring in St. Louis prepared the organization for management of new assessment districts and broadening the base of support, while the consolidation five years later helped streamline governance procedures and eliminate redundancy.

11. A companion organization can provide *involvement for a larger stakeholder group* without compromising the ability to be entrepreneurial.

12. Provide for *appropriate linkages among the organizations* through a degree of overlapping board positions and shared staff.

13. Avoid falling into the *trap of too many board meetings* with attendant preparation and follow-up time cutting into real productivity.

14. *Formalize the distribution of funds and resources between organizations* through written contracts, letters of agreement, or similar documentation.

15. Put "firewalls" in place to *prevent inappropriate comingling of funds.*

16. Having *all shared staff employed by one entity* will provide clarity of reporting responsibilities and facilitate benefits programs.

17. *Avoid confusing the public and members* if actively operating under several names.

18. Be prepared for *transition snags when changing the structure,* including legal details of incorporation or mergers, as well as wounded feelings on the part of "displaced" board members.

19. *Models employed elsewhere are useful guides but should be adapted* to fit the local situation and to fit the management style of the CEO.

REFERENCES

International Downtown Association (IDA). (2004). 2004 Leadership Forum.
International Revenue Service (2003). Allen, Braig, B., Hull, C., Reilly, Francis, J. IRC 501(c)(6) Organizations: 2003 EO CPE Text. Washington: GPO, pp. 4,6.
Osborne, D. and Gabler, T. (1992). *Reinventing Government*. New York: Penguin Group.

Chapter 6

Boards and Committees—Governance

Kate Joncas

INTRODUCTION

Much has been written on developing and managing a nonprofit board. This chapter is not intended to duplicate that information, but rather to cover some of the unique organizational challenges faced by the staff and volunteer leaders of downtown organizations.

Successful downtown executives have both strong private-sector business management skills and excellent nonprofit volunteer and consensus-building skills. Key skill areas include:

- Running an effective organization
- Creating a vision
- Leading and managing
- Volunteer management
- Community consensus building

In many ways, traditional advice for nonprofit management is appropriate and necessary for managing a downtown organization. However, downtown boards are different from other community boards in several significant ways.

One of the most important differences is that downtown boards are often made up of successful business owners—retailers, hoteliers, attorneys, and developers—who can be very demanding, focused on immediate results, and unforgiving of poor outcomes. In addition, their business success may be directly impacted by the decisions the board and staff make. As a result of this high-test mix, downtown association boards can be challenging to manage. For the right staff executive, this can be an energizing and dynamic situation, but with an unskilled executive and inexperienced board chair, it can be a rough ride. Some of the issues described in this chapter should help smooth over some of the potholes.

© 2006 by The Haworth Press, Inc. All rights reserved.
doi:10.1300/5137_07

CONFLICTS OF INTEREST

Downtown organizations are unique in that board members' businesses could be directly impacted by board decisions. This makes for several interesting governance challenges, and one of them is conflict of interest. It can make decision making very complex for the executive and the chair.

Board members often have to vote on a project that directly impacts their business. It gets more complicated when a downtown project benefits one powerful board member but could hurt the business of another. For example, a decision about whether the light rail station is located at First and Pine Streets or Second and Pine Streets could put two influential board members at odds with each other, and it only becomes more interesting if one of them is the chair. Conflicts of this kind on downtown boards are inevitable, and, without an agreed-upon process for considering issues like this, can cause serious harm to the board.

The best strategy is to be up-front about the issue and to acknowledge that conflict of interest could occur. First, board members should sign annual conflict of interest forms. Check with your accounting firm or corporate attorney for examples. Conflict of interest forms stipulate that when a board member sees a potential conflict they need to acknowledge it. Usually these forms are specific to financial ties to the organization, however, this process will enable the chair to bring up the issue in a general way each year, and provide an opportunity to acknowledge that the board will be working on issues where there will be potential benefits and potential harm to individual members. This should help the chair to have a productive and open discussion on tricky issues.

Second, the chair should encourage as open a discussion as possible of the issues, particularly from positions of interest. The board needs as much information as possible to make a good decision, and the chair needs to foster an environment where this kind of frank discussion of self-interest is acceptable. A detailed discussion of how a project helps or hurts specific businesses will help the board get enough information to make an informed decision or come up with a creative solution.

For example, the downtown organization is asked to support an expedited permit process for a new hotel construction project. The expedited permit would allow for a shorter but more disruptive street construction period. The chair is an investor in the project, and there is some board opposition to the permit. The chair declares his interest, cedes his role as chair for the discussion, and abstains from the vote. In open discussion, a board member who owns an office furniture store indicates that she opposes the permit because it will allow the hotel to dig up the street in front of her store for a month and make access very difficult for her customers. She notes that although the hotel project will benefit downtown as a whole, she is likely to suffer a loss of business from a project that will not benefit her, as hotel guests are unlikely to buy office furniture.

This kind of open discussion of business needs could result in a new solution—the hotel could offer a package of discount lunches to the store-owner so she could wine and dine her best customers. The chair needs to foster a climate of open discussion and an expectation that the board is interested in knowing what its members need in order to succeed. If downtown is to be a great place to do business for everyone, the board needs to be educated about its members' business needs.

Third, conflict of interest can be managed by putting the immediate project into a bigger context or longer time frame. Sometimes, even though the impact is primarily on one business, it does affect all of downtown. For example, a construction project that could make access to the department store difficult is a legitimate downtown-wide concern—losing a department store would have negative impacts on the entire downtown economy. Also, reviewing past projects can help individual business and property owners to see that over time, each neighborhood or business type has its turn to get investment and benefits, and conversely to feel the impacts.

ACHIEVING CONSENSUS

Making decisions by consensus (as opposed to taking a vote) is almost always the first choice for downtown association boards. The downtown community, even in a large city, is actually relatively small. A bitterly fought vote with a slim margin of victory can cause you to lose an important board member or two, and most organizations cannot afford to alienate key players. In addition, board members are often intertwined in business deals and want to keep their business relationships. A board member will probably resign from the board rather than lose a business partner over a tough vote.

When attempting to use a consensus model it is important to set appropriate expectations about what consensus is. Do not define consensus as "everyone agrees" with the decision. Consensus should be defined as everyone "can live" with the decision. This is a key distinction that can help to move an issue forward. When checking in with board members it is often more useful to ask, "Can you live with this decision?" instead of "Do you agree with this decision?" That said, the time it could take to reach consensus could be frustrating to business owners who do not like "process." Also, commitment to a consensus decision-making process makes the group vulnerable to "tyranny of the minority," in which one or two adamant and vocal opponents prevent the majority from making a decision.

On any issue that is coming before your board, do your due diligence. The old saying of having the votes counted before you call the question is particularly important in downtown work. It is often prudent to work on an issue quietly to find out how the key players feel about it before it is brought up for open discussion.

Sometimes, an issue is so controversial or mixed in its impacts that it has strong constituencies, both pro and con, on the board. This is a tough spot to be in, as both taking a stand and not taking a stand can be unpopular. If you take a vote and the margin of passage or failure is small, it could alienate half of the board, causing an irreparable rift. If you decide not to take a position, some members will criticize you for being indecisive or soft, or question the point of belonging to an organization that does not have the guts to take a stand. Several techniques can be used when it looks like there are serious divisions over an issue on the board.

Debate by Outside Experts on Both Sides of the Issue

Bring in outside experts on both sides of the issue to debate their points of view and answer questions from board members. This gets the discussion focused away from individual board members, educates all of the members on the issue, and enables the executive and the chair to see who is on each side.

Decision Matrix

Trying to quantify and compare impacts is often very difficult. However, the process of trying to develop a decision matrix and the discussions on ranking benefits and impacts could help to clarify the issue and possibly enable the board to make a decision.

Expert Opinion Panel

Ask a group of disinterested, respected parties to review the issue, ask questions, and make a recommendation. This technique can reduce the emotion behind the issue, get the facts out in a nonjudgmental way, provide support for a controversial decision, and reduce opposition.

Mediator

Every community has a respected elder statesman or stateswoman. The board could ask this person to be a mediator. The mediator could listen to all sides of the issue, ask tough questions, and try to broker a decision everyone can live with.

Change the Focus

If it is clear the entire board cannot agree on a position on the issue, perhaps changing the focus of the issue will provide a point all can agree on. For example, suppose the bus agency is considering bus rapid transit through downtown on either Third or Fourth Avenues. Businesses and property owners on both streets are mixed in their opinions, and the matrix analysis shows relatively equal benefits and negative impacts on each street. The board could agree to not take a position on the location of the project, but to focus on developing and lobbying for a mitigation plan for whatever route was chosen.

SUCCESSFUL RELATIONSHIPS WITH ORGANIZATIONS

In many downtowns, there is a common, cyclical phenomenon of combining community organizations into one umbrella group to achieve efficiency and avoid perceived duplication. Unfortunately, often the next generation separates out the organizations to better serve unique constituencies, only to have the following generation combine the organizations to avoid perceived duplication of effort! For this reason or another, all downtown organizations will engage in a power struggle with another community group. These organizational struggles are often preventable and should be avoided at all costs. They can consume staff and boards, significantly reduce productivity, and can cause the executive director to be fired, pushed out, or to quit in frustration.

Struggles with chambers of commerce over resources and territory are fairly common. Many downtown organizations began as downtown retail subcommittees of their chambers, and in the 1950s and 1960s many of the chambers' biggest members were located in downtown. As suburban growth occurred, the constituent base and missions of chambers changed to reflect the needs of these new members. Chamber membership diversified, adding large suburban businesses, and downtown issues could no longer be the top priority. As a result, many downtown retail committees became independent.

Over time, these former retail committees diversified to include representatives of the broad range of downtown constituencies, including building owners, major commercial tenants, arts groups, and human services. At this point, conflicts between the organizations began to occur. For example, banks often have their headquarters in downtown, and so are asked to belong to both the downtown organization and the chamber of commerce. Businesses, when faced with two invoices for dues, often respond that they don't understand the difference between the two organizations and have resources to belong to only one. This can threaten the chambers' membership base.

Conflicts with economic development organizations are usually over turf. When the downtown organization adds business recruitment and retention activities, this may cause concern in the local economic development organization, which may view these activities as its sole purview and reason for being.

The key to good relations with any peer organization is mission clarity. Following is an example of how the differing missions and activities might be described:

- *Downtown Organizations* are focused on making downtown a great place to work, shop, live, play, and invest. Their mission usually involves business interests and a broad range of constituencies from real estate developers to homeless shelter operators to residents. Downtown organizations also often manage business improvement districts, which provide maintenance and safety services throughout the downtown neighborhood.
- *Chambers and Economic Development Organizations* are focused on making the region or community a good place to do business, and their constituency is often made up solely of businesses. They usually have services focused on business issues and needs, such as health insurance plans and events for business-to-business networking.

Clarifying the missions and services of the various organizations is useful in discussions with the downtown board so that they are comfortable articulating these points to the community. It might be useful to develop a memo, supported by all of the organizations, that clarifies mission differences.

Good communication is also essential to prevent organizational misunderstandings. Hosting an annual meeting of the chairs of major business organizations to discuss and compare work plans can establish a working relationship between the volunteer leaders and prevent misunderstandings. Some communities have found that setting up an informal organization of association executive staff can strengthen all of the organizations by identifying overlaps and potential partnerships.

Funders want to know that community organizations work together to try to leverage one another's resources and avoid duplication. This type of cooperation helps to answer the bank's concern about belonging to both the chamber and the downtown organization. With clear missions and demonstrated organizational cooperation, a strong case can be made that the bank would receive a significant benefit from participating in each organization.

In the case of economic development organizations, a good working relationship can be established by developing an agreement on process. The economic development organization is in charge of recruiting businesses to the region while the downtown organization focuses on recruiting businesses to downtown. If an agreement can be struck based on the operating principle that what is good for downtown is good for the region and vice versa, a mutual sharing of prospects can be arranged.

Information sharing is also a good way to maintain strong working relationships. Organization Web sites should be cross-linked. The downtown site should be the source of information on trends and facts about downtown. It should be linked from the chamber site and the local economic development organization site and vice versa.

TOO MANY ISSUES, TOO LITTLE TIME

The joy of working for a downtown organization is that almost every community issue impacts downtown in some way—which is also the frustration of working for a downtown organization—way too many issues. One of the biggest challenges for downtown executives and boards is that the list of issues they can handle is much smaller than the number of issues that are out there. Prioritizing and choosing issues that are the most important to downtown's future and that matter most to downtown constituents can be difficult. Often the future impacts of projects cannot be clearly defined and compared, and each constituency group thinks its issue is the most important.

The reality of issue management for downtown executives is that there are many more issues to which they must say no than there are those to which they can say yes. A downtown executive will need all of his or her diplomatic skills to tell a constituent that his or her issue is not important enough to become an organization priority. The executive's most effective tool in this case is a clear process for setting annual priorities and a written work plan that cannot be altered except by board action. This gives the executive and the board chair acceptable reasons for saying no but provides a process to alter the priorities when an emergency comes up.

The process for prioritizing issues should include the following test: Does this issue *only* or *mostly* impact downtown, and does the downtown organization have the ability to *make a difference*? If the answer to both of these questions is yes, put it on the list for consideration. If the answer is no, either the issue belongs to another organization—the chamber, the visitors bureau, etc.—or the downtown organization should take the role of *catalyst* instead of *leader.*

Often the type of issue that belongs to another organization is a state or regional project, such as a transportation improvement that goes through downtown. The project may have a significant impact on downtown, but it does not *only* or *mostly* impact downtown. Downtown organizations don't usually have the resources and political clout to lead the large coalitions needed to lobby on the state or regional level. The downtown organization needs a larger organization with which they can partner so that they can focus on the impacts to downtown.

Light rail is an example of a regional project that has big impacts on downtown, but is often too large in scale for a downtown organization to take on by itself. Just going to the project meetings alone could deplete the resources of a downtown organization. However, if approached in partnership with the chamber or regional planning agency, the downtown organization could focus on capacity and design issues in downtown, knowing that the larger organization was focusing on the big picture issues of cost containment and alignment.

An example of the type of issue in which a downtown organization could not be the leader but could have an impact by taking a *catalyst* role is improving recovery/rehabilitation programs for alcoholics. Alcoholism is a societal issue that often has a big impact on downtown—many of the homeless men and women sleeping on downtown streets or aggressively panhandling visitors may be suffering from alcoholism. Trying to reduce alcoholism is clearly beyond the scope of a downtown organization, but the downtown group could be the catalyst for new initiatives by inviting other groups to the table and offering to be a partner. Programs at different levels of government can be very isolated, even if they are serving the same clients. By serving as a catalyst to get different programs talking to one another, new and creative ideas can emerge.

THE NEW REALITY: LOCAL BUSINESS LEADERSHIP IS NO LONGER LOCAL

Many downtown boards are struggling with new business realities. In the 1960s and 1970s, business community volunteer leadership by local CEOs was expected and encouraged. Now, many boards have trouble recruiting new leadership and then engaging those volunteers in their issues. Tables 6.1 and 6.2 depict and compare the changing characteristics of business organizations and their unprecedented challenges. Downtown and community issues have gotten tougher and more complex, and volunteer business leaders have less time, support, and skills to bring to the table. (This discussion is based on material presented by George Corcoran, an exemplary Seattle civic leader and mentor.)

Changes in Private Sector Leadership

Table 6.1 contrasts the characteristics of civic volunteer leaders of the past with leaders of today's communities. A review of the differences points out the challenges downtown association executives and board chairs face. Of course, these are broad generalizations exaggerated to make the point, but these comparisons ring true in communities of all sizes.

The board of "today" needs to be managed very differently than the board of the past. Structure and bylaws need to spell out roles and responsibilities in a way that volunteers who had worked with one another for years did not need. Board members who don't know one another well will rely on rules and procedures to help them interact and make decisions. Board orientation and training are critical, as many board members won't know the organization's history or values. In addition, informal opportunities to get to know one another are key; this will help to ease board discussions later.

Changes in Political Leadership

Many of the changes in private-sector leadership are mirrored in the public sector, making decision making and lobbying at state and local levels more difficult. Table 6.2 summarizes the characteristics of political leaders of the past with current political leaders. The previous caveat about generalization applies.

Nonprofit boards are evolving, impacted by major societal shifts such as globalization and the reduction of public-sector resources. When potential

TABLE 6.1. Comparison of past and present volunteer leadership characteristics.

Characteristics of volunteer leadership	Then	Now
Age	Sixties	Thirty to fifty
Ethnicity/Gender	White and male	A small increase in racial diversity, more women, but still mostly male
Residence	Native to the community with a lifelong network of friends and business associates	Transplant, new to the community, will not know most people on the board
Company Headquarters	Local	Anywhere
Business ViewPoint	Long-term	Next quarter
Political Affiliation	Republican	No affiliation
Community Involvement	Initiate new projects, see a need and organize a response	Responds to requests, does not know the community or other business leaders well enough to initiate a new program
Community Leadership	Broad perspective due to apprenticeship in community organizations	Strategic, targeted, based on business need or company priorities
Public Policy Experience	Extensive due to apprenticeship, probably knows politicians personally	Limited, possibly in another community
Speed of Job	Fast, some free time once at the executive level	Hyper speed, no free time
Position	CEO	State or regional VP, due to acquisitions the HQ is elsewhere
Corporate Support	Company supports participation in local organizations	Participation is viewed as time away from business priorities, is discouraged or limited
Type of Business	Finance, Insurance, Real Estate	Tech style—no time regardless of business type

board members and volunteers have increased pressures at work due to cutbacks and less support from the out-of-town employer for community activities, our downtown boards need to be well managed to attract the best members. In addition to doing the basics of management, downtown directors will need to have sophisticated strategies for decision making that take into account less-experienced board volunteers, and partnerships with a wide range of constituencies to demonstrate efficiency and good value for

TABLE 6.2. Past and present characteristics of political leaders.

Characteristics of political leaders	Then	Now
Age	Sixties	Thirty to fifty
Ethnicity	White and male	More diverse than the private sector, more women, majority still male
Residence	Native to the community with large network of friends, politicians, and business associates	Mix of local and transplant, network may be smaller
Viewpoint	Long-term, based on broad-based support	Probably ran on a single issue or constituency, viewpoint may be narrow
Working Relationship	Collaborative, based on long-term relationships and expectation of need to work together long-term	Partisan, party lines more sharply drawn, campaigns divisive, knows position is short-term
Lawmaking	Legislative-driven, based on experiences of lawmakers	Initiative and poll-driven, shaped by response to narrow constituencies
Policymaking	State capitol	Grassroots, single-issue constituencies
Action	Policy-motivated	Politically motivated, media-driven
Legislative Service	Stability, longevity	Turnover, term limits
Decision-Making Style	Fact- and issue-driven	Poll, media, and single-issue constituency driven
Atmosphere	Trust and camaraderie	Cynicism, individualism, distrust
Business Experience	Yes	No

their investment. A final word, theory is great, but the best way to improve the board is also the simplest—ask members what their best experience is and why—and then implement their suggestions. The organization director's goal should be that board members view the downtown organization as the best board they have ever served on.

Chapter 7

Making the Most of Human Resources

Catherine Coleman

INTRODUCTION

With literally thousands of books written on the topic of personnel and human resources, why is it necessary to include a human resource chapter in a book about business improvement districts (BIDs)? The answer is simple. In many, and perhaps in most business improvement districts, "people" are the single greatest expense. BID ratepayers quite typically are paying for the additional level of service that people provide. In some BIDs, the people are under contract. In other BIDs, the people are employees of the organization managing the BID. In all cases, the successful hiring, motivating, and managing of people can be the difference between an accountable and effective BID and one that does not meet the expectations of the ratepayers.

Jim Collins, in his book *From Good to Great,* states that great companies first get the "right people on the bus" (2001, p. 14). To be a great business improvement district, it is necessary to have the "right people on the bus," and to do this takes a unique blend of technical knowledge and emotional sense.

To Contract, or Not to Contract?

This question is one discussed amongst BID professionals perennially. Both sides of the issue are fodder for debate—there is no absolute or right answer. Rather, circumstances weight local decisions, and the experience of others can only be used as a guide, not as a compass. This chapter does not attempt to enter into this debate. Rather, it is written to provide guidance principally to those business improvement districts that chose to hire their own employees. BIDs that choose to contract for staff, however, must also motivate and build employee passion and many of the same principles of management apply.

doi:10.1300/5137_08

Although the staffing of BIDs is as unique as the communities they support, the most common model combines a cleaning program, a public safety and hospitality program, and a marketing and communications program. It is not unusual however, even in a BID with a "clean and safe" and marketing focus, to find BID staff expertise in the areas of community planning, commercial office or retail leasing, real estate development, and research. It is also not unusual to find BID staff with formal education in managing complex social services programs. What drives the decision of how a BID should be staffed stems directly from the programs and services ratepayers agree to support.

What challenges a BID manager is the diversity of those programs and the people needed to support them. Within a few square feet of office space, highly educated and experienced, salaried professionals often work in close concert with hourly wage cleaning and public safety employees. Sharing the same lunchroom may be people who daily work in air-conditioned or heated comfort while their co-worker in the next seat is exposed on an hourly basis to the ravages of the environment. What binds them is their passion for the betterment of the district they represent, and a good BID manager will regularly reinforce this shared passion.

WHO'S THE BOSS?

In a business improvement district, many people share a sense of ownership and many provide oversight. Typically, an executive director or corporate president manages BID staff. A board of directors typically sets policy, and, depending on the locality, the municipal government may also have oversight authority. Much as shareholders are the ultimate authority in a public corporation, ratepayers are the ultimate stakeholders in a business improvement district. Although ratepayers do not have direct responsibility for staff management, it is not unusual for them to proffer more scrutiny of BID employees than they would others. "It is my dollars that pay their salary," ratepayers might say. Given this level of interest, a good BID manager will set clear boundaries to ensure a chain of command that is clearly understood by employees and ratepayers alike.

GOOD MANAGEMENT BEGINS WITH GOOD EMPLOYEES

How do you get the "right people on the bus?" A simple answer would be, hire the best that you can afford. Monetary reward is certainly a motivator for good performance and an even bigger motivator contributing to longevity. It is, however, only one of the considerations for building a good team of BID employees.

BIDs are not created in a vacuum, and the process of BID creation does not stop with a successful petition drive or a city council ordinance approval. Approval is just the beginning and the time for establishing realistic expectations has begun in earnest—for both the ratepayers and for the employees who will eventually be hired to carry out the wishes of the ratepayers.

From the outset, a wise BID manager will make it clear that the board is in place to set policy, the BID manager is in place to ensure that policy is adhered to, and staff, hired by the BID manager, is in place to implement a work plan. An early action for a BID manager is to define a functional organizational chart clearly showing the lines of authority and establishing the foundation for how programs will be managed.

Well-written job descriptions add to a base of understanding. It's difficult to get what you want if you don't know what you want. The discipline of identifying what one is looking for in an employee greatly enhances the ability to find the right person. Job titles, reporting protocol, academic requirements, character and personality attributes, and even physical requirements to meet the demands of the position can be clearly outlined in a job description. A good job description is also a tool in establishing a salary range. Ranges clearly differ dependent on the locality but finding out the "going rate" will aid greatly in the hiring process.

How employees are found, to an extent, depends on the type of employee sought. Although a newspaper ad might be the perfect way to secure applications for an operations position, advertising in trade organization publications might be the best way to find a department manager. Regardless of the kind of employee needed, some form of communication will be required and there are some simple and basic rules that apply. As much as applicants are marketing themselves to the BID, the BID is also marketing to the prospective employee. Ads and other communication should be written in a way that entices the best, weeds out the nonqualified, and spells out the basic requirements. Be as specific as you can be. If a drug test is required, say so. If only applicants with a valid driver's license will be considered, say so. Working conditions, benefits, and salary ranges are all factors that can both entice qualified employees and discourage the nonqualified.

The hiring process is time-consuming and the responsibility of hiring good employees should not be taken lightly. From initial screenings to interviews, reference checks, background checks, and ensuring that all laws are understood and adhered to, hiring good employees requires organization, skill, intuition, and lots of time.

You've Hired a New Employee—What Next?

Life's greatest disappointments come from unmet expectations. From the first day on the job, it is the responsibility of the employer to establish expectations and the job of the employee to work toward meeting those expectations. Two major factors contribute to effectively communicating expectations.

First, a well-written personnel manual is of paramount importance. The personnel manual is not intended to be a contract. The manual spells out everything from details of the benefit plan to policies and procedures regarding appropriate standards of conduct. Though no one likes to think about termination at the time an employee is hired, a good personnel manual also includes termination procedures. An employee's signature verifies that he or she has received the manual and agrees to abide by its precepts. This can go a long way in resolving conflicts and misunderstandings in the future. The personnel manual should be carefully reviewed and edited by a legal authority specializing in employment law.

Second, and no matter the position, effective training is important to an employee's development and job satisfaction. Written standard operating procedures (or SOPs) for each position are an invaluable resource. Such procedures should be updated frequently, and new employees may even be encouraged to infuse their own knowledge of "best practices" into the written procedures. In a good organization, training does not stop at the end of the first week. Rather, a culture of continuous improvement and continuing education adds to the level of job satisfaction and enhances the contribution an employee can make to any organization.

In larger business improvement districts, a dedicated staff person manages human resource issues and ensures that accepted and legal personnel procedures are followed. In smaller organizations, this responsibility may fall to the BID manager or someone responsible for support to a myriad of BID programs. Regardless of the size of the organization, a system must be in place to document everything relating to an employee's status, performance, and responsibilities. Simple knowledge, such as how long the government requires employee records be held and what those records must include can be the difference between an organization that is in compliance and one that is not. Management of these details is a protection for the organization, and their importance cannot be overestimated.

Everyone wants to know if expectations are being met. Though time-consuming, written employee evaluations delivered verbally to an employee are a wise time investment. Evaluations are an opportunity to document both positive and negative feedback, clear up misunderstandings, and an opportunity to enhance communication. Evaluations are also a unique way to establish and manage individual goals.

MOTIVATING EMPLOYEES AND BUILDING THE TEAM

Many tools exist to help motivate and excite employees and to help build the team necessary to meet the expectations of BID ratepayers. Motivation and team building are not exact sciences. The personality of the BID manager and even the culture of the organization can factor into how this is done. Yet it must be done consciously; it will not happen automatically. Building a cohesive team of motivated employees, however, does not rely on expensive consultants and staff retreats. It takes no money to publicly recognize an employee for a job well done. It takes no money to say "thank you." It takes no money to recognize an employment anniversary in a positive way. It takes no money to provide a listening ear. In other words, sensitivity, support, and genuine caring are not related to budget size and go a long way toward creating a motivational work environment. That kind of work environment is essential to high employee morale and low employee turnover.

KNOW THE LAW AND FOLLOW THE RULES

The "people" business is filled with variables, ruled at times by intuition and often relying on common sense. Employment law, on the other hand, is seldom open to interpretation. In this age of litigation, ignorance of the law is not an admissible defense in court. Despite the complexities of employment law, well-informed managers will make every attempt to have a working knowledge of the laws that apply in their locality. For example, knowing if a literal "pat on the back" can be interpreted as sexual harassment is critical to efficient and effective personnel management. Legally safe personnel decisions should be every manager's goal. Many books have been written on the topic, but one that is especially helpful to those operating in the United States is *Fair, Square and Legal* by Donald H. Weiss (1991). It should be part of every BID library.

Employment laws abound, and the size of an organization and where it operates factor into which laws apply. Following is a brief list of major federal statutes and regulations that cover employment actions in the United States. Note, however, that laws are constantly changing, and trusted legal counsel should be a nonnegotiable line item in every business improvement district's budget.

Civil Rights Act
Family and Medical Leave Act
Age Discrimination in Employment Act
Americans with Disabilities Act
Vietnam Era Veterans' Readjustment Assistance Act
Fair Labor Standards Act
Occupational Safety and Health Act
Immigration Reform and Control Act
Employee Polygraph Protection Act

A BAD APPLE CAN SPOIL THE BUNCH

No matter how adept at hiring, managing, and motivating staff a BID manager might be, there will be times when an employee does not follow the rules or does not meet expectations. Advice to the manager: *be fair and be firm*. Nothing undermines morale and the smooth operation of an organization more than a nonperforming employee who is allowed to go unchecked. Some infractions may be grounds for immediate dismissal. In other instances, an intervention may reverse bad behavior, salvage an employee, and avoid the expense of hiring a replacement employee. Immediate termination should be the action for "zero tolerance" infractions. Counseling or probation may be the action required by other infractions. Regardless of the disciplinary action taken, documentation is a must. Particularly when signed by an employee, documentation is an invaluable defense and record for disciplinary actions taken.

NO NEED TO REINVENT THE WHEEL

In North America alone, more than 1,200 business improvement districts exist. Many of these have been in existence for decades, and many have developed a wealth of resources to support the effective management of personnel. Existing manuals, forms, and documented standard operating procedures in support of personnel management can be an invaluable tool, particularly in a newly created BID. Through organizations such as the International Downtown Association, connection with successful BID programs and their managers can result in the sharing of information and experience. Many BID managers will freely share information. Such sharing can save the recipient time, money, and even heartache. As previously stated however, review of human resource policies and procedures by a qualified legal professional is highly advised and is part of the accountability that BID managers have to their ratepayers.

REFERENCES

Collins, J. (2001). *From Good to Great: Why Some Companies Make the Leap . . . and Others Don't.* New York: HarperCollins.

Weiss, D.H. (1991). *Fair, Square, and Legal: Safe Hiring, Managing and Firing Practices to Keep You and Your Company Out of Court.* New York: AMACOM.

Chapter 8

Financial Management—
Keeping the Numbers Straight

Michael Weiss

GETTING STARTED

Horror stories abound of downtown management organizations with
great ideas that have been translated into wonderful programs, only to fail
as a result of poor internal management. An organization's finances are the
lifeblood of its existence, enabling it to provide funds to sustain its programs. It is essential for a downtown management organization to set up
professional financial systems, to ensure that they are staffed and maintained, and that sufficient oversight exists to meet reporting requirements.
This will engender confidence on the part of board members, and city officials who are often involved in creating these organizations, that the funds
are being well spent.

By nature, Downtown Management Associations (DMAs) have members who are familiar with business practices, in most cases for-profit business practices. However, when it comes to financial management they must
consider the fact that most DMAs are not-for-profit organizations that are
subject to different types of reporting regulations and somewhat different financial management requirements and practices than are for-profit enter-
prises. Although the expertise of for-profit businesspeople is necessary and
helpful, it should not be a substitute for involving members and DMA staff
who have experience in nonprofit financial management

The choice of an accounting system is also an important decision. A
number of well-used and well-documented computer products are on the
market, but it is important that the in-house staff has sufficient training before start up is initiated. Most of the well-known systems provide periodic
updates or upgrades.

The majority of DMAs retain an accounting firm that has experience in
nonprofit or "fund" accounting. You should consult with your accountant to

doi:10.1300/5137_09

ensure that your system is adequate for providing the information that you, your board, and oversight agencies require, and that it has the capacity to grow and be modified should your needs change.

ASSESSMENTS AND REVENUE

Many DMAs and most Business Improvement Districts (BIDs) rely primarily on mandatory assessments collected from property owners or tenants for the lion's share of their revenues. Some groups may receive "seed money" from the local government or the private sector for start-up expenses or special projects.

In the early stages of BID formation questions will arise about the mission and goals of the organization. The answers to these questions generally result in agreement on a series of activities that are desired by the BID members. These program initiatives are then studied in the context of funding available to support them, and often very difficult decisions must be made about the nature and extent of these programs. Funding may not be available for everything that is desired, especially at the beginning.

Setting an Assessment Rate

A new BID generally begins the budget process by agreeing on an assessment formula. An assessment *base* is established related to the square footage, tax-assessed valuation, front footage, or some other standard property indicator. Classes of property may be created within the BID such as development, commercial, industrial, residential, not-for-profit, government or institutional, and each class might have a different assessment base. Some classes, such as government-owned or not-for-profit properties may be exempt or may be required to provide "in-kind" contributions in lieu of an assessment collected by the locality.

An assessment *rate,* or multiplier, must then be established to apply to the base properties to determine the dollar value of the assessment for each property and thus the total assessment revenue available for the BID. If a combination of base factors is utilized, the multiplier for each may vary depending on the type of property to which it is applied. All of this can be very complicated but the bottom line is that there must be agreement of at least a majority of the property owners for the process to proceed.

Of course, there is a lot of give and take required in making these decisions if a balance is to be agreed upon. There is only so much incremental cost that the owners of each class of property are willing to pay. On the other hand, the formula must provide sufficient revenue to support a reasonable array of programs, including administrative overhead that will result in the BID adding value to the area.

PREPARING A BUDGET

An organization's budget is the driving force behind its programs. Almost everything a DMA wishes to do has a cost, and the approved budget is the enabling document that officially allows an organization to expend the funds to carry out these mandates.

The budget preparation process often begins with the appointment by the board president or chair of a finance committee which may consist of board and nonboard members. The board treasurer often chairs this committee. The staff director as well as staff member(s) involved in fiscal matters should attend the meetings of the finance committee. The goal of this committee is to prepare a budget for submission to the board executive committee and to the board of directors for final approval. To save the committee time, staff may prepare a draft budget in addition to providing members of the operative committee(s) with the following documentation:

1. A financial report of the prior year's budget versus actual expenditures and variance to budget. A two- or three-year "look back" is even more helpful in assessing trends.
2. A profit and loss statement that indicates all fund balances, including reserves.

Before a budget can be drawn, an organization should have a clear set of articulated goals. These can emerge from a mission statement and a strategic plan that are regularly reviewed and revised by board and staff. Each year, the goals must be translated into desired program initiatives that become the foundation for the budget process.

The job of the finance committee is to balance the cost of all of the desires for services of the membership against the reasonable expectations of revenue. Discussion may take place at this time regarding assessment increases or programmatic initiatives that may require funding adjustments. Also to be considered is the administrative overhead and staffing necessary to meet these needs.

The DMA should also establish guidelines for maintaining a reasonable reserve fund to cover cash-flow needs and contingencies as well as to provide for capital replacement of office equipment such as computers, copying machines, public safety CCTV or radio systems, etc. It is also wise to consider creation of a capital reserve for purchasing such items as trash containers, benches, lighting facilities, planters, or for capital upgrades such as street paving, special signage, and the like.

A question may arise as to the level of detail required for finance committee and board review and approval. Many organizations prepare two budget documents. The first is a more detailed "breakout," which includes individual salary lines, line-by-line budgets for "Other Than Personnel Services" (OTPS), rent, utilities, telephone, postage, printing, etc., and line-by-line program budgets. In many cases, a board of directors, which has confidence in the staff preparing the budget and in the finance committee review, might be satisfied with a consolidated budget that aggregates many of these specifics. Obviously, this makes the budget easier to read and to digest.

REVENUE

For many DMAs the largest item on the revenue side of the budget is assessment revenue. However, they also have the ability to raise additional revenue through solicitation of government grants, private-sector contributions, or even by "bonding" of a portion of their assessment revenue. They may also generate revenue from related business ventures such as parking, telephone, newsstand or other concessions, or they may seek underwriting of specific projects through advertising or sponsorship opportunities. Some of these strategies may have tax implications that should be thoroughly explored with a knowledgeable tax expert before proceeding.

CASH FLOW

Assessment revenues are often collected by the municipality and then turned over to the DMA. Thus, there is often a lag between receipt of payments and transmittal of funds. Depending on the regularity with which the funds are received, the association must plan for these gaps, with an eye towards evening out the flow of funds required to meet spending peaks and valleys. The creation of a sufficient cash reserve is an important element of financial planning. Generally, a reserve of two to three months of expenses is sufficient to cover these contingencies. It is also possible to arrange for a bank line of credit as a backup to the reserve fund, in the event of an emergency.

EXPENSES

Expenses are indicated separately in categories such as Administration, Program, and OTPS. The draft may break down the expenses of individual programs and indicate allocations for contractual services as well as for staffing of "in house" programs. However, although the finance committee is charged with drawing the draft budget, its members are not the ultimate determiners for programmatic initiatives. Members at large, board members, and staff should drive this function.

Thus, budget preparation is a *process* that consists of a number of iterations prior to final approval. Next, the executive committee and/or the full board of directors would consider, revise as necessary, and approve the yearly budget.

FINANCIAL RECORDS AND REPORTS

Reporting requirements for tax purposes, monitoring by your finance committee, board of directors, external or internal audit, or staff needs will mandate the preparation of regular fiscal reports. Choose an accounting and bookkeeping system that will permit the production of these reports. Some commercially available systems already have standard report formats that are easily accessed, but it may be important to consider a system that can export data to a standard database format if non-standard reports are required. Generally, accountants with experience in nonprofit work are familiar with these products.

Most boards of directors are satisfied with three types of reports:

1. A monthly or quarterly report on revenue and expenses
2. A yearly profit and loss statement
3. A proposed budget report for the next fiscal year

Organizations should prepare a "budget calendar" that lists the dates by which each of the various reports are due for distribution as well as details the various staff and committee deadlines leading to final approval.

Each of these reports should be easily produced from the accounting program selected and all efforts should be made by the bookkeeping staff to keep these records current. Reports are very helpful for board members who are not involved in the day-to-day operation of the organization. This builds confidence that the staff members are "on top" of any budget problems that may arise during the course of the fiscal year.

EXPENSE MONITORING

Monitoring expenses is very important. Quarterly reports are most helpful in this regard. They should be easy to read with sufficient detail to provide current information on the organization's spending compared to budget, but at the same time, not so voluminous as to require members to spend an inordinate amount of time to digest the contents. Spending can be grouped into major categories, with a more detailed report produced for the chief executive, board chair, and finance chair. In a similar way, draft budgets can be produced at two levels: a very detailed report for those preparing the budget and a consolidated report for board members or the general membership.

Quarterly reports' values increase as a management tool as the fiscal year progresses. Significant variances to budget (5 to 10 percent) should be explained. In some cases, they may signal to the fiscal monitors that steps should be taken to mitigate or address major variance. Often, budget adjustments can be made midyear or at the third quarter. This allows the organization to adjust its programs to meet budget mandates. Many organizations set limits on interim budget authority that allow the chief executive, president, or executive committee to authorize spending changes in such cases. Even in the absence of these adjustments, notice to the fiscal watchdogs that one or more line items is not coming in at the original projection is sufficient to avoid comments at the end of the fiscal year, i.e., "nobody told me that there was a problem."

INTERNAL CONTROLS

Internal controls are required to ensure that your organization has fiscal procedures that minimize opportunities for mismanagement, waste, or fraud. Generally, a set of specific written procedures should be in place that spells out mandates when it comes to inventory control, record keeping for time and leave, financial reporting and fiscal management. One of the major weaknesses cited in financial audits is "separation of duties." That is, there are inherent risks associated with the same person performing certain functions relating to the management of an organization's finances.

Responsibilities such as opening envelopes containing funds, recording the receipt of checks, invoices and bills, validating receipt of goods and services, approving invoices for payment, preparation of checks, management of petty cash, check-signing authority, entering information into the association's bookkeeping and accounting system, and bank-statement reconciliation are all tasks that should be separated to the degree practicable. In other words, it is advisable to have more than one person performing these tasks. A balance must be struck between creating bureaucratic procedures that impede the ability to conduct business and the need to meet industry standards for integrity and sound management.

Many small organizations have insufficient staff to fully separate duties and thus are often cited in audits as having deficiencies in this area. Thus, it is important for these issues to be fully discussed with board management committees, for potential weaknesses to be recognized, and, where possible, for remediation to take place. This is a vital issue for most nonprofits where the board of directors may be held ultimately responsible for negligence if cases of malfeasance or fraud come to light. Having a written set of procedures, although not ensuring compliance, at least can shift this responsibility to those charged with its implementation.

AUDITS

In many cases, the not-for-profit incorporation law, local enabling legislation, or other government regulation, mandates that downtown organizations hire an independent contractor to conduct an annual financial audit. In New York City, the Department of Small Business Services, which contractually supervises all BID renewals and BID contracts, requires such an audit. In addition, these contracts are subject to audit by the New York City Comptroller's Office. Thus, periodically, the comptroller's staff conducts its own independent in-depth audits. The comptroller's audits scrutinize the program operations as well as the financial operations, and although they may be critical of the organization, they have been quite valuable in strengthening the management of the association.

Organizations are often given an opportunity to comment on the results of a draft audit before the final product is produced. Meeting with the audit team can assist in imparting a better understanding of their findings, and in some cases, even cause the auditors to modify their recommendations or comments. The independent auditor may issue a management letter that contains a so-called "clean opinion," or it may point out weaknesses that should be addressed. Staff and the board should take this seriously so that the same problem(s) do not appear in future audits.

An audit should be welcomed as a management tool, as it creates an opportunity for an independent view of the group's finances and procedures. This provides yet another level of comfort on the part of the assessment-paying members that their funds are being used according to their wishes, and that there is integrity and sound management of resources.

REPORTING TO YOUR BOARD AND OTHERS

As discussed earlier, financial reports may be shared internally with staff, with various board committees, with the entire board and membership at large, and with oversight agencies. Each downtown association makes decisions as to when, how often, and in what form to communicate financial information to its members. In the absence of this reporting, members can become estranged from the organization and support can erode. This problem can become particularly acute during a contract renewal period or in cases where the association requests increases in assessments to cover inflationary costs or expanded programs.

In addition to the reports already mentioned, an annual report and an open, annual meeting can serve as mechanisms for sharing and discussing the state of an organization's programs and finances. These strategies can also be used to involve and recognize elected officials, government officials, and community leaders in the information flow and decision-making process.

STAFFING AND SKILLS REQUIRED

Many downtown management organizations are rather lean when it comes to management staffing, but fiscal integrity demands that they identify individuals, whether they are paid staff, consultants, board members, or other volunteers, who can ensure that proper management of their finances is guaranteed. Remember, most DMAs are voluntary in that the property owners, commercial tenants, and others have agreed to assess themselves an added fee in order to provide for top-notch services. Thus, it is imperative for the association to have outstanding fiscal procedures and oversight if it is to gain acceptance among its members to permit its work to continue.

Budgeting, accounting, and bookkeeping systems should be set up, as the industry states, using GAAP (Generally Accepted Accounting Principles). Most groups utilize the services of an accounting/audit firm for this purpose. The board of directors should be mindful that sufficient staff time must be allocated to this function. The consulting accountant can assist in evaluating the skill levels of employees and consultants (part-time bookkeepers, etc.), the time necessary, and the mix of staff and outside contractors required to fulfill the tasks at hand.

Depending on the size of the organization, it would be helpful to have one or more staff members who understand the financial management systems, can input data, and produce financial reports. If the chief operating officer does not actually perform any of the day-to-day functions, that individual must have an overall knowledge and understanding and involvement with the financial management issues related to the organization.

Caveat: If one of the board members volunteers himself or herself, or volunteers his or her staff to fulfill some of these functions, the board should be sure that the person(s) assigned has sufficient time, expertise, and *interest* in carrying out these functions while ensuring that there is no conflict of interest in doing so. This is not an area in which to skimp or save money.

CONCLUSION

This is not a chapter to skip. Yet neither does it contain everything you need to know about managing the finances of a downtown association. Hopefully, it will provide some of the basics that will assist groups in their start up as well as provide pointers for those already functioning. To some, this aspect of downtown management is not as much fun as conceiving and managing programs in which the results are more visible. Few awards and rewards exist for doing an outstanding job of managing a group's finances, but there can be nothing so low as an organization that has failed to meet its responsibilities in this arena.

A wealth of supplemental information can be gleaned from the accounting, law, and nonprofit professions from a variety of books, periodicals, trade magazines, and Web sites as well as from courses and workshops sponsored by local universities and professional societies.

One of the best sources of information is the International Downtown Association (IDA). IDA has many programs to provide information, training, and networking for downtown management professions. Check the IDA Web site at www.ida-downtown.org.

BIBLIOGRAPHY

Dropkin, M. and Hayden, A. (2001). *The Cash Flow Management Book for Nonprofits: A Step-by-Step Guide for Managers, Consultants and Boards.* San Francisco: Jossey-Bass.

Dropkin, M. and LeTouche, B. (1998). *The Budget Building Book for Nonprofits: A Step-by-Step Guide for Managers and Boards.* San Francisco: Jossey-Bass.

Jossey-Bass Publishers. Available online <www.josseybass.com>.

Chapter 9

Staffing Structure
and Compensation Management

Dong Soo Kim
David Feehan
Sarah Rose

INTRODUCTION

The International Downtown Association (IDA) conducts a survey of downtown leaders every other year to determine salary and compensation patterns of both CEOs and other staff. This information is in high demand—by executive search committees seeking to determine appropriate compensation levels for CEOs and by downtown administrators as they seek to provide reasonable compensation for staff. The most recent research was conducted in late 2003 by the IDA in partnership with the Norfolk State University (NSU) Social Research Center. This chapter discusses information from that research. In addition to addressing issues of compensation, it offers an assessment of the most current information on CEOs' backgrounds, characteristics, their organizations, staffing patterns, and sources and uses of funding.

ABOUT THE SURVEY

For the survey, a total of 261 structured questionnaires was sent by e-mail and mail from IDA to all its member organizations with CEOs (234 in the United States and 27 in Canada). A total of 118 CEOs returned completed questionnaires to the NSU Social Research Center, an overall response rate of 45.2 percent. The U.S. and Canadian groups were combined in all analyses due to the latter group's low response rate and small numbers and due to the homogeneity of both groups in all respects. When possible, the data gathered from the survey were considered in comparison to data from

doi:10.1300/5137_10

previous surveys to try to identify trends in staffing, compensation, and organizational tendencies.

CEO CHARACTERISTICS

- Survey respondents ranged in age from twenty-nine to seventy-six with a median age of forty-eight.
- Approximately 45 percent of the responding CEOs were female and 55 percent were male, a remarkably fair division of gender for CEO positions. There was a slight increase in the number of female CEOs from previous survey years (2001 and 1999).
- In terms of the highest level of education obtained, there were fairly equal proportions of CEOs with undergraduate degrees (46.2 percent) and CEOs with graduate degrees (44.4 percent). The most popular major fields of education were business administration, public administration, and urban planning.
- Most CEOs had significant field experience, either as a CEO or as staff in downtown organizations. The median tenure in the CEO's current organization was nine years, of which four years were as a CEO. Respondents also on average served for ten years as staff and three years as a CEO in other downtown organizations prior to coming to their current organization.
- Racially, the majority of CEOs were Caucasians (97.4 percent). No African-American CEOs participated in this year's survey, although based on what is known about heads of IDA membership organizations, the number of African-American CEOs seems to be increasing. These CEOs may have elected not to answer the question about race or declined to complete the survey.
- In terms of professional development, respondents reported ongoing training needs that were steady and substantive. When given the opportunity for a sabbatical leave, twenty-three CEOs chose urban study, design, planning, and development as fields of study they would wish to pursue.

DOWNTOWN ORGANIZATIONS

- Most of the organizations (83.1 percent) were located in central business districts.
- Fifty-five organizations had either 501(c)(3) or 501(c)(6) status. Thirty-six had some other corporate form.

- The CEOs represented organizations in cities with populations that ranged from barely 15,000 to over 5,000,000 with a median population size of 220,000. They were more or less evenly distributed among different population categories.
- Organization operational budgets ranged from $32,000 to $13 million with a median budget of $660,000. As might be expected, organizations in smaller cities had smaller budgets while organizations in larger cities had larger budgets.
- Almost all organizations used some measurement to assess their performances. These measurements were varied, however, with different specifications and applications, and with no common, standardized measurement instrument or tool in use.
- Most organizations maintained working relationships with other organizational entities for partnerships. Partnerships with city and county governments were most commonly cited, with 26.5 percent of CEOs claiming that particular partnership.

COMPENSATION

- Surprisingly, only 32.3 percent of CEOs had written contracts with their organization, with the median employment term being two years. Most CEOs with contracts come from the relatively higher budget organizations.
- CEOs' base salaries ranged from $23,000 to $228,000 with an average of $90,590 and a median of $81,500, which has steadily increased over successive survey years.
- The majority of CEOs receive a fringe benefits package averaging 17.8 percent of median base salary, which most often includes health insurance, life insurance, a retirement plan and parking, among other benefits. There was a slight downward trend of the fringe benefits package since the 1995 survey year, although benefits categories have gradually increased over the years.
- The total median compensation of all CEOs, including base salaries and fringe benefits, increased by a modest 28.0 percent from 1997 to 2003.
- Predictably, average total compensation increased as both city population size and organizational budget increased; although high salaries and low salaries within each category did not necessarily follow that pattern (see Tables 9.1 and 9.2).

TABLE 9.1. Total CEO compensation summaries by organizational budget in 2003.

Total Compensation	≤$250,000 (n=21)	$250,001- $500,000 (n=29)	$500,001- $750,000 (n=12)	$750,001- $1,500,000 (n=25)	>$1,500,000 (n=27)
Lowest	$26,000	$30,000	$52,000	$55,000	$76,000
Highest	$190,000	$220,000	$160,000	$250,000	$295,000
Average	$72,760	$84,340	$92,170	$118,200	$151,560
Median	$55,000	$70,000	$81,500	$109,000	$149,000

TABLE 9.2. Total CEO compensation summaries by city population in 2003.

Total Compensation	<50,000 (n=9)	50,001- 50,000 (n=33)	150,001- 300,000 (n=25)	300,000- 750,000 (n=26)	>750,000 (n=19)
Lowest	$39,000	$26,000	$30,000	$50,000	$55,000
Highest	$88,000	$220,000	$186,000	$295,000	$210,000
Average	$62,000	$87,180	$102,440	$130,540	$135,320
Median	$55,000	$73,000	$100,000	$115,000	$146,000

STAFFING

- Staffing patterns vary widely from organization to organization. Among the 115 of 118 responses received, one organization reported eighty full-time staff while thirteen organizations had no staff other than the CEO. The median number of full-time staff was four. Out of these 115 organizations that responded, eighty organizations used part-time staff, ranging in number from one to forty-two.
- The median numbers of male and female staff per organization were two and three, respectively.
- Although the CEOs who responded were virtually all Caucasians, the racial breakdown of staff was much more widely distributed: 59 percent Caucasian, 27 percent African American, 10 percent Hispanic, and 2 percent Asian/Pacific Islander.
- About 30 percent of organizations had the following three most common position categories among their staff: marketing, executive assistance, and accounting/finance.
- Salaries of staff members differed significantly among different organizations and even among various staff categories within an organization. Staff charged with deputy executive functions, planning, real

estate development, and retail management generally commanded high salaries, whereas staff with maintenance, secretarial, reception, and security responsibilities generally received low salaries. The data show that staff salaries of most categories were related neither to city population size nor to an organization's operating budget.

FUNDING

- Most organizations had numerous sources of revenue with significant variation among them. The largest source was assessment district revenue (51.97 percent). It appeared that the sources of revenue had no clear relationship to either the city population or to the size of an organization's budget.
- The largest expense was labor, namely, salaries and fringe benefits of all staff, followed by services. The overall percentage distribution of expenses was remarkably similar to that of the 2001 survey, especially in those two major allocation areas. Staff training and information systems remained the lowest cost areas.

CONCLUSION

The survey data are useful for gathering both point-in-time statistics and for uncovering trends over time. For example, though benefits categories have generally increased, fringe benefits packages have been declining. The findings of the data indicate areas in which downtown organizations might make adjustments. For instance, while anecdotally, IDA sees the increase of racial and ethnic diversity among downtown CEOs, the data still imply a need for continued efforts to recruit minorities to CEO positions.

The data also suggest a use for some uniform or standardized measurement of organizational performance. Categorical variations would occur in measurements from organization to organization, but this standard could provide a useful benchmarking tool for downtown organizations to learn from others' performances.

IDA will continue to use this tool to map out staffing and organizational structure and compensation management patterns over time as business districts proliferate and expand.

Chapter 10

Resource Raising
As a Downtown Management
and Revitalization Strategy

Tom Verploegen

QUALITY, QUALITY, QUALITY

If the three most important words in the real estate are "location, location, location," then the three most important words in resource raising (fund-raising and more) for downtown revitalization are "quality, quality, quality!" Make no mistake about it, quality activities, events, projects, and programs attract quality outside resources.

Quality vision and mission statements, strong business plans and priorities, quality products and activities that heavily promote the resource providers, and follow up after a project or event are all musts for attracting money and in-kind products and services. Exuding quality every step of the way enables a downtown organization to graduate from rapport building to relationship building to reliance building with their resource providers over the years.

That being said, we can now move on to defining resource raising, identifying its various categories, providing examples, emphasizing the importance of research, and ultimately—discussing how to close the deal. Because resource raising is such an enormous topic, this chapter can give only highlights, but hopefully it will provide a helpful framework for structuring a successful resource-raising strategy.

DEFINING RESOURCE RAISING

Resource raising is underwriting in the form of any contribution of money, items, or in-kind services from individuals, businesses, corporations,

doi:10.1300/5137_11

foundations, or government entities that lower the amount a downtown organization must pay.

The resources raised may include not only funds (money), but also property (e.g., donated land and buildings for endowments), labor (e.g., pro bono professional services, event volunteers, court-appointed community service manual labor), and in-kind products and services (e.g., donated or loaned equipment/supplies, in-kind advertising and printing, deferred gifts, etc.).

In this chapter, the term "resource raising" is not meant to address primary or core downtown programs such as special or business improvement districts, membership campaigns, municipal clean and safe contracts, parking management, capital improvements, bonding and the like. Also, it does not address volunteer-driven fund-raisers such as dinner auctions and discount cards. For our purposes, resource raising addresses *secondary,* staff-driven, long-term revenues and in-kind products and services that supplement a downtown management organization's events, publications, projects, and programs. (To research primary downtown programs, see the International Downtown Association (IDA) referenced at the end of this chapter.)

THREE RESOURCE-RAISING CATEGORIES

Resource raising by downtown management organizations has reached more sophisticated and professional levels over the years. An individual organization often uses secondary sources to fund or sustain multiple activities, events, "bricks-and-mortar" capital projects and annual programs all at the same time. Likewise, multiple resource-raising strategies are frequently tailored and used for an individual event, activity, or program depending on available or sought-after resource providers.

Three key categories of sources that an organization can tap to raise the bar on their downtown activities and projects include: (1) private sponsorships, (2) philanthropic donations, and (3) government grants. The International Events Group (IEG) referenced at the end of this chapter (under Sponsorship.com) is another helpful source for defining the differences between these categories.

Sponsorship is cash and/or in-kind fees paid to a downtown management organization for a cause, event, or project in return for the ability to exploit its commercial potential. Sponsorship is undertaken by companies to achieve commercial objectives and should not be confused with philanthropy.

Philanthropy is support of a downtown cause without any commercial incentives. Many individuals and nonprofit foundations are involved in philanthropy purely for the benefit of downtown and the community, not for commercial reasons.

Grantsmanship often involves applying for grants from federal, state, and local governments. In exchange, a downtown organization furthers a public purpose such as safety, education, improving socioeconomic conditions, or exposing more people to the arts, depending on the specific aspect a grant is intended to foster.

Sponsorships from businesses and corporations, philanthropic donations from individuals and nonprofit foundations, and grants from government agencies should all be researched thoroughly to help devise a quality strategy for managing and revitalizing a downtown business district. The next section provides examples of the creative ways downtown organizations are tapping into these three important sources.

RESOURCE RAISING: GENERAL EXAMPLES

Downtown organizations turn to sponsors, donors, and grantors to potentially obtain underwriting from a wide range of resources. Just a handful of examples from the vast world of resource raising include print and electronic media advertising partners, annual programming, banners, cleanliness, communications, community service volunteerism, community development corporations, educational internships, endowments, faith-based partnerships, hospitality, streetscapes and furnishings, loan programs, marketing, placemaking and parks, parking operations, planning and development, preservation, promotions, outdoor public art and sculpture exhibits and murals, capital campaigns for enhanced public facilities, safety and security (crime prevention), downtown wayfinding signage and kiosks, social services, special events, tourism programs, and transit projects, to name a few.

More detailed examples include: social services programs such as homeless outreach, summer youth programs, and day-labor centers; increased use of downtown community courts; in-kind advertising and leveraging media exposure; streetlight banners; space for kiosks; brick pavers bearing sponsor names or trees with sponsor plaques; government grants for transit facilities; vehicles and equipment such as historic train stations, public trolley and shuttle systems and bus shelters; private sponsors for horse-drawn carriage rides; and "safe and sound" ambassador programs. (For more information, see the IDA; National Trust for Historic Preservation's National

Main Street Center; and, Larry Houston's *Business Improvement Districts, 2003*, referenced at the end of this chapter.)

The most common activities with which providers want their names associated are quality community events and projects. Examples from the thousands of special events across the United States, Canada, and beyond include holiday celebrations, the arts, holiday decorations, sculpture exhibits, fashion, music concerts, youth festivals, parades, cultural and heritage events, charitable causes, seasonal activities, theater series, sporting events, and culinary festivals. Find out if there is a festival and events organization in your state. The International Events Group (IEG) is a good source on methods for securing event sponsorship. The International Festival and Events Association (IFEA) is also an excellent resource for event production and management. Both organizations are referenced at the end of this chapter.

RESOURCE RAISING: SPECIFIC EXAMPLES

Following are just a few examples of creative resource-raising methods used by a variety of downtown organizations.

Media Exposure

The Memphis (Tennessee) Center City Commission not only uses celebrity endorsements and produces "live, work and play" profiles in its monthly thirty-minute *Definitely Downtown* lifestyle TV program, but it also receives value-added extra runs and is cross-promoted on downtown hotel channels. Similarly, the Charlotte (North Carolina) Center City Partners teamed up with a local TV station to create a four-part series on downtown that reached 600,000 viewers in its initial airing.

Education

The Philadelphia (Pennsylvania) Center City District secured funding from city, state, and private sources that enabled it to partner with the Philadelphia Technology Alliance to produce www.ePhiladelphiaInsider.com. The Web site's purpose is to retain students in the downtown area by providing them with and helping them find information on housing, cultural events, internships, and jobs.

Annual Programs

The Calgary (Alberta, Canada) Downtown Association has individual sponsors with naming rights for their many annual activities and events including summerHOSTS, Dining Week, Santa Claus Parade, annual meeting, and speakers' series.

Another example comes from The Downtown Denver (Colorado) Partnership, which sells $15,000 platinum sponsorships each year. The sponsorships are exclusive to the industry, and no more than three are sold to prevent diluting the sponsors' impacts. The benefits to sponsors are exposure at each of the monthly member forums, the annual black tie dinner, and the annual meeting.

The Downtown Denver Partnership has also sold sponsorships for its housing program (advocacy, deal facilitation, and marketing). The Colorado Housing Authority was the title sponsor, joined by other sponsors including developers.

Cause Promotions

Downtown organizations across the country support and/or facilitate a number of charitable and health care cause events. The Allentown (Pennsylvania) Downtown Improvement District Authority is involved in the Dream Come True Downtown 500, which raises money for downtown revitalization and for granting the wishes of seriously, critically, and terminally ill children.

Affiliate and Partner Organizations

Separate but subsidiary, affiliated, or partner organizations are often created to manage the resources generated by the parent or downtown organization "holding company." Revenues may come from membership dues, capital campaigns and endowments, special events, transportation management organizations (TMOs), housing corporations, foundations and charitable trusts, and community development corporations. These subsidiary or affiliate entities in turn usually embark on resource-raising strategies.

Significant numbers of downtown organizations have spearheaded or participated in capital fund-raising efforts on behalf of nonprofit institutions. These efforts secure extraordinary gifts and pledges for specific purposes such as public arts centers, cultural districts, museums, permanent art/sculpture collections, theater renovations, and preservation of historic property such as train stations, post offices, parks, and street malls.

The Pittsburgh (Pennsylvania) Cultural Trust, for example, has raised hundreds of millions of dollars over the years for its award-winning downtown cultural and arts district.

Similarly, downtown and neighborhood community development corporations (CDCs) are usually 501(c)3 organizations. CDCs are neighborhood/downtown grassroots-based, nonprofit entities that attract private and public financing/development capital for downtown revitalization efforts such as affordable housing, redevelopment projects, small business lending, start-ups, and growth. Downtown entities using these capital leveraging institutions include larger cities such as New York City, Philadelphia, and Phoenix, and medium-sized downtowns such as Rock Island, Illinois, and Anchorage, Alaska. The 501(c)3 designation of these organizations qualifies their resource providers for tax deductions for their contributions.

Endowments

Property and/or money is sometimes given to downtown organizations or their affiliates to establish endowments. Endowments are structured to retain the principal assets and use the investment income from the principal to help underwrite activities.

One such endowment is the Downtown Denver Partnership's Denver Civic Ventures/Boettcher Permanent Endowment Fund. It was established through a creative redevelopment strategy for a building that generated a $1.3 million permanent endowment fund.

The Roanoke (Virginia) Foundation for Downtown not only transferred about $20 million in properties for a substantial area of downtown, it collected more funds for its endowment fund. Interestingly, this same foundation also raised another $200,000 from the local equestrian community to build a quality stable and office and to provide equipment for the city's downtown Mounted Patrol Unit.

As the examples illustrate, setting up nonprofit 501(c)3 foundations and endowment funds can be effective resource-raising methods. Furthermore, these vehicles can provide longer range financial planning for achieving quality results through ongoing resource raising and management.

THE 5 Ws AND H

Doing research and asking the right questions before making a proposal to a potential sponsor, donor, and/or grantor are essential.

Proper research includes both the "first-hand" method of face-to-face communication and the "second-hand" method using the telephone, computer, library, etc.

Asking the right questions means profiling prospective providers and updating profiles on previous resource providers. Using a journalistic approach, a profile should answer the "5 Ws and the H" about the prospective resource providers:

> **W**ho are they as people, both the decision makers and request processors?
>
> **W**hat are their marketing/donation/grant criteria and strategies, annually, and long-term?
>
> **W**here have they provided funds/resources before?
>
> **W**hen are their structured funding cycles and when are discretionary funds available?
>
> **W**hy have they previously provided resources? (What are their key motivations?)
>
> Finally, **H**ow are they able to provide resources?

Obtaining answers to these internal questions is crucial prior to developing the resource-raising proposal.

A good example of proper profile research comes from the Des Moines Arts Festival's former Executive Director, Mo Dana. She reads *The Wall Street Journal, Fortune,* and many annual reports to find out where companies are spending their marketing dollars and who they are targeting. Then she asks what the (award-winning, nationally sixth-best-ranked) Des Moines Arts Festival has to offer that reaches these companies' demographic targets. This enables her to tailor each sponsors' participation to their specific needs.

Mo has tailored mutually beneficial, on-site arts festival sponsor programs based on pending legislation, upcoming public referendum votes, and the Americans with Disabilities Act (ADA). She has targeted family, student, and local markets, as well as provided statewide art and artist exposure through sponsor-provided funds and creatively incorporated resources.

Understanding community context for resource raising is also critical. Downtown strategists should survey business establishments, nonprofit organizations, and governmental entities in and around their districts to ascertain who else in the community or region is resource raising. This will help identify potential resource-raising conflicts, as well as help discover new providers and pinpoint collaborative opportunities.

As mentioned at the beginning of this section, understanding the key motivation of providers begins with asking the question: Why do sponsors, philanthropic foundations, and governments provide assets to downtown organizations?

The International Events Group (IEG) and others indicate that sponsors provide resources in order to heighten visibility (recognition/exposure), shape consumer attitudes, communicate commitment to a particular lifestyle, enhance business-to-business marketing, differentiate products from competitors, entertain clients, take advantage of merchandising/sampling opportunities, showcase product attributes, drive sales, cross-promote multiple brands, further a cause, and other reasons.

The Internet-based research company fundraising info.com, which has considerable resource-raising experience, concluded that philanthropists and grant providers first consider how much they trust the beneficiary organization and its leadership. After that, they take a more pragmatic look at their own organization's potential capacity, interest, and involvement in a particular event, project, publication, or program. Insights like this make it clear that getting to know resource providers professionally and personally can be quite rewarding in building rapport, relationships, and future alliances.

When using the 5 Ws approach, develop a one-page profile for each entity. Start by profiling the activity or project that the downtown organization represents. Next, profile other downtown and community organizations that are resource raising or have plans to do so. Then, working within the framework created by these first two types of profiles, create a third set of profiles on potential resource providers in the community. Of course, also consider any research done on their histories, marketing information, etc., when creating the provider profiles.

Because every downtown organization's resource-raising activity or program is unique and has its own set of circumstances, there will be many different questions within the 5 Ws framework for each profile situation. When completed, it may be helpful to place these profile sets side by side to more easily visualize and compare the similarities or matching information. This will help make connections and stimulate creative linkages between the downtown organization profiles, the community fund-raiser profiles, and the prospective resource providers.

A review and itemization of all the questions posed in this chapter may prove helpful in selecting applicable questions for the profiling methodology to be developed for each downtown management organization's endeavor.

HOW TO CLOSE THE DEAL

The previous sections of this chapter described a framework for organizing a quality resource-raising strategy. Although the answers to the 5 Ws will vary depending upon each downtown management organization and the resource-raising environment, this framework approach (vision/mission, asking multiple 5 Ws questions, comparing profiles) should produce new perspectives and ideas upon which organizations can capitalize.

This section will highlight some suggestions on how to "close the deal" (getting the resource-raising proposal accepted). Of course, it is assumed that all previously suggested research has been completed in order to accurately target the providers most likely to become involved. Performing this upfront research, then knowing how to make the approach, are valuable in terms of both time management and the resource-raiser's level of confidence during the presentation.

Approaching sponsors, philanthropic donors, and government grantors differs primarily based upon their different motivations, requirements, incentives, and how they want recognition and exposure. The previously described framework will bring this all to light for analysis.

Gaining access to and the attention of these resource providers is also based upon analyzing specific information, ideas, and experiences to develop knowledge-base-driven closing proposals and presentations. Nevertheless, although three different major types of resource provider categories exist (sponsors, donors, grantors), there are some common "how to" close-the-deal approaches for both the written proposal and the verbal presentation. The following section provides a few examples that resource raisers should utilize when applicable:

- If possible, attempt to present the resource proposal face-to-face. If it cannot be done personally, then earlier research interviews should have been attempted with a resource provider's representative. Getting acquainted (if not already) is the first step to building rapport.
- If possible in the presentation process, utilize a volunteer board member or downtown supporter who has a personal relationship with a resource provider. As the business adage goes, "all things being equal, people want to do business with friends. And all things not being so equal, people still want to do business with their friends."
- Initially, concentrate more on targeted resource providers' specific markets/programs rather than putting the downtown organization's needs in the forefront.

- Concentrate more on the expected results/benefits to be leveraged from the providers' resources rather than dwelling on the downtown organization's needs. Customize the proposal to each specific resource provider.
- Emphasize the downtown organization's strengths and needs in concise and winning terms—mission, market, and management (including leadership).
- Presentations should demonstrate an understanding of a resource provider's requirements and motivations in a brief, but visually exciting presentation of benefits to be derived for those involved.
- Be positive! Believe resources can be raised based upon prior research. Do not fear rejection. Again, quality research should provide reasons and confidence for making the proposal to prospective resource providers.
- Generally, by the time the proposal is submitted/presented, 80 percent of the work has been done (research indicating beneficial match). The 20 percent of work remaining is the presentation (10 percent) and the follow-up (10 percent). Follow up with polite persistence.

Many more techniques and strategies can be used to "close the deal." References provided at the end of this chapter, a search of fund-raising on the Web, and literature in libraries will provide an abundance of how-to materials.

The purpose of this chapter, as stated in the beginning, was to highlight professional, staff-driven, long-term, resource-raising strategies. Hopefully, this chapter has provided a helpful approach to consider for producing more sustainable and quality supplemental revenues, and for obtaining more in-kind products and services for downtown management organizations as well as their recognized quality activities (events, publications, projects, and programs).

ADDITIONAL RESOURCES

Books

Larry Houston (2003). *Business Improvement Districts.* Second Edition. Urban Land Institute.

Downtown Sources

International Downtown Association (IDA)

Web site: www.ida-downtown.org
e-mail: question@ida-downtown.org

National Trust Main Street Center

Web site: www.mainstreet.org
e-mail: mainstreet@nthp.org

Fund-Raising Sources

A variety of paid-member and professional fund-raising associations are available. Downtown managers can select those best suited for their particular resource-raising efforts. A number of Web sites are available.

General/Sponsorship/Events

Fundraisinginfo.com
www.fundraisinginfo.com
Association of Fundraising Professionals
www.afpnet.org
Sponsorship.com
www.sponsorship.com

International Festivals and Events Association
www.ifea.com

Philanthropic/Foundation

Council on Foundations
www.cof.org
Community Foundation Locator
www.communityfoundationlocator.org
The Foundation Center
www.foundationcenter.org
GuideStar (national database of nonprofit organizations)
www.guidestar.org

Grants

Federal

Grants.gov
www.grants.gov/FindGrantOpportunities
The Catalog of Federal Domestic Assistance
www.cfda.gov/public/faprshtmi

State

Organizations can research particular state. Arizona given as an example.

Arizona Department of Commerce
www.commerce.state.az.us
Arizona State Parks
www.pr.state.az.us/partnerships/grants/grants.html

Arizona Commission on the Arts
www.arizonaarts.org

Part III:
Operating in a Complex Environment

Most organizational leaders begin the strategic planning process with an environmental scan—a look at the complex systems that surround and interact with the organization. Downtown leaders are no different. Understanding the arena in which you operate is critical to survival. As we enter the twenty-first century, big-city downtowns, main streets, and neighborhood business districts operate in a much more diverse, complex, and challenging environment. Competition is expanding on all sides, and not everyone will survive. Use this section as a way to begin the process of looking backward, forward, and in all directions in order to chart a course that takes you to your desired destination.

Chapter 11

Strategic Planning—Charting the Course

Sandra Goldstein

INTRODUCTION

Sound, strategic planning is essential to effectively manage the many challenges facing downtown business districts. No longer do managers and staff have only the more routine problems of "clean, safe and green." Our complicated, ever-changing world is throwing much more difficult issues our way:

- How do we compete in a regional marketplace?
- How do we deal with traffic-clogged highway arteries leading into our downtowns?
- How will information technology (IT) and at-home workplaces impact our downtown retailers?
- How do we fill our office buildings, which are experiencing double-digit vacancy rates because of corporate contractions?
- How do we effectively provide services on ever-shrinking budgets?

And, there is so much more.

Essentially, in order for downtown managers and staffs to juggle the difficult issues with the plethora of routine matters and still be true to the organization's mission, they must be effective strategists. Managers must embrace strategic planning as a means of organizational focus and high performance. Although strategic planning is essential for both staff and boards of directors, this chapter will deal with the strategic planning process for downtown organization managers and staff.

doi:10.1300/5137_12

WHAT IS STRATEGIC PLANNING?

Strategic planning is a focused, shared effort to "produce fundamental decisions, actions, and work plans which shape and guide an organization in what it does and why it does it" (Bryson, 1995, p. 5). Its major purposes are twofold: respond to the multiple pressures of the outside world by having plans of action before a crisis occurs, and, fashion these plans in such a manner that the organization's vision and mission are intact and respected. Strategic planning creates an intellectual framework upon which an organization can stop being crisis oriented and become focused and value driven. The effort requires a great deal of staff and managerial discipline, but the benefits are well worth the effort.

WHAT ARE THE BENEFITS OF STRATEGIC PLANNING?

The strategic planning process is a journey during which the staff must collaborate, articulate, and elaborate on the organization's vision and mission, and while so doing fashion programs and action plans to bring both mission and vision to life. It's a mind-expanding, practical exercise with a multitude of benefits. First, the process establishes programmatic priorities for each staff member and the organization as a whole. The staff can defer extraneous matters when they arise (as they always do) because they have clear priorities that have been adopted collectively in a strategic manner. Although many emergencies do occur and must be dealt with, strategic planning prevents the staff from going off on time-consuming tangents and permits them to say "no" when necessary. Second, decision making is greatly improved because sound decisions and programs are formulated by the individual staff member and then reviewed collectively by the team and the board of directors to ensure that plans are coherent and defensible. Third, because the organization is focused on specific actions it can be more responsive to problems as they emerge. Last, the staff is infused with energy because it's able to see a complete organizational picture and meet its responsibilities within the framework of an organization built on planning and teamwork.

WHAT ARE THE STEPS
IN THE STRATEGIC PLANNING PROCESS?

Planning strategically is not an esoteric process that only the erudite can achieve. It is a down-to-earth, broadening process that is disciplined, yet relatively simple to do. The planning session itself takes place at a yearly staff retreat, ideally, held off-site. The work plan emanating from this process is operationally reinforced throughout the year. Five steps make up the strategic planning process:

Step 1. Staff Analysis of the Organization's Mission, Vision, and Goals

An organization's mission, vision, and goals are determined at board of directors' retreats. The board, various stakeholders, and the senior staff collaborate in articulating the mission, vision, and goals—but it is only the board that ratifies and codifies the latter. The mission and vision are the organization's raison d'être, and while determined and mandated by the board and stakeholders, the staff's strategic planning session must start with clarifying those essentials. An organization's vision expresses both its deep purpose and its image of a desired future and it is essential that the staff "buys" into this vision, understands it, and knows that all programs must be true to it. The mission provides a sense of purpose. An organization's mission statement and vision should be as succinct as possible while encompassing the organization's essence. The Stamford, Connecticut, business improvement district, known as the Downtown Special Services District (DSSD) has both a vision and a mission, which are reviewed biennially by its board and annually by the staff at its strategic planning retreat. The DSSD's vision and mission are succinct and simple, yet broad enough to form the basis for a very complex work plan. They are as follows:

> The vision for Stamford Downtown is that of a 24 hour/seven day a week city-center for living, working, shopping, dining, education, culture and entertainment.
>
> The Stamford Downtown Special Services District's mission is to create, manage and promote a quality environment for people, which enhances the economic vitality of Stamford Downtown.

Step 2. Formulation of Goal-Related Work Plans in Each Operational Area

Goals are usually driven by the board of directors, but occasionally, are fashioned from the organization's vision by the staff. Goals are always designed to achieve the vision. They are the skeletons from which the staff's work program emerges. Once the work plan is completed by staff and management, programmatic timelines must be attached to each activity. In addition, the strategic work plan must have quantitative outcomes for major programs so that the staff and management are accountable.

Step 3. Collaborative Discussion

New programs and those which may have lost their organizational importance, must be collaboratively discussed. Such discourse helps clarify organizational strategies. New programs must be analyzed for applicability and cost. Those which have lost their relevance, must be terminated. This step is achieved through a SWOT (strengths, weaknesses, opportunities, and threats) analysis, which is subsequently explained.

Step 4. Submission of Work Plans to the Board of Directors

After the work plan is completed, it is presented as a document to the board of directors for edification, suggestions, and approval. The board should review the plan to ensure that it is true to the organization's vision and goals. This will facilitate "selling" the plan to stakeholders.

Step 5. Weekly Staff Meetings to Stay on Track

Weekly staff meetings are an excellent means of keeping the organizational "ship" on "course." Meetings ensure that the staff work plans are "living" programs which can grow, contract, or remain the same. They reinforce the pertinence of the work plan and help staff to stay within the designated time lines.

HOW IS A WORK PLAN CREATED THROUGH THE STRATEGIC PLANNING PROCESS?

The culmination of the strategic planning process is the creation of the work plan, which is the blueprint for the year's programs. A staff retreat (managers and senior staff—away from the office—perhaps at a corporate conference room or a local hotel), away from phones, and work-related problems and distractions is an excellent environment in which to do the brainstorming necessary for this process. It should be held before the budget process before the new fiscal year begins. The DSSD holds its strategic retreat the first week of January, after the holidays and when everyone is rested and in work mode. It takes the organization one full day and two additional half days to complete the tasks and have viable work plans for each department. The agenda for the retreat should include the following: review of mission and vision; creation of goals (or their affirmation if they have already been determined by the board of directors); departmental strategies and tactics for the year, which are geared to the achievement of its goals; assessment of external and internal factors (SWOT analysis) which may determine the efficacy of new programs and viability of older ones; time line, and outcomes. Naturally, a great deal of staff work precedes this retreat. Each staff member comes prepared with a rough draft of his or her department's written strategies and tactics which are then discussed, dissected, and defended. New strategies are presented, deferred or discarded. At the end of the chapter are examples of DSSD's retreat agenda, the organization's vision and mission, its goals, and some of the strategies and tactics of the DSSD's operations department. A SWOT analysis and sample outcomes are provided in Figure 11.1. The retreat agenda is designed to demonstrate how the strategic planning process produces strategies and tactics that emanate from the goals which are in turn derived from the vision.

STRENGTHS	OPPORTUNITIES
• Potential cost savings • Increased quality control • Better control of personnel	• Program expansion to other districts • Produce income as a service provider • Higher retention of personnel
WEAKNESSES	THREATS
• Potential cost increase • Staff intensive • Payroll • Scheduling • Equipment purchase & maintenance • Benefits • Learning curve	• Litigious society exposes DSSD to legal suits • Difficult recruitment because of low regional unemployment rates

FIGURE 11.1. SWOT analysis provides information about internal strengths and weaknesses as well as the opportunities and threats of the external environment. *Note:* Weaknesses and strengths as well as opportunities and threats are often mirror images.

WHERE DO YOU START?

"Strategic planning is the articulation, justification and elaboration of the strategic vision" (Mintzberg, 1994, p. 112). It makes programs operational. Thus, creating the strategic work plan for each department starts with affirming the organization's vision and mission. The strategic work plan must carry out that vision. Therefore, conversation about and real understanding of the vision are essential. The staff must be comfortable with the board's articulated vision. As plans are discussed and reaffirmed, focus should always be on whether the programs are true to the organizational vision.

Whether board-mandated or fashioned by the staff from the vision, a set of goals to achieve the vision must be declared during the staff retreat. More mature organizations may have goals articulated from previous years and just reaffirm them before determining strategies. Goals are clearly defined decisions or policies that lead the staff to fulfill the organization's mission and vision. Goals should always be phrased in action terms. They should start with the infinitive "to" in order to propel thoughts to actions.

Strategies are designed to achieve the organization's goals. Planned strategies suggest clear and articulated intentions. Strategies break down goals into steps, formalizing them so that tactics (the details of how to get something done) can be created. Strategies codify and clarify the goals, expressing them in terms that will make them operational. Tactics elaborate and break down the strategies into specific actions. A progression from vision to tactics is illustrated in Exhibit 11.1. The totality of strategies and tactics along with measurable outcomes and a time line for each program forms the basis of the work plan. During the retreat most of the strategies and tactics are analyzed during a roundtable discussion. Ambassador Programs are generally bid-funded programs that employ workers who patrol public spaces within business districts providing security and hospitality services.

WHAT IS THE SWOT ANALYSIS?

Strategic planning creates value for the organization by providing an intellectual framework for the staff's work plan. A major purpose of this planning process is to alert the organization of potential internal or external stimuli that can positively or negatively impact the organization or its programs. Organizational planning does not happen in a vacuum. Determining the strengths and weaknesses of an organization and the external environment in which it exists are essential if the strategies and programs agreed upon are to be successful.

EXHIBIT 11.1. Strategic Planning: A Progression
from *Vision → Mission → Goal → Strategy → Tactics*

The DSSD Ambassador Program

Vision (Expresses deep organizational values)	⟶	A portion of the Stamford Downtown vision is to create a ". . . 24-hour/seven day a week city-center . . ."
Mission (Organization's identity and purpose)	⟶	A portion of the Stamford Downtown mission is to ". . . manage and promote a quality environment for people . . ."
Goal (Defined decisions)	⟶	In order to achieve a 24-hour/seven day a week environment the board of directors determined that one of the DSSD's goals would be "to plan, initiate, and manage enhanced operational services, which improve downtown's physical environment."
Strategy (means of codifying goals)	⟶	One of the strategies to improve the physical environment is to "address both the perception and reality of downtown safety concerns".
Tactics (Steps necessary to carry out strategies)	⟶	An effective tactic to address safety concerns is to establish an Ambassador Program (a private, supplementary downtown security force with a high visibility profile and which is equipped to deal with the diverse needs of the downtown community.)

Further tactics to establish the Ambassador Program include the following:

1. Determine program funding source and personnel procurement
   * Identify new and current sponsors
   * Go out to bid for Ambassador Program
2. Set up routine system of operations
   * Hold biannual police/Ambassador meetings
   * Hold regular quarterly Ambassador meetings
   * Meet quarterly with vendor to review program status
   * Arrange for vendor to train Ambassadors in public relations/ interaction
   * Continue duties that involve merchant interaction
   * Review daily inventory procedure for potential improvements
   * Arrange for specialty training for Ambassadors by police
   * Arrange for one Ambassador to attend Police Department Citizen's Training

(continued)

(continued)

- Explore potential for Ambassador to police career development program
- Monitor weekly/monthly advance schedules and subsequent hours
- Implement procedure to randomly monitor Ambassador zone coverage
- Monitor AED equipment status reports

SWOT analysis is a tool to provide information about programmatic and organizational strengths and weaknesses in relation to the opportunities and threats certain programs or the organization itself may face. Strengths and weaknesses apply to the internal state of an organization. Opportunities and threats refer to the external world and are future oriented (Bryson, 1995). A SWOT analysis can be conducted on the organization itself or any of its programs. Strengths and weaknesses refer to the organization's internal environment, organizational resources such as personnel, financial strength, work processes, and work ethics as well as performance output. Opportunities and threats refer to the environment outside the organization: societal forces and trends, the economy, the political and social climate, technological change, competition, etc. SWOT analyzes what major external opportunities or threats can be foreseen, or what major internal strengths and/or weaknesses exist within one's organization.

An example of a SWOT analysis for the DSSD Ambassador Program is depicted in Figure 11.1. The figure shows analysis in-house management versus outsourcing of a Security Ambassador Program.

OUTCOMES

Determining outcomes is an essential part of the strategic planning process. The work plan suggests clear and articulated intentions. It must be backed up by formal controls in the form of quantitative outcomes. For example, if you are creating a new marketing program to bring people to restaurants, the following outcomes may be considered: increasing patrons by "x" percent during promotional period (must have figures for previous years for comparison); attracting "x" number of restaurants to actively participate; raising "x" number of dollars from participants to market the program, etc. Staff and managerial performance can then be measured against the outcomes achieved. Exhibit 11.2 depicts outcomes in the Stamford Downtown Ambassador Program.

**EXHIBIT 11.2. Outcomes: Quantitative Benchmarks
By Which Success or Failure of a Strategy May Be Judged**

The following outcomes were set for the Stamford Downtown Ambassador Program:

1. Ambassador coverage to five full-zone circuits per eight-hour shift (currently three).
2. Employ the services of city police and vendors to train each ambassador in at least three new areas of expertise.
3. Schedule shifts to attain coverage 40 percent day (7 a.m. to 6 p.m.)/ 60 percent night (6 p.m. to 10 p.m.) ratio (current ratio is 60 percent day/40 percent night.
4. Procure a second automatic external defibrillator to be carried by Ambassadors on bike patrol.
5. Implement a bike update plan to replace 25 percent of the patrol bikes every nine months.

HOW IS THE WORK PLAN REINFORCED?

Weekly staff meetings are the singular best way to ensure that everyone stays on track. The DSSD holds its staff meetings on Monday mornings. Everyone comes prepared with plans for the week. Particular problems and issues are discussed. The entire staff pitches in with suggestions that help to keep everyone well informed regarding the organization's programs. Quick rundowns of the previous week's unfinished business are articulated. Primarily, the meetings help the staff and managers maintain focus, which is essential due to the long "lead times" of many of the programs. Separate, quarterly meetings with staff should be held just to monitor the progress made on the program time lines.

CONCLUSION

The strategic planning process allows organizations to operate at heightened efficiency by giving focus and definition to its core values. The process is intended to enhance thinking and to facilitate adaptation to changed circumstances. Through the analytical process the organization can determine its core and programmatic weaknesses and strengths, avert threats, and take advantage of opportunities. The work plan resulting from the strategic planning process strengthens the staff's ability to focus on its duties and to deal with problems as they arise. The process increases a manager's ability to plan, lead, and act strategically. In addition, it is an essential component to make others embrace the company's vision. It is the blueprint for organizational success.

APPENDIX A: STAMFORD DOWNTOWN SPECIAL SERVICES DISTRICT

Staff Retreat Agenda (Mon., Jan, 6; Tues., Jan. 7; and Wed. Jan. 8, 2003 [if needed])

Introduction (Executive director/staff)
    I. Quality (Executive director/staff)
        A. What is a "quality" organization?
            1. How do you maintain a quality organization?
            2. How do you benchmark for quality?
            3. How do you establish outcomes for each individual program?
    II. Constituents—who are our constituents? (Executive director/staff)
    III. Review Vision, Mission and Goals
        A. Vision (Executive director)
        B. Mission (Director of operations)
        C. Goals (Director of marketing)
    IV. SWOT Analysis (Staff)
        A. DSSD as an organization
        B. Designated DSSD Programs
    V. Visions for Each Department (Department heads)
    VI. Operations Department—Program: Strategies and Tactics (Director of operations /Director of streetscape)
    VII. Events and Marketing—Programs: Strategies and Tactics (Director of marketing/Program manager)
    VIII. Communications—Directory, Newsletter, Annual Report (Program manager)
    IX. Retail—Programs: Strategies and Tactics (Director of retail)
    X. Office Administration and Management (Office manager)
    XI. Office Practices' Discussion (Executive director and staff)

Vision, Mission, and Goals Statements

Vision

The vision for Stamford Downtown is that of a 24-hour/seven day a week city-center for living, working, shopping, dining, education, culture, and entertainment.

Mission

The Downtown Special Services District is responsible for creating, managing, and promoting a quality environment for people, which enhances the economic vitality of Stamford Downtown.

Goals

1. To foster the downtown's economic growth through a strong retail recruitment and retention program.
2. To ensure the appropriate economic development of Stamford Downtown through comprehensive strategic urban planning and advocacy.
3. To plan, initiate, and manage enhanced operational services which improve downtown's outdoor environment.
4. To attract people to the downtown through targeted special events and marketing programs.

Abridged Excerpts of Operations Department Strategies and Tactics

Goal

To plan, initiate, and manage enhanced operational services, which improve downtown's physical environment.

Strategies and Tactics:

I. Ensure that downtown traffic and parking operations are pedestrian friendly while recognizing the importance of appropriate traffic flow.
   A. Serve as staff facilitator for Traffic and Parking Committee.
   B. Establish 3rd Parking Master Plan
      i. Coordinate and facilitate subcommittee efforts
      ii. Prepare final draft
      iii. Present to city commissions and boards for approval

C. Expand DSSD transportation initiative to newly emerging citywide and statewide issues.

D. Update comprehensive parking plan to be ready to operate during department store construction.

E. Monitor usage of structured and surface parking.

F. Expedite new contract for Bedford Street surface parking lot.

G. Reopen the Spring Street two-way traffic discussion.

H. Address towing practices in private parking lots.

II. Determine downtown patron needs to ensure customer satisfaction

A. Design a Merchant and Property Owner Survey to include parking, traffic, security, and cleaning issues.

B. Arrange an on-site survey of patrons attending five major downtown events: Holiday Parade, Holiday Tree Lighting, Alive at Five concert, Arts and Crafts Show, and Chef's Festival.

C. Design a voluntary online survey to be posted on DSSD Web site.

III. Provide a downtown environment that is clean and well maintained

A. Hire and oversee a supplementary cleaning staff.

    i. Establish funding

    ii. Carry out vendor search

    iii. Establish daily, weekly, and monthly operations procedures

B. Monitor all downtown quality-of-life issues.

C. Address each issue with the correct source on a timely basis.

D. Document resolution of issues which have been addressed.

IV. Ensure Excellent Downtown Lighting

A. Maintain Ambassador streetlight inspection routine.

B. Establish follow-up system for repair status.

C. Streamline and speed up reporting process to city and CL&P.

D. Upgrade lighting in the Library/Caldor alley.

E. Work with city lighting engineer to continue light pole replacement project.

F. Continue and expand upon the holiday lighting program.

V. Establish a Design Review Strategy to guide new development and renovations

A. Institute basic design guidelines for retail facades, windows, and signs.

    i. Determine scope via Board of Commissioners discussion.

    ii. Review scope with zoning officer.

       iii. Form subcommittee to develop and write potential guidelines.
    B. Develop a strategy to encourage rear entrance improvements: "Two front doors."
    C. Monitor process of Bedford Street to a designated Historic Neighborhood District.
 VI. Maintain an enhanced streetscape program
    A. Monitor voluntary newspaper box system.
    B. Participate in development of City Streetscape Design Guidelines manual.
    C. Continue Banner Maintenance Program.
    D. Roll out Hanging Planter Program on Bedford & Summer Streets.
 VII. Maintain and enhance the Downtown Ambassador Program— (see Figure 11.1)

BIBLIOGRAPHY

Beckhard, Richard and Pritchard, Wendy. *Changing the Essence.* San Francisco: Jossey-Bass, 1992.

Bryson, John M. *Strategic Planning for Public and Nonprofit Organizations.* San Francisco: Jossey-Bass, 1995.

Drucker, Peter F. *The Five Most Important Questions You Will Ever Ask About Your Non-Profit Organization.* San Francisco, CA: Jossey-Bass Publishers, 1993.

Harvey, D. and Brown, D. *An Experimental Approach to Organization Development.* Upper Saddle River, NJ: Prentice Hall, Inc., 1996.

Hinterhuber, Hans H. and Popp, Wolfgang. "Are You a Strategist or Just a Manager?" *Harvard Business Review* (January-February 1992).

Mintzberg, Henry and Waters, James A. "Of Strategies, Deliberate and Emergent." *Strategic Management Journal,* Vol. 6, 257-272 (1985).

Mintzberg, Henry. "The Fall and Rise of Strategic Planning." *Harvard Business Review,* (January-February 1994).

Ospina, Sonia. "When Managers Don't Plan: Consequences of Nonstrategic Public Personnel Management." *Review of Public Personnel Administration* (Jan-April 1992).

Rosen, Robert H. *Leading People.* New York: Viking, 1996.

Senge, Peter M. *The Fifth Discipline Fieldbook.* New York: Doubleday, 1994.

Chapter 12

Diversity: Incorporating and Benefiting from Differences

Barbara Askins

INTRODUCTION

What does diversity mean for International Downtown Association members and other downtown and business district managers? Building diversity into downtown management can provide a number of benefits, but is it worth the effort? Downtown leaders have evolved and developed a number of tools and strategies that can be used to increase diversity in downtown organizations.

Since 1954, the International Downtown Association (IDA) and its members have been engaged in activities that bring people together from different areas of the world for the purpose of creating healthy and dynamic city centers. As a membership organization, IDA provides services and products for top executives in the downtown management field. Today, these executives are finding themselves in a position of delivering services and products in a world where there are many changes, not the least of which is a remarkable increase in diversity, from the smallest main streets to the largest megacities.

Among these changes are declining city and state budgets for economic and urban development, the ever-changing economy, the unpredictable stock and bond markets, a burgeoning tourism market, global terrorism, and many other issues that impact the way downtown managers and municipal officials manage cities. These are ongoing topics for downtown managers and leaders who serve, interact with, and develop plans for employees, customers, and visitors.

However, among the most important changes in the world is the growth of an increasingly diverse population; this is having a major impact on the plans and strategies that are being developed for cities, regions, nations, and certainly for downtowns. Populations throughout the world are continuing

doi:10.1300/5137_13

109

to diversify. Focusing on differences and building on inclusiveness are topics being discussed in major corporations, small businesses, public agencies, and not-for-profit organizations.

IDA's members, and especially the authors of this book, recognize the need for adjusting to changes that are consistent with core values but that also address these new changes in effective and innovative ways. IDA began to examine and track the composition and geographical locations of its board of directors and its membership. Although some progress had been made in increasing representation of women and African Americans, it was clear that existing efforts needed to expand and improve. As with any organization, discussion yielded commitment, a lot of soul-searching, and generated dedication and hard work from the entire organization.

Among early initiatives, IDA began a project with universities. The board of directors developed tasks to be incorporated into the strategic plan and developed new organizational policies. Each committee searched for ways to incorporate diversity initiatives into its plans; host cities for conferences worked diligently with the IDA to present workshops and activities that were more inclusive; and IDA's publications were designed to appeal to a more diverse audience.

The effort to make the IDA a more inclusive organization is a work in progress, however, and while the board of directors is pleased with the results and the responses received from its membership, there must be a strong and ongoing commitment to continue these efforts as the organization moves forward.

WHAT DOES DIVERSITY MEAN
FOR DOWNTOWN ORGANIZATIONS?

Defining diversity for any organization is not an easy task. Diversity definitions will vary from organization to organization. However, each organization should be clear that it is committed to including and involving, as well as providing services and opportunities, to those who have been left out of the downtown management and leadership profession.

When IDA first began to discuss its commitment to diversity, the desired results were defined in terms of white women and then black women and black men. However, as the organization continued its efforts, members stressed the importance of looking beyond race, ethnicity, and gender. In addition to the growing population of other racial groups, IDA began to identify many economic development projects being developed by these groups. It became clear to IDA that inclusiveness could also increase the services that IDA could offer its members. Many questions were generated around the economic development initiatives of Hispanics, Native Americans, Asians, international cities, young people, gays and lesbians, religious efforts, geographic locations, and others.

In the book *Winning with Diversity* by Donald M. Norris and M.C. Joelle Fignole' Lofton, diversity is defined as "difference." IDA's work is focused on including the difference.

BENEFITS OF INCLUSION

The benefits of inclusion are many. The workforce and customer base continue to diversify, the world is getting smaller (because of globalization), and it makes good business sense. Diversifying an organization or company is an important issue for managers. In any organization, but especially in downtown organizations, there are daily conversations related to the needs and concerns of minorities, women, and older and younger populations in the workplace. Effective communication, international needs, respect for different holidays and different religions and cultures are all issues that have emerged as reasons to reevaluate goals and objectives. Managers that can include and skillfully work with the changing workforce will likely be more successful than those that do not. Most companies and organizations already have diversification programs, and others are examining how to improve them.

Following are some benefits of inclusion.

- Inclusiveness will help local members prepare to serve their neighborhoods and communities. Members of downtown organizations provide goods and services to diverse employees, residents, and tourists.
- Inclusiveness allows the downtown organization to better serve the global visitor market through greater understanding of the needs and values of its international clientele. Tourism, especially cultural and heritage tourism, is a rapidly growing global phenomenon. One estimate, for example, shows Chinese tourism increasing tenfold over the next decade.
- By serving a more diverse clientele, the downtown organization will be challenged to improve performance, thereby increasing value and providing opportunities to increase membership.
- Downtown organizations will be in a better position to address complaints from minority and international visitors, thereby making them more attractive to those interested in downtown management and leadership. Recruiting a talented and varied staff will be easier.

- Inclusiveness can open doors for examining ways to provide opportunities for investing and partnering with the educational system via scholarships, internships, and joint research projects.

The essence of effective downtown management involves working together to create one place for all. This is why we should diversify.

TOOLS AND STRATEGIES

The 2003 Strategic Plan for IDA included content diversity and development. To appeal to the growing diversity of its members, IDA understood the necessity to develop a program that would offer a diverse set of products and services. IDA members vary with respect to the size of their organizations, size of their cities, years of experience, stages of organizational development, levels of complexity, and more. The lessons learned by IDA can be applied to downtown organizations as well.

- Effective implementation of a diversity strategy requires strong leadership and constant monitoring of program design, content, and member preferences.
- Diverse offerings become even more critical as expectations of constituents are raised through information management and dissemination.

GOALS AND OBJECTIVES

As organizations become more inclusive, many goals and objectives emerge. Consensus should be achieved on the following:

- Create and compile new information related to downtown population and user-diversity trends and issues
- Increase career opportunities for underrepresented groups in the local downtown management field
- Reach out to other related fields and organizations and encourage them to become active in the downtown revitalization effort
- Consult with IDA members from multicultural backgrounds about how to reach diverse audiences and professionals
- Consider consulting firms that have experience providing positive, diverse experiences that are relevant to underrepresented groups

- Contact other professional organizations that have been pursuing diversity to learn from their experience
- Assemble a database of minority downtown professionals and practitioners and encourage a supportive network

ACTIONS OF THE BOARD OF DIRECTORS

To bring focus to a diversity initiative, a downtown organization's board of directors and its chief executive should focus first on things they have the power to change, but should at the same time begin to work in areas where their influence might have an impact. Board diversity can be met by actively recruiting two to three new board members from diverse backgrounds. This goal can be achieved in one year.

A downtown organization can form a task force to work in conjunction with the board's executive committee and chief executive to formulate a plan with measurable outcomes.

In trying to achieve these objectives, the board will undoubtedly realize that a strong approach is needed for the longer term. Policy changes will probably be needed. The executive committee along with the diversity task force should develop and present a policy statement somewhat like the following:

> It shall be the policy of (____) downtown organization that it supports diversity as an important priority, which will be considered and integrated into all aspects of its programs, activities, and policies. It should be adopted unanimously, and the organization should begin its initial efforts of incorporating diversity initiatives into its entire operations.

This policy change, which allows everyone to participate by incorporating diversity into every phase of the operation, is very important. It demonstrates the organization's ability to embrace and understand different cultures and to begin to make choices for future sustainability.

By working through the task force and the board, efforts should continue to increase membership inclusion of diverse business and property owners, as well as representatives of nonprofit organizations in downtown. Diversity in membership should be tracked through an annual survey, and a report should be presented annually to the executive committee and board. A person representing an ethnic or other minority can be appointed to serve on the nominating committee. The organization can continue to use various surveys as a way of collecting information on diversity at the local level to benchmark progress. Local downtown organizations can even undertake efforts to support and pursue the creation of a university graduate program for downtown leadership and management, with a special emphasis on diversity, in order to increase the pool of available talent.

Another possible strategy that the diversity task force might employ is inviting people to a newcomers' reception or similar event. Prospects for membership on the board or on committees can be identified and put into a database that can be followed up through outreach by committee members throughout the year (not only near the board meetings or events).

MOVING INTO THE FUTURE

In the future, managing diversity initiatives will take on added importance. By 2050, the United States will be a "majority-minority" country in which no ethnic group has a majority. This is already true in the state of California. Europe is experiencing increasing immigration from Africa and the Middle East. In Japan, an aging population will literally implode unless Japan opens up to immigration. The commitment must continue, but so must concrete steps with measurable results. As organizations begin to understand the power of diversity, and as they continue to build on inclusiveness with high performance as a fundamental way of operating, the new diverse downtown organization will emerge as a world leader among economic development associations.

REFERENCES

Fignole Lofton, M.C. Joelle, Norris D.M. (1995). *Winning with Diversity: A Practical Handbook for Creating Inclusive Meetings, Events and Organizations.* Washington, DC: American Society of Association Executives.

International Downtown Association (2003). 2003 Strategic Plan. Washington, DC: IDA.

National Center for Policy Analysis (2001). www.ncpa.org/bd/social/sociala.htm.

U.S. Census Bureau (2005). Population Projections. www.census.gov/population/www/projections/popproj.htm.

Chapter 13

Attracting and Keeping Members

Polly McMullen

BACKGROUND AND HISTORY

The lifeblood of any successful nonprofit organization is the support of the constituent group or members it serves. An organization's relationship with its constituents is the foundation for its ongoing effectiveness and is an essential ingredient in the organization's financial stability and continuing viability.

An overview of downtown organizations across the United States demonstrates that their constituent base, and their methods of establishing and maintaining positive constituent relationships, have evolved and changed over the years just as the composition, character, and role of downtowns have changed. In the 1960s and 1970s, the earliest downtown organizations derived their financial support primarily from annual membership dues. As the retail centers of their cities, most downtowns in the 1950s, 1960s, and into the 1970s were the location for large, locally owned department stores as well as an assortment of specialty shops.

A limited number of downtown business organizations existed prior to 1960. Department store owners and specialty retailers were often the backbone and the leadership in local Chambers of Commerce and other civic organizations and downtowns were the focal point of commercial and civic life. With the advent of shopping malls outside downtowns in the 1960s and 1970s, the earliest downtown business organizations were established by retailers to assist downtowns in remaining competitive with outlying shopping malls. These early downtown organizations were primarily retail promotion organizations funded by a voluntary membership who paid annual dues to support a variety of promotional events and activities in order to attract customers.

With the exodus of department stores and other retail shops from many downtowns in the 1970s and 1980s, these downtowns and the organizations that served them faced serious economic challenges. At a time when down-

doi:10.1300/5137_14

towns needed a strong leadership organization to help them transition from their former role as retail centers to the vibrant, mixed-use centers which exist in so many cities today, downtown organizations faced declining membership and decreasing revenues from annual dues. Attracting new, nonretail members and restructuring programs and services from retail promotion to those that would respond to downtown's changing needs required staff leadership with different skill sets and the time to focus on programs and activities beyond membership recruitment and promotion.

In many downtowns, corporate leaders from the nonretail business sector stepped forward to lead, fund, and stabilize their downtown organizations. In other communities, downtown interests were represented and carried forward by other entities, including local governments and Chambers of Commerce. A limited number of downtown business organizations, especially those in larger cities where the downtown represented a significant portion of the tax base, were able to maintain and enhance their membership base and financial vitality through attracting as members major downtown employers and corporations committed to downtown vitality. Other downtown organizations struggled to remain viable during this period with limited success.

The introduction of business improvement districts (BIDs) as vehicles for levying annual assessments to support an array of services and programs was the single most significant event in the ongoing revitalization of city centers and downtowns and in the financial stability of many of the organizations serving them. Today, over 1,500 BIDs exist throughout North America. BIDs are being established outside North America, in places as diverse as the United Kingdom, South Africa, and Australia.

The presence and evolution of BIDs is a phenomenon which has been researched extensively and documented in detail in two publications which were joint projects of the Urban Land Institute (ULI) and the International Downtown Association (IDA) in partnership with consultant Lawrence Houstoun of the Atlantic Group. The first publication, simply titled *Business Improvement Districts* was published in 1993 and a second edition was published in 2003.

Although the widespread success of BIDs has relieved the pressures on downtown organizations to generate their annual operating funds through voluntary membership dues alone, membership organizations have remained an important part of many downtown organizations. This chapter focuses on the membership component of downtown organizations, on how organizations attract and retain members, the type of services, programs, staffing, and dues included in a membership program, as well as examples of "best practices" from both large and small programs.

DOWNTOWNS TODAY:
MEMBERSHIP ORGANIZATIONS AND BIDs

A review of the 2003 membership roster of the International Downtown Association (IDA) reveals 426 downtown organizations and public redevelopment agencies, many of whom operate BIDs and/or membership programs. Of this total, sixty-five operate both membership programs and assessment districts, while fifty-two operate only membership programs.

The downtown organizations operating membership programs or membership programs in conjunction with BIDs encompass all geographic areas of North America, including Anchorage, Alaska, and all different sizes of cities, from Denver, Baltimore, and Dallas, to smaller and midsized cities such as Little Rock, Arkansas, Norfolk, Virginia, Madison, Wisconsin, and Sioux Falls, South Dakota. Some are newer organizations formed in the past ten years; others have operated in one form or another for many decades.

Membership categories and annual dues also span a wide range depending on size of community, budget of the organization, membership benefits, and types of membership. For example, individual annual memberships are available for as little as $35 per year in the Ithaca, New York, Downtown Partnership, and $50 a year in the Downtown Norfolk, Virginia, Council, whereas other organizations such as Downtown Denver Partnership, Downtown San Diego Partnership, and Downtown Dallas Partnership base membership on size of company or number of employees, with corporate members paying dues of up to $25,000 per year.

Newly formed downtown organizations or business associations that are considering creating a membership program as part of their organizational structure should study the wealth of membership information available on the Web pages of downtown organizations included in the IDA Membership Directory. In addition to listings, broken down by city and state, the IDA Membership Directory, available to all IDA members, includes information on each members' organizational structure and Web page address (IDA, 2005).

Membership Income and Annual Operating Budgets

Downtown organizations that operate membership programs, as well as BIDs, view annual membership dues as an important component of their annual budgets. Membership revenues constitute 10 percent, or $180,000, of the $2 million annual budget of the Downtown Spokane Partnership, formed in 1995. The Downtown Denver Partnership also derives approximately

10 percent of its annual budget, or $660,000, from membership dues. The Anchorage Downtown Partnership receives only about 3.5 percent of its annual budget from membership dues, while membership revenue accounts for over 21 percent of the Downtown Lexington Corporation, Kentucky, budget.

DOWNTOWN MEMBERSHIP PROGRAMS AND SERVICES

Regardless of the geographic area, the size of community, or the budget of a downtown organization, membership programs and services among a wide variety of downtown organizations share common themes.

The primary benefit of membership articulated by organizations large and small is the *opportunity to be involved,* to have a voice and to play a role in the day-to-day issues and long-term decisions affecting downtown. This involvement takes many forms, among which are participation on task forces and committees and the opportunity to attend various meetings, forums, and briefings.

The Downtown Austin Alliance, the Pittsburgh Downtown Partnership, the Downtown Lexington Corporation, the Little Rock Downtown Partnership, and the Downtown Spokane Partnership all offer access to service on committees and task forces as a major benefit of membership. Membership materials for these and other downtown organizations frequently list the many committees and task forces that are open to members.

Membership meetings are another mainstay of most downtown membership programs, both large and small. Members of the Downtown Austin Alliance are invited to quarterly luncheons featuring national speakers as well as to a monthly "Issues and Eggs" breakfast series featuring community leaders and public officials. The Little Rock Downtown Partnership offers member forums three times a year on issues impacting downtown, while the Downtown Business and Community Association of West Palm Beach, Florida, holds general membership meetings four times a year.

In addition to active involvement in their organizations, most downtown membership programs also offer access to a variety of information on downtown. Monthly newsletters, e-mail news briefs, presidents' letters, access to mailing lists, monthly board meeting minutes, membership directories, and free promotional brochures are some examples of informational pieces provided to members by downtown organizations.

A wide variety of additional benefits are included in downtown membership programs. Many downtowns offer excellent Web sites and some organizations offer members-only sections. The Downtown Partnership of Baltimore allows members to post job openings as well as promotional information on products and services on the members-only section of its Web site. The Downtown Little Rock Partnership offers LISTSERV access and information exchange via Web pages.

Discounts of all kinds are another member benefit offered by downtown organizations. The Downtown Billings, Montana, Association offers discounted "Park and Shop" stamps and bus passes to its members while the other organizations offer discounts on admission to annual events and festivals. The Downtown Lexington Corporation offers its members first option on sponsorships for downtown events and activities.

Other membership benefits include cooperative marketing opportunities, offered by the Anchorage Downtown Partnership, and promotional flyer distribution and kiosk use offered by the West Palm Beach Downtown Business and Community Association. The Downtown Denver Partnership provides customized research and data to its members while the Downtown Little Rock Partnership offers free use of its boardroom, equipped with state-of-the-art technology, to its members. The Downtown Norfolk Council holds an annual appreciation night for its members at a theater that includes a reception and performance.

Equally important as the programs and services an organization provides to its members is the ability to communicate these benefits clearly and effectively to current members and new prospects. A number of downtown organizations have excellent membership sections on their Web sites, many of which offer online membership inquiry and registration. Downtown organizations with strong membership sections on their Web sites include:

- Downtown Austin Alliance
  www.downtownaustin.com
- Anchorage Downtown Partnership
  www.ancdp.com
- Downtown Partnership of Baltimore
  www.godowntownbaltimore.com
- Downtown Billings Association
  www.downtownbillings.com
- Downtown Dayton Partnership
  www.downtowndayton.org
- Downtown Denver Partnership
  www.downtowndenver.com
- Downtown Fort Worth, Inc.
  www.dfwi.org

- Downtown Lexington Corporation
  www.downtownlex.com
- Downtown Partnership of Little Rock, Arkansas
  www.downtownlr.com
- Pittsburgh Downtown Partnership
  www.downtownpittsburgh.com
- St. Louis Downtown Partnership
  www.downtownstlouis.org
- The Downtown Alliance of San Antonio
  www.downtownsanantonio.org
- The Downtown San Diego Partnership
  www.downtownsandiego.org
- Main Street Sioux Falls, Inc.
  www.downtownsiouxfalls.com
- Downtown Spokane Partnership
  www.downtown.spokane.net

ATTRACTING AND RETAINING MEMBERS: BEST PRACTICES FROM CITIES LARGE AND SMALL

Although providing an array of quality membership benefits and services is the essential ingredient for the continued success of a downtown membership program, a well-crafted strategy for recruiting and retaining members is almost as important to a program's success. Effective membership recruitment and retention depend on three factors: communication, organization, and networking.

1. *Communication.* Clear articulation of the benefits of a membership program—not just once a year but throughout the year—cannot be stressed enough in membership recruitment and retention. Michael Edwards, president of the Downtown Spokane Partnership stresses communicating "constant value-added services" as a key strategy for his organization. All communications materials and member events, from newsletters, electronic communications, annual reports, forums, and informational meetings, should emphasize an organization's value to its constituents.

2. *Organization.* A well-organized membership recruitment and retention program managed by staff with expertise in sales as well as database management is the foundation for a successful membership program. Some downtown membership organizations use an annual

membership campaign staffed by volunteers and conducted at the same time each year as the best approach to membership recruitment and retention. Other organizations, including the International Downtown Association (IDA), conduct membership recruitment and renewals throughout the year.

3. *Networking.* Many downtown organizations utilize board members in attracting and retaining members. Board members are encouraged to provide leads through their business contacts and peers. The Downtown Denver Partnership utilizes board members in its membership retention program. Board members are asked to contact current members to assess their satisfaction and participation levels six months before their renewal statement is issued. Roughly half of its members are contacted through this effort.

The Downtown Denver Partnership staff ensure that new members are on appropriate committees, receive requested information, are aware of and attend events, and, in general, understand what they are getting for their dues. These efforts have resulted in a 90 percent member-retention rate for the past five years.

The Downtown Norfolk Council boasts a 96 percent retention rate and believes the key to its success is seeking out committed people and businesses with a stake in downtown. The Downtown Lexington Corporation reports a 95 percent retention rate and attributes this to including its members in "every phase of planning" through surveys and self-studies.

Other successful membership attraction strategies mentioned by downtown organizations include looking for prospective members in business journal articles and lists and targeted advertising. The Spokane Downtown Partnership has discovered that National Public Radio (NPR) sponsorships are the best way to reach its target market.

TRENDS IN DOWNTOWN MEMBERSHIP PROGRAMS

Interviews with a wide variety of CEOs of downtown organizations across the country reveal an interesting pattern. Regardless of the size of city, the longevity of the downtown organization, or the array of programs and services the organization provides, almost all CEOs report that their memberships are growing, both in number of members and amount of revenue.

Memberships and revenues are growing for a number of reasons. Rose Lucas of the Downtown Lexington Corporation credits a 14 percent increase in membership numbers and 13 percent increase in dues revenue to her organization's approach of "separating ourselves from local government and marketing ourselves in a more aggressive manner."

Mike Edwards of the Downtown Spokane Partnership describes his membership growth as "very positive" in a community where membership development for the local Chamber, Convention and Visitors Bureau and Economic Development Council is a "tough issue." Edwards believes this is due to his organization's ability to "produce results and articulate success very clearly."

Terri Taylor, membership manager for the Downtown Denver Partnership reports that "the most recent year was our best ever." She attributes this to a belief that in uncertain economic times, "people want to be a part of something working to affect change. It is no longer enough to write the check out of civic responsibility or to see their name in print; they really want something tangible from their membership dues."

In Anchorage, Alaska, home to the Anchorage Downtown Partnership, a relatively new downtown organization established in 1997, staff note that they are "increasingly becoming the hub of what is happening in downtown." As their reputation builds, more and more businesses are seeking them out and wanting to join.

Downtown Norfolk Council President Cathy Coleman noted that when her organization's BID was established, she and her board leadership anticipated that it would detract from their membership revenues. Quite the opposite occurred. According to Cathy, "the more we do, the more people want to be a part of it. People love to be a part of success."

If there is a lesson to be learned from these membership trends, it is that strong, proactive downtown organizations who are demonstrating results and clearly articulating these to their constituents are reaping the benefits of their hard work with an increasing number of committed and involved members. At a time when many local governments face budget woes, the core services, advocacy, and hands-on leadership provided by downtown business organizations are increasingly valued by their constituent groups.

REFERENCES

Houstoun, L. Jr. (1993). *BIDs: Business Improvement Districts*. Washington, DC: Urban Land Institute and the International Downtown Association.

Houstoun, L. Jr. (2003). *BIDs: Business Improvement Districts*, Second Edition. Washington, DC: Urban Land Institute and the International Downtown Association.

International Downtown Association (2005). www.ida-downtown.org.

Chapter 14

The Advocacy Role
of a Downtown Organization

Richard T. Reinhard

*Should a downtown organization advocate for its downtown?

Sounds like a simple question. Of course, an organization should be involved in advocating for its neighborhood. In *Democracy in America,* Alexis deTocqueville wrote about Americans and their propensity to form associations: "I have often admired the extreme skill with which the inhabitants of the United States succeed in proposing a common object for the exertions of a great many men and in inducing them voluntarily to pursue it" (deTocqueville, 1831-1832).

In other words, associations advocate. However, the question is a bit trickier than that, as we will see.

An executive director of one downtown organization e-mailed the Board of Directors of the International Downtown Association, "I am trying to determine if any of your organizations have a formal policy in regard to which issues you will or will not advocate or support. My organization is increasingly being called on to advocate for:

1. specific property owner issues where they are seeking a variance to the zoning or building code;
2. design standards such as use of pedestrian walkways downtown; and
3. large projects that may be great for downtown but do not comply with existing height and setback restrictions.

---

*This chapter is a compilation of responses from various International Downtown Association Members. The data and correspondence were gathered through an extended period of time using the IDA's electronic LISTSERV, Brain Trust, which asks members to respond to a specific question (in this instance "Should a downtown organization advocate for its downtown?"). All individuals noted within this chapter were authors of their expressed ideas.

doi:10.1300/5137_15

These issues, while important, are consuming my staff's time. We need to determine where our efforts can best be utilized."

To paraphrase the former head of the Downtown Stratford-upon-Avon Association in the United Kingdom: "To advocate or not to advocate, that is the question."

Downtown organization veterans respond that the advocacy issue depends upon three things: organizational structure, consensus, and the downtown plan.

ORGANIZATIONAL STRUCTURE

Advocacy depends, at least in part, on the type of organization that is involved. According to James Cloar, president of the Downtown St. Louis Partnership.

> I have long felt that the advocacy role is very questionable for a Business Improvement District organization. . . . There is a question of appropriateness of taking a position on something contrary to that of people who are required by law to fund your activity.

Cloar noted that Downtown St. Louis has separate entities.

> The Downtown St. Louis Partnership, funded by voluntary dues and sponsorships, is our advocacy voice. The Community Improvement District, funded by mandatory assessments, does not take positions, though we do advocate generally for Downtown as part of our marketing and campaign image.

Cathy Coleman, executive director of the Downtown Norfolk Council, pointed out, "Our Board took the position that we are not a 'Civic League,' and, while we monitor what is going on with private property and business issues, we only get involved on a policy level if there is an issue that affects the overall health, wealth and vitality of Downtown."

CONSENSUS

> A good rule of thumb when dealing with potentially controversial issues is to make sure you have a "supermajority" of supporters, approaching unanimity or at least broad consensus . . . and work closely with your Board Chair to make sure that he or she will support you in enforcing the deliberative decision-making process, convince everyone

around the table to speak up during debate, and stand by the group decision. (Peter Armato, director of Special Projects, CEO for Cities; former head of downtown organizations in Providence, Bellevue, Washington, and Savannah)

"We have avoided 'taking sides' in disputes involving one local property owner's interests versus another," said Michael Weiss, executive director of Brooklyn's MetroTech BID. He offered an example: A developer proposed building a 1-million-square-foot building to house state courts adjacent to a new hotel. He approached the BID for support. The BID Board, with representation from both the developer and the hotel, declined to involve itself in this controversy. Eventually, the City decided to support the building of the court structure.

However, Cloar noted that a downtown organization executive is "rightly expected to be the voice of and for Downtown redevelopment activity. You just have to be sure to achieve the right balance between action and advocacy, say 80-20 percent. And getting in between two private interests is to be avoided."

THE DOWNTOWN PLAN

My experience has been that it is critical to have a comprehensive plan that your Downtown organization was actively involved in developing, preferably in partnership with the City, before jumping into case-by-case zoning, land use and . . . urban design issues. (Peter Armato)

The comprehensive plan can serve as the filter for your review of projects, thus bringing logic to your recommendations or your decision to not even consider certain proposals. . . . The planning process builds a community of interest around issues that can help your organization weather the inevitable criticism you'll take for getting involved in advocacy that may favor one Downtown interest against another.

Jeff Sanford, president of the Memphis Center City Commission, agreed with the importance of a plan. Armed with a strategic plan that has been adopted as public policy, and with certain other guidelines (e.g. zoning laws, historic preservation requirements, special district redevelopment goals) in hand, we try to make rational, defensible decisions relative to our support or nonsupport. . . . We often work to move parties and their positions toward compromise, when we believe the results will still fall within the bounds of our plans and guiding principles or advance the cause of

Downtown development. . . . We're called upon almost daily to determine what is and what is not in the best interests of Downtown. . . . Sometimes we're popular; sometimes we're not!

REFERENCE

deTocqueville, Alexis (1831-1832). *Democracy in America.*

Part IV:
Marketing and Communicating

If a tree fell in the forest, perhaps no one would hear it. But if a tree falls in downtown, your job is to communicate effectively with a whole range of downtown visitors and stakeholders. Marketing and communicating require not only responding to emergencies; they also require actively working to create positive and memorable experiences for those visiting downtown for the first time and for those who use it every day. This section examines how downtowns are operating in the new "experience economy" and how they are using the latest technologies to communicate quickly, effectively, and inexpensively.

Chapter 15

Creating the Downtown Experience:
The New Fundamentals
for Downtown Programming

Stephen J. Moore

The American downtown, formerly the psychological and social center
of American life, relinquished its prominence, stature, and place to shopping centers more than a quarter century ago. Shopping moved indoors as
the new town center heralded quarry tile, climate control, Muzak, and security. Though the longing for holiday department store windows, tea rooms,
and the city-street hustle and bustle never fully subsided, the purchasing of
apparel and household goods now overwhelming takes place in one of the
40,000+ enclosed malls and strip centers that dot this country from coast to
coast.

This, of course, is old news. The numbers and causes and scenarios explaining downtown's downward plunge have been rehashed time and again.
Restudied and revisited often, we are more fluent in the growth of the suburbs than we are in the tools and tactics that are necessary to remake the
downtown. The forces that conspired to bring on the demise of the downtown are as gone as the department stores themselves.

Arguably, it is no longer of value to know the economic muscle of the
nearest edge city or Wal-Mart. It just doesn't matter. It is *nice* to know but
not what we *need* to know to move forward.

MAKING SHOPPING FUN AGAIN

With neither the time nor the inclination to shop for fun, the American
consumer is increasingly avoiding malls as a pastime. Shopping is now,
more than ever, a chore.

It has stopped being useful for those of us who market the American
downtowns to make comparisons between shopping centers or suburbs and

doi:10.1300/5137_16

downtowns. We are moving now in different directions more divergent than parallel and there is no looking back. The consumer attitude about free time has changed so much that time and money spent promoting the downtown as a place to shop may have the unintended consequence of reminding the consumer that shopping is an obligation. The typical regional mall shopping trip of today is shorter and less frequent than it was a decade ago and is driven by three powerful motivations: find it, buy it, and get the hell out.

Now more than ever, we in the downtowns are breaking new ground, solving new problems, and packaging an old entity in new ways. We are like Hush Puppies shoes—both hopelessly out of fashion and the new thing, well positioned for resurgence.

NEW FUNDAMENTALS

Downtown organizations can, though, impact and accelerate the success and the reacceptance of downtowns greatly, yet this has more to do with local celebrity, small events, and opportunities to learn than it does with sales promotions and hype.

If Gilmore and Pine (1998), the authors of *The Experience Economy*, are correct in their assertion that downtown is a stage and downtown managers are producers, directors, and actors, we can begin to see what we do in an entirely different light.

For example, safety ambassadors in some cities have been given permission and instructions to gather at high visibility locations around lunchtime and launch into songs or skits. Business improvement district (BID) cleaning staff can perform their daily cleaning activities with a bit of drama and style.

Street musicians might be encouraged rather than discouraged. Some BIDs have even organized street musicians, giving them specific locations and times in exchange for nominal stipends and the BID's blessing to put out a hat or guitar case for donations.

Street vendors can also be organized and assigned locations through city ordinances. Perhaps these vendors be given training so that their interactions with downtown customers are pleasant and memorable.

Sales associates in retail stores can certainly be part of the show. A great example is Amy's Ice Cream shops in Texas. This small chain encourages its staff to perform like Benihana chefs, chopping and massaging ice cream and fresh fruits on a cutting board, then tossing the scoop in the air and catching it in acrobatic ways in a serving cup or cone. The ice cream is great—the entertainment value is greater.

SEVEN AREAS OF PROGRAMMING

So what is it that we as marketers do? Where do we place our priorities and resources? Where should we aim our efforts to have the biggest and most lasting impact? In the absence of the new streetscape plans or leasing plans do we have a role and can we make a difference? The answer is emphatically, yes.

One of the distressing curses of working in downtown organizations is that we have a tendency to become blinded to the assets we have around us. For instance, we see the parks, the cafes, the building façades, the cultural institutions every day and soon they become part of the wallpaper. Yet we are surrounded by incredibly valuable assets of all kinds, and it is our challenge to reopen our eyes and rediscover the treasures that we can use in very creative ways.

Our history, museums, and merchants are our greatest assets. They provide uniqueness, place, and identity.

We must be willing to design and lead a long-term campaign that is unlike our work to date. Seven distinct areas of emphasis are suggested for the new downtown marketer:

1. Promoting downtown merchants as celebrities.
2. Promoting the museums and cultural institutions as the new downtown anchors.
3. Promoting local history as the context for the experience of the downtown.
4. Programming smaller, more frequent events.
5. Promoting a 24/7 mind-set among all of the downtown stakeholders.
6. Creating different criteria for new businesses, e.g., actors in the experience.
7. Becoming a concierge: scripting the trip/organizing the trip/creating itineraries for locals and visitors alike.

These seven strategies are a good recipe on one hand, and just a start on the other hand. They give downtown marketers a framework in which to create events and opportunities to produce excitement and sales.

Promoting Merchants As Celebrities

Purpose: What to do

- Identify key merchants in the business district as "good copy" candidates.
- Augment the branding of the business district by identifying and celebrating the merchants as a "must see" for visitors and locals.
- Identify the key relationships for locals to "get" the experience of the downtown.
- Draw attention to the person not the product.
- Create "star maker machinery."
- Determine the role of merchant as celebrity.
- Declare the downtown as a unique, one-of-a-kind experience based on its "characters."
- Promote the "characters," the taste masters, the hubs of activity, the arbiters of cool, trendsetters on fashion, authorities on food, and the pulse of the community.

Benefits: Why do it

- An opportunity for publicity, which is cheaper and better than ads.
- Characters are essential to the branding of a place as an experience.
- Celebrity merchants are the source of creative direction to an agency or branding team.
- An action plan with merchants at the center is an *opportunity to lead.*
- The merchants and their stories provide for unique positioning for the downtown that is not goods-acquisition based.

Intended Results

- A higher profile for merchants, chefs, business owners, and community thought leaders.
- A group of trendsetters identified with the downtown.
- The downtown merchants become the go-to sources of what is happening in the community for fashion, food, and entertainment.
- These high-profile characters are an engine for publicity for the downtown.

Promoting Cultural Institutions As Anchors

Purpose

- Solidify the branding of the business district by identifying the cultural institutions as the anchors for the district.
- Use the local cultural icons as the hub for the identity of the business district.
- Maximize the image, programming, collections, and distinction of the cultural institutions.
- Package the downtown trip as a larger, more significant event than a trip to a mall.
- Draw the attention of the customer away from a one-dimensional convenience shopping trip to a larger, more valuable, culturally anchored trip.

Benefits

- Create a unique position that the business district "owns" regionally/nationally.
- An action plan with cultural institutions at the center is an *opportunity to lead.*
- The cultural institutions and their stories provide for unique positioning for the downtown that is not goods-acquisition based.

Intended Results

- Enrich the context of the downtown by association with cultural programming.
- Attract a longer, more valuable trip.
- Fill the niche of an experience trip which is closer to the needs and desires of a broader customer base.
- Establish a high-profile cultural community as a driver of both the identity of the downtown and traffic into the downtown.
- Position the downtown as a place worth visiting and an experience worth having.
- Create for the merchants cultural sponsorships and tie-in opportunities.
- Establish the cultural calendar as a merchandising calendar.

Creating History and Heritage As the Context for the Downtown

Purpose

- Solidify the branding of the business district by establishing it as a special place with a unique past and a story to tell.
- Maximize the experience of the place by making history come alive, for both the everyday and the occasional visit to the downtown.
- Package the downtown trip as a larger, more significant event than a trip to a mall.
- Draw the attention of the customer away from a one-dimensional convenience shopping trip to a richer and more meaningful trip with a significant past.
- Add history as an everyday dimension to the experience of the business district.

Benefits

- Create a unique position that the business district "owns" regionally/ nationally.
- The history of the downtown provides a unique position that is not goods-acquisition based.

Intended Results

- Enrich the identity of the downtown by making its history come alive.
- Attract a broader variety of trips including cultural tourist, historians, etc.
- Fill the niche of an experience trip that is closer to the needs and desires of a broader customer base.
- Establish history and heritage as drivers for the identity of the downtown.
- Package the history of the downtown as a family opportunity to learn, and a compelling reason to visit the downtown.
- Position the downtown as a place worth visiting and an experience worth having.

Special Events Programming

Purpose

- Solidify the branding of the business district by establishing it as a special place where something is always going on.
- Maximize the experience of the place by planning large, signature events and smaller, frequent, ambient events for the everyday and the occasional visitor to the downtown.
- Package the downtown trip as more entertaining than a trip to a mall.
- Program the larger signature event as an icon for the business district.
- Program the ambient event as an everyday dimension to the experience of the business district.

Benefits

- Create an events reputation that the business district "owns" regionally/nationally.

Intended Results

- Generate publicity for the downtown at a rate of ten times the ad budget.
- Generate increased trip satisfaction for downtown users.
- Attract target audiences to specific events.
- Drive traffic to the downtown.
- Establish the reputation of the downtown as always having something to do and see.
- Published event calendar as a driver for publicity.
- Position the downtown as a place worth visiting and an experience worth having.

Working Toward a 24/7 Downtown

Purpose

- Position the downtown as a broadly attractive, must-see destination to the widest possible audience.
- Maximize the experience of the place by planning large, signature events and smaller, ambient events for the everyday and the occasional visitor to the downtown.

Benefits

- Create events reputation that the business district "owns" regionally/nationally.

Intended Results

- Generate publicity for the downtown at a rate of ten times the ad budget.
- Attract target audiences by time of day.
- Establish the reputation of the downtown as always having something to do and see.
- Maximize shoulder hours/seasons.

New Business: More Than a Store

Purpose

- Develop criteria for new leasing at street level.
- Position the downtown as attractive to potential merchants who fit the criteria of contributing to the downtown as a place to be experienced.
- Solidify the branding of the business district by establishing that this is a special place with unique merchants who participate in creating the downtown as a place to be experienced.

Benefits

- Create a clearly defined merchandising plan.
- Mobilize a group beyond the broker community to identify and attract qualified street-level uses.

Intended Results

- Increase occupancy rates.
- Increase synergy between merchants, cultural institutions, and restaurants.

The Concierge: Scripting the Trip

Purpose

- Market downtown on a one-to-one basis and not on a mass (trade-area) basis.
- Solidify the branding of the downtown by affording visitors the opportunity to customize their trip.
- Create a relationship with the downtown users.

Benefits

- Attract a more valuable trip.
- Create events reputation that the business district "owns" regionally/nationally.

Intended Results

- Attract target audiences by time of day.
- Establish the reputation of the downtown as always having something to do and see.
- Maximize shoulder hours/seasons.

CONCLUSION

In conclusion, these seven strategies are a starting point. With a modest budget, or even on a shoestring, a downtown marketing professional can create experiences that reward, satisfy, and lure back downtown visitors and shoppers. These are intended to stimulate creativity and experimentation. Downtowns have incredible assets that shopping malls can never own or duplicate. It would be a shame to ignore them.

REFERENCE

Gilmore, J. and Pine, J. (1998). *The Experience Economy: Work Is Theater and Every Business a Stage.* Boston: Harvard Business School Press.

Chapter 16

Marketing the Shopping Experience

Maureen Atkinson

INTRODUCTION

Marketing the shopping experience, or retail marketing, is different from other kinds of marketing that you will do for your downtown because it has a key goal—to attract customers to your retailers and get them to buy something. Remember that when we talk about the shopping experience, we include:

- stores that sell merchandise (e.g., craft shops and women's clothing stores);
- services (e.g., dry cleaners and copy shops);
- food, beverage, and entertainment services (e.g., restaurants, cafes, and bars); and
- cultural and sports venues (e.g., art galleries, theaters, and ball parks).

Other factors that should be kept in mind when creating your retail marketing plans include the following:

- *Overall image or brand of downtown.* This will have significant impact on how you market your retailers. If your message about downtown is intimate and historic then your retail advertising cannot be loud and abrasive.
- *Nonretail events and activities.* Although we deal with marketing the shopping experience separately in this chapter, in practice, you should carefully coordinate retail and nonretail events. For example, a Santa Claus parade may not by itself be a retail promotion. However, if you plan other activities (e.g., a pre-Christmas sale) at the same time, then retailers can take advantage of the crowds attracted to downtown.

doi:10.1300/5137_17

DOWNTOWN'S SHOPPING IMAGE

Before setting out a retail marketing plan, it is critical to settle on the retail image that will be communicated. This image must be based on the existing mix of businesses in downtown. Key issues related to developing the image include the following:

- The image should convey the most appealing side of shopping in downtown.
- It must relate to the needs and desires of the target market.
- The impression should be different from other competitive shopping environments. Differentiation is often the only way that downtown can compete with shopping environments that may have more selection or lower prices. Remember what you choose as your points of differentiation must be relevant to the target customer and based on the reality of what your retailers are capable of delivering.
- The image should not "oversell" the reality. It is better to under-promise and over-deliver rather than to disappoint visitors.
- The theme for marketing the shopping environment should complement the overall theme or brand for downtown.

Once a theme or image has been confirmed then a retail marketing plan should be developed. Although your marketing plan can change on a year-to-year basis, your overall theme should remain consistent. Repetition of a consistent message will help the downtown story penetrate faster and more thoroughly by using the same resources.

Visual and audio symbols, such as brand marks or taglines, are tools that can be used repetitively to reinforce the shopping image.

THE RETAIL MARKETING PLANNING PROCESS

Retail marketing, whether it is advertising, promotion, or special events should all be done as part of a larger plan. Simply running a few ads at Christmas or launching a back-to-school sale will not get payback on the investment. A well-thought-out plan with key measurements will help ensure that downtown's limited resources are maximized.

The best planning process includes the following steps.

Step 1: Develop a Planning Group

A planning group should involve retailers. Although this may seem self-evident, many downtown organizations find it difficult to get busy retailers to participate. Marketing is one place where retailers may feel that their input will be valuable, so make sure that your best retailers are part of this group. Most of your retailers will already be doing some promotion on their own. If these efforts can be coordinated and additional resources applied, the results will be greatly enhanced.

In addition to having better coordination of promotions throughout downtown, involving retailers will also bring more knowledge and experience to the working group. Although this is generally an advantage, it will be important for retailers to see the big picture, and not just be focused on what works for their business or area.

This planning group may sometimes be divided into subgroups. Often, downtowns will have special-interest groups (e.g., bar and restaurant owners, special districts, etc.) that work together to develop their own initiatives. These subgroups can be very effective, but should work within the overall marketing plans.

Step 2: Agree to Targets and Objectives

An important first step for the working group is to set clear, measurable objectives for the retail marketing plan. Although it may be difficult to measure progress, the working group should be required to show results from the resources used in marketing.

Marketing programs should be designed to accomplish the following:

- Build awareness of downtown shopping.
- Create an understanding of how downtown shopping is differentiated.
- Build a liking or preference for downtown shopping among the target market.
- Turn preference for downtown shopping into visits to downtown for shopping purposes.
- Turn shopping visits into purchases.
- Turn purchases into return visits and purchases.
- Produce loyal customers.

No single event or ad can accomplish all of these goals; however, over time a good marketing program should focus on these goals. When setting out measurements, ensure that you are as specific as possible in retailing to time frames, sales gains, traffic increases, etc.

Following are examples of goals that are specific and measurable:

- Create awareness in 70 percent of the target market by the end of year one.
- Have 70 percent aided recall of key promotional themes or benefits among the target market.
- Have 65 percent preference for shopping downtown for specific purposes among the target market.
- Attract 40 percent of the target audience to shop for specific purposes over a specified period.
- Generate a 65 percent return shopping visit rate among downtown shoppers.

Obviously, these measurements will require that regular market research be done to ensure that the goals are being met. The research can be done as part of an overall plan which will give information for other key programs that the downtown organization is operating. As such, the research budget should not be charged completely to the marketing program.

In addition to customer awareness and behavior measurements, other measures of actual retail sales increases can be made. In the United States, where sales tax data are available for small trade areas (e.g., California), the change in retail sales can be measured accurately. In other cases, where data are not available, confidential surveys among downtown retailers can be initiated. Retailer surveys are less accurate and depend on a high level of participation to ensure that you are receiving a clear picture.

Although actual sales may look like the best measurement to evaluate a retail marketing program, many other issues affect sales, which are not related to the marketing program. The arrival of a large, new retailer, or the loss of an old one, can affect the results dramatically. In addition, actual retail sales changes should be measured in the context of the rest of your city. A modest increase in sales may be good when compared to decreasing retail sales among downtown's competitors.

Step 3: Agree to Target Market Segments

As you can see from the goals set in Step 2, clearly identifying key target market segments is critical to the success of the retail marketing program. Although downtown tends to have a broader set of target customers than any individual retailer, clear definition of the customer segments that will contribute the most sales to all downtown retailers is a very important process.

A good rule of thumb in identifying key target markets is that the closer those potential customers are to downtown, the more likely they are to be customers. This is especially true if your retail base is made up primarily of convenience-oriented and/or service businesses. Often customers do not want to travel far for businesses such as fast-food outlets or convenience stores. However, customers will travel farther for furniture stores or unique restaurants. The other rule of thumb is that the greater the number of certain kinds of retailers you have, the more likely that you will attract from a wider geographic area. Make sure that you are realistic in your target market planning so that you are not wasting your marketing funds on customers who are unlikely to come downtown.

Following are some examples of target markets. They are listed in the order of their exposure to downtown.

Downtown Workers

These potential shoppers are in the downtown five days a week and form the backbone of the shopper base for many downtowns, especially for specific kinds of businesses (e.g., fast-food restaurants and cafes). However, the extent to which downtown workers will be a key customer group for you will depend on the number of workers in downtown and the kind of work that they do (e.g., low-paid clerical workers will not be as attractive as well-paid managerial or professional workers).

Other Regular Downtown Visitors

In addition to offices that bring workers, many downtowns have facilities that attract regular visitors to downtown. Local universities and colleges are examples of attractors. As in the case of local workers, the number of students and the kind of courses that they are taking can have a strong impact on how attractive these potential customers are to downtown retailers.

Irregular Visitors to Downtown

This target market can include local residents who come downtown for entertainment or other facilities (e.g., theaters, sports facilities, or nonretail facilities such as doctor's offices, hospitals, or even post offices). These visitors will already be in downtown and may be interested in using downtown merchants. However, remember that the primary reason why these visitors come is not for shopping. Be realistic when it comes to estimating their potential. It is also a good idea to think about subsegments within these groups. For example, when assessing sports fans, young, single adults may have more potential for downtown restaurants and bars than families.

Downtown Residents

This group is likely to spend the highest proportion of its overall retail shopping expenditures downtown. However, for most downtowns, the number of residents is relatively low so their comparative importance as a primary target for marketing may be small. If this is the case, in-store promotions and signing may be the best way to attract these customers without spending a lot of money.

Local Residents

These residents live within a wider neighborhood area. In small communities, it will be the whole community; in larger communities it will be neighborhoods close to downtown. The composition of the local neighborhoods and the makeup of the retail base will dictate how important this group is.

Regional Residents

This group will be the largest in number, but also the most diverse. In order for a marketing plan to be effective, this target must be subdivided. Not everyone will be a potential customer. The retail base will determine the key target segments.

After analyzing these potential customers, the marketing planning group should prioritize on whom it will spend its money. Once key segments have been identified, they will be used as part of the planning process in other steps (see Exhibit 16.1).

Step 4: Develop Budget Allocations

The overall retail marketing budget should be developed on a yearly basis. This allows the planners to allocate the total budget over the most important merchandising periods. It may mean that most of the budget is spent in the fall and Christmas, and only a small proportion is spent in the spring, because the fall is when there is the greatest potential for sales success.

EXHIBIT 16.1. Macro versus Micro Marketing

Macro marketing is also called "one-to-many" communications. Macro marketing focuses on strong marketing messages that are relayed to a broad audience. Typical macro marketing media include newspaper and network television. Micro marketing focuses on a much narrower form of communication. In micro marketing a relatively small target audience is identified and the communication form that will reach that group most effectively is chosen. Media, such as direct mail, e-mail, and in-store media are micro marketing vehicles because they tend to be "one-to-few" communications.

Marketing professionals are now choosing micro marketing over macro marketing for a number of reasons. Micro marketing is more effective if the target audience, media, and messages are all aligned. Unlike macro marketing in which a broad message is transmitted to many viewers who are not interested, micro marketing has a very specific target. If done properly, micro marketing is far less expensive to use. This makes it ideal for the average downtown organization where marketing budgets are tight. The challenge of downtown organizations is to ensure that they have the proper tools for micro marketing. This includes a database on the target markets.

The process for allocating the budget is to first determine the sales patterns for downtown retailers. Once this is done, the budget is allocated in roughly the same proportion starting with the most important merchandising period, which is usually Christmas. Make sure that significant amounts are allocated, because this will be where the greatest successes are achieved. It may mean that you will have no marketing activity at certain times of the year. This makes sense if resources are limited and the goal is to maximize productivity. Though there may be some pressure from retailers to drive sales in slower periods, this is almost certainly a waste of money if customers are not in a shopping mood. The old adage "Shoot while the ducks are flying" also applies to the timing of promotions.

Most downtowns expand their marketing budgets by soliciting co-op advertising dollars; this can be done by promoting in conjunction with other interested parties. Examples of potential downtown sponsors include:

other downtown facilities (e.g., sports arenas that have significant budgets);
local nonretail businesses that want a higher profile; and
national brands that want to be associated with a local event (e.g., a beer company related to a "Taste of" event).

A downtown's success in attracting additional co-op advertising funds will depend on having a strong professional advertising program and a good story to tell potential co-op partners. Good market research can help the planning group to develop the reasons why potential partners should join forces with downtown.

In addition to co-ops, downtowns typically ask retailers to contribute additional funds for specific marketing vehicles. For example, a directory of downtown businesses may be subsidized by selling display advertising to local businesses. In some cases, local media will help sell advertising spaces to local businesses and provide space for an overall downtown message. This can be done in flyers, newspapers, radio, and cable TV.

All of these expenditures make up the overall budget for marketing. They should all fit into the plan developed in Step 5.

Step 5: Create the Marketing Calendar

Once goals have been established, target markets are agreed upon, and budgets are finalized, it is time to develop a marketing calendar. Remember that your communications tools go beyond media and events. The experience of downtown is the most powerful medium in reaching your customers. Figure 16.1 illustrates some of the ways that downtowns communicate with their customers.

The marketing calendar is a great planning and communications vehicle, because it encapsulates all the activities that are happening in one easy-to-read document. The calendar is also ideal for communications to members and other stakeholders.

The marketing calendar should have several levels of information. These levels are as follows:

- basic calendar dates (e.g., Christmas and Thanksgiving);
- overall events that organizations are putting on in downtown (e.g., Santa Claus parade);
- advertising (include specific themes and media);
- promotions that are specific to retailers;
- release of in-store, back-up promotions that enhance advertising; and,
- any other activities that are relevant to marketing.

Downtowns with small budgets typically create the calendars themselves with the help of freelance professionals. However, downtowns with larger budgets will work with an advertising and promotions agency to create the marketing calendar. When working with an agency, it is important to

FIGURE 16.1. Downtown communication tools.

have clear, measurable goals so that the effectiveness of the agency can be assessed.

Once the calendar is developed, it should be disseminated to all stakeholders. Get it into the hands of the retailers early enough so that they can time their own store events to coincide with larger events. The calendar should be established at least four months in advance of the promotion dates.

Make sure that the calendar is widely distributed. The first distribution should go to all retailers as soon as it is finalized. This will encourage retailers to develop in-store promotions to reinforce downtown events. The easiest and least expensive way to send out this information is through e-mail. Most retailers, even in smaller towns, now have e-mail. A limited number of hard copies should also be printed and distributed as required. Encourage retailers to let you know about their special events so that they can also be included in the calendar. If a famous author is signing books at your downtown's bookstore, this should be included in the final calendar.

Closer to the date of the promotions, the finalized calendar should be distributed to the general public, particularly those who are part of your key target markets. Downtowns can distribute the calendar in any number of ways including the following:

- Posting on the downtown's Web site.
- E-mailing to a list of interested potential customers (make sure that recipients have a way of opting out of being on the e-mail list).
- Mailing to interested potential customers.
- Distributing at downtown information outlets (e.g., visitors center and hotels).
- Printing in the newspaper.
- Any other distribution methods that will reach the target audience.

Step 6: Implementation Plans

Although the planning stage is very important, good implementation is "where the rubber meets the road." It will be better to take on fewer projects and do them well than to do many, poorly implemented projects. This is particularly true if the downtown organization is counting on volunteers to do the work.

Downtown management should have alternative plans for most elements of the promotional calendar. Specifically, events should always have a disaster backup plan, which can include an alternative "rain" date and/or another venue.

Successful retail marketing includes a strong in-store presence of the promotion. This means that customers will not only see the promotion on the streets of downtown, but stores will reinforce the promotions. Implementation should include recommendations and tools for retailers to participate in a promotion. Examples of effective in-store promotions include:

    window displays,
    contests (some contests include visiting multiple downtown stores),
    feature displays,
    seminars and demonstrations,
    point-of-purchase signs, and
    bag stuffers.

Step 7: Review and Measure Results and Make Warranted Changes

The marketing planning group should meet at least twice a year, but preferably quarterly, to review the results of the promotions. A more formal, written review should be produced on a yearly basis. These reviews should be done on a very detached basis. Each promotion should be evaluated to see if it met the goals set for it. Although hard numbers, such as the number of attendees and reported increase in retail sales, are useful, the key will be to relate the achievement of goals to the cost of the promotion. These goals should be set in Step 2.

All promotions, even those that have been carried out for many years, should be analyzed in the same way. This regular review should end by categorizing each promotion as:

- repeat the promotion in the same way, or
- repeat and make changes to enhance results, or
- cancel and try something else.

By taking this systematic approach to analyzing your promotions, you will ensure that they remain fresh and strong.

Chapter 17

Electronic Marketing

Andrew M. Taft

The Internet, and affordable, easy-to-use software applications allow downtown organizations to communicate their rapidly changing message twenty-four hours a day, seven days a week. Graphic content, special effects, and interactive features involve the viewer in ways that printed marketing tools and direct mail cannot. Although these advantages give downtown professionals new and compelling ways to communicate the downtown story, new technologies present challenges that should be recognized as readily as their more appealing features.

Electronic marketing falls into two distinct categories, active and passive. As with print, outdoor, and broadcast advertising, e-mail newsletters, LISTSERVS, and other forms of distribution require action on the part of the sender to actively position the message.

Once created, Web sites are passive. They sit on a computer until someone calls up the information. A key to successful use of these active and passive communications tools is to maximize the likelihood that they will be viewed.

ACTIVE ELECTRONIC MARKETING

E-newsletters

E-newsletters are a remarkably inexpensive way to communicate quickly with members, property owners, the media, elected officials, and other stakeholders. Using standard word processing software, timely and colorful layouts featuring photos and graphics can be copied and pasted into your e-mail message and distributed to thousands within a matter of minutes. Many downtowns send weekly e-newsletters, while others send bulletins as topics arise (see Exhibit 17.1).

doi:10.1300/5137_18

EXHIBIT 17.1. E-mail Newsletter Do's and Don'ts

Don't include the name of all recipients on the "To:" line. This shares your list with others, makes the e-mail larger and exposes your list to spammers.

Do place your distribution list in the "Blind CC:" box.

Don't make the e-mail so large that it takes a long time to download.

Do use modest, file-sized graphics that capture the imagination or clarify a point.

Don't type and send! The immediacy of e-mail tempts writers to send messages before documents are adequately proofed. Get your e-newsletter proofed as thoroughly as you would proof a printed document.

Do put the date on your e-newsletter and archive. They are a wonderful resource for downtown and organization history.

Although e-newsletters are a convenient, inexpensive way to keep in contact with your audience, remember that some key recipients may not have e-mail access. Overreliance on e-mail to the exclusion of other forms of communication can leave some stakeholders uninformed. Another downside: spam.

"Spam" is not just "pork shoulder and ham," as the good people at Hormel would have us believe. Unwanted spam e-mails are the scourge of the Internet, and users of e-mail newsletter distribution risk having their message lost in the morning ritual of deleting overnight spam. To avoid having your carefully prepared e-mail discarded with the rest of the junk e-mail, try these techniques:

1. Make sure that the "From:" line is quickly recognizable as being from you or your organization. If it is not clear at a glance, you are likely to be swept into the trash with the Viagra peddlers.
2. Make sure that the "Subject:" line is also clear. "News from Downtown XYZ . . ." or another simple subject line will capture your audience's attention.
3. Make sure recipients want your message. Give them an opportunity to unsubscribe.
4. Keep the content brief and snappy. Long passages on the screen are difficult to read. Use more detailed content in your printed newsletter.

5. Send your e-mail during the day so that it is not deleted with the overnight spam.
6. Keep image file sizes small to ensure a quick download.

Because Internet service providers (ISPs) are becoming more aggressive in screening spammers, large distribution lists may need to be sent in sections. Be sure to adapt your sending routine to your ISP's spam screening method. A simple call to your ISP explaining your situation should result in helpful advice.

Building Your List

Building your list of e-newsletter recipients starts with board members, general members, elected officials, government staff, media, and property owners. Offering a subscription to your newsletter on your Web site, mining e-mail addresses from business cards, providing e-mail sign-up sheets at public meetings and other techniques can be used to quickly develop a long list of interested parties.

LISTSERVS

By using the Internet, rapid communication among multiple parties is easy. Downtown organizations can host online discussions via e-mail. For example, a property owner e-mails the downtown organization with an idea that deserves discussion among key stakeholders. This message is quickly forwarded to a list of targeted parties who are encouraged to "Reply to All" and share their thoughts with the rest of the group. The Internet also features free LISTSERV discussion forum services.

Although not a sales marketing effort, electronic communication enhances membership. Members, property owners, and other stakeholders can become more involved in your organization by providing meaningful input.

Electronic Brochures

Compact disk technology allows the creation of elaborate electronic brochures featuring on-disk information, special effects, music, video, and seamless Internet interactivity. These brochures are developed to launch automatically when inserted in a computer CD drive and can be stored on disks no larger than a business card.

CDs can be immediately engaging, visually impressive, and evoke strong emotions. Many e-brochures imbed links that launch Web-based information sources, thus expanding the information content and referral capacity of the disk immeasurably.

CD technology requires an action on the part of the recipient: putting the disk in the drive—a significant weakness. For this reason, compelling packaging is critical to enticing the viewer to load the disk. Disk duplication fees are modest and e-brochure design can be relatively simple and inexpensive. As with all digital marketing, strong consideration should be given to the speed of upload and operation.

The compact-disk-based e-brochure is the equivalent of handing someone your Web site; it bridges the active-passive divide.

PASSIVE ELECTRONIC MARKETING

Web Sites

For any group with a communications requirement, the Internet is a valuable resource. Web sites behave like a twenty-four-hour staff member, always ready to instantaneously share printed information, data, and graphics with anyone in the world. Once established, and for a low monthly fee, your downtown information waits for visitors from around the world. It requires no postage, no long-distance phone bills, and no delay.

Management is important. A common failing in Web sites is stale information. Because Web sites facilitate easy updating, downtown organizations often include details that they would not ordinarily put in printed brochures, e.g., targeted opening dates, meeting dates, occupancy figures, etc. As a result, unless it is refreshed on a regular basis the detail becomes dated. Dated material detracts from the credibility of the organization and the Web site as an information source. (See Updating in the following section.)

Because most visitors to a Web site are already interested in the subject matter, you can regard them as qualified prospects. For downtown organizations, these could be prospective members, residents, merchants, office tenants, developers, or shoppers. Efforts should be made to capture their interest, encourage feedback, or inspire a visit to downtown. Making the Web site an interesting, informative, and fun experience can accomplish this.

Components

Web site components vary dramatically among downtown organizations. Simple, streamlined sites contain text information about the center city, a "contact us" link, and a few interesting photos. This kind of Internet presence can be perfectly appropriate for many downtown organizations.

More advanced Web sites include membership enrollment forms and on-line payment ability, event registration capability, interactive parking maps, 360-degree views of the downtown, short films, mapped merchant information, geographic information system (GIS) features, and links to other relevant sites. Although there are many sophisticated downtown sites, a few worthy of note are: Seattle, Denver, Portland, Baltimore, and the Times Square BID.

Developing a Web site should begin with the question: "What do we want the site to accomplish?" If the answer is, "We want to tell people what we do," a simple site may do the job. If the answer is, "We want to create a one-stop shop for information about downtown and our organization," then a more complex site is in order. Establishing a simple site can be accomplished with off-the-shelf software. Complex sites require the services of a Web site designer and can cost thousands of dollars. Streamline your Web site creation process and lower costs by reviewing other sites and identifying what you like and do not like about them. Make a simple map of what you would like your site to do and share these ideas with your Web site designer. Refer the designer to elements of your favorite sites. This homework will reduce costly design hours and the stress of "trial and error" design. See Exhibit 17.2 for a list of good Web site attributes.

UPDATING

Periodic review of every page in a Web site is recommended. Downtown organizations of all sizes should have in-house Web-site-text-update ability. Using in-house text updates, dated material can be revised and Web designer fees can be reduced. Building the capacity to update text from your

---

EXHIBIT 17.2. Good Web Site Attributes

1. Quick download times.
2. Organization contact information on the home page. Make it easy for people to contact you.
3. "Contact Us" page offering phone numbers, addresses, and e-mail addresses.
4. "Return to Home" link on every page reduces chances of getting lost in your site.
5. Top-tier menu on each page makes jumping to the main subjects easy.

office is easy, and basic Web site updating techniques can be learned in less than an hour.

When establishing your Web site, be sure to ask the designer about the following:

- FTP (file transfer protocol) access between your computer and the Web host
- FTP software
- connection instructions
- updating instructions

MAXIMIZING THE POTENTIAL OF YOUR SITE

Just because a Web site is passive, you don't have to be. Maximizing visitation to your site should be a goal of your marketing program. The "if you build it, they will come" fallacy is as true for Web sites as it is for bricks and mortar. Because Web sites are a passive media form, i.e., requiring visitors to seek out the site, marketing the URL is as important as marketing a retail destination. See Exhibit 17.3 for some free and easy Web site marketing tactics.

URL Positioning

Unless Web users know exactly what your site address is, they will be searching for you. Make your site easy to find by ensuring that the most frequently used Web browsers rank you among the top listings.

One way of improving your search engine position is to pay for placement. ISPs, placement services, and others are familiar with strategies that enhance visibility to Web crawlers. These firms will charge a fee to ensure that your keywords are cataloged correctly to increase the likelihood of major search engine placement.

EXHIBIT 17.3. Free and Easy Web Site Marketing Tactics

- Place your Web address on business cards, letterhead, brochures, event banners, and other promotional tools.
- Feature your Web site on e-newsletters and imbed the link in e-newsletter stories that relate to your site's content.
- Refer to your Web site in slide shows and public presentations.
- Make the Web site address easy to remember: www.downtowncity. com.

EXHIBIT 17.4. Google Tip

- At the time of this writing, Google was the portal for fully one-third of all English language Internet searches.
- The Google ranking algorithm places emphasis on Web sites that have their address linked on other sites.
- This is an advantage for membership organizations. Try to get your Internet address link placed on as many member or colleague Web sites as possible.
- Google notwithstanding, placing your link on other sites is another free way to drive traffic to your Web page.

Google (see Exhibit 17.4 for Google tips), MSN, Yahoo, and other search engines employ automated Web crawlers that seek out keywords and phrases in sites. These words are then matched to search requests. Be sure to match your text with themes that are sought by Web users. For example, the text on your site's home page should contain the words "downtown cityname," preferably more than once. These text words (not graphic images) will be recognized by the crawlers and cataloged. When someone using a search engine types in "downtown cityname," your site will be among those provided. To increase your chances of more prominent placement, make sure the words you expect to be used to find you are part of your "keyword" listing.

Registration of your site will include "keyword" submissions. These submissions are a shortcut to listing and are a proactive step in making sure that your site is cataloged correctly. Avoid generic, single-word terms such as "downtown" and "cityname," etc. Linking these words in the same way that searchers input them increases your chance for higher placement. For example, searching for "cityname" could result in hotel, restaurant, travel, municipal, and a host of other listings. Using "downtown cityname" should place your site near the top of listed sites.

Other downtown-oriented keyword strings such as "historic preservation cityname" and "cityname parking" should also be submitted. Remember to use these keyword strings within your Web site.

FEEDBACK—SUSTAINING THE INFORMATION SEARCH

Remember that your Web site is not an end in itself. The site is a tool to inform, persuade, entertain, or move to action. For downtown organizations, action is the most important product of a Web site initiative.

Whether the ultimate action is buying a building, purchasing a home, leasing office space, opening a store, shopping or dining in downtown, center city organizations tailor their marketing plans to invoke an action. Before those actions occur, however, effective communicators attempt to sustain the information search by providing quality information quickly. The downtown Web site is a portal, a door through which those interested in downtown can pass for more information.

Hopefully, the downtown Web site will provide useful data, but even the most comprehensive sites will still leave many with unanswered questions. Make sure to sustain the search for more information by encouraging feedback. Downtown organizations want to know who is looking for information so that they can provide more service and track success. Provide staff phone numbers and e-mail addresses on the site. People and relationships sell downtowns; Web sites are an introduction.

Another good feedback tool is provided by ISPs. Each month, statistics on your Web site usage can be compiled and e-mailed to you for review. This information will show when the site was accessed, what pages were visited, domain names of visitors, images accessed, etc. These data will help you track what people are searching for and can help guide new content decisions. Placement of contact phone numbers more prominently in these areas can generate more leads.

GUERILLA MARKETING

Although not often used by downtown organizations, electronic "guerilla marketing" is making inroads on the Internet. Effective guerilla marketing is sometimes defined as low-cost, high-concept, alternative marketing. A funny, recent example was an advertisement stenciled onto the back of a streaker who interrupted an internationally telecasted soccer game. The segment ran on news stations worldwide, drawing extraordinary attention to the product at a very low cost.

On the Internet, guerilla marketers get their message across using interactive games, funny or amazing videos, and other eye-catching content. The trick is to create a forwardable desktop experience that is so unique, entertaining, or different that people who receive it pass it on to other like-minded people. Usually, the product drives visitation to a Web site where the advertiser's core message is found. Guerilla marketers use clever content to access the distribution channels of others to spread their message.

For downtown organizations, a guerilla tool could include time-lapsed video of an exciting construction project. A unique video like this would be distributed to many others beyond the original downtown distribution list.

Reference to the downtown organization or Web site could be included in the video to drive traffic to the site.

Whether active or passive, effective use of electronic media can help downtown organizations communicate effectively with their constituencies, market their organization or downtown, and answer questions from around the world . . . even while the staff sleeps.

Part V:
Managing Downtown's Many Elements

Urban planner. Event director. Real estate developer. Community organizer. Marketing expert. Social worker. Security specialist. Housing manager. These are but a few of the roles downtown managers find themselves in every week. Yet does this mean that the downtown manager must be a "jack of all trades, master of none"? Or does it mean that the successful downtown leader becomes just expert enough in many areas to make wise decisions when appropriate or to assemble needed experts and engage in collective decision making? This section outlines seven key areas most business district managers should know at least something about.

Chapter 18

Clean and Safe—Basic Requirements

Rob DeGraff

The perception of escalating problems from transient street people was common in major urban centers in the late 1980s. Individuals sleeping in doorways and loitering in groups, aggressively begging, or publicly intoxicated created fear and apprehension among many downtown users. Evidence of public urination and defecation, litter, and graffiti sent the message that these areas were less than safe. These behavioral problems appeared beyond the control of municipal governments suffering from years of stagnating revenues and a series of court decisions that invalidated municipal ordinances designed to give the police tools to address these issues.

Demands from downtown business communities that the government address these concerns were often met by protest that scarce police resources were needed elsewhere in the community to address serious safety issues such as gang violence. As a result, early business improvement district (BID) planning efforts focused on how the private sector could address these issues. Many of the programs developed by BIDs were directed toward creating a "clean and safe" environment downtown.

CLEAN PROGRAMS

Cleaning programs focus on sweeping up the debris that accumulates on downtown's streets during the day and in the evening. Cleaning crews generally operate five to seven days per week, beginning work early in the morning before the business day starts and functioning until late afternoon or early evening. Cities vary in their approach to these tasks. Most downtown associations contract with private-sector janitorial companies to deliver the service. Often, those companies have invested in technology such as the large vacuum sweepers that are operated by one person walking behind the machine which literally suck up all the dirt, stray papers, and

doi:10.1300/5137_19

cigarette butts that have accumulated on downtown sidewalks during the prior twenty-four hours.

Portland, Oregon, initially eschewed the high-tech approach, opting to employ formerly homeless individuals using brooms, dustpans, and large garbage cans on wheels to remove the trash in downtown. This low-tech approach created entry-level employment opportunities for individuals who were trying to rebuild their lives. This program was a significant contribution from the former Association for Portland Progress (APP), Portland's downtown association (now part of the Portland Business Alliance), toward the broader community's effort to address the problem of homelessness in the central business district.

In addition to litter collection, cleaning programs often also include sidewalk pressure washing and graffiti removal from at least the public property (telephone poles, letter boxes, etc.) within the right of way. Pressure washing cleans chewing gum and other sticky and staining substances off the sidewalks, maintaining their attractiveness and sending a message to downtown users that this is a well-maintained environment. When BIDs provide this service, it is usually done on a rotating basis, covering each block face within the district one or more times per year.

The presence of graffiti also creates a negative impression of downtown that BID cleaning programs work to negate. Actually, graffiti removal represents a bridge between the "clean" programs of the BID and their "safe" programs. Graffiti vandalism is a crime. Graffiti is also widely associated with gang activity, even though in many cases, it is the work of "taggers," generally young people whose only crime is defacing property with their unique "signature." Although defacement is reason enough to actively work to remove graffiti, the fact that, to the untrained eye, all graffiti is an indication of gang activity increases BIDs' motivation to remove it. No district wants to be perceived as gang turf.

Graffiti takes many forms. Marker pens, spray paint, and a variety of decals are just a few of the common ways vandals leave their signatures. Different surfaces and different kinds of graffiti markers result in a variety of techniques for removal. Choosing the wrong method to remove graffiti can result in permanent scarring of the surface being cleaned.

Monetarily, one of the most expensive tagging methods has been the use of ultra-sharp instruments to "etch" tags into display windows and metal surfaces often found on new buildings and in elevator cabs. This method has spurred the application of clear plastic sheeting to these surfaces since, once damaged by etching, it is often necessary to replace the glass or metal to remove the tags. The plastic absorbs the damage and is relatively inexpensive to replace.

The risk of permanently scarring a building's surface has required BIDs to work closely with the owners of vandalized private property. Some BIDs have negotiated liability waivers from the victim/owners before the BID undertakes graffiti removal.

A final wrinkle to graffiti removal relates to tags applied to the upper stories of buildings. Workers' compensation and insurance issues usually keep BID graffiti crews from removing these tags. In Portland, a city ordinance places an affirmative duty on property owners/victims to remove graffiti tags applied to their buildings above the ground floor, though even by the spring of 2004 it had yet to be enforced.

SAFE PROGRAMS

Portland, Oregon, was the location of one of the first BIDs to focus on clean and safe services as the core of its mission. As the story goes, the leaders of the Association for Portland Progress went to the chief of police and offered to pay for ten additional patrol officers to be dedicated to patrolling downtown Portland (at a cost of about $500,000). The chief thanked the business leaders for their support, said he could really use the ten additional officers, but if he had the personnel, he would deploy them in seriously gang-affected neighborhoods across the river from downtown. He said that it was his responsibility to put police resources where they were needed most. He suggested that if APP wanted enhanced security for downtown, the organization should hire security personnel of its own. The security program of Portland's BID, "Downtown Clean and Safe," was the result of this conversation.

Several important questions need to be answered once the decision has been made to provide some kind of supplemental security presence in downtown public spaces. Questions include:

- How "hard" or authoritarian will the security presence be?
- How will the personnel be armed, if at all?
- What will their uniforms look like?
- Will they have a quasi–law-enforcement role or will they be positioned as goodwill ambassadors for the downtown?

The answers to these questions will depend upon local conditions including the problems to be managed, the attitudes of the elected officials asked to implement the BID, and the attitudes of the local police force toward the BID. The latter is especially important since, in order to be effective, it is imperative that the BID and police personnel work well together.

Most BIDs contract with professional private security companies to deliver these services. Portland adopted a unique, two-tiered approach—their security contractor employs retired police officers who are armed and out-fitted in uniforms that project a strong law-enforcement message. The BID also deploys goodwill ambassadors, who dress in distinctive uniforms that do not send an authoritarian message, to provide information to tourists and other users of downtown.

In some cities, the police deliver the BID services under special con-tracts, either by dedicating regular-duty personnel to downtown or allowing the BID to employ off-duty police personnel to supplement regular patrols. Winnipeg, Canada, took a completely different approach, creating a pres-ence through their "Clean Team." Comprised of young people, Winnipeg's "clean team" sweeps up litter, entertains and dispenses information, as well as discourages antisocial behavior.

The goal of each of these efforts is to discourage difficult behavior by putt-ing personnel on the streets of downtown that will also interact positively with the majority of downtown users. Personnel can, at a minimum, provide "eyes and ears" for the police charged with managing difficult behavior while providing useful information and directions to downtown users.

The working relationship between the BID security program and the po-lice is crucial. Some programs develop the relationship by having those po-lice officers detailed to patrol downtown and the BID security personnel share "roll call" at the beginning of each shift. Others enhance the working relationship by carrying one another's radios so they can easily communi-cate. Some programs have been able to upgrade equipment so that they and the police have radios that share a common frequency thus making direct communication possible.

In Portland, the BID purchased mountain bikes and donated them to the precinct that covers downtown. Although common today, officers deployed on bikes was relatively new in 1989. It moved the regular officers out of their patrol cars and made them more accessible to the BID security person-nel who patrol on foot.

The spread of community-based policing methods across the country, in conjunction with the development of BIDs, has facilitated the development of working relationships between BID security programs and the police. The BID personnel are another partner as police seek to interact with mer-chants, property owners, and residents in problem-solving efforts.

SPECIAL PROGRAMS ENHANCING SAFE PROGRAMS

As BID supporters became engaged in providing what had been hereto-fore municipal services, they came to better understand the interrelated na-ture of the criminal justice system. They realized that improvements or modifications to elements of that system, besides officer patrols, could increase the impact of their "safe" resources if those other elements were given BID support.

The Community Court

The Community Court program was one of the first BID forays into additional elements of the criminal justice system. Much of the antisocial behaviors that BIDs seek to inhibit with their security patrols are, at worst, misdemeanors. In a typical major city with overcrowded jails, conviction of such crimes results in no real sanctions for the perpetrators. The Times Square BID in New York City was the first to support the creation of a community court, an alternative to the regular district court. In Community Court, guilty offenders are given community service as their punishment. In addition, the court seeks to connect offenders with social services that will help the offender deal with underlying problems such as alcohol and drug addiction, which may be motivating the individual to engage in illegal activity.

In Portland, the BID provides the supervision for the community service work crews made up of those convicted in Community Court. This is another bridge between the BID clean and safe programs. Community service work crews do large clean-up projects, such as cleaning up under freeway overpasses. In these instances, the BID cleaning program either lacks the resources, or the site of the project is just outside BID boundaries (yet close enough to impact the public perception of downtown).

The Neighborhood-Based Prosecution Program

In Portland, the Multnomah County district attorney created what is called the Neighborhood-based Prosecution Program. Inspired by community policing, a deputy district attorney is assigned to a district and works cooperatively with all interested stakeholders to solve public safety problems.

In downtown Portland, the assigned deputy works closely with police, BID security, and other private security organizations on a number of projects that address crime problems in the BID. The DA took over coordination of the Downtown Security Network (DSN), that was created by the Portland Business Alliance, formerly the Association for Portland Progress, as a forum for information sharing between the police, BID security, and private security providers. The Portland Police Bureau alerts retailers to such things as shoplifting rings, bad-check passers, and other kinds of retail fraud. When high-profile events or demonstrations are planned, the police use the DSN to brief private security personnel about expected problems or precautions.

The downtown DA has been instrumental in successfully prosecuting several prolific graffiti vandals. Portland's cleaning program has been documenting graffiti with digital cameras for years. The prosecutor has argued, and local courts have agreed, that different pieces of graffiti can be linked together (thus to the same perpetrator) by a process similar to handwriting analysis. The damage inflicted on any one building by a tag is likely only sufficient to charge the perpetrator with a misdemeanor. Linking multiple tags to the same individual increases the dollar value of the damages to the level of a felony crime—which carries the penalties of incarceration, large fines, and restitution.

The BID employee who manages the image database of graffiti tags (built by the BID) has been certified as an expert witness for purposes of connecting individuals apprehended in the act with other pieces of graffiti. As a result, the Portland police, the downtown DA, and the BID have successfully prosecuted a number of prolific graffiti vandals resulting in prison terms, heavy fines, and restitution orders to compensate the victims. After almost a decade of steadily increasing numbers of tags removed by the BID cleaning program, peaking at over 70,000 tags removed in one twelve-month period, graffiti vandalism in downtown Portland declined significantly since the project's inception.

Education

Security programs have spawned a number of education efforts sponsored by BIDs. In Portland, Clean & Safe Fairs are events in which the BID sets up informational displays in the lobbies of major downtown office buildings. These displays provide tenants and visitors with brochures on street smarts and personal security, office security, shoplifting prevention and information, and referral lists of important city and county offices. In this way the BID works to deliver value to tenants of downtown, many of whom pay for BID services through their leases.

Panhandling Vouchers

A number of programs have created panhandling vouchers as an educational tool and to promote an alternative to giving cash to those asking for money. In Portland, homeless service leaders testified that, to their knowledge, many panhandlers use the money they receive to support alcohol and/or drug habits which contribute to their poverty. Redeemable only for food and services, panhandling vouchers provide those asked for money with a humane alternative to just saying "no." They also direct those begging to services that may succeed in helping them address their problems.

Mental Health Outreach

BID security personnel or the police may not have the appropriate skills to manage or influence the difficult behavior of some individuals. Specifically, individuals misbehaving because of serious mental illness will often respond more positively if they are contacted by professional mental health outreach workers. Recognizing this, Portland's BID supports Project Respond, a mobile team of mental health outreach workers who respond to calls for service from the BID, the police, or other downtown businesses. This team can often convince persons suffering from mental illness to accept services, thus getting them off the street and into a facility where their problems can be comprehensively addressed. Portland's BID has also been an active supporter of funding for the CHIERS Program, which is a similar outreach effort focused on assisting seriously intoxicated individuals on the streets of downtown by transporting them to detox.

ORDINANCES

Many BIDs have identified problems with city codes designed to manage street disorder. Many ordinances from the late nineteenth and early twentieth centuries have been invalidated by the courts because they overtly discriminated against protected classes of individuals (i.e., minorities) or are now interpreted as infringing on constitutionally protected rights. Some BIDs have gotten involved in efforts to rewrite these ordinances so that they conform to current judicial interpretations but still provide a tool for police to use when attempting to manage difficult behavior on the streets.

Ordinances against begging or panhandling have been invalidated as infringing on freedom of speech. As a result, they have been rewritten in some communities to regulate the supplicant's behavior (as they are asking for money rather than the act [speech] of asking). Thus, they cannot behave aggressively, cannot block someone's path down the sidewalk, and cannot make bodily contact with someone they are asking for money or behave in a generally harassing manner if they are refused. Ordinances have also been adopted, with BID support, regulating where individuals can beg, specifically banning such behavior proximate to automatic teller machines, at transit stops, or at other locations where the target of the request may not have the freedom to move away from the supplicant.

The city of Seattle, Washington, passed an ordinance against sitting and lying on the sidewalk in a commercial district during business hours. The ordinance was supported by advocates for the elderly and disabled, and people who have difficulty maneuvering on downtown sidewalks crowded with those loitering, begging, or sleeping in the right of way.

Although controversial to civil libertarians, these ordinances have generally been upheld by courts as reasonable exercises of the local government's right to manage the public's right of way.

ACCOUNTABILITY

Accountability is fundamental to most BIDs. Is the BID accomplishing its goals and how do we measure success? Measuring the success of cleaning programs entails counting the number of graffiti tags removed, the gallons of trash collected, and the number of blocks pressure washed in a given period. Safe programs have a harder time measuring success. Data on crime are largely confined to serious, person-to-person and property crimes, events BID security efforts are not really designed to impact. In Portland, the BID tracks graffiti incidents and the number of times its personnel observe someone panhandling. The Portland city auditor conducts an annual citywide survey of citizens, measuring how they feel about the community. It specifically asks residents if they feel safe in their neighborhoods. The number of respondents saying that they feel "safe" or "very safe" in downtown Portland has gradually increased since the BID has been put in place.

Clean and safe programs are some of the most tangible enhancements BIDs bring to revitalized downtowns. They are perhaps the most dramatic manifestation of the increased role that the private sector has played in shaping our central cities as we begin the next century.

Chapter 19

The Public Realm and Urban Design

Jill M. Frick

INTRODUCTION

To understand the range of urban design issues that have become the work of many downtown management organizations, one can look at four basic elements of the public realm: building appearances and facades, sidewalks, roadways, and open spaces.

Building Appearances and Facades

Many downtown organizations offer assistance to property owners, often in the form of matching grants, for improvements to building appearances and façades. Programs and projects may include historic preservation and storefront treatments, signage design, window displays and merchandising assistance, vacant window programs, and interior and exterior lighting.

Sidewalks

Improving the design and comfort of the pedestrian experience on the sidewalk itself is often a priority for downtown management work programs. Design and comfort improvements to sidewalk areas may include the upgrade or addition of sidewalk treatments and pavers, pedestrian scale lighting, wayfinding signage, sidewalk cafés and outdoor dining, sidewalk kiosks, tree plantings, landscaping and seasonal plantings, banners and seasonal decorations, and amenities and street furniture. Sidewalk amenities and street furniture improvements often include the design and placement of newspaper boxes, bicycle racks, benches, trash cans, and more.

doi:10.1300/5137_20

Roadways

To address issues of access and parking, downtown management organizations take on a range of design projects. These may include traffic-calming initiatives such as narrowing streets at select intersections and converting one-way streets into two-way streets; alley improvements; adding parking or improving the configuration of parking; gateway signage and roadway treatments that can provide a sense of arrival; or transit systems such as circulator buses, light rail, and trolley systems.

Open Spaces

With the goal of creating a sense of place, downtown management organizations can undertake many efforts to create or improve open spaces including the renovation of existing public parks and open spaces, construction of new parks and public spaces, and installation of murals and public art.

THE IMPORTANCE OF GOOD URBAN DESIGN

The design of a downtown greatly influences how successful the downtown will be. The creation of an environment that is inviting and comfortable lends not only to a sense of confidence on the part of the public, but also a confidence and commitment on the part of private developers and investors. Good urban design strongly impacts the social and economic vitality of a downtown.

The quality of the public environment can make the pedestrian experience memorable, creating a positive image, a sense of community pride, a desire to linger, and a desire to return. Danish architect Jan Gehl observed the relationship between the quality of outdoor spaces and the rate of occurrence of outdoor activities. In a poor physical environment, people take care of their necessary activities in the least amount of time. However, in an appealing and attractive environment people will take more time for what Gehl calls "optional" activities such as browsing store windows, sitting on a park bench, or enjoying public art. The frequency of optional activities in the public realm increases the likelihood of what Gehl calls "resultant" activities which are defined as the chance encounters and conversations of strangers.[1] In terms of the social viability of downtown, downtown management's goal is to not only attract people to the downtown, but also create a memorable and interesting experience that will result in an increased length of stay and an increased likelihood to return.

In addition to attracting social activity, well-designed public spaces attract development investment. Whether it be the renovation or development of a park, a streetscape initiative, or a development plan, improvements to pubic space spur improvements to existing properties as well as private development of offices, housing, and retail. After suffering severe decline and becoming a haven for drug dealers, New York City's Bryant Park reopened in 1991 after four years of renovation. The Bryant Park Restoration Corporation and the Bryant Park Management Corporation, a business improvement district of neighboring properties, were responsible for the park's restoration and currently manage the space with a budget six times the level under prior city management (http://www.bryantpark.org/park-management/overview.php). Today, seven million square feet of office and retail space surround the park. According to a study conducted for the Bryant Park Restoration Corporation, leasing activity increased and office rental rates increased in the years following the renovation of the park. In terms of the economic viability of downtown, by improving the public environment, downtown management's goal is not only to foster improvements to private property, but also to attract new investment and development.

GUIDELINES AND PRINCIPLES OF URBAN DESIGN

Downtown managers can use a number of urban design principles to guide their efforts and initiatives to improve the design of the public environment.

Diversity of Use and Balance of Activity

A successful downtown is one that can attract different people at different times. Attracting large numbers of people to downtown alone is not enough. Creating pedestrian activity at different times is an important ingredient. "By offering people a wide variety of reasons to visit and stay in the heart of the city throughout the day and evening, it is possible to attract more people, more frequently and for a longer period of time."[2] Cities are creating successful twenty-four-hour downtowns by combining complementary, but diverse uses including office, residential, cultural and entertainment, restaurant, and retail.[3]

Compactness

Compactness creates a critical mass as well as ease of access and continuity of the pedestrian experience. In her book *The Life and Death of Great*

American Cities, Jane Jacobs discusses compactness in terms of the need for small blocks. "Frequent streets and short blocks are valuable because of the fabric of intricate cross-use that they permit among the users of a city neighborhood."[4] Long blocks can keep people separate who are downtown for the same reason at the same time, thus limiting the critical mass and frequent interactions. The same is true of gaps in the urban fabric that create discontinuity of the pedestrian experience and significantly reduce pedestrian activity. This can occur when downtown anchors and activity centers are located too far apart from one another, or when the storefront continuity is interrupted by surface parking or vacancies.

Intensity of Development

Maximizing the intensity of development while at the same time protecting the continuity of street-level activity can be a challenge for downtowns that lack appropriate zoning codes and guidelines. New construction needs to be scaled appropriately with the downtown's existing buildings and street-level spaces. "The city center plan, development regulations, and the review process must specify how buildings should relate to the street and set standards for the quality of street-level spaces."[5]

Accessibility

Downtown streets need to provide access for both automobiles and pedestrians, but giving pedestrians enough space first will encourage walking and strengthen the vitality of the downtown. According to Johnathan Barnett, "A sidewalk needs to have about eight feet clear, the amount of space needed so that two couples walking in opposite directions can pass each other comfortably without having to shift into single file."[6] Barnett suggests another five feet are needed to add room for pedestrian amenities such as street lights, trees, signs, parking meters, and street furniture. He also suggests adding another five feet to sidewalks where outdoor cafés or sidewalk kiosks are desired.

A well-designed, pedestrian-oriented downtown can become a one-stop area in which a person makes a single vehicle trip, uses one parking space, and makes multiple stops easily on foot.[7] However, vehicular traffic circulation and parking also need to be convenient and efficient.[8] Attention needs to be given to providing convenient, short-term, on-street parking as well as long-term, peripheral parking.

Linkages

Downtown activity centers should be connected by continuous, interesting pedestrian linkages. According to William H. Whyte's observations, "the distance that people were likely to walk in New York City was five north-south blocks, which adds up to about 1,250 feet, or a little less than a quarter of a mile."[9] Shopping center developers find the limit between anchor tenants to be approximately the same at 1,200 feet.[10] According to Whyte, in order to get people to walk a five-minute distance you need to create an interesting experience. Pedestrian traffic will decline in environments that contain blank walls, vacant storefronts, or parking lots directly fronting the sidewalk. Interesting pedestrian connections can be created by integrating distinctive streetscape elements, open spaces, and active street-level uses.[11]

DESIGN AND PLANNING PROCESS: INTERNAL VERSUS EXTERNAL STRATEGIC PLANNING

Downtown organizations undertake strategic planning initiatives to set a vision and mission for their organization. Many of the same principles and skill sets needed to undertake such "internal" strategic planning efforts are directly transferable to the work of downtown organizations in "external" strategic planning. In the same way that an internal strategic plan defines what the organization does and provides a roadmap for how to do it, an external strategic plan for design and development defines the what, why, and how for the physical environment. "A good plan helps define the rules of the game for all the players, and along with the tools used to implement it, provides a predictable framework for decision making and a basis for coordinating public and private investment."[12]

The degree to which downtown organizations get involved in external strategic planning can "range from detailed plans intended to guide redevelopment and open-space investments to less formal visioning exercises undertaken to develop consensus on goals and priorities."[13] Through varying levels of planning efforts, downtown management organizations define a vision for the physical environment and identify the changes needed to make their commercial area more competitive.

HOW DOWNTOWNS USE DESIGN TO CREATE
A SENSE OF PLACE

There are countless examples of how downtowns organizations are using the principles of urban design to improve the public environment resulting in a more livable and memorable downtown. The following are just a few examples of downtown management projects and programs aimed at improving the public environment.

Streetscape—Houston's Cotswold Project

Houston's Cotswold Project Phase One is more than a simple streetscape project—it is truly about creating linkages. The goal of the project is to create a pedestrian-friendly environment in the north end of downtown and to link the Theater District on the west through the Historic District and Harris County Campus to Minute Maid Park on the east. The result is a transformation of the area from a collection of separate and distinct sites into a richly textured urban neighborhood. In the first phase of the project, improvements were made to thirty-four blocks in the downtown, and when complete, the entire project will improve over 100 blocks.

The Houston Downtown District played a significant role in the design and planning stages of the project. The Cotswold Foundation, a group of local businessmen, prepared the original plan. The Houston Downtown District then worked with the Cotswold Foundation to bring together the downtown stakeholders and to gain the city of Houston's support for the project. The planning process involved a series of workshops which included local owners and businesses, local civic groups, and the transit agency. The project required the preparation of a downtown-wide transportation plan to demonstrate that the proposed narrower streets, wider sidewalks, and introduction of angled parking did not negatively impact traffic flow and overall access to downtown. The Houston Downtown District managed all aspects of planning, design, and construction including street and utility construction.

The heart of the project is Preston Avenue where eight fountains, special sidewalk treatments, accent lighting, and public art are used to create an attractive "signature corridor." The entire project involves numerous streetscape improvements including

- New water lines, sanitary sewer lines, and storm sewer lines
- Reconstructed or asphalt overlays of all streets
- Relocated overhead utilities

- Wider sidewalks, sidewalk extensions at intersections, pavers in high-profile areas
- Street trees, hedges to screen most parking lots, accent plants, and irrigation
- New traffic signals and street lighting
- Street furniture, wayfinding signs, water fountains, and public art
- Creation of 386 metered on-street parking spaces in the first phase and over 1,100 metered parking spaces throughout the entire project

The majority of funding for the Cotswold Project came from the city of Houston and from incremental parking meter revenues from the addition of new parking spaces created by the project. The Houston Transit Authority is providing funding for the parking and transit improvements on two key downtown streets, and the Harris County/Houston Sports Authority integrated its ballpark streetscape with the project design concepts. Property owners funded upgrades at building approaches and basement vaults under the sidewalks, and community nonprofits have contributed to landscaping and streetlight treatments. The Houston Downtown District funded the wayfinding signage and maintains most of the streetscape improvements, except the fountains which are maintained by the city.

Use of Vacant Spaces—San Jose's Phantom Galleries

The San Jose Downtown Association (San Jose, California) created the Phantom Galleries program which combined the goals of putting magic into the downtown pedestrian's daily journey and providing local artists with additional venues for exhibits. The program enlivens vacant storefronts in downtown San Jose with creative, colorful art exhibits provided by local artists. A two-block area is the core of the program with fifteen locations that are rotated bi-monthly. The project has spurred surrounding businesses to spruce up their own windows to fit in with the flow from one exhibit to the next.

Public Art—Ann Arbor's Historic Street Exhibit Program

The Ann Arbor, Michigan, Downtown Development Authority has brought the past to life with sidewalk exhibits that celebrate downtown's history and historic architecture. A viewer standing on the sidewalk sees the past and present juxtaposed on a series of historical markers. Using transparent glass frames, the markers are placed so that the viewer can compare a historic image of the site with the reality of the present. The markers also contain additional images, maps, and bronze replicas of historic artifacts that provide an element of surprise, discovery, and amusement. The project has encouraged the public to recognize and preserve the community's identity and has encouraged tremendous civic pride.

CONCLUSION

Good design of the public realm in downtown is critical to creating a sense of character and vibrancy. Design that facilitates getting around, and encourages lingering will boost downtown's economic and social dynamism.

NOTES

1. Barnett, Jonathan. *Redesigning Cities.* Chicago: Planners Press, American Planning Association. 2003. p. 17.

2. Paumier, Cyril B. *Creating a Vibrant City Center.* Washington: Urban Land Institute. 2003. p. 12.

3. Jacobs, Jane. *The Life and Death of Great American Cities.* New York: Bantam Books. 1964. ch. 8.

4. Ibid, p. 186.

5. Paumier, p. 14.

6. Barnett, p. 217.

7. Paumier, pp. 54-55.

8. Ibid, p. 15.

9. Barnett, p. 236.

10. Ibid, p. 236.

11. Paumier, p. 16.

12. Ibid, p. 155.

13. Houstoun, Lawrence O. *Business Improvement Districts, Second Edition.* Washington: Urban Land Institute. 2003. p. 93.

Chapter 20

Managing Hospitality

James E. Peters

As much as we try to be different, our lives revolve around five basic activities: eating, drinking, working, socializing, and sleeping. Interwoven among each of these activities are relationships with family and friends, concerns about our health and safety, personal enrichment, and the quality of life in our communities. What we do and how we perform the basics affect the quality of life.

Hospitality—the process of creating environments incorporating each of these basic activities—is a daily part of our lives. It is also a unique vehicle for community organizing and development.

The word *hospitality* is derived from an Arabic word *ghosti* meaning host. A second meaning for the same word is guest. This concept, as when host equals guest, defines true hospitality—when the host shares a "common interest" with the guest.

Businesses comprising the "hospitality industry" are a vital part of any community, and include many different types. Bars, cafes, restaurants, taverns, hotels, motels, convention centers, sporting arenas, country clubs, golf courses, night clubs, dance clubs, and food service operations in colleges, at airports, at schools, and in shopping malls comprise the industry. Some sell or serve alcoholic beverages, and some do not.

As the hospitality industry sector expands and maintains high service standards, other retail and professional business sectors benefit. In the same way, as the hospitality industry engages in high-risk practices, e.g., operating in violation of codes and community norms, all other business sectors can suffer. Assaults, vandalism, noise, and other safety and security problems are often linked to the irresponsible members of the hospitality and retail licensed beverage industry.

doi:10.1300/5137_21

PERSPECTIVE

Imagine you are hosting a dinner party for ten guests. Among these are two who are vegetarian, two on Weight Watchers, three who do not drink alcohol, one allergic to seafood, and one who everyone knows has a serious drinking problem.

Parking in your neighborhood is limited. You plan the menu, shop for the food and beverages, make room in your refrigerator and closets, and clean your house. Your guests arrive, sample your appetizers, exchange greetings, and arrange themselves at the dinner table. Then, just as you begin serving, someone comes from the bathroom to tell you the toilet is backing up.

As the last guest leaves, you survey your living room, the dining table, and the kitchen. Knowing you have to leave in the morning for a three-day trip you have no choice but to clean and remove all of the trash.

Now imagine that these ten guests were staying for a week and you had to serve them three meals a day. What about your neighbors? Shopping? Cleaning? Storage?

Imagine even further that you decide to open a restaurant with 300 seats open seven days a week from 8 a.m. to 2 a.m.

Finally, suppose you then became a business district manager and your board decides that a way to revitalize the neighborhood is to create a dining and entertainment district, bringing in a dozen or so businesses with fine dining, family dining, entertainment, and cafes for the late-night crowd. Your task is to create an 18/7 (18-hour day/7 days/week) district. It must appeal to all ages and incomes, integrate the hospitality businesses among the growing housing units being built, and sustain the mix of other retail and professional businesses that have kept the district viable for the past thirty years.

TRENDS

Merging economic, political, and demographic forces are redefining street life in America. Planning efforts over the past decade have steered growth toward urban areas and encouraged in-fill and redevelopment in existing neighborhoods. At the same time, there has been a renewed interest in an urban lifestyle in neighborhoods with dining and entertainment.

The "bookend generations" of aging "baby boomers" and the even larger cohort of "millennials" want to live in an area that supports a vibrant social life. As a result, downtown and urban residential populations have increased dramatically.

San Diego urban designer Howard M. Blackson III observes,

> We need to raise our standards for creating public space. Talking of walkable communities seems to define our communities by our mode of transit rather than our mode of being. Personally, I'd like more than just walkable. I'd like most stayable, hangable, lingerable, standable and sitable. People don't always want to be going somewhere. They want to be somewhere.

The local cafes, restaurants, night clubs, fairs, festivals, and other hospitality venues provide the "somewhere" people are looking for.

Opportunities for more vibrant neighborhoods challenge urban planners and business district managers as they work to stimulate tourism, reestablish street life, and enhance quality of life. Demands on public services, government licensing and enforcement agencies, as well as potential conflicts with residents on noise, trash, public safety, parking, alcohol abuse, and traffic increase simultaneously.

In meeting the challenge to develop and sustain neighborhoods and urban communities two important questions surface:

1. What are emerging trends and issues affecting the city's dining and entertainment businesses, the communities in which they operate, and the future development of both?
2. What are the existing and potential resources available to address these issues, preempt symptoms of future problems, and promote downtown and urban areas as vibrant places to both live and socialize?

2020 VISION

The year 2020 will mark three major demographic milestones that will shape social and economic trends throughout the country: baby boomers will be age sixty and over, Generation X will be in its prime, and millennials will come of age.

Baby Boomers over Sixty

Long the primary force in defining American culture, the last of the baby boomers will begin turning sixty in 2020. Unlike previous generations, boomers are expected to continue working, start second careers, and indulge themselves in leisure activities. The number of people in the over-sixty age group will double to 70 million during the first quarter of the twenty-first century.

Generation X in Its Prime

Known as the "lost generation," the Xers will enter senior positions in business, elected offices in their communities, and continue to be involved in raising their families. Though fewer in numbers than the other generations, they sparked the interest in movement back into downtown environments.

Millennials Come of Age

Born of the boomers who started parenting late and the early Xers, this generation is often known as the "protected" generation, i.e., "Baby on Board," "Just Say No," etc. Raised during a relatively peaceful era, economic prosperity, and access to unprecedented amounts of information through technology, this generation will be a major social and economic force, and is likely to be the most traditional and conservative in generations.

Boomers and millennials are shaping the growth in urban life as each seeks more "space for sociability." According to a University of Michigan study (2002), on average, more than 40 percent of those between ages eighteen and thirty report going out three or more times a week, while only 15 percent of those overage thirty do. As this age group grows by more than 11 million people over the next decade, combined with those over age sixty with more time and money to spend on leisure activities, community planners will be overwhelmed with those wanting more dining and entertainment establishments.

HOSPITALITY, SAFETY, AND DEVELOPMENT

Hospitality and tourism are vital to the social and economic vitality of most cities, yet there is often no permanent unifying mechanism for communication among stakeholders representing hospitality, safety, and development organizations to facilitate information and resource sharing or systematically assess current and future issues and trends.

The matrix of these three primary sectors merge to form the greatest opportunity for the most productive planning to enhance hospitality and tourism while avoiding the typical conflicts that arise in mixed-use districts.

In most cities, especially older ones, the tangle of dining and entertainment establishments often represents a patchwork of the history of neighborhood development. Because the local tavern or restaurant may represent the touchstone of many families, celebrations, and business deals, their connection to the community cannot be underestimated. Like the layers of paint in an old house, many of these businesses are social, political, and economic institutions that show the history of a city.

Interwoven in this patchwork may be newer businesses, perhaps corporate owned, reflecting stages of neighborhood development. Within each layer is often a new set of codes, regulations, and controls.

As previously mentioned, the addition of new dining or entertainment businesses taps infrastructure for water, sewer, energy, and access for deliveries and trash removal. The infusion of more people into these environments can add vibrancy, but for some it may represent an intrusion in personal space and quality of life.

Among the greatest challenges in converting a downtown commercial "9 to 5" district into an 18/7 mixed-use district are physical and policy restrictions. Many districts are based upon paper goods retail trade, offices, office supply retail, clothing stores, bookstores, and other types of businesses requiring few public services.

Adding more dining and entertainment businesses, especially those operating beyond midnight, creates special issues in key development factors.

Transportation

As the district evolves, there may be greater demands for parking, especially as evening hours begin. In the evening, security demands in parking areas increase, yet often it is during these hours that security staff may not be working. One of the ironies of the evolution of development is that while there may be more people working in the district in offices during the day, there are more people on the street in the evening. During the day, people park and go to work; in the evening they may linger in the parking area and use their cars for illegal activity including drinking and drug use.

Renovation

Modifications to a building to accommodate a dining or entertainment business can often be inhibited because of zoning restrictions, especially in historic districts. Working through the labyrinth of bureaucracy can be daunting enough to discourage development, especially by an independent entrepreneur.

Resources

As with your dinner party, resources for space, water, sewerage, energy, storage, and trash removal for a dining or entertainment business exceed that of a traditional office or retail business.

Security

High-volume dining and entertainment districts mean a high volume of potential public safety issues. In some districts, thousands of people can be in clubs until late hours, and then spill out onto the streets. Normally, in the young-adult category, they linger on the sidewalks, parking lots, and streets as part of the sociability of a night out. Concerns about noise and disturbances lead to more demands on police services.

Access

One inhibiting factor is access for delivery trucks and trash haulers. In historic districts, alleyways are often narrow and when dumpsters, which are required by a high-volume business, add to the mix then access becomes more difficult. Restrictions on truck traffic limit access and sometimes trash may not be removed. In an office district, this would not be an issue, but a dumpster filled with organic matter during a hot summer day can be problematic.

Pedestrians

Dining and entertainment districts can add vibrancy especially when there is a commitment to pedestrian convenience. Pedestrian safety becomes even more critical during late-night hours, when some people may be impaired and at risk both as drivers or walkers. Street security, public facilities, good lighting, and taxi stands are all important to accommodate the late crowds.

Smoking Bans

One outcome of smoking bans in cities is the growth in outdoor seating and street life, especially in more temperate climates. However, street life has had a number of unintended outcomes. To accommodate smokers, many businesses add outdoor seating, or smokers congregate outside of entrances. Failure to properly plan for the patios can put a business in jeopardy

of violations and fines. Outdoor seating may add to occupancy requirements for fire safety inspections. Many alcohol regulatory agencies require
new applications for additional seating and for serving alcoholic beverages.
Without approval, businesses may face a penalty. Outdoor food service can
also contribute to pests and rodents seeking scraps of dropped food, especially on slotted decks without access for cleaning below. Heat lamps with
propane containers may require approval from the fire department; awnings
may in fact violate the smoking ban because the seating is no longer "outdoors."

Noise

Of all the controversial issues of mixed-use districts, noise is at the top of the
list. The story usually evolves like this: A city has an old warehouse or buildings in an old district not being used. Zoning codes are changed to allow a concentration of licensed-beverage businesses including restaurants and night
clubs. The area becomes popular. Vacant loft space is converted to housing or
new housing units are built on vacant lots. Residents move in and begin to complain about the noise and the clubs are blamed. Increased enforcement results
in resistance by the business owners stating, "We were here first, it is like moving next to an airport and then complaining about the noise."

Workforce

Consumer expectations are increasing. The variety of foods, beers,
wines, mixed drinks, coffees, and teas being offered requires greater knowledge of preparation of these items. Sophisticated register systems and
equipment require better training. Increased awareness of public health and
safety related to diet and alcohol requires more responsibility. Adding more
hospitality businesses may place a drain on the pool of qualified managers
and staff available in the workforce.

LEARNING BY EXAMPLE

Many cities have stories about the opportunities and challenges in planning and managing a dining and entertainment district. Following are a few
stories to provide some insights.

Delray Beach

Listed as one of the "ten most enlightened suburbs" by *Utne* magazine,
this coastal Florida city has gone through major changes in the past decade.

Key to its evolution was a strategy to build Main Street by infusing it with fine dining establishments and restricting truck traffic. Today the city is vibrant, growing, and a jewel of success. According to Marjorie Ferrer, executive director of the Downtown Development Authority, Delray Beach, Florida, success didn't come without lessons. First, as restaurants came on line, residents and other businesses had problems with plumbing backups. In time, the city realized the sewer system was overtaxed and it became necessary to install new lines at a great, unanticipated cost.

Like small manufacturing plants, restaurants require raw materials and produce parallel waste. Delivery trucks and trash haulers compete for the narrow alleys, as well as residents and visitors walking from parking lots through the alleys. Besides developing a routing system for truck traffic, the city recently launched its "You have a nice backside" campaign to encourage businesses to maintain the appearance of the alleys.

San Diego

San Diego, California, is a laboratory of change, especially its highly successful and touted Gaslamp Quarter. Evolving from a blighted district of transients and adult entertainment parlors it has become one of the nation's most vibrant dining and entertainment districts. Spurred on by visionary leadership and a unique open-air shopping center, restaurant and entertainment businesses began to sprout and fill vacant spaces and replace the blight. The continual expansion of the Convention Center and surrounding high-rise hotels and housing complexes added visitors to the growing number of residents patronizing the establishments.

A downtown ballpark, home of the San Diego Padres, and development of East Village have added even more impetus for continued development and expansion of the Gaslamp Quarter. Although originally designated as a dining and entertainment district, conflicts with residents were limited. The popularity of the area led some developers to convert old warehouses into residential spaces.

Two years ago, a jazz club opened, the first African–American-owned business in the district. Popular among visitors and residents, local neighbors grew increasingly frustrated with the noise coming from the club and patrons leaving in the early morning. The debate could have been scripted. The new residents moving into their California price-inflated condos complained. The business replied with the "we were here first" and the old "moving near an airport and now you complain" argument began. Residents not satisfied pursued legal action that spawned similar action against other businesses.

Eventually, the club owners, deciding that their legal costs exceeded the potential to maintain a viable business, closed the establishment.

Working through the San Diego Hospitality Resource Panel, an alliance of key stakeholders came together and recognized the current and future issues from planned development. As the award-winning City of Villages General Plan was announced, many believed the next phase would be a closer examination of the various zoning standards and codes, especially relating to noise.

The Mixed Use Advisory Group evolved from these meetings and was officially recognized by the City Council Land Use and Housing Committee. City staff from key agencies were assigned to meet with representatives of residential and business organizations to make recommendations for adapting to the city's growth and mixed-use districts.

Washington, DC

Downtown Washington, DC, is home to many professional and government agencies and organizations. Currently involved in massive renovation and rebuilding in conjunction with the new convention center, residential housing, hotels, restaurants, and retail businesses are spreading throughout the district.

The downtown club zone meetings started after a national hotel franchise opened a $23 million property with thin, historically preserved windows in the middle of the club zone. Needless to say, guests with rooms facing busy F Street were not getting restful sleep on weekend nights. The hotel was at risk of losing its franchise. The stage was set for a bitter fight replete with calls to the police, protests of liquor licenses, and other hostile acts between the hotel and the clubs.

Yet the fight never happened. Instead, representatives from the hotel, the clubs, the Downtown DC Business Improvement District, the nascent downtown residential community, the police, and property management firms started meeting every Wednesday to hash things out. The meetings were sometimes contentious, sometimes frustrating, and hardly the solution to all of the parties' problems. However, they created an atmosphere in which everyone felt they could be heard, where everyone's right to exist on equal footing was respected, and where people sought common solutions.

The clubs made some changes, such as staggering their closing times, redirecting foot traffic away from the hotel and the apartment buildings, and entering into a contract with the police through the BID for a substantial peacekeeping detail on busy nights. The hotel installed interior window soundproofing, at a cost of about $250,000.

The results have been impressive. Customer complaints at the hotel dropped to practically nil. Crime dropped in downtown too. The residential community gained a voice in what has long been a strictly business neighborhood, and an ongoing networking forum was established to address concerns and share ideas.

Athens

With seventy restaurants, music clubs, bars, and coffee houses, downtown Athens, Georgia, is as popular with the 35,000 students, faculty, and staff of the University of Georgia as it is with the burgeoning residential and convention market attracted by the amenities of a mixed-use, historic downtown.

In response to the challenges brought on by sharing of space by multiple markets and industries, the Hospitality Resource Panel (HRP) was formed in 1999 to enlist the support of both the dining and entertainment industry and the local government in managing growth responsibly. This dexterity has enabled the HRP to rally the private and public private sector community around a shared vision of a clean, safe, and commercially viable hospitality district.

As the homegrown rock bands R.E.M. and the B-52s, among others, became international, the club and restaurant scene grew even more. Some saw this as success while others wished for the old days, especially in the summer as odors from the restaurant and clubs made the downtown experience unpleasant.

A task force was formed, and following some finger pointing and blame, conflicts were discussed and solutions defined. It was apparent that much of the odor from the spillage on the sidewalks came from the restaurant and club trash. Plastic bags left on the sidewalks leaked and fermented in the hot summer sun.

First, the HRP coordinator spent some time examining the situation and soon discovered that many of the older trash hauler trucks had lost a plug in the truck bottom and therefore as the bags were crushed, the fluids drained onto the streets.

Second, the local code required businesses to put trash in plastic bags on Monday, Wednesday, and Friday on the sidewalk by 5 p.m. to be picked up at 11 p.m. This policy was fine when the downtown was primarily a 9 to 5 business district, but with the growth of the number of hospitality businesses leaving the trash out, especially on Friday night as people came downtown to dine, became a real problem.

Trucks were repaired, trash pickup schedules were changed, and faucets were installed on the street to hose down the sidewalks for any spillage that might occur.

CONCLUSION

Responding to demographic, social, and economic trends and increasing demands for more "space for sociability" requires city planners to take a broad view and answer three primary questions:

1. Do you really want a new district?
2. What scale are you thinking of?
3. Who is involved in planning and decision making?

Do You Really Want a New District?

Be careful what you wish for. Consider the implications. A dedicated area for dining and entertainment may increase tax revenues, civic appeal, and the job base, but it also burdens road and parking systems, infrastructure, peace and quiet, and neighborly relations.

Are you looking to serve the neighborhood, or to bring in outsiders? Are you looking strictly for nighttime uses, or are you trying to create an eighteen- to twenty-four-hour district? Will your district serve people of all ages? Families? Adults only? Teens and college students? The answers to these questions have substantial impact—on parking, traffic, noise, quality of life, enforcement, and other areas.

What Scale Are You Thinking Of?

Do you have the infrastructure in place? This involves more than just roads and parking. Restaurants, bars, and clubs are huge consumers of gas, electricity, water, and sewer utilities. Do you have the capacity for a large concentration of food and beverage establishments in a small area in your downtown? Are you setting your aging systems up for failure? Will businesses experience slowdowns or shutdowns because you have to tear up the roads and sidewalks to repair old pipes or lines? Can your alleyways accommodate the trash trucks and delivery vans?

Do you have the municipal services to make sure the streets are well maintained and safe? Is there sufficient law enforcement? Will you be asking the businesses to provide these services through a Business Improvement District or Main Street effort?

Who Is Involved in Planning and Decision Making?

Are you creating a district out of whole cloth, or are you identifying an area growing on its own? Either way, there are a lot of stakeholders who should be included in the process. Localized decision making, with an emphasis on open communication and proactive discussion forums, is key.

RECOMMENDATIONS

1. A mixed-use district (business, residential, etc.) that offers commercial choices (different cuisines, price points, age groups) is optimum. Avoid the desire to completely isolate the district geographically or by type. In mixing uses, develop strategies that anticipate intrusive activities and quality-of-life problems (e.g., noise, trash, panhandling, loitering, litter, late-night hell-raising, vandalism, public urination, foul odors).
2. Provide orientation programs for new businesses before they open and offer owner/manager training on strategies for working with neighbors and conflict resolution. Find ways to assist businesses, accommodate multiple markets: young adults, young professionals, visitors/conventioneers, older adults, and families.
3. Maintain a scale appropriate to your city and district. Avoid inflexible regulations and zoning—the nature of commercial districts is that they evolve and shift. Be proactive—plan additional resources for growth, including licensing and permitting agencies, law enforcement, public works, and workforce development.
4. Develop city-supported incentives to draw diverse businesses. Update building and zoning codes to accommodate redevelopment of stagnant areas. Get key stakeholders to form coordinating councils (city, county, state) that consolidate planning and code requirements.
5. The ideal district features convenient, sufficient, and well-maintained public accommodations (parking, bathrooms, phones, bike racks, and trash cans), and offers clear signage and traffic management with an emphasis on safety and pedestrian friendliness.
6. Employ attendants to keep the public and establishment bathrooms clean and safe. Use ambassadors to direct traffic and address panhandlers. Establish panhandling zones. Motivate proprietors to take ownership of area in terms of litter control. Develop a wide-scale street-cleaning system. To improve transportation access, offer free shuttles (from campuses, apartment buildings, subway stops, remote garages, etc.), extend public transportation hours, identify and develop shared-use

parking (i.e., school lot by day, dining/entertainment lot at night). Build pedestrian tunnels and bridges.

7. Find a neutral facilitator for conflict resolution. Be inclusive while identifying stakeholders. Don't forget to include the businesses, police chief or sheriff, or the fire department. Focus on commonalities to find a shared vision—don't get bogged down in the areas of disagreement. Organize venting sessions to allow the honest exchange of opinions, and then spend the rest of the time moving forward. Break issues into manageable segments.

REFERENCE

Party Animals Are a Rare Breed After College, ISR Study Finds, with Drinking and Drug Use Declining As a Result (2002). The University of Michigan, News and Information Services; Available online at http://monitoringthefuture.org/pressrelease/jb_bookpr.pdf.

Chapter 21

Transportation Management
and Downtown Revitalization

Elizabeth Jackson

DOWNTOWN AS A HISTORIC TRANSPORTATION HUB

Central business districts (CBDs) were designed, first and foremost, as transportation hubs. Whether it's the evolution of Boston or Boise, the development of downtown was predicated on the strategic location of transportation. From harbors, to roads, to rail, and then highways, downtowns grew around the intersection of commercial transportation routes. Trade and transportation are inextricably linked.

Downtowns maintained their dominance as the hub for multi-modal transportation well into the 1950s. Although highway development quickly followed the introduction of the mass-produced automobile, the trend toward decentralization did not take hold until after World War II. The National Interstate Highway and Defense Act of 1956 and home loan policies for war veterans that favored new construction over existing home purchase served to draw households away from the central city. Real estate developers saw the opportunities provided by public policy and built suburban shopping centers. The rest is (sub)urban history.

Early attempts to staunch the flow of investment to the suburbs only accelerated the deterioration of the CBD. The construction of highway bypasses and ring-road systems, intended to remove truck traffic from surface streets, only succeeded in diverting *all* traffic to the perimeter. Many downtown development leaders of the 1960s and 1970s—even into the 1980s—adopted an "if you can't beat them, join them" attitude and lobbied for an array of "suburbanizing" initiatives such as pedestrian mall development, one-way road pairing systems, and the creation of massive amounts of surface parking. The outcome? Downtowns were left with gaping holes in the building fabric, confusing and unnecessary circulation systems, and even fewer shoppers, employees, and visitors using the district. The more that the

doi:10.1300/5137_22

national transportation system moved to support auto transit, the less downtown's system of rail and public transportation mattered to economic development.

TRANSPORTATION AND DOWNTOWNS OF THE FUTURE

Since the mid-1980s, downtown leaders have been forging strategic partnerships to redefine and revitalize their central business districts. Now, after nearly two decades of success, downtown management groups are turning their partnership-building expertise to *infrastructure*—the key to the long-term viability of the CBD. When it comes to the infrastructure of transportation, downtown leaders are embracing transportation *choice* as an essential element of downtown revitalization.

Everything in Western culture is about choice. With unprecedented levels of mobility, people are making work, housing, schools, recreation, and cultural choices based on where they want to be, not where they have ended up. If downtowns are to achieve "24/7" status, they must provide *options*— in housing, entertainment, work, recreation, and *access* to these amenities. That means downtown organizations must become involved in managing a transportation system that includes automobile access, public transit, commuter options, pedestrian mobility and safety, and bicycle access. Gone are the days when a downtown can assess its transportation infrastructure by the number of short-term parking spaces it supplies.

With the advent of high-speed wireless telecommunications, to replacement of 100-year-old water, sewer, and electrical service, downtown leaders face infrastructure needs that transcend the boundaries of their districts . . . *and their control.* Downtown organizations have succeeded in the past by drawing a line around a geographical area and applying an integrated system of management, marketing, planning, and development strategies within that boundary. Yet what of systems that extend beyond the CBD, systems that are controlled not just by municipal government, but by county, regional, state, and even federal entities? How do downtown management organizations insert themselves into this environment and carve out a solution that keeps downtown's transportation priorities on the table?

URBAN TRANSPORTATION BASICS

Few elements of urban infrastructure are as complicated as transportation. When it comes to creating a *system of transportation choice* that supports downtown revitalization, the choices expand and the players become more numerous.

Elements of the Downtown Transportation System

Virtually every central business district provides some or all of the following transportation amenities:

- *Surface streets*—usually a modified grid system—that serve the commercial needs of the property and business owners within the district.
- *On- and off-street parking*—On-street parking is almost exclusively reserved for short-term parking needs and is targeted to shoppers and other patrons of the district . . . not day users such as employees or employers. Off-street parking provides longer-term options for day shoppers, employees, employers, and others such as college students and residents who need parking for hours at a time.
- *Bypass roads, interstate highways, on- and off-ramps*—These are higher-volume roadways that, for the most part, help drivers avoid the CBD. On- and off-ramps provide access to and from the highway, often without consideration for the physical impacts on the built environment of downtown.
- *Rail systems*—In major metropolitan cities, freight rail still operates through the CBD. In the Northeastern United States and many parts of Canada, passenger rail still operates. A few cities provide intercity commuter rail systems such as the Virginia Railway Express (VRE) and the MARC Train Service in Maryland, both serving the greater Washington, DC transportation corridor.
- *Subway systems*—The largest cities operate subway transit systems, most of which are designed to move suburban workers to downtown employment centers.
- *Bus systems*—Many more cities operate gas- or electric-powered bus systems, most designed to serve city residents and suburban areas. Most bus lines still operate on a hub-and-spoke system, with the CBD serving as the hub.
- *Light-rail systems*—A growing number of cities are investing in light-rail, fixed-route transportation. These systems are not as oriented to moving travelers between the suburbs and the CBD, and offer suburb-to-suburb connections as well.
- *Commuter bus and vanpool services*—Private and county- or state-funded programs exist to encourage workers to leave their autos at home and commute to their jobs by van or long-haul bus.

- *Downtown circulator buses*—Special shuttle buses are operated in some central business districts to encourage downtown workers and shoppers to park once and still visit multiple downtown destinations.
- *Sidewalk, crosswalk, and bike lane systems*—The sidewalks and crosswalks serve as the transportation system for pedestrians, while bike lanes and bicycle racks are the backbone of the growing bicycle transit system. Though only a small percentage of downtown's users will arrive by bike, virtually everyone will be a pedestrian for at least some part of each day.

Who Manages the Transportation System?

The complexities of urban transportation systems demand many managers. The following are the typical managers of the aforementioned modes:

- *Surface streets*—Local roadways are usually managed by the local municipality, or county or metropolitan government, depending on how far the roads extend.
- *On- and off-street parking*—On-street parking is almost always the responsibility of the local municipality. Off-street parking in most cities includes both publicly and privately managed sites. Public off-street parking is usually managed by city hall or its designee.
- *Bypass roads, interstate highways, on- and off-ramps*—High-volume roadways are usually managed by either the county or the state departments of transportation.
- *Rail systems*—Management of rail infrastructure can be very convoluted. Rail track is often privately owned, and leased to public-sector railcar operators.
- *Subway systems*—Subway systems are usually inter-jurisdictional and controlled by a metropolitan transit authority.
- *Bus systems*—in smaller markets, the local municipality operates public bus systems. Larger systems are usually managed by a metropolitan or county authority.
- *Light-rail systems*—Light-rail systems are usually regional in nature and managed by a metropolitan transportation authority or county government.
- *Commuter bus and vanpool services*—Commuter transit services can be either privately managed or run by metropolitan or county transportation departments.
- *Downtown circulator buses*—These small systems are sometimes operated by the local transportation authority, the downtown development

group, or even the chamber of commerce/convention and visitors bureau.

- *Sidewalk, crosswalk, and bike lane systems*—Sidewalks are the exclusive domain of local government, but crosswalks and bike lanes are "owned" by the jurisdiction responsible for the roadbed. Bike racks can be a municipal or private-sector obligation.

Short Primer on Transportation Finance

As if the choices in transportation, and the layers of management were not enough, funding for public transportation is inscrutable in the extreme. In short, the following are the most common sources of financial support for transportation.

Federal Funding

In 2004, more than $275 billion dollars were appropriated for reauthorization of the Transportation Efficiency Act for the 21st Century—TEA-21 for short. The largest spending bill after defense, federal funding for transportation supports all fifty state departments of transportation, as well as metropolitan planning organizations (MPOs), and special project grants for regions, counties, and municipalities. Funding formulas are complex, grant competitions stiff, and "earmarks" (read: pork-barrel appropriations) numerous.

State Funding

Usually supported by state gasoline taxes, state funds are used to match federal dollars and are, for the most part, focused on highway development. Some states, such as California, pass through the majority share of their funds to the municipalities and counties, where transportation decision making is customized to local needs. Some states have passed statewide sales tax initiatives to provide further funding for special transportation projects.

Metropolitan, County, and Local Funding

Metropolitan transportation authorities are usually supported by contributions from all participating jurisdictions, as well as by federal and state funds. County and local funding comes from general funding, special taxing tools, and grants from the state and federal governments.

Fare Box Revenue

The smallest proportion of funds for transportation comes from the fare box—meaning bus and subway fares, toll road revenue, and other forms of transportation user fees.

MANAGING TRANSPORTATION— ROLE OF THE DOWNTOWN ORGANIZATION

How do downtown management organizations get involved in providing transportation choice? They do this by researching the need, creating and managing effective programs, and advocating for appropriate public investment.

Research

Integrating transportation priorities into the downtown development plan is essential. Following are eight areas that should be researched when developing an integrated transportation network. Each requires an analysis of current supply, performance, and management; projected demand, planning, and locational impacts; gaps in supply and management; and current sources and uses of funds.

Traffic Circulation and Management

Traffic circulation and management involves mapping current vehicular traffic patterns around downtown; identifying where and when bottlenecks occur; and clarifying how the system is currently managed—especially when it breaks down.

Parking

Analysis of parking involves mapping existing supply of on-street, off-street, public, and private parking, including space sizes, fees, hours, and penalties; surveying valet parking establishments and parking locations; identifying enforcement rules and realities and plotting enforcement problems; locating peak usage, particularly in relation to nearby oversupply; and calculating gross economic impact of current parking supply.

Transit

Transit analysis involves itemizing the types of public and private-sector transit alternatives; assessing the quality of the physical inventory, including rolling stock, shelters and stops, and signage; analyzing schedules for frequency, on-time performance, and usage; assessing locations of stops and shelters relative to employment concentration, visitor destinations, and residences; conducting inventories of existing commercial development around stops and shelters; and collecting examples of current marketing and advertising efforts to promote transit.

Pedestrian Flow and Management

Analysis of pedestrian flow involves conducting "footfall" counts; analyzing quality of sidewalks and quantity/quality of crosswalks; assessing traffic signalization and pedestrian crossing times; conducting inventories of sidewalk, intersection, and crosswalk lighting; and plotting locations of pedestrian accidents.

Cyclists

Analysis of cyclists includes developing an inventory of bike messenger companies' fleets; mapping bike lanes and existing bike racks (and their condition); plotting informal bike routes; analyzing current bicycle ordinances, penalties, and enforcement; and surveying the current number of bike commuters.

Public Space

Managing public space involves analyzing the interaction of transportation modes, including how pedestrians and bicyclists share the sidewalks; where buses idle between departures; and how freight deliveries interfere with sidewalks, parking, alleyways, and crosswalks.

Ingress and Egress

Managing ingress and egress includes mapping arterial entranceways and exits; analyzing them in relation to pedestrian concentrations, residential areas, and anticipated new development; assessing quality; and identifying enforcement rules and realities.

Development Demand

Analysis of development demand involves surveying existing office, commercial, civic, and residential transportation demands and projecting the impact of planned development on the current system.

Roles for the Downtown Organization

Armed with the facts about the current supply, condition, and operation of the transportation network, downtown organizations can play important roles in improving transportation management.

Transportation Management Organizations (TMOs)

TMOs have been created to allow governments to subcontract certain activities associated with transit operations. Many downtown organizations are taking on the TMO role in their communities, with activities including promotion, managing and enforcing parking in city-owned parking lots and structures, serving as the sales office for parking and transit passes, and managing public-sector ridesharing and vanpooling operations. (See Exhibit 21.1.)

Public Space Planning, Design, and Management

Most downtown organizations are involved to some degree in the planning and design of downtown open space. These organizations can add value to streets and parks by suggesting improvements to intermodal connections, circulation, wayfinding, public space maintenance—including bus stops and shelters—and by supporting new information technologies that help direct drivers to parking, alternative routes, etc.

Transit-Oriented Development

Mixed-use projects that connect to transit are proving to be a growth market in many suburbs; connecting new development in the CBD to an improved transportation network can give downtown a competitive advantage. Downtown management organizations can help by crafting incentives that encourage developers to build with transit in mind. Incentives include transfers of development rights, density bonuses, and reductions in parking requirements. Although the organization cannot enact the incentives, it does

EXHIBIT 21.1. Downtown Organizations
with Transportation Management Organizations (TMOs)

Bellevue Downtown Association
www.bellevuedowntown.org
Bethesda Urban Partnership, Inc.
www.bethesda.org
Buckhead Coalition, Inc.
Buffalo Place Inc.
www.buffaloplace.com
Center City District
www.centercityphila.org
Central Atlanta Progress
www.atlantadowntown.org
Central Dallas Association
www.downtowndallas.org
Central Houston, Inc.
www.centralhouston.org
Central London Partnership
www.c-london.co.uk
Charlotte Center City Partners
www.charlottecentercity.org
Downtown Denver Partnership, Inc.
www.downtowndenver.com
Downtown Fort Worth, Inc.
www.dfwi.org
Dublin City Business Association
www.dcba.ie
Georgetown Business Improvement District
www.georgetowndc.com
Main Street Meridian
www.meridianms.org
Pittsburgh Downtown Partnership
www.downtownpittsburgh.com
St. Petersburg Downtown Partnership, Inc.
www.stpetepartnership.org
Tampa Downtown Partnership
www.tampasdowntown.com
The Downtown Business Alliance Of Provo, Inc.
www.provodowntown.com

have the credibility to develop the ideas and advocate for their creation by government.

Location-Efficient Mortgages

Likewise, downtown organizations can work to promote the creation of what are known as location-efficient mortgages. These mortgages allow people buying homes near transit routes to include the savings associated with riding public transportation into their qualifying income. Supported by the Federal National Mortgage Association (Fannie Mae) and local banks, this incentive program is currently operating in more than ten U.S. communities including Philadelphia and Seattle, El Paso, and Burlington. This could be a very valuable tool in marketing downtown housing to a wider variety of buyers. (See Exhibit 21.2.)

Tax Incentives for Ridesharing and Transit Passes

Downtown organizations are promoting tax breaks for employers who provide ridesharing services or underwrite transit costs as employee benefits. Encouraging more employers to offer these services helps reduce the demand for expensive downtown parking and increase the use of public transit.

Custom Transportation Services

Downtown organizations often extend their ambassador staff for special projects. Some use ambassadors to supplement traffic management during rush

---

EXHIBIT 21.2. Useful Resources

- Location-efficient mortgages:
  Federal National Mortgage Association (Fannie Mae)
  www.fanniemae.com
- *Business support of transit:*
  National Business Coalition for Rapid Transit
  steveschl@aol.com
- Transportation policy and transit-oriented development:
  Reconnecting America
  www.reconnectingamerica.org
- Context-sensitive transportation and public space design:
  Project for Public Spaces
  www.pps.org

hour or special events, or offer late-night escort service for downtown employees going to transit or parking facilities, particularly satellite parking areas.

Circulator Bus Systems

Other downtown organizations develop or manage low-cost or free circulator buses in the downtown area. These buses reduce the use of autos during the day and encourage downtown employees and visitors to explore more of the area. The Downtown DC Business Improvement District Corporation is currently working with District of Columbia officials to create and manage such a system.

Advocacy

Changing the transportation system is exceedingly complex. Transportation decision making takes place on a very large playing field, not limited to local and county governments, but involving MPOs (metropolitan planning organizations), state departments of transportation, federal agencies, and congressional committees. However, downtown development leaders are in a good position to influence transportation planning, policy, and funding by delivering business support rarely mobilized around issues of transportation. Following are strategies that downtown organizations can use to be involved in transportation planning.

Have a seat at the regional transportation-planning table.

Downtown development interests need to be represented in regional transportation planning. Board-level participation may be limited to local governments, but working or advisory committees should provide an opportunity for the downtown business community to get involved.

Support the public participation process.

Transportation planning requires public input. Downtown organizations can host these public participation workshops in the district and help shape the plan.

Lobby at the state and federal level.

The business community has influence with elected leaders that other interest groups do not. The more informed downtown organizations become, the more they will form policy priorities that they can lobby for. Although some downtown organizations are prohibited from lobbying *local* government, they may be able to advocate at the state and national levels. If limitations on advocacy do exist, individual business leaders can be prepped to carry the standard on behalf of downtown.

Promote what the downtown organization can do.

Along with planning and policy, downtown groups can partner with transportation authorities and MPOs to promote and manage the system. Most of the projects described previously were created through partnership agreements and existing resources.

Advocate for integrated management.

Too often, regional transportation networks are fragmented, poorly coordinated, or inefficiently managed. The downtown business community can promote more coordinated, cross-jurisdictional governance and help broker better partner relationships.

THE BOTTOM LINE:
CREATING TRANSPORTATION CHOICE

More than ever, decisions regarding major infrastructure are being made on the *regional* level. Regional decisions significantly affect the fortunes of downtown. In order for transportation systems to contribute to long-term, sustainable downtown development, they must:

- Be reliable, run frequently, and maintain a high level of quality and condition in the rolling stock
- Improve their image with the general public and be seen as a viable— even preferable—alternative to auto transport
- Tie transportation options to new development—particularly development of new residential units, entertainment venues such as arenas, and employment centers
- Improve the supply and operation of parking—creating a truly *integrated parking system*
- Create incentives to encourage auto users to try public transportation

Twenty years ago, downtown management organizations had neither the experience nor the influence to affect transportation decisions. Today, downtown groups and their leaders have the talent, credibility, and insight to affect the future of transportation. The competent downtown management organization must get involved in transportation research, planning, and management in order to guarantee that the transportation system works *for* downtown, not against it.

Chapter 22

Parking: Finding Solutions

E. Larry Fonts

America is addicted to free parking, yet parking downtown requires cash. That unfortunate reality is a disincentive to visitors, tenants, and prospects for leasing office space. In survey after survey, the hassle of paid parking ranks right up there with the fear of crime for most downtowns.

The first-time experience of visiting a parking garage is confusing. How much will it cost me once I pull a ticket? Where can I find a space that isn't reserved for a monthly parker? Do I have enough cash to pay when I leave? Do they take credit cards? Once I park, how do I get to street level? You can avoid some of these concerns by parking in a surface lot, but some additional concerns crop up: Is the lot attendant for real or a con artist? Is it lighted after dark? Is my car a target for break-ins?

In most downtowns, crimes related to automobiles comprise the majority of FBI index crimes. Theft of the auto, auto parts, or personal items taken from the auto, account for 52 percent of the crime reported in downtown Dallas annually. Together, the fear of crime, the price, and customer confusion create the "hassle factor" of downtown parking.

PROVEN OPTIONS

In most cities, private companies dominate commercial parking. Many properties, such as department stores and office towers, have parking facilities to meet the needs of their customers, but seldom is the number of spaces adequate to meet their total need. The marketplace of commercial lots and garages meets the excess demand.

Public agencies have entered the marketplace as well. Municipal parking garages, often financed by parking authorities, can play a significant role in aiding the retail base by providing "shopper rate" parking, an accepted public purpose. Parking meters can be effective in meeting short-term needs if not otherwise consumed by handicapped users.

doi:10.1300/5137_23

Satellite or peripheral parking lots with shuttle service to the core can meet the desires of cost-conscious customers, and the park-and-ride lots found in all cities play a small role in reducing the demand for downtown parking. By far, the most significant means of reducing parking demand is public transit.

Parking validation programs abound in central cities, mostly in support of retail districts. Perhaps the most extensive program is in Seattle where the Downtown Seattle Association employs the "City Park" program. In almost 200 lots and garages, tokens are redeemed for $1 off the posted rates. The tokens are issued by merchants at the rate of one for every purchase of $20. More purchases equals a lower parking fee.

Valet parking is a big item in Dallas. The Dallas Downtown Partnership sponsors a single valet provider that allows the patron to deposit his or her car at one location and pick it up at any of five locations in the six-block retail district. The operator contracts with neighborhood parking garages to store the vehicles.

IMPROVE THE APPEARANCE

The "broken windows" theory states that if a garage or surface lot is well maintained and shows pride of ownership it will be respected. Those that don't meet that standard are subject to abuse. In downtown Dallas, surface parking lots are ugly, poorly maintained, and the source of the majority of crime. New lots and garages are required to meet set design standards, but existing lots have little incentive to improve. Recent efforts by a few responsible owners are raising the quality for new garages and lots.

The Central Dallas Association has taken the lead to change city ordinances to require all lots to meet the standards for new lots—fencing the perimeter, night lighting, and landscaping. To calm the squeals of financial ruination, matching grants are offered through the tax increment financing (TIF) for the lots within TIF district boundaries and by the business improvement district (BID) for the remaining lots. Within three to five years all surface lots should be in compliance. The goals are obvious: to define the boundary between public and private space, to improve the appearance of the lots, and to ensure adequate night lighting for safety.

IMPROVE PUBLIC SAFETY

Improving public safety in surface parking lots is a program undertaken cooperatively by the business improvement district and the Dallas Police

Department central business district (CBD) unit. The partnership initiated the "Take/Lock/Hide" program to advise the general public to "TAKE their keys," LOCK their car," and "HIDE their possessions." At a well-attended press conference, printed materials were distributed, and equipment was displayed. Reflective signs were distributed at lots and garages and installed on streetlight poles to inform the general public to "Lock, Take and Hide." These defensive tactics go a long way toward reducing targets of opportunity.

Part of the safety program involved the purchase by the downtown improvement district (DID) of the "Skywatch" tower. The Skywatch tower is a hydraulic lift with an observation cabin mounted on a trailer. Similar to a "cherry picker" lift, it is outfitted with a large, air-conditioned cabin with smoked-glass windows and power for computers or other electronic equipment. The cabin can be elevated to twenty-two feet, providing a multi-block area of surveillance. Experience shows that the tower serves its purpose. Auto theft and auto burglary decrease wherever it is placed. Often, the tower is unmanned, but due to the smoked windows the burglars don't know that.

This effort supplements the "Eagles Nest" observation program of the Dallas Police Department and the cooperative release of private video surveillance tapes by building security directors for police investigations. Property managers of high-rise buildings are periodically asked to make available a vacant corner office for police officers to use high-powered binoculars and sighting telescopes to observe infractions and radio to ground forces, who are out of sight nearby, for immediate apprehension of perpetrators. These practices have reduced incidence of auto theft and auto burglary and thus the overall crime rate, which is down 62 percent since 1994 when the DID was established and these programs were implemented.

PROACTIVE STRATEGIES

Public parking authorities can be an advantage for some cities. They can offer "shopper" parking for limited periods at reduced rates. Examples can be found in many cities. The key its to have them operate to the advantage of the business interests of downtown, not the general fund.

Portland, Oregon, contracts the operation of its public parking garages to its downtown business group. The revenue gained helps to support other downtown initiatives. It doesn't hurt revenue when Portland establishes a "cap" on the number of spaces allowed downtown. This is a familiar model to many cities. Being managed by nonprofit interests allows for a more flexible operation. For example, discounts can be tied to festivals, retail promotions, sporting events, or to valet parking systems.

Outsourcing the function of parking-meter reading and enforcement allows for similar benefits to downtown. A handheld computer makes this job much more accurate and efficient. Just as car rental agencies at airports issue billing receipts upon arrival, these devices can record real time enforcement. Parking meters exist to regulate the use of available curb space with the charge for the space seemingly incidental. In reality, they become a significant revenue generator for city hall as a proprietary function of government.

PEGASUS PARKING

So far, we have talked about ways to improve the safety and appearance of surface lots and how to provide more relevant management of public parking spaces. Yet we are still left with the question of how to reduce the "hassle factor" of paying for parking: one neither owns nor controls parking spaces; paying for parking is an economic necessity.

Nonprofit organizations have no influence over pricing, and in very few instances would a local government attempt to control pricing. So, if you can't affect price, how can you improve the situation? The answer is to affect service levels.

This is a story of how a solution to a parking problem evolved to a new concept called Pegasus Parking. The issue of parking was addressed during a strategic planning session of the Central Dallas/ Transportation Management Association (CD/TMA) in 1998. The goal was modestly stated as finding ways to "improve the parking experience." There was not a lot of guidance, but there was enough to get started.

Subsequent brainstorming sessions outlined some criteria:

1. *Use technology.* The parking industry is notoriously a hands-on-cash business. Pilferage is an issue. The use of technology might provide for better accounting for transactions if it could overcome the obstacle of computer-illiterate minimum-wage employees.
2. *Avoid staffing.* Anything that would increase the cost of a parking operation is working at cross-purposes.
3. *Improve air quality.* Anything that eliminates the lines at entrances to parking facilities, given the volume of vehicles involved at morning rush, would be a plus.
4. *Pursue the program as a business.* A nonprofit has little currency with a business operator. The statement: "I'm here from the government and I want to help you" doesn't go far. Good intentions are not enough

to do business. Parking must be undertaken as a business offering a valuable service.

Using Technology

Dallas is home to the company that introduced the Tolltag. The North Texas Tollway Authority (NTTA) was the first in the nation to use the Tolltag on the Dallas North Tollway. When first introduced, it was priced as a premium service. Experience dictated that it become a discounted service, since the use of the Tolltag improved the performance of the toll road by increasing the thru put at the toll-booth. These efficiencies led to barrier-free designated lanes at toll plazas. Today, there are over 800,000 Tolltags in use on the numerous toll facilities (roads, bridges, tunnels) operated by the North Texas Tollway Authority (NTTA).

The E-ZPass in the New York Thruway/New Jersey Turnpike corridor uses the same Dallas-made Tolltag under a different brand name. Similar applications can be found in Florida, Georgia, Oklahoma, Canada, and California, to name a few. Other radio-frequency-read tags have entered the market, but the Tolltag has the greatest market penetration.

The breakthrough idea was to consider the parking collection booth as a tollbooth at a toll plaza. Compatibility of equipment would augment the opportunity to interface parking with toll roads and perhaps even airports, such as DFW International and the city-owned Love Field, which is home to Southwest Airlines.

The question then became how to make this application attractive to the owners of parking garages. By issuing Tolltags to all monthly parkers at a garage, the operator garnered the thruput advantage of this technology (less hassle of waiting to enter and exit). The owner also gained the advantages of both electronic recording of *every* transaction and also accessing a wider base of Tolltag users for intermittent hourly parking (premium rates). The opportunity also existed to use the system for monthly billing, thus ensuring the ready availability of capital through credit card transactions rather than the typical thirty-day billing cycle with all the paperwork processing involved.

Finally, the required equipment was an add-on to the existing gate controllers and did not require their replacement. Familiar equipment could be retained since the new system simply overlays existing equipment. A value-added service could indeed be offered to the garage owner.

Next, consideration was given to the customer—the ultimate concern. The Tolltag system offered safety (as the car approaches the gate lifts), no stopping at the ticket spitter (you don't have to roll down the window), and the comfort of knowing that whatever the charge, your credit card will handle it (no fumbling for correct change). Quick in—quick out—no hassle! Customers believe the system works "like magic." It also imparts the feeling that the customer is getting VIP treatment. For the business traveler, the issuance of a monthly statement that details every transaction aids in expense account reconciliation.

To make the system truly impressive it had to expand its utility to a regional program of toll roads, bridges, tunnels, airports, and parking garages. The New York state region had partially accomplished this with toll roads, bridges, and tunnels, yet it still lacks the interface with regional airports and hasn't considered private parking garages.

Finally, the system had to be structured as a business entity, not as a social endeavor. Civic motivations were behind the idea—the promise of cleaner air as a result of shorter lines at entrances. Given the name Pegasus, the new system offered a consolidated approach to what was then a fractured delivery system.

The Central Dallas Transportation Management Association (CD/TMA) took the lead to develop such a program. As a certified vendor to Federal Transit Administration agencies, it could enter into contracts with public agencies. Using a federal grant, the CD/TMA began work to outline the program and to develop a prototype. The beta test site proved the viability of the concept.

What became apparent early is that the idea needed the protection of a federal trademark, so Central Dallas Association (CDA) filed the trademark application, which was subsequently approved and since renewed. Pegasus Parking in now a nationally registered service mark.

BUSINESS ISSUES

The prospect of a nonprofit running a legitimate business held two problems: a successful business could warp the public purposes of the parent organization, and, if successful, the nonprofit would have to pay unrelated business taxes. This posed a real problem. If Pegasus Parking became successful, CDA risked losing its civic way and if the unrelated business taxes became substantial, CDA could lose its nonprofit status.

The Girl Scouts came to the rescue. Accountants discovered IRS rulings that allow the Girl Scouts to sell their cookies and retain their non-profit status. The concept is a third-tier subsidiary, wholly owned by nonprofits.

The for-profit entity, Pegasus Parking Ventures, Inc., pays all taxes, yet it can remit royalty fees for the trademark and dividends back to Central

Dallas Association and remit dividends to the other shareholder, Dallas Civic Ventures, Inc., a charitable 501(c)(3).

Next came the formulation of a Memorandum of Understanding with the NTTA and the airports and the establishment of a clearinghouse for the system. Fortunately, a clearinghouse already existed that serviced the NTTA. It was agreed to continue with that service. Next came business rules that created peer-to-peer relationships with each entity guaranteeing the transactions of its customers. Each service provider sets up a $40 prepaid credit card account for each of its customers. Each transaction draws against the prepaid balance. When the prepaid account reaches a low threshold, the clearinghouse replenishes the account from the individual's credit card.

The Pegasus Parking program opened in 1999 with a beta test site garage and the municipal airport, Love Field, as a demonstration facility with joint use of the NTTA facilities. The acceptance of the Tolltag at DFW airport required a separate Memorandum of Understanding. In the subsequent years, the Pegasus program has grown to 12,000 customers and is financially sound.

EXPANSION OPPORTUNITIES

Two major program expansions are underway at the NTTA. The clearinghouse function will be taken in house, and final testing is proving successful for handling the electronic transactions for the Harris County (Houston) Tollroad Authority. This step portends a multi-city system with the Tolltag used interchangeably in either city. This can only make intercity travel more enjoyable.

The North Texas Council of Governments is evaluating the use of Tolltags for High Occupancy Toll (HOT) lanes in newly widened freeways and existing High Occupancy Vehicle (HOV) lanes. This would be an easy extension of the system.

Results from travel pattern analyses are another basis for expansion opportunity. With 800,000 Tolltags in use in the metroplex, sampling cohorts are readily available. Each tag application must include vehicle data, driver's license, and address. The Pegasus application authorizes use of location data for analytical processes but must be limited to zip-code area. From a downtown perspective, transaction data from parking garages, combined with zip codes, allow identification of the home-to-work trip of the workforce. Fortunately, zip code and travel zones have been largely coordinated through geographic information system (GIS) mapping.

The Pegasus parking program is now exploring the option of franchising its system to other cities where the Tolltag is in use.

SUMMARY

Downtown parking, a liability in a world competing for office tenants and shoppers, can be made into a more convenient and pleasurable experience. The Pegasus program demonstrates one aspect of removing the "hassle factor."

Chapter 23

"Best in Class" Parking Operations

Dennis Burns

INTRODUCTION

Parking is an essential element of a downtown's infrastructure and, when well managed, it can contribute greatly to efforts to develop and sustain healthy and vibrant downtowns. Convenient, safe, clean, and affordable parking is critical to attracting and retaining retailers, restaurants, office buildings/tenants, and all other types of development. In this chapter, we will explore the characteristics of "Best in Class" parking operations and how they can contribute to the success of your downtown and discuss the skill sets needed by parking professionals whose job it is to "tame the parking beast."

PARKING 101: CHOOSE ANY TWO

One element is common to every study and every downtown—parking is always a source of frustration and contention. It is amazing how emotional an issue parking can be. This is because it affects people so directly. Think about it—how many other areas involve issues of personal safety/security, finance, convenience, wayfinding, accessibility, and customer service? Parking creates the first and last impression of your downtown. How can that "parking experience" best be managed?

An interesting dynamic about parking is illustrated in Figure 23.1.

Everyone wants three things when it comes to parking: (1) they want there to be plenty of it; (2) they want it to be very convenient; and (3) they want it to be inexpensive (and preferably free). Unfortunately, you can have any two, but not all three. This ushers in the need for a policy decision.

doi:10.1300/5137_24

1. If you choose to have inexpensive and convenient parking you will likely not have enough. This option may be acceptable if you want to use the lack of spaces as part of a demand management strategy to encourage the use of transportation alternatives.

2. If you choose to have inexpensive and enough parking it will not be very convenient. With this choice you may be adopting a strategy that utilizes less expensive remote parking supported with shuttle operations.

3. If you choose to have convenient and enough parking, it will not be cheap. This often-preferred approach typically means you have chosen to develop structured parking. The average construction cost for surface lot parking ranges from $1,500 to $2,000 per space. Above-grade parking structures average between $8,000 and $12,000 per space. Below-grade parking can range between one and a half to two times the cost of above-grade structures. Another consideration that is often overlooked is that operating, utility, maintenance, and security costs are significantly higher with structured parking.

In downtown environments the choice is most often made to have "convenient and enough" parking. This strategic decision, and the significant capital investment it requires, creates the need to ensure that these investments are well-managed and responsive to the communities they serve.

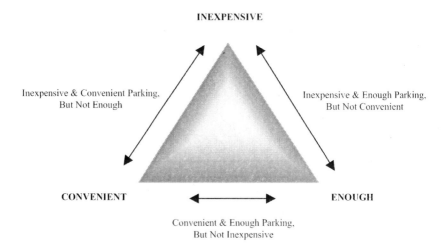

FIGURE 23.1. Choose any two.

CHARACTERISTICS OF EFFECTIVE
PARKING PROGRAMS

Based on evaluation of numerous parking systems of various sizes and complexity, a set of twenty characteristics, which, when combined into an integrated programmatic approach, can provide the basis for a sound and well-managed parking system. A parking system that has all twenty of these characteristics is well on its way to being in a class apart from the majority of parking systems. The ultimate goal is a system that provides professional management, understands the role it plays in contributing to the larger objectives of the downtown, and is responsive to the community it serves.

In the following sections we will briefly explore each of these characteristics. This is not intended to be an exhaustive review of each area, but rather just enough of a treatment to give the reader an idea of how each characteristic contributes to an effective parking system.

1. Clear Vision and Mission

Truly effective parking systems have a clear vision and a well-defined mission. The development or periodic reassessment of the parking system vision/mission statements should be an open and inclusive process involving a wide range of downtown stakeholders. Typically, the following groups should be included in the public input process:

- City officials (including elected officials, planning staff, transit agencies, etc.)
- Downtown development agencies
- Downtown business associations
- Downtown property owners
- Downtown merchants
- Downtown employees

A parking system's vision and mission statements should have one overriding goal: to see that the parking system's purpose and direction is tied to and supportive of the larger community's strategic development plan. Parking can support the health, vitality, and development of a downtown in many ways. Having a professionally managed parking program that presents clean, safe, attractive, and well-maintained facilities is perhaps the most visible dimension. Other attributes include providing an adequate supply of parking overall, and the appropriate allocation and management of those resources to best support the various businesses that depend on them for their success. Successfully meeting these goals promotes downtown business retention and attraction.

The parking system administrator should play a key role in providing educational support to community leaders about the importance of parking and the role(s) parking can play (and cannot play) in meeting community objectives. Staying abreast of the latest technological developments related to parking systems can broaden the options available to improve parking system management effectiveness and efficiency. Common problems for downtowns are promoting turnover of short-term on-street spaces without being perceived as "unfriendly" or "heavy handed," or providing more convenient customer payment options. The use of new technology to support the mission and vision can have a profound impact on the perception of the parking system and how it is contributes to achieving the goals of the downtown it serves.

In effective systems, parking's financial responsibilities are well defined and understood. This is a critical component of the vision/mission, as it directly impacts the perception of whether the parking system is meeting its financial obligations and expectations. Part of this important discussion relates to whether the parking system is expected to be subsidized by the city's general fund, or other revenue sources such as tax increment financing, contributions from business improvement districts, special assessment districts, etc., or whether parking is expected to cover its own operating and maintenance costs, but not debt service. Or, is parking expected to cover all costs and generate additional revenue? Deciding which of these options is feasible for your community depends on a number of variables.

2. Parking Philosophy

A succinct statement or statements reflecting your philosophical approach to parking can provide clarity when communicating to your patrons, stakeholders, and staff. Some examples of "parking philosophy" are noted as follows along with a brief commentary.

Parking Isn't About Cars . . . It's About People

This statement reflects an understanding that parking is not simply the act of temporarily storing cars, but it is, in fact, more about addressing "people" needs at the transition from the vehicular to the pedestrian experience. Under this philosophy, issues such as facility cleanliness, safety, lighting, wayfinding, and customer service move to the forefront. Functional design elements that directly impact user comfort such as stall widths, turn radii, walking distances, etc., also take on special importance.

People Don't Come Downtown to Park

This concept reinforces the reality that parking, while an important support function and critical infrastructure element, is not the reason people visit your downtown. For the downtown to be successful there must be good restaurants, interesting retail businesses, and other special attractions. Even the best-run parking system with well-designed facilities will not "attract" people to come downtown. However, poorly run operations or dysfunctional facilities can definitely be excuses for people *not* to come downtown. The fundamental principle behind this philosophy is threefold: (1) the role of parking is to support other downtown activities; (2) eliminate parking as a "reason *not* to come downtown;" and (3) recognize what parking is *not,* i.e., an attraction.

Parking Should Be a Positive Experience

For years Carl Walker, Inc., an international parking engineering and consulting firm, had a slogan: "Parking should be a non-event." This notion has undergone a qualitative evolution making parking not just a "nonevent," but actually a "positive experience." In their book *The Experience Economy,* Joseph Pine and James Gilmore (1999) address the concept that, especially in America, what customers are actually purchasing are "positive experiences." One expression of this transition can be seen in the health care arena. Have you noticed that the lobbies of newer health care facilities have taken on the feel of grand hotel lobbies? At one hospital, the look and feel of a new bed tower lobby (marble, glass, air-conditioning, etc.) was extended into the parking structure elevator lobbies to extend that welcoming experience. Similarly, the more extensive customer service training required for hospital reception desk staff was also required for parking attendant and valet parking staff.

Parking Is the First and Last Experience

Most customers' first and last impressions of any venue really begins and ends with their parking experience. You might enjoy the best meal followed by a fabulous evening of entertainment in the downtown, but if you have to circle and circle to find a parking space or are accosted walking from your car to your destination, this will taint your whole experience. Follow this up by an encounter with a surly, gum-chewing attendant upon exiting the parking facility and guess what you'll be talking about the next day (it probably won't be the delicious meal you had at Gino's).

Parking Should Be Friendly, Not Free

There is no such thing as "free parking." One of the ongoing challenges that downtowns face when it comes to parking is cost. Because of land values, densities, and walking-distance issues, parking structures are here to stay in the downtown environment, and with them is the need to charge for parking in one form or fashion. The perception that parking at the mall is "free" doesn't help (even though it is not true). Even if you promote "free parking" as a marketing concept, someone is paying for that parking. Either through increased taxes or an increased cost of goods or services, the cost of providing parking is still there. This philosophy recognizes this reality and focuses instead on providing a friendly, well-managed parking experience.

Parking Is a Component of the Larger Transportation System

Surprisingly, parking often gets divorced in people's minds from being a component of the larger transportation system. Structured parking, because of its cost, is often the reason that development projects "don't pencil" (to use developer lingo, meaning the project would not be financially viable). By considering parking in the larger context of a broad range of transit and transportation alternatives, demand management strategies (including shared parking policies) can be developed that help reduce the amount of parking required, especially in urban areas where good bus transit, light rail, taxi service, and increasingly in-town residential developments can be found. Developing programs that integrate complementary parking and transportation strategies is a hallmark of this philosophy.

3. Strong Planning

One consistent characteristic of well-managed and forward-thinking parking programs is strong planning. The first step in developing a well-managed parking planning function is to have a solid understanding of existing parking resources. Documenting the basics is fundamental. Following are some basic planning tenets that should be considered:

- Parking inventory is complete and up-to-date (includes both public and private parking).
- Parking inventories are subdivided by type and use of space.
- Parking utilization, by type of spaces, is known and trends tracked.
- Changes in supply are documented.
- Changes in utilization are tracked and understood.

- Periodic parking supply-demand studies are completed.
- Quality parking maps are available and up-to-date.

Key planning tools that parking departments often overlook or don't understand are land-use data. Successful parking systems develop relationships with city or regional planning agencies so that valuable land-use data, information on proposed developments, downtown planning maps, etc., can be obtained and used in crafting parking planning strategies. When reviewing a strategic parking plan, look for the following items:

- Are land use data readily available and up-to-date?
- Is historical parking development well documented?
- Is planning for the next parking development "on the drawing board"?
- Is parking represented and participating in other types of community studies, e.g., downtown strategic plans, marketing studies, retail studies, economic development studies, transportation studies, traffic studies, etc.?
- Have strategically located potential parking development sites been identified?
- Are future parking development sites "land banked"?
- Are potential sites assembled to achieve an adequate footprint size to develop efficient parking structures (300 to 325 sq. ft. per stall)?
- Have parking lot and structure design guidelines been developed?
- Does the organization incorporate a "Program Criteria Document" approach to parking structure design projects to effectively integrate operational elements early in the design process?

4. Community Involvement

One common problem with struggling parking programs is that they are operated only to satisfy a narrowly defined set of internal objectives (typically focused on revenue generation). Successful parking programs understand that their larger purpose is to support the downtown and the businesses that create and sustain downtown vitality. Parking systems should develop close and cooperative working relationships with other community groups such as economic development agencies and downtown business associations.

This does not mean that the parking system exists simply as a tool to be manipulated by these organizations. The parking operation has its own goals and objectives. For example, if the parking system is operating under a mandate to be self-supporting, it may not be able to subsidize a downtown validation program, even though the local downtown business associations might desire this. However, acting as partners, a mutually beneficial solution can be devised to meet the overall objectives of both organizations whereby costs are shared or alternative funding sources are obtained.

Another significant area of potential partnership is downtown and parking system marketing. In many successful downtowns parking cosponsors or shares in downtown marketing and promotional initiatives. The downtown business association, the chamber of commerce, and other groups promoting the downtown should include parking information in their publications, and parking publications should promote the current programs of the other agencies. This cooperative relationship creates an impression of a well-managed downtown and positively advances the image of the downtown.

Successful parking operations actively solicit public input from a variety of sources including: public forums, parking task-force groups, "parking advisors"—people who have demonstrated an interest in parking issues (sometimes characterized as "complainers") and who are recruited to provide input on an occasional basis. The key to success is to listen to the concerns of your customers, act promptly to resolve the issues (or engage and educate them on the "real issues"), and then *follow up* to make sure their issue has been satisfactorily resolved. By doing this, you short-circuit that stream of negativity, which too often circulates among downtown customer groups, and you can begin to build a network of parking system supporters.

5. Organization

Whether a city department, a quasi-independent parking authority, an arm of an urban renewal agency, or the responsibility of a downtown business association, an important question is whether the parking organization is structured and staffed to best achieve its stated goals.

Some basic questions to ask related to the issue of organizational structure include:

- Are all parking operations to be managed through a centralized operation, or can other departments or agencies get involved in limited parking operations?
- Is parking to be managed in-house?
- Should certain functions be outsourced?
- Are there advantages to a hybrid approach?
- Does the current organization/staffing plan provide the right mix of skills, talents, and abilities?

- Is staffing as efficient as possible? Are there tools in place to evaluate staffing adequacy, efficiency, and program effectiveness?

When evaluating which organizational option is most appropriate for your particular downtown, consider the following criteria to evaluate the relative advantages and disadvantages of each model.

- Best supports economic development
- Is most efficient
- Is most customer friendly
- Is most politically feasible
- Is most focused on the vision
- Is easiest to achieve
- Is most responsive to business and stakeholders
- Is most financially viable
- Provides the most effective coordination

Another component of the evaluation process is to identify the program elements for which the parking system will be responsible. Following is a list of potential program elements:

- Overall leadership and management
- Program definition and development
- Parking system revenue control and accounting
- Manage parking facilities
- Contract management
- Marketing/promotion/information
- Parking planning and coordination
- Community outreach and education
- Equipment and technology specifications
- Equipment and technology maintenance
- Parking enforcement
- On-street parking management
- Meter collections
- Meter maintenance
- Employee parking
- ADA compliance
- Parking facility maintenance programs
- Develop consolidated financial reporting system
- Special events parking management
- Parking resource allocation

- Rate setting
- Residential parking permit programs
- Special program development
- Service and information center (parking hotline)
- Wayfinding and signage
- Customer service programs
- Validation programs
- Valet parking programs
- Parking and transportation demand management
- Facility safety/security/risk management

6. Staff Development

Unlike property management, public administration, etc., there are no formal educational programs for parking management. You cannot go out and hire someone from the latest crop of college parking graduates. However, this is beginning to change. The International Parking Institute (IPI) has a highly regarded and reputable educational/certification program called the Certified Administrator of Public Parking (CAPP) program that is administered by the University of Virginia. For the most part, parking professionals are still learning as they go and bringing with them numerous skills and perspectives imported from a variety of previous work experiences.

One characteristic of the most successful parking programs is recognition of the unique knowledge, complexity, and broad skill sets required to be successful in parking. These programs invest in parking-specific training and educational opportunities to develop their staff into parking professionals. The following is a list of options to consider to actively promote parking staff development within your parking operation:

- Support participation in the International Parking Institute and the IPI's CAPP program.
- Support participation in local, state, regional, and national parking associations to create networking and peer-to-peer communications. These associations also provide the best access to parking-specific training opportunities for various staff levels from frontline to administrative.
- A recommended best practice is to conduct an operational peer review. An operational peer review involves having a representative from a similar municipal program critique your downtown parking program with a "fresh set of eyes." Typically, this service is reciprocated. This

is generally a low-cost initiative that can be set up directly or through the local, regional, or national parking association and is an effective way to gain and share parking knowledge.
- Build a parking resource library. Following is a basic bibliography of resources that can increase your staff's knowledge of the parking industry.

Stehman, R. (Ed.). (2001). International Parking Institute. *Parking 101, A Parking Primer,* Manuscript. Fredericksburg, VA.

Weant, Robert A. and Levinson, Herbert S. (1990). *Parking.* Washington, DC: Eno Foundation for Transportation.

Chrest, Anthony, Smith, Mary S., and Bhuyan, Sam (2001). *Parking Structures, Planning Design, Construction, Maintenance and Repair.* Third Edition. Boston: Kluwer.

Urban Land Institute (2000). *The Dimensions of Parking,* Fourth Edition. Washington, DC: The Urban Land Institute and National Parking Association.

Institute of Transportation Engineers (1987). *Parking Generation.* ITE Publ. No. IR-034A. Washington, DC: Author.

The Urban Land Institute (1983). *Shared Parking.* Study coordinated by the ULI in association with Barton-Aschman Assoc. Inc. Washington, DC: Author.

Illuminating Engineering Society of North America (1998). *Lighting for Parking Facilities.* Publ. No. RP-20-98, Second Edition. New York: Author.

7. Safety, Security, and Risk Management

The importance of providing a safe environment in your parking facilities cannot be overestimated. The actual and perceived security within your facilities impacts the success, not only of the parking operation, but also of the businesses supported by those facilities.

Planning for security in your parking facilities should begin during the design of new facilities. If you are inheriting existing facilities, a security audit of all facilities is highly recommended.

The concept of "crime prevention through environmental design" (CPTED) provides useful tenets for architects, facility planners, designers, and law enforcement/security and parking professionals. CPTED concepts help create a climate of safety in a parking facility, on a campus, or throughout a downtown, by designing a physical environment that positively influences human behavior. These concepts can also be used to retrofit environments to address specific security issues as they develop or to address emerging concerns as conditions change.

CPTED builds on four key strategies:

1. territoriality,
2. natural surveillance,

3. activity support, and
4. access control.

- *Territoriality:* People protect territory that they feel is their own and have a certain respect for the territory of others. Fences, pavement treatments, art, signs, good maintenance, and landscaping are some physical ways to express ownership. Identifying intruders is much easier in a well-defined space.
- *Natural surveillance:* Criminals don't want to be seen. Placing physical features, activities, and people in ways that maximize the ability to see what's going on discourages crime. Barriers, such as low ceilings, solid walls, or shadows, make it difficult to observe activity. Landscaping and lighting can be planned to promote natural surveillance from both inside a building and from the outside by neighbors or people passing by. Maximizing the natural surveillance capability of "gatekeepers" such as parking lot attendants, maintenance personnel, etc., is also important.
- *Activity support:* Encouraging legitimate activity in public spaces helps discourage crime.
- *Access control:* Properly located entrances, exits, fencing, landscaping, and lighting can direct both foot and automobile traffic in ways that discourage crime.

These principles can be blended in the planning or remodeling of parking facilities and other public areas. In parking environments, the following specific strategies are recommended:

- Higher floor-to-floor heights to improve openness
- Glass-backed elevators
- Glass around or open stairwells
- "Blue light" security phones
- Security screening on the ground level
- Eliminate potential hiding places (for example under stairs, within storage areas, etc.)
- Low-level landscaping
- Ensure that all your facilities are well lighted and meet or exceed the recommended minimums for parking facility lighting as established by the Illuminating Engineering Society of North America (IESNA).
- Develop facility lighting standards. Provide consistent lighting levels in all facilities.

- Integrate security offices, parking offices, retail shops, etc., into parking facilities to provide increased activity levels.
- Integrate parking attendants, cleaning and maintenance staff, shuttle drivers, etc., into your parking security program.
- Incorporate safety and risk management issues into a weekly facility walk-through checklist.

8. Effective Communications

Best in Class parking operations actively engage other community groups to help define how the parking system can best support the objectives of the businesses and the community at large that depend on a parking system that works. As an outside consultant coming into a downtown to evaluate some aspect of a downtown parking program, it is not uncommon to find the parking system at odds with the downtown association. Although there may be as many reasons for this "disconnect" as there are personalities involved, there appear to be at least two primary underlying reasons:

1. Downtown associations are driven by efforts to revitalize downtown areas and see parking costs as one element that places them at a competitive disadvantage (compared to the perception of "free parking" at the malls/suburbs). Parking system managers are being pushed, usually by municipal governments, to generate revenues. The bottom line is they lack a shared vision and therefore are pulling in opposite directions.
2. The second major issue typically has to do with service-level expectations. Downtown associations tend to have higher expectations in the areas of customer service, facility cleanliness, security, etc. It is not that the parking system administrators do not value these same qualities, but there is a cost associated with providing these programs and limited budgets to support them. The irony is that revenues are often reduced by not providing these higher levels of service.

The first steps toward resolving this problem are improving communications and defining a shared vision/mission. A clear understanding of the issues and potential solutions is the kick-off point for developing the mutually beneficial approach. Developing a set of "guiding principles" for the parking system is a good starting point for crafting a successful collaborative relationship.

Successful programs also have well-defined relationships between various departments, especially other support departments, such as: Maintenance, Security/Police, Communications, Facilities Management, Planning, etc.

Finally, successful parking programs are in touch with their customers and actively solicit input through meetings with major downtown employers, customer surveys, Web sites, parking "hotlines," and public forums.

9. Consolidated Parking Programs

Taking a systems approach to parking is an important dimension to creating a comprehensive and effective parking program. Having control of all or most aspects of parking can contribute to a more effective operation because of the interactive nature of parking as a system.

For example, having control of off-street, but not on-street parking can lead to problems if the rates for the various types of parking are not kept in the proper balance or relationship. Or, not having control over parking enforcement practices can hamper efforts to promote or improve turnover to support downtown retail businesses or to support special downtown events.

Ideally, the parking system should control off-street, on-street, and parking enforcement operations. All parking-related revenues should first go to fund parking programs, including preventative maintenance, maintenance reserves, parking system/downtown marketing, planning, and new parking resource development. If additional revenues, in excess of operational needs, are available, they should be banked as reserve funds for future parking development projects or returned to the general fund for discretionary spending.

10. Financial Planning

The parking system's financial expectations should be well-defined and understood. For example, is the parking system expected to be:

> A self-supporting entity?
> A profit/revenue center?
> A support service sustained by other primary revenue sources?

With the exception of airports, some university systems, and some very large municipalities, parking programs are rarely capable of being totally self-supporting. Many factors affect whether parking can be self-supporting: market rates for parking, parking mix (percentage of transient versus monthly parkers), availability of on-street parking revenues, availability of parking enforcement revenues, politics, and economic development policies. For systems that cannot achieve true financial self-sufficiency, a common goal is to cover all operational costs but not debt service costs. Debt service costs are typically subsidized by the general fund, tax increment financing revenues, in-lieu parking fees, or other sources.

An important principal in developing a successful parking program is tying revenues to the larger vision and mission of the downtown it is intended to serve. Development of a downtown strategic plan that incorporates not only market and land-use strategies, but also critical support infrastructure such as parking, transit, pedestrian access, freight mobility, loading and unloading, etc., is an excellent means for defining the relationships of all these components and establishing clear goals and direction. Once the vision and mission have been set, investigation of other possible sources of parking revenues may be desired. Alternative parking revenue sources might include:

- On-street pay parking (if that does not already exist)
- Parking enforcement
- Tax increment financing districts
- In-lieu-of parking fees
- Special parking assessment districts

Other important financial planning elements that are recommended for all parking systems include:

- A consolidated parking financial statement that tracks all sources of parking revenues and expenses.
- Parking revenues and expenses that are well managed and books that are regularly audited.
- Annual operating statements published in an annual report and available for public review. (For an excellent example of this, check out the annual parking report posted online by the Calgary Parking Authority (www.calgaryparking.com.)
- If a private parking operator is used to manage day-to-day operations, an annual parking operations and financial audit is recommended.

11. Creative, Flexible, and Accountable Parking Management

Different land uses, environments, and user groups require different parking management approaches. A one-size-fits-all approach does not work. A variety of parking management strategies should be employed to address different needs, such as:

- Visitor parking
- Employee parking
- On-street parking
- Reserved parking
- Residential parking
- Special-use permits
- Accessible parking (Americans with Disabilities Act)
- Shared parking
- Parking allocation plans
- Loading/unloading zone parking

Another key management principal is the need for strong and accountable parking revenue control systems. This begins with the purchase and installation of a parking access and revenue control system specified to meet your system's needs.

All the components of the system should be utilized to their full potential. Many parking systems purchase an expensive software system and use less than 10 percent of its capabilities. Using standard parking access and revenue control system reports and creating customized reports can provide enhanced management information, improved understanding of operational dynamics, and ultimately increased system utilization and efficiency.

Another characteristic of effective parking programs is that they have mapped out audit trails and developed systems to provide acceptable levels of control and accountability. Because of the large revenues generated, revenue control and accountability are key parking management issues.

Developing policies and procedures for anticipating and managing losses of parking supply (both temporary and long-term) is another basic parking management responsibility. Some key elements in this area include:

- Planning for and communicating losses of parking supply.
- Ensuring adequate capacity to handle short-term parking supply losses.
- Effective plans to manage routine maintenance projects, including customer communications and contingency plans.
- A full understanding of the financial impacts of these projects on revenue streams.
- Defined parking replacement cost policies.

Development of an annual parking report can have a number of positive impacts for a parking system. It identifies key departmental issues and challenges, promotes departmental achievements, documents the "state of parking" to the stakeholders, creates a record of "system history," and builds credibility and confidence in the department.

Other parking management elements include:

- Well-defined parking policies and procedures.
- Development and maintenance of parking facility operations manuals.
- Well-defined and implemented facility maintenance programs.
- Parking system marketing programs.
- Effective parking and wayfinding signage programs.

12. Operational Efficiency

Another area to investigate when assessing a parking program is the overall efficiency of the parking operation. Parking system efficiency has several dimensions, depending on how the system is managed. The first area to be scrutinized is the management responsibilities of the system, i.e., what programs the department or organization is responsible for implementing. Once this has been defined, organizational structure and staffing plans are analyzed.

Development of some form of benchmarking or comparative analysis to measure costs and performance to similar operations is highly recommended. Benchmarking can be a tricky business—make sure you are comparing "apples to apples." Some basic benchmarks make sense for downtown parking operations:

- Parking revenue per space
- Total operating cost per space
- Administrative cost per space
- Maintenance cost per space
- Citations issued per enforcement staff (full time equivalents)
- Parking citation collection ratio

Other operational areas can also yield significant savings. For example, facility lighting. Utility costs are integral budget elements in managing a parking structure, but by placing the exterior bay and rooftop lights on separate circuits with photo-cells, 25 to 35 percent of the facility's lights can be turned off during the day, saving significant amounts of electricity.

Another area worthy of investigation is staffing costs in the late evening hours when the income generated is less than the staffing costs incurred. In these situations, the use of automated cashier units can be an effective alternative.

13. Comprehensive Facilities Maintenance Programs

Few things make a greater impression on first-time downtown visitors than the cleanliness and maintenance of parking facilities. Beyond first impressions, however, few areas provide a greater potential return on investment than a comprehensive parking system maintenance program.

A few best practices related to parking facility appearance and maintenance are noted as follows.

- Paint interior surfaces to enhance the perception of cleanliness and safety and to improve lighting levels.
- Develop a comprehensive preventative maintenance program for all essential systems.
  — parking access and revenue control systems
  — elevators
  — lighting and energy management systems
- Organize and track parking facility warranties in a binder. Schedule warranty inspections six months prior to warranty expiration. Document with digital photos and results of inspections.
- Schedule regular facility condition appraisals and develop a prioritized program of facility maintenance repairs.
- Set aside adequate maintenance reserve funds based on a prioritized facility maintenance action plan.

Parking facility maintenance can be grouped into four categories:

I. *Housekeeping.* This work is typically conducted by in-house staff and consists of basic cleaning, sweeping, slab wash downs, etc.
  A. Sweeping of the stairs, elevator lobbies, and floors on a regular basis
  B. Trash collection on a periodic basis
  C. Slab wash downs on a semiannual basis
  D. Floor drain clean out (including sediment basket clean out)
  E. Cleaning of stair enclosures (stair, elevator, and storefront glass)
  F. Cleaning of doors, door frames and glass on a periodic basis
  G. Cleaning of signage, elevator floors, doors, walls, parking equipment, etc., on a periodic basis

H. Cleaning of restrooms, cashiers' booths, offices, etc., on a regular basis
I. Daily walk-through of the facilities by operator to confirm that housekeeping is being performed

II. *System Maintenance.* This includes tasks necessary to ensure proper operations of systems and components.

A. Landscaping
1. Maintenance—leaves, lawn, trees
2. Plantings (annual)
3. Fencing—posts, chains, etc.
4. Planters

B. Painting—spot, or seasonal painting

C. Parking equipment maintenance
1. Spitters, card readers, computers, booths, gates, etc.
2. Annual maintenance contract with equipment supplier
3. Parking equipment will usually be replaced every seven to ten years

D. Fire protection
1. Maintenance contract is anticipated
2. Drain sprinkler systems periodically
3. Testing (twice per year)

E. Lighting—lamps should be replaced every two to three years
1. Fixture repair and isolated replacement included in operations—generally more economical to replace fixture when ballast goes bad
2. Fixture replacement every twenty years (included in capital expenditures)
3. Lens replacement every six years (with lamps, included in operations)
4. Lamp replacement on an as-needed basis (current)—operator to review scheduling lamp replacement, by level, to maximize light effectiveness, and to maintain economy. (Note: lamp intensity depreciates significantly, well before burnout.)

F. Elevators—elevator service contract and maintenance/repairs are generally provided by an outside maintenance firm
1. Periodic cleaning of equipment will be reviewed
2. Improve maintenance to reduce breakdowns

G. Electrical/mechanical/plumbing maintenance
1. Offices/restrooms/cashiers' booths
a. HVAC (heating, ventilating, and air-conditioning)
b. Exhaust fans
c. Plumbing fixtures

          d. Hot water heaters

          e. Lighting

   H. Electrical equipment—general and emergency cleaning/maintenance

    I. HVAC equipment—general and emergency cleaning/maintenance

       1. Mechanical ventilation

       2. Elevator tower ventilation system

    J. Emergency power/lighting testing and maintenance contract

       1. Generator: maintenance contract

       2. UPS system: maintenance contract

   K. Plumbing—general clean out

   L. Domestic water maintenance

       1. Drain wash-down lines annually

       2. Sump pump inspection

   M. Doors and hardware—periodic inspection and lubrication (malfunction, sticking, etc.)

   N. Signage

       1. Illuminated signs—replace lamps

       2. Replace damaged signage periodically as required

   O. Snow removal/deicing

III. *Annual General Maintenance and Repairs.* Annual general maintenance would usually be performed by outside contractors, although in some cases the operator's staff may perform the work. This work is not typically included in a capital cost budget and may be combined with the System Maintenance category.

   A. Concrete repairs—isolated concrete slab, beam, joist, tee, topping, etc., repairs. In some cases, periodic concrete repairs (every five years) are included; however, isolated repairs between the five-year intervals should be anticipated.

   B. Masonry repair—isolated masonry repair should be anticipated (spot tuckpointing, damaged masonry unit replacement, resetting capstone, etc.).

   C. Sealants/expansion joint—repair/replacement of isolated sealant (floor and façade) or expansion joint failure (not included under the five-year warranty). Leaking at slab cracks may also require sealant installation. Leaking joints should be repaired as soon as possible after discovery, and evidence of leaking should be removed.

   D. Deck coating—isolated deck coating repairs (not included under the five-year warranty). Wear of the topcoat should be repaired prior to damage to the underlying base membrane.

E. Painting—painting touch-up (spot/seasonal painting) should generally be performed as damage is observed. Repainting of exposed steel and concrete surfaces would be performed every ten to fifteen years, and parking stripes reapplied every three to five years.

F. Graffiti removal—graffiti removal should be completed as soon as possible after the application

G. General electrical repairs and maintenance—isolated corrosion damage, switchgear maintenance, panel maintenance

H. Light fixture repair/replacement—individual light fixture repair or replacement will require immediate attention

I. HVAC—office, restroom and elevator HVAC repairs

J. Plumbing—isolated replacement of drain lines and floor drain grates. Isolated clean out of drains/lines. Periodic sump pump repairs.

IV. *Periodic Repairs, Protection, and Improvements (Capital Expenditures)*. This work is generally performed by outside contractors and will consist of replacing/repairing damage to waterproofing or structural elements.

Annual Maintenance Costs by Category

Cost of housekeeping, operations, and operator maintenance, will vary based on specific operations requirements but will approximate $350 to $450 per space per year.

Annual general maintenance and repair costs will approximate $0.10 to $.15/sf per year ($35 to $50 per space per year), depending on condition and type of structural system.

Periodic repairs, protection, and improvements (capital expenditures)— the maintenance reserve fund can likely be lower during the first ten years of life, and increased to accommodate improvement planning budgets. For a new structure, this item may range from $75 to $100 per space per year for the first ten years.

14. Use of Technology

Best in Class parking operations almost always have a comprehensive and integrated parking access and revenue control system that offers the following benefits:

- Consistent operations and features for customers
- Simplified/consistent training for staff and auditors

- Similar equipment and models for simplified maintenance and less costly parts stocking
- Consolidated, system-wide reporting and management information

Staying informed of new technologies can help provide the parking department with the best tools available to achieve its goals. New technologies can help you—and your staff—work smarter, not harder.

Other benefits of incorporating new technologies are improved overall efficiency and effectiveness, reductions in operating expenses, improved management controls, and the ability to implement seamless, customer-friendly payment-system options such as Internet payment options.

15. Parking System Marketing

Parking system monitoring is one of the most overlooked aspects of parking system management. An effective parking system marketing and promotions program will set your parking operation apart from the ordinary. The following is a list of "action items" that can help launch a new program or enhance an existing one.

- Develop a consistent parking system brand
  — The brand should promote the image you want people to have of the system
  — It should reinforce the positive aspects of the system, e.g., "Free and Easy Parking," "Visit Downtown and Parking Is On Us," etc.
- Use consistent signage to tie the system together
- Tie in parking to all downtown promotional materials
- Expand and improve parking system Web site
- Develop new employee/tenant parking brochures or info packets
- Develop parking "e-bulletins"
- Designate a parking spokesperson
- Have regular personal contact with customers
- Develop parking deck floor identification (themed graphics, music, etc., could be considered an extension of a local public arts program)
- Develop cooperative relationships between public and private parking operations to promote efficient use of resources for large public events
- Develop a parking information database
- Use the billing system to distribute system info and promotional materials
- Utilize "guerilla marketing" techniques (creative/low-cost concepts)

16. Customer Service Programs

Downtown businesses depend on a parking system that works and contributes to an overall positive downtown experience. Because parking is the first and last impression customers visiting the downtown will have, providing a high level of customer service is critical. When weighing the importance of customer service, consider these statistics:

- An average business never hears from 96 percent of its unsatisfied customers.
- On average, for every complaint received, there are twenty-six customers with problems.
- The average unsatisfied customer tells nine to ten people about their problem.
- Customers who have had the problems solved tell, on average, five people.

A strong customer service program can provide the following benefits:

- Helps create a more "friendly" atmosphere
- Improves the image of the Parking Department and the downtown
- Contributes to increased facility utilization (and therefore revenue)
- Contributes to increased acceptance of, and adherence to, parking regulations

What are some characteristics of bad customer service?

- Indifference
- Unfriendliness
- Runaround
- "Joe Rule Book" (an employee who adheres exactly to the rules instead of offering customers some flexibility)
- Not listening
- Getting the brush-off
- Just going through the motions
- No follow-up

What are characteristics of good customer service?

- Being friendly and respectful
- Allowing customers to fully explain their situation, without interruption (let them vent)

- "Actively listen" to what your customers say
- Ask questions seeking clarification
- Maintain eye contact
- If the customer is making a complaint, always apologize for the situation (and mean it!)
- Explain what you *can* do for the customer, not what you can't
- Always remember that tone of voice and body language convey meaning
- Walk through the service process with the customer, explain the options
- Help the customer understand the options and achieve a level of buy-in
- Make sure they know you are there to help
- Always conclude a service opportunity with a "thank you"
- If possible, follow up with the customer to see if the solution worked and if they are satisfied

Other recommended strategies to improve customer service include:

- Focus on employee training and good hiring practices—hire friendly, attentive, outgoing, knowledgeable attendants
- Increase personal contact between the parking system manager, stake holders, and customers
- Institute performance measurements and utilize them for company and employee incentives
- Create and implement a parking services program (battery jumps, lockouts, flat tires, escorts, audio book checkout, etc.)
- Implement a "parking hotline"—(immediate response, centralized, easy to remember)
- Improve Web site and links (use as a customer service tool, pay fines, order information, such as downloadable maps, rate schedules, special event info, etc.)
- Measure program effectiveness (customer surveys, etc.)
- Implement a secret shopper program to evaluate customer service
- Develop a new employee parking brochure/information packet to make it easier for larger organizations to get their employees into the system

17. Special Events Parking

Coordinating parking for special events, almost more than any other parking management activity, requires a coordinated and cooperative effort with the larger community. Some of the keys to success in this area include the development of a well-defined special events policy and detailed system for coordination of special events.

Another important dimension is strong relationships with the key stakeholder groups that are active in the downtown. Providing practical incentives for city departments and other groups to communicate with the parking department in their planning processes early on is critical. Examples of the incentives parking can provide include special services such as: coordination services, parking validations, waiving of parking enforcement, etc., for those who participate in the special event planning process.

Finally, be consistent in providing a high level of service to those that work with the parking system. Conversely, provide disincentives for those that ignore the special events parking policy or chose to not include parking in their planning.

18. Effective Enforcement

Having an effective parking management program requires that the rules and regulations be enforced. The key to an effective parking enforcement program is attitude, consistency, and fairness. Best in Class operations have adopted the philosophy of being customer focused not revenue or violator focused.

The following are enforcement program elements to ensure that your program avoids some common pitfalls.

- Define who is responsible for day-to-day parking enforcement. Set up a central phone number that everyone knows to call for information regarding parking enforcement (eliminate the runaround).
- Ensure that parking rules, regulations, and consequences are clearly posted.
- If towing or booting is a possibility, be sure that the number to call for towed/booted vehicles is clearly posted.
- Define how enforcement revenues are to be collected and used.
- Define who sets enforcement policies.
- Have a clearly stated process for adjudicating parking citations.
- Define who has the authority for towing, booting, or other enforcement practices.
- Make paying for parking citations as easy as possible.
- Provide incentives for early citation payment and disincentives for late or nonpayment.

19. Parking and Transportation Demand Management

Because the cost of providing parking can be so high, strategies to manage parking demand are an important consideration in parking system planning. Incorporating parking and transportation demand management also ties into environmental goals and objectives such as the desire to reduce pollution, decrease traffic congestion, reduce reliance on single occupant vehicles, etc.

When evaluating options to reduce parking demand, integrate transportation demand management strategies into your parking program philosophy. A few best practices include:

- Use parking rates as a tool to promote desired behaviors.
- Take advantage of employer-paid and employee-paid pretax benefit options.
- Promote carpool/vanpool programs.
- Provide preferred parking for carpools/vanpools.
- Subsidize mass transit passes for downtown employees.
- Provide a "Guaranteed Ride Home" program for those who participate in alternative transportation programs.
- Integrate bicycle racks and storage lockers in parking facilities.
- Show transit stops on parking maps.
- Provide remote parking options and promote park and ride options on the parking Web site.

20. Awareness of Competitive Environment

Another characteristic of effective parking programs is that they are keenly aware of their competitive environment. They actively monitor private-sector parking operators for changes in rates, new services offered, new technologies being used, etc. One of the most fundamental practices that all parking programs should engage in is a formalized process for evaluating parking market rates. Parking market rate surveys should be conducted biannually to help maintain an awareness of the competitive climate. This information can also be valuable during annual budget planning.

Another dimension to staying competitive is being aware of what parking systems in other municipalities are doing. What has been tried? What has worked? What hasn't worked? Participating in state and regional parking associations, sending key staff to parking conferences, and implementing a peer-review process.

CASE EXAMPLES: EXCEPTIONAL PARKING PROGRAMS

Tempe, Arizona

The business improvement district known as Downtown Tempe Community, Inc. (DTC) manages the parking system in Tempe, Arizona. DTC has consolidated virtually all private parking in the downtown to be managed as a comprehensive parking system to meet the needs of downtown businesses and municipal buildings. The city owns no public parking structures. The DTC has succeeded in turning a collection of individually owned private parking lots and decks and city-owned on-street parking spaces into a cohesive and seamlessly run parking system, complete with a successful validation program common to all facilities and an integrated marking and promotional campaign.

The parking system has over 9,300 off-street parking spaces and over 600 metered spaces.

Of particular interest in Tempe is its experience with on-street parking system technologies. A few years ago DTC boldly launched a program to convert all on-street and many off-street parking lots to a pay-by-space system based on "multi-space meter technology." This technology, while much improved in recent years, is still considered fairly progressive and some would argue difficult to use and understand. Tempe did an excellent job of educating the public and marketing the new concept. Overall, the program worked well but always suffered from one major complaint—user inconvenience.

Tempe has recently made the decision to abandon multi-space meters in favor of dual-headed, single-space, electronic Duncan parking meters. The bottom-line advantage, according to DTC Executive Director Rod Keeling, is that everyone intuitively understands standard single-space parking meters, and the convenience to his customers cannot be matched by the multi-space meter technologies.

Boise, Idaho

The off-street parking component of the downtown public parking system in Boise, Idaho, is managed by the urban renewal agency known as the Capital City Development Corporation (CCDC). The on-street program is managed by the City of Boise. The CCDC has an impressive record, not only of spurring development in the downtown area, but also of using tax increment financing funds to develop well-planned and strategically located public parking facilities as an incentive to attract additional development. With over

5,000 structured parking spaces in the downtown core (75 percent of which are public facilities), downtown Boise has seen significant growth over the past decade.

The on-street program, which has over 1,100 metered parking spaces, recently upgraded its meters to new, electronic meters. These meters feature a twenty-minute "free" button and a smart-card payment option. On-street and off-street rates are calibrated to make long-term parking more attractive thereby promoting increased turnover and utilization of on-street spaces.

Although Boise has some of the cleanest and best-managed parking facilities, the CCDC is embarking on a new program to: enhance customer service programs, revise its parking validation program, upgrade parking system technology to improve management information, strengthen communications with key downtown stakeholders, and create a positive public information and marketing program.

A long-term challenge for the Boise parking system is to integrate the on-street and off-street parking programs.

Fort Collins, Colorado

Downtown, the heart and soul of Fort Collins, Colorado, is characterized by an abundance of locally owned retail shops, restaurants, and entertainment establishments. The availability of customer parking in downtown lies at the core of the mission of Fort Collins' Parking Services Division. The division aims to encourage turnover in a customer-friendly way.

With over 9,700 parking spaces, capacity is adequate for current needs. However, 68 percent of the spaces are off-street, and the majority of those are privately owned and underutilized. The city is actively working to implement a major recommendation of its downtown strategic plan that calls for enhanced public/private cooperation in the management of downtown parking.

Implementation of the new downtown strategic plan also calls for a focus on the pedestrian. Fort Collins will build an integrated program providing for parking needs on the periphery of the downtown's core, thus enhancing the pedestrian infrastructure, and providing a wayfinding system. This supports Fort Collins' efforts to promote a "Park Once, Pedestrian First" concept.

These strategies, among others, are expected to enhance and protect the economic vitality of a vibrant downtown. Long-range parking resources will be developed in conjunction with residential, office, and retail development as it occurs. The future is very bright for parking in downtown Fort Collins, Colorado.

SUMMARY

The importance of parking, one of the most visible and often controversial elements of a downtown's infrastructure, is often underestimated. Parking, when well managed, can be a key component in attracting and supporting new development and is essential to sustaining healthy and vibrant downtowns.

REFERENCE

Pine, Joseph, and James Gilmore (1999). *The Experience Economy: Work Is Theatre & Every Business a Stage.* Boston: Harvard Business School Press.

Chapter 24

Managing Downtown's Social Behavior

Elizabeth Jackson

INTRODUCTION: FURTHERING THE SOCIAL ENVIRONMENT OF DOWNTOWN

Downtowns regain or maintain their vibrancy by imbuing their districts with social activity. Parades, festivals, and sporting events create instant venues for sociability, but it is shopping, theater, dining, sightseeing, strolling, or lingering in a downtown square that provide the social fabric of the successful central business district.

At the same time, downtowns also provide refuge for homeless people. Downtowns are more likely than other areas to have nighttime shelter, indoor public space, free or minimal-cost food, emergency medical care, rest rooms, and shower and laundry facilities. These necessities are within reach of people who are homeless and have no access to private transportation. Because they have no housing, bathroom facilities, or employment, homeless people are certainly more likely than other city residents to panhandle, loiter, urinate or defecate in public. People who have serious mental illnesses or use alcohol and drugs are more likely than others to become homeless; and, therefore, some persons become intoxicated, use drugs, or, in some cases verbally abuse others on downtown streets.

These are behaviors that shoppers, employers, visitors, and residents find objectionable. This, in turn, affects the ability of downtown organizations to conduct business, attract and serve customers, or engage new investors. Therefore, successful downtown management organizations need to address the issue and devise strategies to reduce these behaviors. Downtown organizations have often responded by advocating laws and strict enforcement to prohibit loitering, panhandling, outdoor encampment, littering, sales and use of illegal or controlled drugs, and public urination and defecation. Many downtowns are adopting other strategies that have long-term possibilities of reducing incidences of objectionable behaviors.

doi:10.1300/5137_25

UNDERSTANDING THE PROBLEM

To address the problem, downtown management organizations must have a clear understanding of objectionable behavior and the characteristics of the people concerned. A downtown organization can collect, over a relatively brief period, data on the type, frequency, and locations of the behaviors of concern, and match them to the number and characteristics of the people who behave in these ways. This information will inform downtown organizations how much of the problematic behaviors are caused by homeless people and whether these persons have a serious mental illness or substance abuse problem. The data will also establish a baseline for a strategy and assess its effectiveness.

TOOLS OF RESPONSE

Enforcement, Adjudication, and Incarceration Strategies

Most communities have local ordinances to deal with one or more problematic behaviors. Although laws prohibiting loitering, panhandling, outdoor encampment, littering, sales and use of illegal or controlled drugs, and public urination and defecation exist, their effectiveness is completely dependent on the ability to enforce them.

Though this strategy may have immediate impact, in many cases, that impact may be short-lived. Many jurisdictions have vacated their loitering laws because of successful constitutional challenges. Severe backlogs in district courts and local jails in other jurisdictions have discouraged police officers from making arrests related to "quality-of-life" infractions. When presented with the option, local law enforcement prefers to focus its attention on making drug-related and solicitation arrests, for which the chances of prosecution, conviction, and incarceration are better. Furthermore, persons arrested are back on the streets after a relatively brief time in local jails.

Community Courts

Several cities are doing more to enforce quality-of-life ordinances—and aid those on the street in need—by creating what are called community courts. A community court is an official division of the local district court system set up to deal only with misdemeanors and petty crimes and authorized to issue alternative sentencing after conviction. Alternative sentences can include court-ordered community service, mental health treatment, and/or drug and alcohol rehabilitation. Community courts work closely with downtown management organizations, outreach networks, clinical service providers, and rehabilitation services to make sure that services can begin immediately after legal proceedings. Another variation, with the same intent, but without the necessity of sentencing, is pretrial or presentencing diversion.

Community courts may be effective in providing persons with treatment that they may otherwise not seek. They may also provide homeless persons with the housing and services they need, may have sought, but have not received. Possibly the largest obstacle to reducing incidences in downtown resulting from the behavior of homeless people is the lack of housing and needed services. Housing and services, perennially in short supply, have recently been cut drastically by states and localities facing severe budget shortfalls. Community courts cannot solve the problem of downtown homelessness, but they may help persons who are homeless and whose behavior may be of most concern to downtowns.

Human Services Strategies

Homelessness is an economic and social issue of national proportions that particularly affects downtowns. Reducing homelessness and related behaviors are not assignments solely for downtown organizations; but, downtown organizations can ensure that public and private resources are directed to homelessness and focused on downtowns.

To do so, downtown organizations need to form partnerships and coalitions with other organizations that support, influence, and provide, needed housing, services, and income supports. Many public and private organizations, acting separately, may each address a small part of the myriad of basic needs, but, each has a different purpose, usually not focused specifically on homelessness. The result is a set of services—complex, underfunded, and fragmented.

The purpose of partnerships is to provide or obtain services, income supports, and housing. Initially, such collaborations often begin with the most visible and immediate need—outreach service programs. Housing and employment efforts often come later—once the partnership is solidified, credibility is established, and the partnership's leaders commit to longer-term initiatives.

Several rules of thumb may be important in addressing homelessness through a human services partnership approach:

1. An expectation that human services will eliminate homelessness and related behavioral incidences is not realistic, or required, in order for a

downtown organization to adopt a human services strategy. Adopting a human services strategy is a wise choice if its benefits (a reduction in behavioral incidences) exceed costs or a target level.

2. Downtown organizations and collaborating human service organizations serving homeless people will likely have differing motives for addressing homelessness; it is expected and appropriate. Similarity of motives is not a prerequisite for a successful partnership.

3. Accountability is an important component for selecting a human services strategy and partner. The partners need to set objectives and outcomes and collect data to assess results.

4. Downtown organizations are not expected to, and need not, spend significant organizational funds to address homelessness. Access to decision makers, support, and modest, but flexible, funding for emergency service needs, are valued and appropriate contributions.

Partnerships have addressed the array of human services, most particularly outreach and networking, shelter and supportive services, and long-term assistance. Shelters are not enough: to reach the chronic homeless, partnerships must create a continuum of care including steps to obtain shelter, services, and eventual independent living. In addition to ensuring direct services to homeless people, downtowns can further partnership goals by providing skills and assets in communications.

Outreach and Networking

Coordinating and extending outreach. Many agencies and organizations are out on the street attempting to help. Downtown organizations should seek partnerships with agencies that have experienced outreach workers, with good connections to social services, mental health and employment resources. The most effective outreach is provided by *coordinated* teams that are multidisciplinary and professional, ensuring that the team can assess and address a person's needs and help him or her receive care from existing service providers.

Programs such as the Times Square Consortium's Mobile Treatment Teams and the San Diego Homeless Outreach Team employ this on-the-street, multidisciplinary approach. Others, such as the Homeless Coalition of the Gulf Coast, convene service agencies on a regular basis to streamline existing outreach, avoid service duplications, and promote the availability of help to the business community, the media, and the general public.

Improving outreach hotlines. Downtown business owners, customers, and employees often feel powerless in the face of homelessness. Establishing and promoting the presence of dial-in hotlines is one way of engaging the community in reducing homelessness without resorting to 911 calls, police complaints, citations, or arrests. Downtown organizations can be particularly valuable in helping to create and then promote the existence of hotlines.

Portland, Oregon's, Project Respond provides a call-in hotline that is widely promoted by the business community. The Downtown Phoenix Partnership's goodwill ambassadors promote the use of the city's twenty-four-hour call center by distributing information to the people they get to know on their rounds: downtown shoppers, visitors, business owners, and the people hanging out on the street. Likewise, the Downtown Cleveland Partnership promotes the community's "care line"—a phone number that alerts the police and the Salvation Army's three service providers to send an outreach team to the person in need.

Shelter and Supportive Services

For people living on the street, finding shelter is a constant worry. With shelter, most people can then consider the next steps toward recovery. Yet for a minority of the homeless population, other means of contact are required before they can move toward shelter and beyond.

Emergency shelters. Virtually every American city has one or more shelters serving homeless people, many of them located in or near downtown. Shelters help to reduce the number of people sleeping on the streets, in vestibules, or under overpasses, thereby aiding in the goal of improving the quality of the public realm. Downtown business organizations can work to improve shelter conditions, provide ambassadors or cleaning staff to maintain the area surrounding the shelter, and promote the availability of emergency shelter housing to the people in need, as well as the general public.

Drop-in centers. Drop-in centers are a critical component of a system of care for people living on the street. Centers often serve as the first point of entry for providing services and can be the first step in a process of recovery that can return the individual to a safe, productive life. Finally, drop-in centers provide a daytime alternative to living on the street that nighttime shelters do not.

Many downtown business leaders have been reluctant to support drop-in centers, fearing that such facilities will only attract more people from around the region. Those downtown organizations that *have* participated in creating drop-in centers have learned that such centers help to reduce incidences of behavior, address pressing medical and social needs, and demonstrate to the community that something is being done to help.

The Downtown Services Center (DSC) in Washington, DC, is an example of a successful day center. Located in a downtown church with an existing meals program, the Downtown DC Business Improvement District renovated the property and provides management for the twenty human services partners that were invited to bring "satellite" operations to the center. In addition to two meal programs, the DSC offers shower and laundry facilities, a weekly medical clinic, mental health outreach, and help with Social Security and Veterans' benefits.

Long-Term Assistance

Providing shelter and access to needed services is only part of the solution to getting people off the streets and into productive life. Once homeless people avail themselves of these services, they need access to housing, job preparation assistance, and even employment placement.

Creating job training and placement programs. Many individuals living on the streets of downtown have work experience and can, with help, re-enter the workforce. For example, people who have serious mental illnesses can be helped to receive treatment, training, if needed, and be placed in jobs that fit their needs and skills. Downtown organizations are well suited to help, by providing venues and faculty for training programs, coordinate job placement, and even provide jobs within their own operations.

The Downtown Services Center (DCS) in Washington, DC, offers employment assistance to its clientele, with an average of ten people finding permanent employment each month. Several other downtown organizations directly employ people who are formerly homeless and who have completed substance abuse rehabilitation, or are under treatment for their mental illness, including the Downtown Seattle Association, the Association for Portland Progress (now part of Portland Business Alliance), and the Times Square Consortium.

Developing transitional and supportive housing. Transitional housing with support services is often useful in moving people out of the shelter system and on their way to complete independence. Supportive housing is even more essential to those persons transitioning from homelessness and struggling with severe and persistent mental illness. These individuals may never live completely independent lives and may always need housing options that provide case management, health care, and other social services.

As with drop-in centers, there is concern that supportive housing will impede other economic development initiatives of the district, particularly market-rate housing development. Yet downtown management organizations are coming to the table to support well-designed and sited transitional housing by offering real estate development expertise and private-sector advocacy.

Central Houston, Inc. has contributed both influence and funds for additional, single-room occupancy housing with support services. The Downtown Lexington Corporation (DLC) in Lexington, Kentucky, supported the development of the faith-based St. James' Place, a 100-unit single-room occupancy with support services, by helping navigate through potential opposition from neighborhood groups and individual businesses.

COMMUNICATION

Gaining support for partnerships—and keeping or *expanding* that support—is accomplished through effective communication. Downtown management organizations excel in communication, given their depth of expertise in public relations, marketing, and media relations. Among the communications tools used are the following:

- Directories of services, distributed to downtown employers, employees, shoppers, and visitors.
- Detailed homeless-outreach guidebooks, distributed to office building concierges, libraries, shopping center managers, and others, to provide detailed how-to information when interacting with unruly or homeless people in front of their facilities.
- Feature article placements and other media coverage designed to educate the public about avoiding panhandling and offering information about alternative ways to help.
- Coverage of the outcomes of the partnership through the downtown organization's annual reports, periodic newsletters, Web sites, and annual general meetings.

Internal communications are every bit as critical. Homeless partnerships are complicated and somewhat fragile, given the differing motives of their members. Keeping the partners "in play" requires the following:

- The leadership should meet, at least quarterly, to discuss program outcomes and policy needs. If there is significant opposition to elements of the program, the leadership needs to devise the appropriate response. If dissension appears within the rank and file of the partnership staff, leadership has to negotiate the resolution.
- Frontline staff should meet regularly, weekly if necessary, to discuss specific issues arising from the services. At least quarterly, the staff

should get together to review program effectiveness and make recommendations to leadership about program changes or new program development.

- Once a year, both staff and leadership should conduct an intensive planning session, e.g., a retreat, to look at the "big picture" and set specific goals for the coming year.
- E-mail LISTSERVs or password-protected access to private pages on the partners' Web site. This will help foster real-time communication between the staff, and will give the leadership the chance to check in on the dialogue from time to time.

PICKING YOUR PARTNERS

Many groups and institutions play a role in improving social behavior and connecting people to the help they need. Partners must understand the values and motivations, the services offered, and the potential brought by each group to the overall effort. Most of the following agencies and organizations exist in every community and have a role to play in the solution to inappropriate public behavior.

Public Agencies

Publicly funded and positioned within the local government structure, public agencies are charged with providing public health, mental health, homeless outreach, shelter, and emergency services to the greatest number of qualified individuals. These agencies are sometimes grant makers themselves, establishing requirements and monitoring nonprofit caregivers. These organizations provide potential partnerships with not only expertise, but also connections to the public-sector environment of policymaking, budget development, regulation, and program evaluation.

The City or County Police Department

Charged with maintaining the peace and promoting the health, safety, and welfare of the community, local police forces are often the first to intervene with people misbehaving on the streets. Many police officers have established relationships with individuals who are homeless and know the circumstances of their homelessness. Likewise, the police are aware of which members of the street population are *not* homeless, but are simply panhandling, trafficking in or using drugs, or otherwise engaging in illegal behavior. In short, the police are perhaps the most informed about who is truly in need and who is simply preying upon the homeless community, or using them to conduct petty crimes of opportunity. As part of a partnership, they can assist by separating the petty criminals from the truly needy individuals and help direct those in need to the help provided by the partners.

Nonprofit Agencies

Nonprofit organizations provide much of the assistance to persons experiencing homelessness and suffering from mental illness, substance abuse, and other disabilities. They are passionate about their work and, because of chronic funding challenges, are constantly on the lookout for opportunities to improve and extend their reach. Competition for funding among agencies is common, but generally speaking, nonprofit organizations communicate freely and attempt to help one another out when they can. Unfortunately, nonprofit organizations often see the business sector as prime advocates for arrest-and-detention strategies that hurt rather than help individuals struggling with homelessness.

The Faith Community

Congregations of virtually every faith have, for years, plugged holes in the safety net for individuals suffering from homelessness. By creating *social ministries,* faith organizations provide shelter, food, clothing, health care, daycare, job training, and counseling to persons in need. As part of a cooperative partnership, the faith community can provide direct access to the general public—the people who attend their churches, synagogues, and mosques—and help build broad-based support for coordinated outreach.

Advocates

Advocates for homeless persons include a wide array of organizations that in most cases include human service agencies, including governmental organizations. Downtown organizations can, and should, join and be an influential partner in any such coalition. Some advocates will likely be organizations that emphasize a constitutionally protected right of homeless people to association, assembly, and speech. They may assert that people living on the streets, including people who loiter or panhandle, have a right to remain there, and that government or society has no legal basis to remove people from the street or provide treatment. It is both challenging and useful for downtown organizations to communicate with such organizations; in some cases, these organizations and downtown organizations can reach mutually acceptable understandings of acceptable and enforceable behaviors.

The Media

Local radio, television, newspapers, and Internet news services can be formidable allies in eliminating homelessness and addressing street behavior. They are certainly interested in the issues surrounding homelessness and occasionally explore the circumstances of individuals living without shelter. As partners, the media could significantly advance the level of understanding in the general population, and could help raise awareness, support, and even funding for the projects of the partnership.

Of course, there may be other partners in your community, and the partners listed may or may not behave in the ways described. The point is that *partnerships must develop a mission and program of service that give each participating organization a connection between their work in the partnership and their goals within their own operation.*

BUILDING PARTNERSHIPS

Simply put, for partnerships to succeed, the partners must *meet.* Initial meetings set the tone for the relationships and help protect against future misunderstandings. Downtown organizations often initiate the partnerships because they seek the expertise, or need access to the services, or desire to better understand the issues surrounding homelessness. The initial few meetings should accomplish the following goals:

- Focus the on identifying and endorsing *shared* interests.
- Identify current activities, client populations, and missed opportunities.
- Unearth, address, and dispense with old antagonisms and misunderstandings.
- Describe the current funding environment in order to get beyond any perceived competition for resources.
- Prioritize ways to team up to extend current programming and address missed opportunities.

These are not small tasks. Coalitions require the involvement of more than one service organization and may involve more than one business group. If past relationships have been particularly tense, initial meetings may need to be facilitated by a mutually respected third party—the mayor, a popular opinion leader, someone from the faith community—willing to serve as a *neutral party*. Meetings should elicit discussion from all the participants, and control those who may attempt to dominate or derail the effort.

Structuring the Partnership

Successful partnerships require a management structure that accomplishes the following:

- Establishes agreed-upon goals.
- Supports the delivery of services.
- Develops active internal and external communication.
- Anticipates and overcomes obstacles.
- Secures needed resources.
- Encourages innovation and continuous improvements.
- Maintains collegial relationships between the partner organizations.

The *structure* of the coalition can take on any number of forms. The three most common are described as follows.

1. *The organization is led by one of the partners*—This format is employed when one of the partners is seen as providing the most capacity to support the partnership. Capacity is often measured by the partner's depth of staff and funding resources, its relationships with external decision makers, and the level of trust it has with the members of the partnership. In Washington, DC, for example, the Downtown DC Business Improvement District serves as the management entity for the Downtown Services Center—a one-stop shop providing everything from meal programs, to health care, to employment services, and laundry and shower facilities. In addition, the DC BID runs its own outreach program and provides business-based advocacy for citywide policy and program improvements. In 2002, the DC BID set aside 5 percent of its multimillion dollar budget for homeless services programming; in 2005, that amount increased to 6 percent of an overall budget that was over $9 million.
2. *Partners share tasks but maintain separate management*—Many partnerships choose to remain separate, but with parallel management structures for their shared programs. The reasons can be many. Sources of funding may not allow for blending resources or setting up a third-party management structure; the nature of the work being

created does not warrant a new management system; and/or the initial levels of trust between the partners makes keeping the management in-house more comfortable. Dozens of communities employ this approach. Baltimore, San Diego, Philadelphia, and Portland partners simply modify their current operations to maximize the potential that comes with working together.

3. *Newly formed organizations*—Some downtown and social services agencies have found it advantageous to establish entirely new organizations to manage the work of the partnership. In some instances, such as Times Square in New York City, the conditions were so severe and the relationships so new, it made sense to create a new organization as "neutral turf," through which each of the representative organizations could build their relationships. In other areas, like Mobile, Alabama, the faith-based organizations lacked the infrastructure to support the new partnership. They saw the creation of the Homeless Coalition of the Gulf Coast as a way to knit together existing social service programs, government resources, and the interests of the business community, and demonstrate to the public that they were serious about addressing the needs of individuals and families living without shelter.

MEASURING SUCCESS

Because of the highly visible nature of street behavior—and the backlash that is generated when people attempt to minimize behavioral incidents—it is critical that these coalitions track the outcomes of their efforts. Downtown management organizations are very familiar with establishing benchmarks for effectiveness and then reporting outcomes. Likewise, social service providers keep statistics about the effectiveness of their programs. The challenge is to establish benchmarks and standards of measurement that meet the goals of both the business community and the service-related partners.

Establishing Benchmarks

A benchmark is simply the baseline from which progress is measured. Solid information on number, type, location, and time of each behavioral incident in a one-month interval, for example, is a starting point. Each of these incidences can then be matched with the characteristics (but not the name) of the person—whether he or she is homeless, his or her age, shelter use, serious mental illness, or substance abuse. These data empower the partnership to redirect resources to more important initiatives, create entirely new initiatives, and/or advocate for policy changes. In short, the benchmarks should drive program development and partnership formation.

Standards of Measurement

With benchmarks established, partners identified, and programs of work designed, coalition members must create objective standards to measure progress. Here, the goals of the individual members of the partnership can complicate the process. For example, the business community may expect to see a net reduction in the number of homeless people within a specified period of time, while social service providers may see an increase in the number of people using services—regardless of their homeless status—as a completely legitimate standard of measurement. Meal providers may see an increase in the number of people seeking food as a measure of success— more people are coming in off the streets, eating, and moving closer to other forms of help—while public sector leaders and business interests may see that as evidence of a problem that is escalating. Given the tenuous nature of the partnership, time and effort must be made to (1) identify all of the partners' measures of success, (2) negotiate a core of commonly held measures, and (3) gain consensus on the expected outcomes. Beyond this core set of endorsed standards of measurement, each partner organization is free to establish its own additional means to define progress.

Reporting Outcomes

All the hard work of establishing benchmarks and agreeing to a core set of measurements is lost if the coalition does not commit to a system of reporting outcomes. The nature of the programs will largely dictate the process for reporting progress. For instance, if one of the projects is to create multidisciplinary homeless outreach teams, standards of measurement may be (1) to increase the number of street contacts made, (2) to increase the number of contacts that result in clinical, shelter, or job placement assistance, and (3) to move a certain number of homeless individuals into permanent housing. Given the three discreet measures, reporting should be quarterly for the first measurement, twice annually for the second, and annually for the third.

Again, all partners should be involved in creating the reporting schedule and methods of communication. The downtown organization, however, is typically equipped with communications staff, media contacts, and communications instruments (Web site, newsletter, annual report, etc.) and can, as its contribution to the partnership, take on a greater role in the reporting functions.

CONCLUSION

No single organization—no single partnership for that matter—will eradicate homelessness and problematic street behavior. Yet partnerships that include the business community have certain advantages.

First, the downtown business sector has a perspective on the impacts of homelessness that most social services organizations do not. Those impacts are not only economic, but social as well. If citizens avoid downtown because of the persistent presence of homeless people, then part of the social safety net for homeless people is threatened. The economic health of the downtown district will impact the business community's ability to support those who support the homeless.

Second, downtown organizations have resources, particularly staff talent, that can extend the reach of social service programs. With coordination and training from the social service partners, downtown staff resources can provide additional on-the-street outreach. With a framework for communication, the downtown staff can assist with critical data gathering, analysis, and reporting.

Third, downtown organizations have proven themselves very effective in advocating for additional resources. Typically, downtown associations seek to use their influence to move the social service agenda forward. In recent times, they have also helped to build support for capital investments, such as the development of drop-in centers and transitional and supportive housing.

Fourth, downtown management organizations have established public relations, information management, and media programs, all of which can be used to educate the community on the realities of homelessness and promote the results of the partnership which include more people living on the streets being reached and connected to services and reintroduced into productive society.

Finally, business leaders have years of experience in building coalitions, heading off conflict, and building on mutual goals. They often have the ear of policymakers that the social services community may not. They can marshal support from the private sector when needs or opportunities arise.

Conversely, downtown organizations are very clear about the benefits of partnering with the social services community. Clinical expertise, experience with homeless people on the streets and in shelters, data gathering and reporting experience, and access to a different set of constituent groups all make social service partners indispensable to the business sector's homeless efforts.

What is *really* required to bring these divergent interest groups together is an agreement that homelessness is an unacceptable condition in our wealthy, democratic society; that every interest group has a right to its own motivations; and that strategies can be devised to employ each partners' resources, address each partners' needs, and contribute to the ultimate goal.

USEFUL RESOURCES

Following are additional resources for information on successful downtown partnerships.

National Organizations and Agencies

- International Downtown Association (IDA), ida-downtown.org. For a PDF version of the IDA publication *Addressing Homelessness: Successful Downtown Partnership,* go to the IDA Web site and then click on "Publications." *Addressing Homelessness* is available free of charge and can be downloaded in PDF format from the Web site.
- Corporation for Supportive Housing; www.csh.org.
- National Coalition for Homeless Veterans; www.nchv.org.
- Interagency Council on Homelessness; www.ich.gov.
- National Alliance on Mental Illness, www.nami.org.
- National Alliance to End Homelessness; www.naeh.org.
- Policy Research Associates; www.prainc.com.
- Projects for Assistance in Transition from Homelessness (PATH); www.pathprogram.samhsa.gov.

Local Programs

- Downtown DC Business Improvement District; www.downtowndc.org/DevInit/Homeless/services.html.
- Downtown Partnership of Baltimore; www.godowntownbaltimore.com.
- Times Square Alliance; www.timessquarenyc.org.
- Downtown San Diego Partnership; www.downtownsandiego.org.
- Homeless Coalition of the Gulf Coast.
- Portland Business Alliance; www.portlandalliance.com.

- Downtown Phoenix Partnership; www.coppersquare.com.
- Downtown Cleveland Partnership; www.downtownclevelandpartner
  ship.com.
- Downtown Seattle Association; www.downtownseattle.org.
- Central Houston, Inc.; www.centralhouston.org.
- Downtown Lexington Corporation; www.downtownlex.com.

Chapter 25

Getting the Right Consultant
for the Right Job

Richard Marshall

The success of development and redevelopment projects is determined by many factors—the vagaries of political will, the economics of place, and community opinion, amongst a host of other things. For many business improvement districts (BIDs) getting involved in these projects for the first time is a daunting undertaking. There are aspects of projects in which staff simply lack experience, and, consequently, they may mistakenly believe that hiring design and planning consultants, for example, will automatically solve their problems. This is not necessarily the case. The success of any project depends on the selection of the right consultant for the right job.

This chapter sets out a road map of steps and considerations that city managers and BID staff could follow to select an appropriate design or planning consultant. The one fundamental factor that any client should consider is the qualifications of the firm for the specific project to be undertaken. The question remains: How can one match the best qualifications for the best project and be sure that the consultants hired are the right ones for the job? The answer lies in the first step of the selection process, which is clearly determining the goals for your project.

SETTING GOALS FOR THE PROJECT

Consultants get jobs through a variety of means. They get work from repeat clients; they respond to requests for proposals (RFPs) and submit statements of qualifications (SOQs); they win work through referrals; and occasionally they win work simply by meeting people at dinner parties. Generally, the larger the project, the more formal the procurement process is. For government agencies, accountable to the people they serve, the need for clearly articulated selection criteria is critical. The RFP process, when done well, provides a level of confidence for the client, the consultant, and

doi:10.1300/5137_26

the public that the selection process is fair and that the best team has been hired for the project. First, however, clients must clearly articulate the objectives, set a deadline for when the work must be completed, and establish what is expected from the consultants.

After determining the objectives of the project, the clients will be in a far better position to determine if they need an urban designer, an urban planner, an architect, a landscape architect, an engineer, an economist, an environmental consultant, a public outreach consultant, or some combination of these. For larger redevelopment projects, several entities may need to come together to determine the objectives and to scope out the project. These entities might include the mayor's office, the planning office, the redevelopment agency, the BID, other public/private agencies or the public works office, etc. Not only does this allow others to help determine what might be needed for any particular effort, it also reduces parallel and conflicting efforts that might be going on in other departments or agencies. This joint session (or sessions) should establish a clear set of goals and a clear scope of work for the future consultants. It should also establish the evaluation criteria by which the consultants will be judged.

Another player in setting goals and objectives should be the public. Involving the public requires that departments or agencies organize scoping meetings to establish a mechanism for public input. This might take the form of a series of public meetings or the creation of a public advisory committee. Essential to the long-term success of any project is the public's inclusion in the goals process. In addition to determining the overall goals for the project, it is essential to include the public in the development of the evaluation criteria. For contentious projects, there should be no ambiguity as to the objectives of the project and the process by which the consultants will be chosen.

ISSUING THE REQUEST FOR PROPOSAL

Once the agencies and the public have had input into the objectives, critical issues, and the program of the project, and the evaluation criteria for the consultants have been established, the RFP can be issued. The RFP should include a detailed format and time frame for the consultants' responses. From a consultant's perspective the best RFPs are those that clearly define the objectives, the program, the process, and the deliverables for the project as well as the evaluation criteria for selection. Consultants will then determine if they are able to comply with the expectations of the client. They will carefully develop their approach to the project and their teaming strategies based upon what they see in the RFP. For large or complicated projects consultants will often team together to provide a range of services with one consultant taking the lead.

REVIEWING THE SUBMISSIONS
AND INTERVIEWING THE CONSULTANTS

The review of the submissions should be done by a panel of individuals drawn from a range of departments or agencies. Evaluations of the proposals should be carefully based on the evaluation criteria established in the RFP. Time should be allowed for this process, but the ultimate goal is to narrow the field of qualified firms to a "short list" of three to five firms to be interviewed.

Once a short list has been established, interviews are conducted and the short-listed firms are ranked. The number of short-listed firms will depend on the size of the project. Between three and five consultants are normally asked to come to the interview, and the interviews usually occur over one or two days so that each of the interviews can be compared and ranked. A set of questions should be prepared by the selection committee based upon the critical issues of the project and the responses submitted. The consultant teams should be asked to give a brief presentation at the start of the interview.

Several things should be taken into consideration during the interviews. How well does the consultant communicate his or her ideas? This will be very important for public presentations. Does the consultant display evidence of creative thinking? Will the consultant be able to creatively solve problems? Does the consultant bring value to the project? Does the consultant have a balance of local experience and experience from other locations? Do the areas of expertise being presented match the services required to deal with the issues and objectives of the project? In addition, the client should seek to determine a comfort level with the consultant.

Clients of any kind have to understand that they are entering into a long and sometimes difficult partnership with their consultants. A partnership based upon mutual respect is preferable to a relationship in which the consultant thinks the client has no value to bring to the project *and* preferable to one in which the consultant expects to be given all the answers. The best relationship is one in which each member of the project team feels comfortable with and values the input of the other. The interview process should establish a level of expectation from the relationship. The more comfortable a client is with their consultants, and vice versa, the better the project will be.

Get a very clear understanding of whether or not the consultants present at the interview are those that will actually do the job. Too often, consultants have an "interview team" that is different from the "project team." This is particularly true for the principals of the firms. How often will you see them? What is their specific role? Make sure that the people with whom you develop a relationship in the interview process will actually be the people who will be doing the work.

MAKING THE DECISION

The decision of which consultant to choose should be based on the qualifications and capabilities presented by the consultants and how well they match the services required to deal with the issues and objectives of the project. It should also be based on the results of the interviews and the level of comfort the clients have with each consultant. Once the clients are happy with their choice of consultant, they should then enter into a negotiation with the top-ranking consultant about fees, program, and scope. At this point, very clear expectations should be established. For the ultimate success of the project, a partnership needs to be established between the client and the consultant.

DOING THE WORK

A good working partnership is based upon clear communication and valuing one another's contribution. For this to be successful, the client's project manager needs to be present at important team meetings to ensure that the decisions upon which the consultant is acting are correct. This is not to say that the project manager should be present for every consultant work session. Consultants do need some time alone to discuss and test ideas that the project manager may feel are "off track," but these are an essential part of a creative process. However, the consultant should never meet with policymakers or the public (or the press!) if the project manager is not there. This is important for the political aspects of development projects. After all, it is the client who is ultimately responsible for the project, not the consultant. A clear understanding of client "boundaries" will mean that the project will move forward smoothly.

CONCLUSION

Engaging the right consultant for the right task is really the last act of a process of determining what the objectives of any project are. Clearly articulated objectives mean well-established expectations. Consultants hate to get involved in projects in which the expectations are unclear. Some projects require a more fluid set of definitions, but as long as everyone appreciates this fluidity the project team can move along. Consultants work for a living, and the old anecdote that "time is money" is the very basis of the consulting game. Fee proposals are based upon an estimation of delivering a set of services and products within a determined time frame. If the time frame extends or the deliverables change, the consultant's formula of time and money will be upset. Consultants love certainty and only embrace change if there is an associated adjustment to their fees. Understanding the motivation of your consultants will give you a far better relationship with them. (Paying invoices in a timely manner is probably good for the relationship, too.)

Part VI:
Discovering Downtown's Development Secrets

Downtowns and business districts are as much about the soul of a community as they are about bricks and mortar or dollars and sense. Yet without the buildings and the businesses that make up downtown, there would be no heart and no soul. Therefore, it is imperative that downtown managers understand how economic and physical development work. Equally important is knowing how to work with developers, lenders, construction companies, retailers, and other business owners on the private side, and with city planning and economic development staff on the public side. This section provides a primer for the novice and more sophisticated analysis for the experienced downtown manager.

Chapter 26

Economic Development for BIDs

Gary Ferguson

A DEFINITION OF ECONOMIC DEVELOPMENT

From their earliest beginnings, communities across the United States have embraced a straightforward definition of economic development that centered on growth. The civic goal of young American communities was to grow. Growth associations became standard community initiatives. Yet few parameters were established for growth. For a growing America, the prevailing mantra for cities was "bigger is better."

Growth typically had three components: jobs, investment, and tax base. Growing cities needed jobs for their residents. Success could be measured in the dollars and cents actually invested into projects. Public officials were particularly eager to reap the new tax benefits accruing from the new investments and jobs.

As American cities matured, traditional growth measures became less relevant. Growth of a metropolitan area did not necessarily translate into prosperity for the central city. Edge-city development competed for the very tax base sought by the central city, luring away talent and resources while leaving behind the costly task of caring for the less fortunate and less mobile. Even when jobs were located within the central city, they did not necessarily embody the full measure of a successful city. In a commuter age, living in a central city was no longer necessary. Cities, particularly their downtown centers, have been forced to consider wider ranging definitions of community betterment. Making a city a better place for people to want to live became as important, if not more significant, than simply seeking job growth.

A more contemporary definition of economic development focuses on guiding and directing growth to achieve a desirable quality of life. Under this definition, no single factor dominates. Safety can be a measure of success. So too could be the quality of schools. Culture, arts, and a downtown

doi:10.1300/5137_27

with a sense of character and identity could all factor into a definition of quality. Communities may also define quality of life in their own style.

DOWNTOWNS AND ECONOMIC DEVELOPMENT POLICY

BIDs have been late to embrace economic development as a core element of their work. In many communities the task of economic development was delegated to a community-wide or regional organization charged with job and tax-base growth. Whether that organization was a chamber of commerce, growth association, city agency, or independent economic development entity, it usually had little in common with downtown organizations such as BIDs. Base-job creation was industrial in nature and occurred in business parks at the periphery of town where land was inexpensive and construction costs for horizontal low-rise structures was low. (Base jobs are considered primary, wealth-creating positions that create the need for supporting goods and services. Base jobs encourage related, spin-off, and multiplier vendor, retail, and service-sector jobs.) The complex mix of programs undertaken by downtown programs simply did not seem to fit the commonly held mold of economic development activity.

For many BIDs and downtown programs, it has been a challenge to be included at the community economic development table. Inclusion carries important benefits. It signifies that the community has embraced a broader definition of economic development that acknowledges urban quality-of-life issues. Inclusion opens the door to corporate and public resources that otherwise may be targeted solely to industrial development. It also positions downtown to be a player in the very competitive arena for jobs and investment.

POINTS OF DIVERGENCE AND CONVERGENCE

Downtowns and their BIDs routinely confront differences between the traditional industrial development model and a much broader downtown interpretation of economic development. Among the items that cause confusion and angst are:

- *Mixed-use projects:* Industrial projects are single use in nature. Mixed-use urban projects that blend office, retail, housing, and possibly entertainment do not readily fit job creation formulas, defy normal single-purpose financing, and are typically not eligible for traditional financial incentives.

- *The presence of retail:* Retail is usually viewed by traditional industrial development practitioners as soft. Retail jobs are not considered base jobs. They exist only because *there are* base jobs. Retailers compete against one another within the marketplace, making it difficult or even impossible to offer incentives for new businesses.
- *Housing:* Residential development seems to have nothing in common with industrial development. In fact, traditional economic development experts generally regard housing development as another consequence of base-job creation.
- *The relevance of location:* To geographically defined organizations such as BIDs, location matters. Critical mass and synergistic relationships are important. One block may determine the success or failure of a project to a district. Industrial developers have less affinity toward location. Instead, they seek to satisfy the needs and specifications of targeted businesses, often irrespective of their location within the market. The rewards are the jobs and the tax revenue. Exact location is less important.

Despite these differences, a growing number of downtown programs have found ways to affiliate and link with traditional industrial development organizations. Just as there are items of divergence to overcome, so too are there points of convergence to nurture. These include:

- *Office jobs:* The office sector provides a powerful engine for local economies. Often taken for granted, office jobs can provide a wide range of salaries, including many of the region's highest-wage positions. Office jobs can also have longevity and provide for career advancement. They meet most, if not all of the criteria set by industrial developers for quality jobs.
- *Technology jobs:* Downtowns have proven to be excellent environments for technology based jobs. Entrepreneurs and the people who work for them have shown a preference for creative, dynamic environments provided by downtowns. Technology jobs count in the eyes of traditional industrial developers.
- *Back-office jobs:* Back-office operations offer the potential for large volumes of jobs. Although wage rates tend to be modest, the reward of many positions tends to overshadow resistance to low wages. Once again, traditional industrial developers seem to identify with back-office industries.
- *Serving low- and moderate-income persons:* Many federal economic and community development funds require targeting low- and

moderate-income persons. Downtowns have unique advantages for serving these populations that suburban or greenfield locations do not have. Public transportation systems typically have hubs in downtowns, making them readily accessible to low- and moderate-income workers. These same workers may struggle to access jobs located at the periphery of the community.

THE ROLE OF BIDS IN ECONOMIC DEVELOPMENT

BIDs must make two basic decisions pertaining to economic development. First and foremost, they must decide to become engaged in the local economic development process or skip economic development intervention altogether. If a BID decides to tackle economic development, there is a subsequent decision: What will be the scope and level of its intervention?

Economies and markets can be left to run on their own. BIDs can choose to focus on noneconomic factors, e.g., improving the physical environment, and hence set the stage for investment activity. However, many BIDs discovered that just because their programs were silent and "hands off" in regard to the marketplace, other interests in the region were not. Government policies and decisions regularly affect the marketplace. The actions of private developers and leasing agents representing other competing commercial areas affect the marketplace. Even if a BID chooses not to engage in recruitment and retention activities, other competing entities may and probably are at work wooing businesses away from their district.

Markets are not static; they are remarkably dynamic organisms. At a given moment any number of forces are at work shaping and influencing the direction of the marketplace. Competing commercial properties routinely vie for prospects. New properties are introduced and must seek occupants. Perceptions of investment opportunities throughout a metropolitan area shift with the introduction of new projects, new governmental policies, and public opinion. Deciding to remain aloof from the economic process allows the forces of the marketplace to solely shape the future of the BID. Many BIDs have come to the conclusion that some intervention, even if it is limited in scope, is better than taking a chance on the roulette wheel of the marketplace.

ECONOMIC DEVELOPMENT INTERVENTION

BIDs approach economic development strategies from different starting points. Some districts have robust marketplaces while others struggle to attract any new investment. Some districts are well served by an infrastructure of real estate development professionals, including brokers, leasing agents, and private developers. Other districts struggle to attract the interest of any real estate brokers and developers. This variation in starting points means that BIDs will necessarily adopt different strategies for achieving their economic development goals.

Strategies are neither right nor wrong. Each BID must assess its own unique character and select models and programs that suit its own situation. City size often has little relationship to the model selected. A large New York City BID may have little need for many advanced economic development strategies if it is well served by the real estate community. Conversely, a small city with little or no real estate professional interest in downtown may need to adopt strategies that compensate for this absence. Selecting appropriate intervention strategies requires BIDs to undertake careful analyses of both the district marketplace and the metropolitan region.

THE BID AS DATA MANAGER

At a most basic level, BIDs can assemble and disseminate data. Economic decisions of all sorts rely on data. One of the simplest intervention strategies is to make sure that appropriate players in the development process have access to their desired data.

Data needs for economic development activities can be wide ranging. Prospective businesses may be interested in a statistical profile of the district. Retailers may seek information on the types of existing stores within a district. They also crave information on sales volumes and sales per square foot. Office businesses often seek information on available services and amenities and labor pools as well as transportation and parking options. Developers seek market data to help substantiate demand for space. Nearly everyone looks for data that provide a strong, positive picture of a district as a place to invest. Tenants seek information on available space. Investors look for data on properties available for acquisition.

BIDs can assume important roles in assembling and disseminating data to the key players in the economic development process. Obvious candidates for data are business and investor prospects, but other key groups are crucial to the economic development process. These groups include real estate brokers, leasing agents, building managers, property owners, real estate appraisers, bankers, secondary and bond market representatives, and government officials. All play some role in business development and all have data requirements. When BIDs provide data they are often able to shorten, simplify, and in some instances reduce the costs associated with economic development decisions.

How data get disseminated is a key consideration. Some BIDs simply respond to inquiries, providing data on an as-needed basis. Others will make certain that data pertinent to industry segments is uniformly disseminated to all. For example, appraisers will be particularly interested in lease rates. Providing such data in a newsletter or bulletin format to all appraisers helps keep them informed about BID conditions. The Internet has also become a popular method for making data readily accessible to large groups of potential users.

One key category of data is "available properties or spaces for lease" within the district boundaries. Realtor multiple listing service (MLS) directories generally do not contain complete rosters of available commercial spaces and properties. Many properties and spaces are shown by owners or proprietary leasing companies that do not subscribe to MLS services. By collecting data on the full range of properties and spaces, BIDs acquire a powerful database unique to the marketplace. This uniqueness will cause businesses and real estate industry participants to seek out BID information and give the BID a role in the business development process.

Maintaining and updating data are important commitments for any BID program engaged in this intervention strategy. Data can help a BID become part of the development process, but only if they are current, accurate, and reliable. Periodic updating is essential.

THE BID AS A BUSINESS FACILITATOR

Sometimes simply providing data is not sufficient. Once a program passes along its data, what happens next is generally unknown. Programs that only provide data have no way of following or guiding prospects. Subsequent decisions are left to the whims of others.

The next level of intervention in the development process involves "making connections." The BID becomes a conduit or *facilitator,* linking the prospect with private-sector individuals able to consummate deals. Such individuals are typically real estate brokers, building managers, or property owners.

As data managers, BIDs assemble information on available properties and provide it directly to prospects or brokers. The inquiring prospect may or may not act on the data. The BID generally loses contact with the prospect at that point. Yet as a business facilitator, the BID *retains* contact and performs at least two additional steps:

- screen and qualify possible locations and spaces; and
- places prospects in direct contact with the individuals responsible for the leasing or selling of desirable properties.

This allows the BID to assume a more active role in the development process, acting as both a screener and a conduit for the leasing industry. Most real estate professionals welcome this value-added assistance. Screening helps them to qualify leads, saving time and increasing the likelihood of success. Direct referral to landlords ensures that connections are made rather than relying on the initiative of prospects or brokers to make contact.

An excellent example of the facilitator model in action is the Site Seeker program operated by the Downtown Dayton Partnership (DDP). When a prospect approaches the DDP seeking information on available properties, pertinent requirements and specifications about desired space needs are obtained. These are summarized into a blind solicitation and issued via fax or e-mail to a list of building managers, leasing agents, and property owners. Interested agents and owners send responses to back to the DDP, which then assembles them into a packet for the prospect. After the prospect selects space options to investigate, the DDP staff makes introductions with representatives of the targeted properties. The Site Seeker program creates substantial added value to both property owner and prospect, winnowing out ill-suited matches. The program remains engaged in the development process, at least until the referral is passed off. By this time, however, the chances of success are improved.

MANAGING PROSPECTS

Business prospect facilitation makes sense when there is a strong cadre of dedicated, motivated, and loyal real estate professionals working to promote downtown properties. Sometimes, however, the real estate industry serving BID properties may not be particularly motivated or loyal to downtown. Real estate professionals often represent multiple properties in different areas of a region, not all downtown. Prospect referrals generated by a BID may resurface in other locations outside the district, steered there by agents who "simply couldn't make a downtown deal happen." Sometimes, referrals are not acted upon. The agent may be too busy or simply unmotivated. In any case, downtown loses.

In these instances, programs may choose to adopt a more assertive "case management" model of development assistance. In these programs, BIDs remain connected to the prospect throughout the entire development process. BID staff serve as case managers, tracking the progress of prospects and providing targeted and specific aid and assistance whenever necessary.

A case management approach can make good sense. The process of bringing a prospect and a landlord to a signed lease is often a rocky, tumultuous journey. At any stage of the process, a deal-ending problem can arise. Real estate brokers make their commissions by "closing" deals. Prospects that consume inordinate amounts of time or which require overcoming too many difficult hurdles may simply not be worth their expenditure of effort. This is where BID staff can make important contributions, managing prospects and helping to solve issues that might otherwise doom a deal.

Case management is an extremely labor-intensive strategy. Prospects will expect BID staff to be available and involved throughout the entire development process. If the BID program is simultaneously working with a number of prospects, the hours and days devoted to case management can multiply rapidly. Yet, such in-depth assistance has its rewards. Prospects are seldom lost due to any lack of motivation or loyalty by a broker or agent. Success rates are improved as BIDs work to reduce the number of pitfalls faced by prospects.

BIDs also gain hands-on knowledge of the real issues that make or break real estate deals. Among the issues likely to be encountered in any case management program are providing desired tenant or customer parking, building permit and code issues, build-out negotiations, and business financing. BID staff act as troubleshooters and mediators, seeking solutions that keep a deal on track. This could mean securing sympathetic interpretations from city building departments, securing and packaging financing, and finding financial incentives.

One example of this approach was the success of the Ithaca, New York, Downtown Partnership (IDP) in helping to land Dynamic Patterns, a start-up, paint-your-own-pottery business. The IDP helped to find the lead, qualify spaces, assist in the development of a business plan, and provide assistance with overcoming issues with the local building department. The IDP remained engaged in the process from start to finish, helping to ensure the eventual signing and opening of this novel business.

START-UP AND EXPANSION BUSINESSES

Industrial development programs have long known and downtown programs have discovered that most new jobs are created locally, by new or expanding locally based entrepreneurs. Businesses recruited from outside of the community may get media headlines, but the majority of jobs created in any given metropolitan statistical area (MSA) are generated from within the MSA, not from outside.

The importance of the metropolitan region to new job creation is a key factor to consider when structuring a downtown economic development strategy for both retail and office businesses. Two of the best strategies for new job creation pertain to start-up businesses and expansions of existing businesses.

Many downtowns serve as de facto incubators for start-up businesses. Downtowns often have an extremely broad range of rental rates, including considerable low-cost space. Such space can be attractive to new start-up businesses unable to immediately afford standard market rents.

Working in conjunction with universities or governmental programs, BIDs can take a leadership role in supporting and encouraging start-up firms. In Grand Junction, Colorado, the Downtown Development Authority was a key partner in a community effort to build a small business incubator in the West End of its downtown. The incubator, known as the Western Colorado Business Development Corporation, became an important part of the community's economic development strategy.

Street vending and pushcart programs can be excellent routes for growing new retail businesses. Gaining market knowledge and street savvy from vendor carts can position an entrepreneur for the jump to a fixed storefront location. A number of downtown programs, such as Downtown Crossing Association in Boston, support active street vendor programs.

Business expansion represents an unheralded yet extremely important part of an economic development program for downtowns. Expansions are often quiet and understated. Yet they regularly churn out large proportions of new jobs and investment. Between 1999 and 2001, roughly half of the new retail space occupied in downtown Ithaca, New York, was the direct result of expanding businesses.

Expansions, whether they are retail or office, provide an important and powerful story that needs to be transmitted to the media and the public. An expansion is by definition a success. It sends a powerful signal to the community that the downtown district is a location where businesses can succeed. Cataloging and "telling the expansion story" should be a key part of any business recruitment marketing effort.

Expansions may happen without any intervention and the BID may simply be relegated to reporting and celebrating the event. However, such a passive strategy has limitations. If an expanding business needs additional space, it becomes a candidate for relocation elsewhere outside of the district. BIDs sometimes take proactive measures to identify prospective growing businesses and assist them to grow within the downtown district.

BUSINESS RETENTION STRATEGIES

Proactive business retention is a relatively new addition to downtown economic development programs. Long a standard component of industrial development programs, business retention is a crucial and logical part of any advanced economic development program.

Recruiting new businesses is an expensive enterprise. The ratio of prospects to actual signed new business leases is almost always low. Considerable time and money can be spent recruiting new businesses. Hence, retaining and growing existing businesses is smart economics and good policy.

Visitations

Industrial development programs often include visitations to existing businesses as part of their core work. Teams of staff and community volunteers pay visits to industries on a scheduled basis, to learn about issues or opportunities that might require attention. Too often, communities learn about an impending relocation of a company out of their market at the very last minute. They then frantically try to identify reasons for the decision to leave and fashion a response. Usually this effort comes too late to reverse a process that has been gaining momentum for months. Visitations help to diagnose such situations before they become chronic.

BIDs have begun to adopt similar visitation strategies for their retail, commercial, and corporate businesses. Visitations make sense on several levels. They provide direct face-to-face communication. They allow for an on-site inspection of the facility to determine if there is overcrowding or a noticeable thinning of staff or product. They also help introduce the BID program to businesses that may not be active in community and downtown affairs.

The Downtown Dayton Partnership launched a comprehensive office visitation program in the mid-1990s. When the program was first undertaken, many firms reported that their visit was the very first time anyone from either downtown or the public sector had ever come to talk with them. Businesses felt doted upon. Issues were uncovered and addressed on a case-by-case basis. As the Dayton program demonstrated, good communication and proactive case management are key to successful business retention.

Making visits a priority is a crucial step in the retention process. Many cities are served by private firms selling business databases that include the lease expiration date. Expiration dates provide programs with a timetable for establishing visits. Most leases require advance notice for extension or renewal. Hence, it is usually necessary to schedule visitations at least twelve months prior to lease expiration. If private data sources are not available for purchase, programs may need to collect such data on their own or, at last resort, estimate when leases may come due.

Visitations require a commitment of considerable time, not only for the visit, but also for the inevitable follow-up and case management. Sometimes volunteer labor can assist in the visitation process. Dayton made use of its downtown Rotary Club to assist in visits. Rotary members volunteered to make visits to preidentified businesses, and completed questionnaires that extracted important information about business satisfaction and growth. Use of volunteer clubs can extend the reach of BIDs. Such volunteer help, however, requires careful organization, supervision, and care to avoid possible conflicts of interest.

Technical Assistance

Visits represent only one way to address business retention. BIDs can also offer technical assistance on a wide array of topics to business groups or to individual firms. Such assistance might include expansion financing assistance, promoting overseas sales, retail window display advice, and encouraging more e-commerce.

However, there are limits to a BID's capacity to improve the operation and profitability of businesses. Particularly with retail, intervention strategies can run up against the will and aptitude of the business owner. Technical assistance requires both a knowledgeable teacher and a willing student. Many businesses are simply unwilling to include others in their personal decision making, regardless of the potential benefits.

In the early 1990s, the Downtown Haverhill, Massachusetts, Partnership launched a pilot program called Project Profit. The program was designed to provide intensive technical assistance to a select number of key retail businesses. A consortium of experts representing a broad range of business disciplines was assembled to work one-on-one with the target businesses. The goal was to strengthen the participating businesses and improve the likelihood of retention.

The pilot program lasted one year and was subsequently discontinued. Despite hand picking the businesses, the selected stores were often reluctant to share key business data and failed to follow up on recommendations. A postassessment of the program determined that there was insufficient motivation for the businesses to be invested in the program.

Well-managed, strong businesses are often the most willing to accept technical assistance or self-help seminars. Businesses most in need of help are often the least likely to seek assistance. BIDs considering technical assistance initiatives need to carefully assess the reach of such programs and be realistic about the limits of technical assistance in promoting retention.

MAKING PROJECTS HAPPEN

Not all downtown development is centered on businesses. Downtowns offer a number of development opportunities for entertainment, culture, office, residential, retail, education, parking, and all combinations of mixed-use investment. Project development, rather than business development, can be the focus of another segment of economic development strategy.

BID programs can facilitate project development in several incremental ways. At the most elementary level, BIDs can help define a vision of their district for the community. This process creates a blueprint for the future, a portrait in both words and pictures. Visions and the strategic plans that emanate from them help public and private investors understand what projects are possible and why they should make financial commitments to these projects. Strategic plans have become common tools used by downtown programs to shape and guide investment decision making. Without a plan and a vision, investors will find it difficult to commit to projects. Plans put a project into context and envision the future. They are important economic development tools.

A slightly more interventionist approach to project development involves the BID assuming a predevelopment and project formulation role. Projects, even exclusively private-sector driven projects, do not always spring forth without assistance. The BID can help germinate projects. Project formulation involves conceptualizing the parameters of a project, engaging in preliminary analysis to demonstrate its feasibility, and thereafter using this work to market the project to a private or public developer.

Dayton's efforts to build a downtown minor league baseball stadium illustrate the role of a BID in project formulation. The Dayton BID identified baseball as a priority for the community and conducted the early research on all phases of the project. Committees were formed to investigate stadium design and funding and team recruitment. A Baseball Task Force chaired by a leading community business executive was launched. By the time the project was passed on to the city for implementation, there was a clear picture of how the project would work, where the team would come from, what sites would be considered, and how the project could be funded. Without this early project-formulation activity, the stadium project would never have advanced.

Sometimes, BIDs choose to intervene even more aggressively to ensure that a project is implemented. Predevelopment functions, often performed by developers, can be undertaken by the BID or a development affiliate of the BID. Among the actions that are most often tackled are feasibility studies to demonstrate market potential, detailed business and financing pro forma preparation, and property-site assembly. Such actions may be necessary to entice private developers to step forward.

In Ithaca, New York, the BID spearheaded a housing market study of its downtown district conducted by a national residential market research firm. The purpose of the study, jointly funded by the BID and the city, was to demonstrate absorption capacity for market-rate residential units within the BID's boundaries. The firm contracted to undertake the work had a strong national reputation in both the banking and residential development industries. The results of the study provided quantitative evidence of a robust market for residential units. The study was used to convince private developers of the opportunity for residential development, saving them up-front investigative time and money.

Land banking is another tool used to facilitate project development. In many cities the obstacle to development is property assemblage. By assembling and holding properties for future development, BIDs can guide and control growth.

In certain circumstances in which private development is not abundant, a BID may choose to act as its own developer. A small but growing number of BIDs have created subsidiary or separate local development corporations (LDCs) capable of undertaking any or all phases of normal development. These LDCs can be sole developers or partners with other investors and developers. The downtown Rock Island, Illinois, program has had an active and successful local development corporation for over a decade. It has partnered with private developers to undertake several key mixed-use downtown projects that were seen as catalytic for downtown development.

Serving as a developer or development partner represents the most sophisticated and complex approach to development intervention. It carries the direct reward of the BID being the driver of development activity. This benefit, however, does not come without risk. As active development partners, BIDs assume an element of risk in the success or failure of a project. BIDs that dabble in active development roles will need to structure themselves to isolate the risk. They must understand both the pros and cons inherent in deals and be prepared for any outcome.

INTERVENTION OPTIONS: CONCLUDING REMARKS

BIDs can play a role in shaping and guiding the character of their districts. This naturally occurs when BIDs assume active roles in service delivery, making districts cleaner and safer for users. It can also happen when BIDs decide to become directly involved in the economic market-place. Economic development strategies enable BIDs to move from passive observers to active participants in the effort to shape local economies.

No two BID programs will or probably should have the same economic development strategy. A minimalist strategy may be as appropriate as a complex, sophisticated strategy. The key question to ask is whether the selected strategy is appropriate to the local district's needs and conditions.

Chapter 27

Residential Development:
Creating a Living Downtown

Dan Carmody

HISTORICAL TRENDS

Over the past twenty years residential development has become an important growth sector for downtowns regardless of their size. This is a significant departure from how our urban areas grew in the preceding 100 years. Fogelson (2001), in *Downtown: Its Rise and Fall, 1880-1950,* examines the urban forms that evolved in American's formative years and identifies a uniquely American urban characteristic—the separation of workplace from place of residence. This separation was largely a manifestation of the rapid urbanization and immigration occurring in the late 1800s, during the height of the Victorian era. Fear of the unwashed masses and their detrimental affect to the moral or physical health of one's family fueled the separation of work and residence by a growing middle class. Advances in transportation technology, first rails and then freeways, made increasingly longer commutes possible.

Three elements contributed to overcoming this historical tendency toward separation and encouraged the growth of residential use in our downtowns: congestion, demographics/lifestyle, and obsolete structures.

Congestion

In large urban areas, more households and an increasing female labor force, combined with the separation of work and residence, increased traffic congestion. Much of the demand for housing within or near major downtown employment centers is the result of intolerably long commute times.

doi:10.1300/5137_28

Demographics/Lifestyle

Yet even in smaller metropolitan areas without traffic congestion, residential development has also increased. Demographic trends have worked to divide the housing market into more segments. Specifically, the 2000 census reveals that households with one or two persons make up nearly 60 percent of all households, that average household size has decreased to 2.57 people from 3.14 people in 1970, and that only 24 percent of all households have school-age children (Fields and Casper, 2001). Trends throughout the age spectrum have increased the fragmentation of housing markets. Young people are waiting later to get married; younger couples are waiting longer between getting married and having children; a stubbornly high divorce rate splits households; older couples are living longer, and those surviving the death of a spouse live even longer. For most of these groups, the traditional suburban paradigm of safety, streets, and schools is not as important, and the detached single-family home is not as appropriate as it is for the traditional family with school-aged children.

Closely linked to smaller households are lifestyles with greater emphasis on such amenities such as the arts, entertainment, and culture that urban areas can better provide than suburban or rural areas. Bohemian enclaves, gay and lesbian neighborhoods, and arts colonies have sprung up in most markets. The sexuality of downtown living, as characterized by the popularity of such TV shows as *Sex and the City* and *Friends,* indicates a full turning from the Victorian values that worked against downtown living.

Supply of Obsolete Structures or Low-Density Fringe Areas

The third and last factor is the availability of a large supply of obsolete structures of all types and sizes in downtown and fringe areas in cities of all sizes. Masonry and frame construction buildings with small column bays are not suitable for redevelopment for the uses for which they were originally built. The cost to retrofit older office space to meet current telecommunications and mechanical specifications in most markets is more than the space will generate in rent. The residential boom in older cities began when demand generated by congestion and/or demographic/lifestyle considerations met the supply of low-cost, obsolete buildings. New construction typically followed as market dynamics were tested by conversion of obsolete structures to residential use.

In the newer cities of the south and west such as Charlotte, North Carolina, where the local leadership inspired construction of much more dense downtowns, redevelopment of the low-density fringe areas of downtown occurred in response to congestion and the civic desire to have a more dense urban center in an era when new office space was not as concentrated at the center.

HOUSING'S LINK TO ECONOMIC DEVELOPMENT

The focus of economic development has shifted from transportation and raw materials to the workforce. Cities that have successfully grown downtown housing markets also seem to be the most economically vibrant. Lifestyle gurus such as Rebecca Ryan and Richard Florida have detailed the correlation between a region's economic success and its ability to attract and retain young and talented workers. Creative people want to live in creative places, and the interesting urban neighborhoods in and around downtown are preferred for many of the most talented members of the workforce.

Photos from south of the Loop in Chicago highlight this dramatic change in economic development. Figure 27.1 from the 1970s shows the Rock Island Rail Line converging on downtown, evidence of Chicago's railroad-related explosive growth in the late 1800s. The same location shown circa 2000 (Figure 27.2) is a dense urban neighborhood with a wonderful lakeside vista for talented workers.

FIGURE 27.1. 1970s Rock Island Rail Line converging on downtown.

FIGURE 27.2. Image of the same downtown Chicago location shown in Figure 27.1 taken in 2000.

RESIDENTIAL DEVELOPMENT PREREQUISITES

During the 1970s, when downtowns were in their worst condition, it was difficult to attract daytime workers, let alone permanent residents. In the early stages of revitalization, cities worked to stabilize downtowns before turning to residential development as a way to grow downtown. Downtowns that have experienced housing growth first worked to make it cleaner and safer and then conceived strategies that mobilized civic investment. Such elements as streetscapes, waterfronts, cultural amenities, and stadiums added sizzle to the downtown. Once minimum safety and cleanliness standards were achieved and a demonstrable, and long-term civic commitment to downtown was in place, it became possible to attract housing developers, home buyers, and higher-income renters.

Another important prerequisite for downtown housing in smaller cities, especially those that do not have major rail or expressway systems separating downtown from adjacent neighborhoods, is stable neighborhoods adjoining downtown. Working in historic core neighborhoods reveals important lessons about the local housing market that developers can later apply to downtown housing development.

Financial Incentives

Once these prerequisites have been met, it is time to consider developing downtown housing. Downtown organizations have a variety of roles to play in stimulating housing development including: conducting market research on the housing market, marketing housing opportunities to developers, expediting and packaging assistance to developers, or serving as a community-based developer. Understanding the financial incentives available to assist with housing development is critical because they often determine how much and what kind of housing will be developed in the downtown.

HOUSING MARKET BY SECTOR

Four components comprise an urban housing market:

- *Affordable rental.* Existing rental units that provide housing for households earning as much as 120 percent of area median income or new rental housing built with public financial support that limits the incomes tenants may earn in some or all of the units.
- *Market rate rental.* Existing rental housing that has rents which require household income above 120 percent of area median income to service (income × 30 percent > rent). Also, new rental housing that has no income limits.
- *Affordable owner.* Existing owner-occupied housing available to those at or below 120 percent area median income or new owner-occupied units built with public funding that limits the income of some or all of the households purchasing the units.
- *Owner market rate.* Existing owner-occupied housing available to those at or above 120 percent area median income or new owner-occupied housing that has no houshold income limits for those purchasing the units.

Developing a sustainable downtown requires a strategy for participating in all four quadrants. Although most cities would like to have nothing but upper-end, owner-occupied housing, interesting and exciting urban neighborhoods have a dynamic mix of uses and incomes. Struggling artists and musicians, entry-level workers, hospitality and service-sector employees all contribute energy to a successful downtown but need affordable housing options. If affordable housing is not integrated into an overall strategy, poorly designed projects may dampen market-rate interest and continue the pattern of economic integration that has been the curse of central cities.

Also, from a market development standpoint, it is often difficult to go from no housing market to high-priced condominiums. Mixed-income projects that utilize favorable financing to assist with affordable housing development can help to grow the market in an incremental fashion, starting with more moderately priced units.

AFFORDABLE HOUSING

Many funding sources are available to assist with affordable housing development, but a key concept is median income. The United States Department of Housing and Urban Development (HUD) publishes income figures for each metropolitan area. Very low income is typically defined as less than 40 percent of the area median income. Low income is between 40 and 59 percent of the area median income, and moderate is between 60 and 80 percent of the area median income. These income limits vary greatly from one metropolitan area to the next. This is best indicated by the fact that during the late 1990s, 34 percent of Silicon Valley's (California) 20,000 homeless people had full-time jobs, with many of them making more than $50,000 per year. Affordable programs vary greatly. Some allow participation of families with incomes as high as 125 percent of area median income. The important point is that affordable housing programs can offer profound financing tools to both improve housing opportunities for people with few options and help build market-rate housing in areas that have little urban housing.

The tools available to build affordable housing can be used in very creative ways to build mixed-income and mixed-use projects. In most cities, however, affordable housing development is conducted by either social service agencies or by for-profit developers, neither of which may have as their goal the sustainable evolution of a downtown residential neighborhood. Learning the nuances of affordable housing development enables downtown groups to advocate for projects that support the creation of a viable downtown neighborhood *in addition to* the need to provide shelter (the focus for most housing advocates) or maximizing developer fee income (the focus of most for-profit developers).

Development Is a Team Sport

Housing development, like all forms of development, is a team sport. Assembling a strong team is a critical step. Architectural and engineering, construction, financing, marketing, and property management are required skills. Although building owners, investors, and building users often lead such teams, many communities are increasingly undertaking community-led development to accomplish projects the for-profit developers cannot or will not tackle.

URBAN HOUSING IS DIFFERENT

The design of urban housing is different from its suburban counterparts. Building new housing developments close to the sidewalk to improve the public realm is critical. Accommodating the automobile is more challenging and needs to be done with minimal impact to the primary elevation of buildings. Building and fire code issues need to be carefully addressed both in new construction, and, more importantly, in the conversion of older buildings to residential use. New building codes, specific to building renovation, have provided more flexibility in dealing with renovation issues without sacrificing the health or safety of residents.

Neighborhood Amenities

What matters most to those willing to live downtown? Convenience and a pedestrian-friendly lifestyle are central concerns. Most downtown households continue to own an automobile but many eliminate one car from the family budget. The resulting increases in disposable income can be used to purchase more housing or more nearby urban amenities.

Building Amenities

Fitness workout areas are important. If they are not available in the immediate neighborhood the project may have to include a fitness center. Social facilities are also important. Rooftop decks with patios and hot tubs provide a place for entertaining or gathering with neighbors. High-speed Internet access is now a basic amenity. Security systems are important to overcome lingering safety concerns, especially for those returning from the suburbs. Rental housing has more flexibility in meeting parking needs while ownership housing generally requires secure, adjacent, and covered parking.

Unit Amenities

Raw and "honest" architecture featuring exposed building elements is attractive to urban buyers looking for an alternative the textured gypsum board, vinyl-sided, suburban tract house. Minimalist, partitioned spaces with oversized windows and high ceiling heights are typical of the features that make urban living compelling (see Figures 27.3-27.5). Since most downtowns are adjacent to waterfronts, views are often very desirable assets for downtown housing development.

Market Rate Incentives

The Federal Historic Tax Incentives Program provides a major subsidy for conversion of buildings on the National Register of Historic Places. Developers can gain a federal tax credit valued at 20 percent on allowable construction costs. In larger projects the tax credits are sold to investors, typically for 90 cents or more per dollar of federal tax credit. For each $1,000,000 in allowable costs, the developer can cover $180,000 from the sale of tax credits. One drawback to using this tax credit is that projects must be income properties for a period of at least five years making it difficult to do owner-occupied projects.

The Federal Historic Tax Incentives Program requires that the property undergoing renovation is listed on the National Register of Historic Places, and there is a highly detailed design review process to ensure that work contemplated and executed is consistent with historic design guidelines. Following these rules and regulations costs money, takes time, and may increase construction costs.

Some states such as Missouri, Louisiana, and Kentucky have developed state historic tax credits mirroring the federal law giving developers the ability to use both federal and state tax credits in the same project. That same $1,000,0000 investment may yield as much as $360,000 in a combination of state and federal tax credits.

Tax-increment financing also allows for substantial help to finance housing of all kinds including market-rate housing.

Mixed Use/Mixed Income

The strength of downtowns has always been their diversity of use and their role as the one place the entire community calls home. Housing can play a key role in preserving the diversity of downtown by enabling the artful recycling of class C office buildings and white elephant buildings such as former department stores or hotels. These blighting influences can be converted to mixed-income housing, and, by using affordable housing finance tools, reduce the financial risks of reinventing these key historic buildings. A healthy mix of modern, competitive office space and mixed-income housing in vintage buildings also helps to spur retail development.

FIGURE 27.3. Tall ceiling heights, exposed brick, an open floor plan, and a great view are sought-after unit features.

FIGURE 27.4. Fireplaces, exposed duct work, and structural elements are other desirable urban-living elements.

FIGURE 27.5. Affordable housing is often successful when it is indistinguishable from market-rate housing. The economic status of this tenant is not discernable from looking at this photo.

Estimates show that the typical downtown resident spends three to four times what the typical downtown visitor spends on goods and services. Increasing the population of downtown in terms of both workers and residents helps to fuel retail sales growth.

CONCLUSION

As downtowns resettle with residents some great side benefits have occurred. Downtowns are safer, with more sets of "vested eyes" keeping a close tab on things twenty-four hours a day. Downtowns have a profound new political weapon—voter bases have expanded. Last, it has become easier to attract office employers and retailers because the environment has improved with fewer blighted buildings and more people on the streets. Residential development has grown and urban areas have become more vibrant.

REFERENCES

Fields, J. and Casper, L. (2001). America's families and living arrangements: March 2000. *Current Population Reports,* P20-537. Washington, DC: U.S. Census Bureau.

Fogelson, R. (2001). *Downtown: Its Rise and Fall, 1880-1950.* New Haven: Yale University Press.

Chapter 28

Retail Revitalization and Recruitment

Maureen Atkinson
John Archer

It's hard to imagine a more important aspect to urban and town life than retailing: from food and beverage offerings, to personal services, to entertainment and culture—retailing creates the places where people both meet and get their needs met. Although larger towns and cities have more people employed in offices or light manufacturing than retailing, retailing is what gives a city its character. Retailing is what local people, visitors, and investors judge the city's core by, declaring it either "vital" or "dead." So beyond paying and generating taxes, creating employment, and serving shoppers, retailing is the face and heart of your community. Investors, office locators, residents, convention organizers, tourists, and shoppers all make their spending decisions based on how alluring a downtown retail area is. Think about it: Is it more fun to visit downtown San Francisco or Dallas? Would you rather work in Manhattan or Newark, New Jersey? Will your investment be more rewarding in Atlanta or Buffalo?

Due to the highly competitive nature and the fact that most of our cities are oversupplied in terms of retail, retail recruitment has become increasingly more challenging for private leasing companies and individuals, as well as for public agencies.

UNDERSTANDING RETAILING

Retailing is a very special industry. Because we all experience it on almost a daily basis, it is easy to assume that the shopping environment "just happens" and that opening and managing stores is a simple business.

Following are some basic principles of retailing.

100 Percent Customer Driven

Retailing is a direct mirror of society, the market segments present in the trade area, and particularly the residents in the trade area. When a downtown tries to force high-end retailing into its core with no up-market residential population in it or nearby, the plan is bound to fail. For example, downtown Cleveland's Tower City, with no up-market residents within five miles, opened to great fanfare, but lost all its high-end retailers in five years.

Retailing follows and serves a market. Retailing does not lead or go in first. The economics of operating a store or service are so fragile (just a 2 to 7 percent profit is typical) that anything less will put a retailer under. This is why locating just one-half block off a main street, or expecting stores to pioneer in locations will not work.

Hypercompetition

Retailers face a wide range of competitors. Not only do suburban malls pose direct challenges, but there are also new formats such as "big box" category killers, lifestyle centers, cataloges, and Web sites. Downtown's challenge is to serve even more demanding consumers in an overstored, hypercompetitive environment. However, by finding the right opportunities and niches, your downtown retail core can flourish and add to your city's vitality.

The Basics in Place

Retailing success requires that the basics be in place. Basics include a vibrant street scene with pedestrian traffic (at 500 to 1,000 per hour at peak shopping times in large cities), more than 95 percent occupancy, and use in the evenings and weekends.

Timing is the critical issue in tackling retail revitalization. Key to this is retail retention and recruitment programs so that early discussions build logically toward the goals, and problems do not arise later on.

Retailing is obviously very visible. An office building can be virtually vacant and people would not know about it. Yet when one or two stores close or a department store closes, the media often react negatively and/or out of proportion to the situation.

CREATIVE PLANNING

Successful retailing requires creative thinking. Trying to replace what "went dark" with another store and selling the same old stuff will not work.

What *will* work is preparing a strategy and action plan that will meet the key economic goal of turning shopping outflow into inflow, so that more people will come downtown to use your city's core rather than leave it to spend dollars and time elsewhere. This can only be done by creating a total retail experience that is both right for your city and right for your target market—one that is wanted, unique, and superior.

To begin the process of developing an appropriate and competitive retail base, you must have a pretty clear picture of how you want your downtown to look in the end.

Figure 28.1 illustrates the retail process.

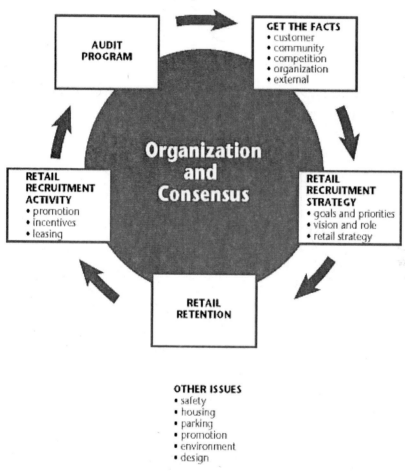

FIGURE 28.1. The retail process.

THE PROCESS

The process of retail recruitment is an ongoing one. The five steps in this process include (see Figure 28.1):

1. get the facts,
2. develop a retail recruitment strategy,
3. conduct retail retention programs,
4. organize retail recruitment activities, and
5. audit the programs.

As discussed earlier, there is a right way and a wrong way to go about retail revitalization and recruitment. There are no shortcuts: each of the steps is necessary for success.

Get the facts to make decisions that are appropriate to your specific situation. Then, move on to develop a strategy that takes into account both your starting position (determined from the fact finding) and your vision for what your downtown will be in the future. Prioritizing areas for emphasis, this strategy should be accompanied by measurable goal statements.

The Retail Recruitment Process and Organization

Start the retail revitalization and recruitment process with a task force of people who are critical to the program's success. Obviously, this group must include:

- The person(s) in the BID responsible for success, plus support functions such as marketing.
- Key retail property owners.
- Leading leasing agents from national and local firms.
- Key city staff.
- Civic/political leaders.
- Support staff/consultants.

Be prepared to establish the following.

- Expectations.
- Time lines and regular meetings.
- Budgets backed up by research, database, and marketing.
- Broker information and exchange meetings.
- Task force management guidelines.
- A communications program with *all* retail property owners and retail tenants.

Once the strategy and goals have been set, direct action can take place. A successful recruitment program will focus on retail *retention* first to make sure that the *existing* retail base is strong before building on it. Only after all this preliminary work is completed should retail recruitment activities take place.

This process is never really over; complete reviews of your activities and new fact-finding rounds must be relaunched to keep up to date on what is really happening.

The following sections outline in detail what each step involves. The process is circular; it should be never ending, not just a one-time event. Individual situations and retail environments are constantly changing. Downtown organizations must track these changes and adjust their process constantly to keep their downtowns alive.

One final word of advice: retail recruitment should never be done in isolation, but constantly connected to the many other issues affecting it.

REVITALIZATION AND RECRUITMENT
ACTION-PLAN SCHEDULE

Organization and Consensus (6-12 months)

- An organizational process that involves the majority of stakeholders committed to your vision and goals.
- Someone responsible for coordinating and/or cheerleading the retail revitalization and recruitment plan.

Fact Finding and Analysis (6-12 months, concurrent)

- Information needed to make strategic decisions and to assist landlords and retailers in making expansion, moving, investment, or leasing decisions.

Retail Revitalization and Recruitment
Strategy Decisions (3 months)

- Decision on the retail economic revitalization strategy for your downtown and its component districts.
- Identification of gaps and opportunities by district, block, and property.

- Identification of action needed for holistic strategic alignment and market-demand weaknesses.
- Budgets for action.
- Commitments for joint public/private sector support.
- An informal organization of BID leadership and real estate brokers/landlords who will meet regularly to strategize retail recruitment.

Retail Retention (Ongoing)

- A program of retailer strengthening and retention that will help align existing stores/restaurants/services with the strategic direction.

Retail Recruitment Activity (Ongoing)

- Arrange and set priorities.
- Prepare materials and promotions.
- Decide on incentives.
- Begin leasing and attracting developers.

STEP 1: GET THE FACTS

Collecting factual information is an absolutely essential first step in creating a recruitment action program. The data collected will create a base of information from which to work, rather than having to rely on assumptions or opinion; it is a critical "reality check."

This information will help you:

- determine what kinds of businesses you want and do not want in your downtown;
- establish information essential for the actual recruiting and promotional leasing materials; and
- keep you up to date on market change so that you can modify your recruiting plans as required.

The data that you will need to collect fall into five different areas:

1. customers,
2. community,
3. competition,
4. organization, and
5. external environment.

Customers

Following are the questions you must be able to answer about your customers:

1. Where is your trade area?
2. How many people go through the downtown or are in the trade area?
3. What are their characteristics regarding income, age, lifestyle, etc.?
4. How are customers changing?
5. What do customers use the downtown for?
6. What are customers' attitudes toward the downtown regarding things such as safety, cleanliness, etc.?

Community

Community-related fact finding for the purpose of retail recruitment involves gathering information on the existing retail base and other downtown facilities. An extensive base of information outlining what actually exists in downtown will help you create a better strategy and will make your downtown easier to sell. Important information on your downtown should include:

- Total retail and service space broken down by commodity.
- Both the total amount and individual size of vacant space.
- Sales per square foot.
- Rental rates.
- Other traffic generators: facilities such as municipal offices, large office buildings, key employers, parking, transit, and sports and cultural facilities should be noted. In smaller communities, a post office can be a very important traffic generator. These can all contribute to the marketability of downtown retail space.
- Major geographic characteristics: map these so that the impact of rivers, railways, hills, and large vacant lots can be assessed. Data that are useful for retail recruitment relate to the number of potential consumers in downtown. Retailers will use these for comparison to other locations. These data include:
  — pedestrian counts
  — daytime population
  — size of office and residential complexes
  — quantity, rooms, and occupancy of hotels
  — parking spaces within districts.
- Be realistic about parking

Competition

- Who are the competition's customers?
- How is the competition positioned regarding things such as price, fashion, and service?
- What are the competition's weaknesses?
- What is your competition's recruiting activity?

In order to look for gaps in the marketplace, be prepared to visualize your downtown's position in terms of market-segment appeal against your competition's. See Figures 28.2 and 28.3 for examples of positioning exercises.

Organization

Information on your organization should be compiled for inclusion in any recruitment materials you plan to send to prospective tenants. In addi-

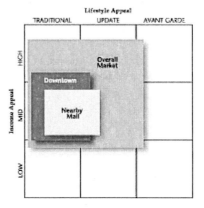

	No. of Stores	Approx. Sq. Ft.
Downtown	11	14,050/2%
Mall	12	
Total	23	

FIGURE 28.2. Retail audit and analysis. (Commodity: Gifts.)

(*Note:* Stores in this commodity category are equal to those in the mall, and the two shopping areas together form an exceptional draw. There are gaps in: general contemporary, contemporary home, imports, collectable toys (e.g., bears, dolls, antiques), and gadgetry.)

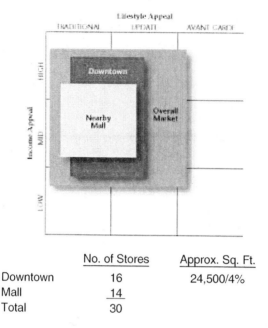

	No. of Stores	Approx. Sq. Ft.
Downtown	16	24,500/4%
Mall	14	
Total	30	

FIGURE 28.3. Retail audit and analysis. (Commodity: Menswear.)

(*Note:* An unusually strong group in numbers and quality, as typically menswear, etc., is underrepresented in nonmall shopping districts. As well, there is good balance between traditional and update appeal. Possible gap in "outdoors" wear and jeans specialist.)

tion, knowledge of your organization's abilities and opportunities, gleaned through collecting this information, will help you assess appropriate strategies in the following step of this process.

Organizational facts include:

- the name of your organization;
- who runs it;
- how is it staffed or operated;
- how is it funded;
- what kinds of programs it offers;
- what is its purpose or mandate;
- what is its relationship with other private and public bodies such as city hall; and
- marketing and special events.

External Environment

Your ability to attract retailers also depends on many factors that relate to issues outside of your community. Be a student of what is happening in retailing outside downtown.

- Do you know what local and regional retail businesses locate in towns or cities your size?
- What do franchisers require in terms of space, size of market, etc.?
- What are the latest retail trends?
- Can you attract new users?

Collecting the Facts

Many techniques can be used for collecting information. These methods include:

- Census information
- Sales tax information
- Intercept surveys (face-to-face interviews with select target customers)
- Trade area surveys
- Merchant surveys
- Internet sources

The following list includes especially helpful Internet services.

Name	Address	Subjects Covered
Global		
World Tourism Statistics Service	www.world-tourism.org	tourism
Claritas	www.claritas.com	population estimates
United States		
Bureau of Labor Statistics	www.stats.bls.gov	office, other
CBS MarketWatch—Market Data	www.marketwatch.com	retail, industrial
Department of Foreign Affairs	www.dfait-maeci.gc.ca	government, culture, tourism
Hospitality Net	www.hospitalitynet.org	events, hospitality
ICSC Research	www.icsc.org	government, retail
ITA Tourism Industries	www.tinet.ita.doc.gov	tourism.
National Retail Federation	www.nrf.com	retail

The North American Real Estate Review	www.narer.com	office, industrial
SportsTicker	www.sportsticker.com	events
Urban Land Institute Web site (real estate)	www.uli.org	office
U.S. Census Bureau	www.census.gov	office, culture, residential, other
Canada		
Colliers International Market	www.colliers.com	office, residential, industrial
The Conference Board of Canada	www.conferenceboard.ca	conferences, events
Statistics Canada	www.statcan.ca	office, retail, hospitality, residential, industrial, other
Strategis	www.strategis.ic.gc.ca	office, retail, events, industrial, other
MapInfo/Compusearch	www.compusearch.ca	secondary information

Analysis

Simply collecting information is not enough. Your downtown will better serve its target customer and outperform the competition by analyzing the data you have collected.

Gaps in your retail mix can be determined numerically, but the process requires an accurate retail inventory, accurate sales-per-square-foot data, and information on consumer spending within the trade area. Professionals who have the necessary expertise should conduct the analyses.

Effective strategic plans build on strengths. Factors on which to build your retail recruitment plan should therefore include:

- *Commodity strengths*—In what areas of retailing is downtown clearly dominant or stronger than its closest competitor?
- *Lifestyle strengths*—Is your downtown the destination for any particular group of consumers, e.g., traditional/high income, or avant-garde/low income?
- *District strategy*—Each node should have a distinct role, target market segment, and strategy.
- *Other Nonretail attractions*—Do other attractions such as museums, theaters, or offices in your downtown bring potential shoppers to the area? If so, what kind of retail operations are likely to appeal to them?
- *Other strengths*—Can downtown depend on political or emotional support from the community? How can this be used to make the retail recruitment effort stronger?

Clear identification of these strengths will be critical to your success. Problems and opportunities can be identified by comparing your situation with that of others. Incorporating a perspective of how retailing and downtowns are changing will bring creativity to your recruitment process.

STEP 2: RETAIL RECRUITMENT STRATEGY

All too often, people involved in retail recruitment, development, and leasing skip this step entirely. Instead of analyzing the facts, setting goals, and planning a strategy, they jump right to trying to attract stores. This frequently leads to failure. Too often we've seen "the right store" go into the wrong location (e.g., not in their target market's district or block) and flounder. Then the downtown is raked over the coals as being a place where retail does not work.

A recruitment strategy is critical because it will: allow you to effectively make use of your actions and resources (funds, time, and volunteer efforts); ensure that your downtown maintains a competitive position in the marketplace; and build a unique niche or role for the commercial component of your downtown.

How recruitment is carried out is critical, too. If it is done in isolation, or just by developers, city hall, or any single group alone, then, most probably, it will not be successful. The planning and implementation of a downtown recruitment strategy should involve everyone who can benefit or be affected including developers, local property owners, retailers, bankers, city staff, politicians, local citizens, institutions, and leasing agents.

By ensuring that the preparation of the strategy is a collective effort from the start, a groundswell of both general and specific support will arise. Involving the property owners or retail landlords is particularly important. They must buy into your plans for the future retail mix and see how it makes sense for all of downtown, as well as for their property. A presentation of the results of a market analysis is a good bridge to retail recruitment and ensures that the strategy developed is based on reality.

A Clear Vision for Downtown

As previously stated, failure is virtually guaranteed if there is not a clear vision of the commercial role of the downtown in your community. This applies both overall and for each of the downtown nodes or subdistricts. Hopefully, your community will already have a vision of what it will be in five, ten, or twenty years. If not, then now is the time to come up with a vision that includes specific details about retail.

Downtown can be:

- the regional center *or* the community center
- a tourist Mecca *or* a place for locals and nontourists
- a service center
- the food and entertainment center
- mainly serving the downtown worker
- only up-market *or* mainly discount/value oriented *or* outlet dominated

Visions for Downtown's Subdistricts

In addition to your vision of the entire central area, there must also be a clear, distinct, "minivision"—including a specific role for each of the districts within the downtown. This ensures that these districts are acknowledged and that their diverse character is a benefit to the total community. Too often, districts are not understood, and incompatible roles are forced upon them.

The following district options should be taken into account:

1. *Specialty Lifestyle Shopping District*
   - Up-market traditional and contemporary such as Michigan Avenue, Chicago; Pine Street area, Seattle; Newbury Street, Boston; and Bloor Street, Toronto
   - Major role for tourists and affluent local residents
2. *Traditional Main Street*
   - Mix of moderately priced apparel; accessories; food; personal services; national, regional, and independent stores; e.g., State Street, Chicago
3. *Merchandise or Commodity Districts*
   - Jewelry, e.g., Elizabethtown, Tennessee; 47th Street, New York City; Broadway, Los Angeles; Downtown Santa Fe, New Mexico
4. *Value Districts*
   - Discount stores, secondhand and pawn shops, outlets; e.g., Chestnut Street, Philadelphia
   - Too often looked upon with disdain, but important in any medium or large city
5. *Experience Districts*
   - Arts and culture; e.g., LoDo, Denver; Cultural District, Pittsburgh; Avenue of the Arts, Philadelphia
   - Includes galleries and studios, often with home-decorating studios or design-related stores and services

6. *Service Districts*
   - Underground "PATH" system in Toronto, below the financial district; underground tunnels in Houston; underground shops in Rockefeller Center, New York City; and service streets such as 17th Street in Denver; Lexington Avenue, New York City
   - Serves office staff and businesses from lower-rent space or in space that is not at street level due to the class AAA office buildings taking up all of the space at ground level
7. *Special Downtown Features*
   - Farmers' or public markets, e.g., Reading Market, Philadelphia; Nashville Public Market; Pike Place Market, Seattle; Farmers' Market, Roanoke, Virginia; St. Lawrence Market, Toronto
   - Can be an effective service to local residents and big traffic builder for local merchants

Downtown Commercial and Retail Goals

Part of what is involved in retail recruitment is committing to a goal or objective. This means understanding how to get people to reduce their shopping expeditions outside of downtown by creating a shopping, service, dining, and entertainment environment that not only keeps people, but also draws people into your downtown.

Goals should be specific in terms of creating new stores and cafés, filling vacancies, increasing the number of transit riders, creating jobs, and increasing the taxbase—and, of course—attracting retailers to achieve all of this.

To reach these goals and to realize your vision, you need a clear-cut strategy for all of downtown and for each distinct district in it.

Strategic Alignment

In order for the commercial and retail components of a downtown and its districts to be exceptionally successful, there must be both alignment and operational effectiveness between the key elements in a retail area. The four key elements include:

1. Accessibility
2. The offering
3. The environment
4. The support elements

Retail Strategy Development and Review

For each district, primary and secondary target market segments need to be specified and the district's strengths and weaknesses identified. In developing your strategy, these strengths should be built upon to create a unique market niche. Weak aspects of the district should be dealt with only if they are a major barrier to the district's operational effectiveness. Strengths upon which to build could mean a particular retail commodity, services, or cultural attractions. Weak elements to improve on include parking, safety, and cleanliness.

In addition, review the inventory of retail space and any other information or research that will help reveal market potential and gaps in what would be an "obvious" ideal mix of retailers, such as missing a shoe store when there are a lot of apparel stores.

Before making any decisions, complete a reality check to ensure that your retail strategy will work. (Contact a consultant or real estate broker for assistance.)

- Will this strategy make the area distinct and fill a niche for target market shoppers? Explain how it will be better for shoppers.
- Does the strategy build upon the strengths of the district before filling weaknesses? What are those strengths?
- Based on the identified strengths, what types of stores or services can be linked to complement and improve one another?
- What important gaps need to be filled in?
- What community strengths (not retail/commercial) can be used to build a unique retail character? For example, downtown offices can support pharmacies, sundries, or accessory stores for impulse purchasing; museums and galleries can support cafés; and special events can expose infrequent visitors to the services and charm of downtown.

Complete the following checklist:

Downtown Retail Recruitment Strategy
- ❑ Creates uniqueness
- ❑ Builds on strengths within each district
- ❑ Builds on strengths in the overall community
- ❑ Fills identified gaps
- ❑ Has a viable target market
- ❑ Has a long-term advantage

Specific Retail Recruitment Strategy

Now you can get specific. Start from the bottom up with each district. Based on your analysis determine:

- the ideal number of stores and square feet per commodity and in total;
- the specific types of stores that fit the character of the district; and
- the hierarchy of shopper needs (see the following).

Within your total community or district, how adequately are the various levels of shopper needs looked after?

1. Basics/convenience
   - basic groceries
   - cards, film
   - hardware
   - drugstore
   - personal services, e.g., cleaners, barbers, financial services
   - basic apparel
   - office services and products

Are all these services covered? Are they in convenient locations?

2. Mid-level needs
   - fast food
   - moderate apparel

Is there an opportunity to broaden the offering? (e.g., ethnic fast food, specialty book stores)

3. Expression/lifestyle level
   - fashion
   - restaurants
   - specialty foods
   - hobbies, recreational, leisure
   - electronics
   - decorating
   - home furnishings

Can downtown go beyond the standard national brand offerings and be the center for one-of-a-kind shops, cafés, galleries, and events?

4. Experience
   - movie theaters
   - live theater
   - clubs
   - specialty restaurants
   - museums and galleries

- music venues
- sports
- special events

Can downtown be the undisputed regional center for educational, cultural, sporting, and social experiences?

Each district will have its own hierarchy. Also, each district should try to build one or more unique commodity strengths that will adequately serve the local market and in turn draw shoppers into your community.

Tip: Building on strengths will create "retail gravity." For example, if one downtown district contains an exceptional furniture store, adding other home furnishing specialists to the retail mix in that district will build retail draw and position the district in the minds of consumers as *the* place to shop for all their home furnishing needs.

This creates "destination shopping" and the opportunity for other related commodities to benefit from additional traffic.

Destination Shopping Benefits

entertainment	←——→	restaurants
hobbies, toys	←——→	children's wear
retail food	←——→	pharmacy, services
services	←——→	impulse shopping, cafés
fast-food strip	←——→	automotive

When doing this exercise, think about ways to make the physical linkages between complementary districts as effective as possible.

This step concludes with the setting of specific goals, by district and by type of store, with target dates to finish leasing. This is just the beginning of the retail recruitment process, but it is the most important part because it confirms what is needed to make downtown successful as a retail destination. It brings together the resources that will make the process a winner. The challenge now is for the downtown organization to implement the plan and to continue to review the plan as circumstances change and as new retailers open.

Chapter 29

A Guide to Developing a Retail Base

H. Blount Hunter

BACKGROUND

Downtown areas of U.S. cities functioned as central business districts for mercantile activity, employment, and civic life until post-World War II suburbanization shifted much of the focus of American life away from city centers. The migration of retailing to malls in suburban neighborhoods stripped downtowns of their vital shopping function. The cost of allowing downtowns to move from multipurpose destinations to single-purpose places was high. Many downtown areas were reduced to single-purpose employment areas—vertical office parks that turned into ghost towns after 5 p.m. Other downtowns retained their civic institutions of arts and culture and their tourism venues. After shedding many layers of civic purpose, many citizens regarded downtown as obsolete and unnecessary. Now, many downtown managers are charged with guiding the development of retailing for a new generation of downtown patrons. Often, this task is assigned before a downtown has regained its role as a vital place in the community—before it is "ready for retail."

When fully functional, downtown areas serve as unique "crossroads" locations where residents, visitors, and workers convene for a variety of purposes. Concentrating multiple layers of consumers in a downtown setting generates significant expenditure potential for retail goods and meals. Over the past two decades, experience has demonstrated the importance of restoring downtowns as well-rounded, mixed-use districts and centers of unique activities with broad appeal and regional drawing power. Experience has also taught that restoring the retail base is most successful after important destination activities and traffic generators are in place and functioning successfully. Except in highly unusual circumstances, retailing is a poor excuse to use to lead a downtown repositioning strategy; instead, retailing is the culminating layer of achievement in downtown revitalization.

doi:10.1300/5137_30

Many downtown managers, politicians, city planners, and well-intended residents are inclined to demand the return of retailing long before conditions are appropriate. This pressure is responsible for many false starts and frustrations as retail initiatives are attempted before conditions for success are present.

This chapter presents a general process that downtown managers can follow to pave the way for retail revitalization. This process is not a one-person endeavor, nor is this a short-term task. Professional assistance may be required for best outcomes. Every community has different circumstances; however, these steps demystify the process and break a big challenge into a series of manageable steps.

STEP 1: CREATE AN "INVENTORY" OF DOWNTOWN ATTRIBUTES

An assessment of downtown strengths/weaknesses and opportunities/ challenges begins with an inventory of key institutions and "reasons for being."

1. What is the size of the daytime workforce?
2. What key institutions are clustered in downtown, and what are their attendance counts?
3. What tourist attractions are in downtown, and what are their attendance trends?
4. What is the scope and content of the existing mercantile base (restaurants, shops, and services)?
5. What is the viability of downtown retailers and restaurants as measured by sales volume and sales trends?
6. What is the inventory of parking?
7. What are vehicle counts at major intersections?
8. What are the crime statistics, and what is the trend?
9. What is the population of downtown residents, and what is their demographic profile?

Downtown's attributes form the basis of its current use. Its present conditions and future potential can be identified through this inventory.

STEP 2: DEFINE THE NATURE OF DOWNTOWN'S RETAIL CHALLENGE

The downtown manager must make a candid assessment of the nature of downtown's retail challenge. What are the issues facing downtown from a retail development perspective? Examine where downtown falls on the continuum of "completely vacant to completely occupied." Be honest in an assessment of where downtown falls on the continuum of "obsolete retailers/ marginally viable retailers to contemporary tenancy/economically viable retailers." Does downtown have any sustainable retail niche today?

Major aspects of the self-examination include:

1. What is the prevailing occupancy rate of retail space?
2. Are retail spaces occupied but with suboptimal tenants?
3. Have negative factors (such as pornography) caused prolonged vacancy of spaces?
4. Is the existing retail space suitable for contemporary retailers in terms of dimensions and ceiling height, or is the space functionally obsolete?
5. Is the retail space in downtown concentrated in the best location relative to parking and major activity generators?
6. Are key retail locations being used for nonretail purposes such as offices?
7. What is the physical condition of vacant retail buildings?
8. Are key retail spaces owned by cooperative landlords?
9. Is vibrant retail so decentralized that it loses its impact as a critical mass?
10. Is the current downtown retail base oriented predominantly to downscale consumers?
11. Are unrealistic rent expectations preventing leasing activity?

This process requires discipline and a willingness to examine factors beneath the surface and should include merchants, brokers, and property owners. This is an internal self-appraisal, so be rigorous and don't hold back. The only way to affect change is to confront issues head-on.

STEP 3: EVALUATE PREVAILING USAGE AND CUSTOMER PERCEPTIONS OF DOWNTOWN

For many reasons, the downtown manager should also complete a comprehensive and objective assessment of downtown's use by local residents. This provides an opportunity to assess strengths and weaknesses—from the perspective of current patrons as well as intended users of downtown. This can be an eye-opening experience that helps to focus attention on the barriers that need to be removed before downtown can aspire to retail development.

Many research techniques can be used including focus groups and community charrettes (stakeholder participation) (qualitative) and random telephone research (quantitative). The questions you'll be asking are similar to "who, what, when, where, why?" The goal is to understand who is using downtown and who isn't using downtown; what are the predominant visit generators; how frequently trips occur for various reasons; where patrons live; the key demographics of users and users' likes and dislikes about key attributes of downtown. Be careful to utilize appropriate research methodologies. Consumer surveys conducted within downtown lack the ability to reach nonusers, and Web-based surveys with self-selected respondents are inadequate tools for this assignment.

Downtown use should be measured for a variety of motivations or trip purposes including shopping, dining, entertainment, professional errands, and other nonwork purposes. The goal is to establish an overall "penetration rate" for downtown as well as "usage rates" for key motivations. Assessing frequency of visits for specific purposes provides another dimension of understanding.

Key outcomes of the quantitative research are an objective measure of downtown's "reach and frequency" along with prioritized trip motivators and demographic profiles of users and nonusers. The insight will be useful in understanding how fully the market has embraced downtown and for determining the reasons they are oriented to downtown. This consumer perspective will be useful in evaluating retail development options.

STEP 4: DOCUMENT DOWNTOWN'S TRADE-AREA DRAWING POWER AND ITS MERCANTILE AND DINING SUCCESSES

Nothing captures the attention of retailers like verifiable success stories of other retailers. For this reason, it is important to document the successes of downtown restaurants and retailers.

Retailers generally seek established markets signified by sustained traffic and predictable market coverage. Retailers generally make site decisions based upon their understanding of the geographic market to be served from a specific location. The site selection model that has prevailed in the United States is a "suburban model" based upon a "divide and conquer" approach of carving a region into a limited number of trade areas or geographic niches with dominant site opportunities. Every metropolitan market has been carved into a series of mall trade areas with readily understood consumer demographics. Retailers match their store location decisions to the shopping center trade areas that most closely serve their needs.

In many cases, downtown areas draw from extended geographic areas covering their entire host metropolitan areas. A downtown may provide a level of market coverage that would require multiple suburban store locations. This is counterintuitive to retailers weaned on the suburban site selection model. Downtown drawing power can be documented through user research; it provides a perspective of market coverage that can supplement a suburban site strategy or in some cases even supplant a suburban multi-store market-coverage strategy. Retailers who misapply the suburban site model to a downtown site opportunity may assume that downtown's market is limited to the typical three- to seven-mile radius of a regional mall, when, in fact, downtowns tend to draw patrons from a ten- to twenty-mile radius. Documentation of downtown's extended drawing power must be one of the retail development tools readily available to downtown managers.

STEP 5: IDENTIFY DOWNTOWN'S MOST SUSTAINABLE COMPETITIVE RETAIL NICHE

Downtown's retail niche cannot be determined in a vacuum; the region's retail hierarchy must be taken into consideration. Downtown's functional strengths must be matched with market voids when identifying competitive opportunities. Optimally, one or more aspects of strength will enable downtown to carve out a unique and sustainable niche that is not directly competitive with suburban retailing.

1. Will downtown's mercantile base focus on food, services, and convenience retailing primarily for workers and tourists?
2. Is downtown uniquely suited to become a specialty niche for arts, hand-crafted goods, and antiques?
3. Can "comparison-goods" retailing in downtown be competitive with suburban offerings?
4. Does downtown have one or more destination retailers or other anchors that can be used to attract complementary merchandising?

STEP 6: PINPOINT THE RETAIL "BULLS-EYE" AND ACKNOWLEDGE THE NEED FOR A CRITICAL MASS

Most retail revitalization initiatives attempt to restore retailing to a traditional shopping street. Although most downtown managers will not have the luxury of starting with a clean slate, it is important to pinpoint the strongest site for retailing and work to concentrate new activity at the "bulls-eye" where exposure and accessibility are highest. Unless circumstances permit the concurrent introduction of a significant mass of retailers, define a primary retail zone with the capacity of accommodating a critical mass of tenants. A cluster of new merchants will achieve higher visibility and greater drawing power than the same number of tenants scattered over a broad area. Scattered retail development has less impact than concentrated development.

STEP 7: TARGET THE MOST APPROPRIATE RETAILERS FOR SUCCESS

Any retail development strategy has short-term candidates and "stretch" prospects based upon long-term aspirations. Retail revitalization efforts can be easily thwarted if inappropriate retailers are targeted in advance of market support. The volume and demographics of downtown's users will dictate which retailers are appropriate candidates. The regional retail hierarchy also influences the opportunity for downtown retailing when voids can be identified or as niches are eliminated for competitive reasons.

In most cases, local entrepreneurs are the key to the early stages of retail revitalization. These merchants are usually the first to perceive market potential, and they have the flexibility to tailor their offerings to the market they perceive. Local retailers are less bound by rigid store prototypes and can more readily adapt to the unusual space configurations typically present in downtown retail buildings. Avoid defining success in terms of leasing space to national retail chain tenants. National chains may never acknowledge the customer base that local retailers perceive in downtown settings. National chains are highly risk averse and are willing to wait until local merchants have proven a market before committing to highly speculative locations. Chains are more than willing to wait until risk is eliminated, even if the cost of deferring is higher rent. In addition, most chains have strict co-tenancy requirements and rigid criteria for floor plans that make it difficult for them to secure locations in urban settings. Chain proliferation makes it doubtful that downtown can create a unique niche if chains are the predominant element.

The merchandise content of pioneering retail tenants will tend to skew toward specialty goods that reflect downtown's key uses. For example, it is unrealistic to expect to create a significant cluster of apparel merchants if downtown lacks a viable department store. However, it is highly realistic to expect interest from artists and artisans if one of downtown's primary trip generators is a museum or arts center. Similarly, if downtown hosts a critical mass of restaurants and entertainment venues, it would be reasonable to target merchants of compatible goods such as books, tapes/CDs, gourmet products, and many types of gifts, as these items can be purchased on impulse by patrons drawn to downtown for dining and entertainment.

Tenant recruitment is a specialized endeavor. The downtown manager can do much to generate prospect lists and establish rapport with potential tenants. Downtown managers traditionally collect pertinent statistics, business facts, and "good news" stories for leasing packages. Downtown managers also review local economic development programs and incentives for applicability to retailers.

Most retailers would prefer to join an established retail node rather than to participate in the speculative creation of a new retail district. Ironically, the very merchants who would have the biggest impact on establishing or transforming the image of a retail node are the most reluctant to lead the transformation. Remember, merchants react to the immediate opportunity for profit and the probability of success rather than the quaint architecture of a prospective storefront or the opportunity to be a "pioneer."

So, although it may be tempting to attract exclusive merchants or national chains as "trophies," it is best to begin the retail revitalization process with entrepreneurial merchants who will be successful.

STEP 8: GROOM DOWNTOWN
FOR LONG-TERM RETAIL EVOLUTION

Just as most downtowns lost their retail base in a slow bleed, most downtowns will regain their retail base in an incremental, evolutionary process. In limited cases, market conditions support large-scale development opportunities for an urban retail center. In these instances, strong co-tenancies can be created in effective critical mass clusters.

Retailers operating in downtown today may not be the tenants that are ultimately desired in downtown. The downtown manager must acknowledge that retail content is dynamic. The downtown manager must be strategic in guiding tenant recruitment programs. Grooming downtown for long-term retail evolution is critical to directing the future tenant base and merchandise mix. The goal is to strengthen and improve each generation of retail tenants.

Success begets new retailer interest, while the inevitable failures of individual retailers represent opportunities to tap into the market for replacement tenants with greater probabilities of succeeding. The downtown manager is advised to maintain a list of desired prospects and to create ongoing relationships with potential merchants in order to quickly capitalize upon opportunities to strengthen the mix. Existing merchants can serve as ambassadors for downtown; they can help sell the opportunity to brokers or prospective merchants.

A PRACTICAL MODEL OF DOWNTOWN RETAIL EVOLUTION

Many small- and medium-sized communities need a practical model for retail revitalization. Communities without downtown department stores and without clusters of mainstream retailers must take the first steps toward building a retail base that can evolve to include a broader variety of retail uses and tenant types and a more competitive merchandise offering.

No universal prescription exists for downtown revitalization; however, a model that has been employed successfully in a variety of cities uses family entertainment programming as the basic element in a strategy to stimulate traffic and reduce barriers to downtown usage. Fun, family programming can establish the appeal of downtown—first as a "special place" then as a place to be enjoyed routinely because of its unique characteristics and enjoyable setting.

Restaurants are the initial commercial response to consumer perception of downtown as a "place" and an entertainment destination. Restaurant development should be encouraged as a means of reinforcing downtown as a destination. Enlightened restaurateurs flocking together to create a "restaurant row" understand that downtown's general drawing power augments each restaurant's individual drawing power. Once restaurant development provides a sustained and consistent base of patrons, the area can be positioned to capture the interest of local retail entrepreneurs. Given certain economics, these pioneers can survive by trading low cost of entry with upside performance.

Initially, shopping will not be a major trip generator for downtown. In the early stages of retail revitalization, retailers will feed upon traffic drawn to downtown for entertainment, dining, and other nonshopping motivations. Over the long haul, as the merchandise offering expands and the critical mass of shops increases, shopping will optimally become one of the key trip generators for downtown. Pioneering merchants will survive on their individual destination customers and impulse purchasing by entertainment- and dining-driven patrons. Tenant recruitment efforts should focus upon local destination merchants whose loyal following can become an asset to downtown.

As a critical mass of retailing becomes established, merchandising can expand to include "comparison goods" such as apparel. As the breadth and depth of merchandise offerings increase, shopping may emerge as a primary trip generator on par with other established downtown visit motivations. When this occurs, downtown retailers benefit from a location that offers spin-off patrons from nearby trip generators in a busy, mixed-use place as well as a steady stream of destination shoppers responding to its retail content.

Chapter 30

"One-of-a-Kind" Regional Attractions

Donald E. Hunter

During the formation and early days of American cities, it was taken for granted that the community's primary public, corporate, and civic facilities would be located in the downtown area. No one questioned the downtown location for government offices, local and federal courts, main libraries, civic auditoriums, and other facilities that were considered "one-of-a-kind."

In the private sector it was always assumed that local banks would have their headquarters downtown; professional service firms such as accountants, attorneys, and architects were downtown; local corporations in regional offices preferred downtown locations and signature buildings rather than campus facilities in outer areas; and, downtown was the regional retail center with department stores attracting shoppers for destination shopping trips which, in turn, supported smaller shops and restaurants.

CYCLES OF CHANGE

During the second half of the twentieth century, as American cities experienced several cycles of economic and social turmoil, it no longer was taken for granted that these facilities needed to be downtown. County governments moved many functions to outer areas and campus-type settings, in many cases only leaving symbolic courthouse structures behind. Libraries and civic facilities expanded elsewhere as metropolitan areas grew, often following the people to the suburbs. Corporate changes such as growth, mergers, acquisitions, and consolidations resulted in corporate headquarters changing locations, often out of the downtown area and, in many cases, out of the city entirely.

The out-migration of retailing resulted in the closing of downtown department stores as new stores were developed in regional malls. Locally owned banks were no longer locally owned and no longer in need of a symbolic downtown headquarters. Even professionals such as attorneys and

doi:10.1300/5137_31

accountants discovered that they no longer needed a downtown headquarters or even a downtown location. Free parking in suburban parking lots was often the excuse for moving, along with safety concerns, high taxes, overpriced real estate, and difficulties associated with growth and expansion in the downtown area.

Throughout these transitions, downtown advocates recognized that the damage done from these out-migrations was more than just the loss of the facilities themselves. The symbolic loss, and the ancillary developments that went with them, often hurt the downtown area as much or more than the loss of jobs and economic activity. A number of techniques were attempted during the second half of the 1990s, with varying degrees of success, to stem the outflow of important "one-of-a-kind" facilities.

REVITALIZATION IN DOWNTOWN

The good news is that during the past fifteen years this situation has changed substantially. Successful downtown revitalization activities of the 1980s and the 1990s, coupled with failures associated with the suburbanization of many one-of-a-kind facilities contributed to these trend reversals.

For example, major cities that built their one-of-a-kind sports facilities in a suburban area suffered attendance losses, and in several cases, the loss of a professional franchise to a competing city with a downtown facility. Metropolitan areas with limited public transportation in suburban areas recognized that constituents and customers needed better access to governmental facilities. Demands for larger and bigger civic and tourist-related facilities such as performing arts and convention centers posed difficult siting and usage problems in the suburbs, and could function better downtown.

In addition, governments and downtown supporters championed more aggressive public/private partnerships that allowed many one-of-a-kind facilities and complexes to come back to downtown (where they belong). Success stories associated with the move and location of these facilities in downtown areas proliferated. By the year 2000 it was clear that a location in the core area, the heart of the metropolitan area, was the preferred location for most, if not all, of the one-of-a-kind facilities that served all metropolitan residents and many visitors from outside of the metropolitan area.

From the standpoint of downtown development, public- and private-sector leaders and managers now seek to locate their mixed-use developments, major civic and governmental facilities, sports and performing arts facilities, certain educational and institutional uses, and a variety of other major facilities that are "people generators" in downtown. Those facilities that clearly depend upon extremely large sites and low land costs (e.g., theme parks, regional malls, university campuses) may still favor outer locations due to necessity. They trade off access and convenience factors because of their destination nature and the fact that their customers/users will seek them out wherever they are.

However, most other destination attractions and facilities that are singular in nature, or for which local markets can only support a single facility, are increasingly seeking the numerous benefits associated with being downtown. Even multiplex cinemas, which require a large footprint at a relatively low cost and large volumes of parking, which customers expect to be convenient and free, are coming back to dense downtowns in a vertical configuration with shared parking arrangements. These businesses, in turn, anchor and benefit from restaurants, bars, stores, offices, hotels, apartments, and other entertainment venues in downtown mixed-use developments.

The downside is that these major new downtown developments with their "one-of-a-kind" facilities are not easy to put together. Exceptional leadership and political support is necessary, along with enlightened and creative financing, site assembly, and management/marketing skills. Nevertheless, successes proliferate through North American cities, and the aggressive public/private partnerships necessary to realize these projects are becoming more commonplace.

Downtown leaders and managers need to look beyond the "soft stuff" of programs, projects, and processes, and get involved in the "hard stuff" of bricks and mortar developments that not only improve the look and character of the downtown area, but more importantly, bring jobs, residents, visitors, expenditures, and tax flows back into the downtown area in a major way.

Chapter 31

Managing the Politics of Downtown Redevelopment Projects

N. David Milder

INTRODUCTION

Increasingly across the United States, the name of the game in downtown revitalization is shifting from district management to redevelopment. It's not that district management has failed—far from it—but for the first time in decades, scads of developers are looking for downtown projects. Admittedly, the crown jewels behind most of our visions of downtown revitalization are significant real estate projects that are designed to both enhance our central business districts (CBDs) economic vitality and make them even more attractive central social districts.

Consequently, the primary focus of many downtown leaders is shifting from such concerns as "crime and grime," façade improvements, streetscape renovations, and promotions to such challenges as assembling viable development sites, attracting developers, and determining proper densities and use mixes for significant real estate developments, etc. Although downtown leaders usually welcome their growing involvement in viable redevelopment projects, all too many initially fail to recognize—often, until it's too late—just how "political" redevelopment projects are. Consequently, they are very reactive and ineffective when the inevitable political brouhahas emerge.

An earlier and shorter version of this chapter appeared in the *Downtown Idea Exchange* newsletter, May 15, 2004 issue. The author would like to thank Peter Beronio, Spencer Ferdinand, Beth Lippman, Mary Mann, Rick Mariani, and Marvin Reed for their comments on and contributions to this article.

doi:10.1300/5137_32

REDEVELOPMENT PROJECTS ARE PRONE
TO GENERATING CONFLICTS

Downtown leaders should understand that redevelopment projects, by their very nature, usually motivate some residents and businesspeople to oppose them and often there are community groups ready to organize, mobilize, and finance this opposition:

- Redevelopment projects can have an adverse impact on some local residents and businesses. Most directly affected are the residents and/or businesses who may have to be relocated in order to assemble a viable redevelopment site. A good relocation program can convince them to accept a project; a bad relocation program can create project enemies who are easily perceived by the public as victims.
- In a geographic ring immediately around a project site, you are likely to find people who fear that increased traffic congestion, increased demand for available parking, building shadows, refuse odors, etc., will adversely affect their homes or businesses. These people are usually easily mobilized by efforts to oppose the redevelopment project and often provide the most skilled and intractable opponents of a project. They can't be won over by relocation.
- Most communities have "protector" organizations concerned about such issues as: not burdening the school system with more students, historic preservation, protecting the community's trees and open spaces, etc. These organizations might find "principled" reasons to object to a redevelopment project. In addition, communities often have merchant groups and neighborhood associations, organizations with strong latent missions to protect the interests of their members. Consider, for example, a possible merchant mobilization to a Wal-Mart coming into your downtown. Protector organizations often provide the organizational spines and political skills for campaigns opposing downtown redevelopment projects. They are the mechanisms through which opposition to redevelopment in a community is "scaled up."

Downtown leaders should also be aware that even widespread public support for their redevelopment projects may be amorphous and insufficient to motivate active political support on their behalf. The appreciation of the benefits of a downtown redevelopment project—and thus political support—is likely to be dispersed within the residential community and geographically located in a broad ring. This ring is more distant than the one where residents and businesses who are impacted negatively by environmental factors are located. For these distant project supporters, the benefits are likely to be perceived as Mancur Olson-like "public goods" such as clean air and pure water. The better retailers, skating rink, new museum, etc., that a project might provide may be great ideas, but *their* bottom-line attitude is: "If the project happens, great; if not, oh well!" They are content to let others in the community make it happen—or fail trying. For downtown leaders, the challenge is to make these supporters feel more strongly and directly impacted by the project.

Project support from the downtown business community is absolutely essential, but it may be discounted by some residents, civic activists, and political leaders as self-serving.

SOME DO'S AND DON'TS

Following are some suggestions for handling a number of the political problems associated with downtown redevelopment projects.

1. *Have an area-wide, agreed-upon plan before soliciting developers.* Years ago, the Regional Plan Association interviewed most of the big developers in New York City to find out what would get them more involved in the outer boroughs' downtowns. Their overwhelming answer was for the city to prepare area-wide plans that would designate development sites, with their allowed uses and densities, and, establish environmental, parking, and traffic parameters for the surrounding areas. Such plans may be the gold standard for dealing with redevelopment areas. For the developers, comprehensive, area-wide plans mean that most of the important potential conflicts that a project might provoke are resolved before the developers become involved—and this promises huge reductions in risk and front-end costs. However, for downtown leaders and/or city redevelopment officials, creating such plans means they must still deal with the conflicts that the area-wide plan would enable the developers to avoid. Doing this well requires money, time, and a strong, consensus-building process—assets that they often lack.

Because of time constraints, it is almost impossible to create an area-wide plan after a proposal for a redevelopment project is placed on the table.

2. *Prepare a compelling case for your project.* All too often, downtown leaders are so involved in attracting a developer and getting the deal done that they don't pay enough attention to creating a compelling brief for their project. Formulate ways to make the project's benefits psychologically immediate and tangible to residents. This will motivate more active support for the project. Residents need to understand how the project will protect

against property tax increases, add jobs, create affordable housing for local residents, bring in retailers that the community wants, etc.

Some types of data may be persuasive and trigger action, e.g., statistical data showing how a project will bring down property taxes, reduce crime, increase jobs, etc.

However, as Rick Mariani, an official at New Jersey Transit with a long history of involvement in downtown revitalization projects, has aptly noted: "I've learned that people don't change their behavior based on what they know; they change it based on what they feel." The case also has to push the right psychological buttons, and stories are a great way of doing this. For example, the case for a retail project might feature a narrative showing how much choice in shops and merchandise it will provide; or how the busy, time-pressured life of a "Super Mom" in the "outer impact ring" might be made easier because the project will significantly reduce the time she spends on shopping chores.

General praise about how great, big, or beautiful your project will be won't cut the mustard.

3. *Conduct a well-planned and timely public relations campaign to present the case for the project.* This campaign should begin well before any pivotal make-or-break vote about the project occurs. In addition to well-placed stories in print and electronic media, this should also involve presentations to key community groups and decision makers.

4. *Don't let your mayor be your strategist, planner, or developer.* The role of the mayor can be absolutely critical. Some mayors want to be the city's redevelopment guru, energizer, and deal maker. Almost invariably, this creates strong political turbulence. Citizen support for the mayor's redevelopment project(s) becomes inseparable from political support for the mayor. Ideally, you want the mayor to be able to support a project without the project being perceived to be under his or her political ownership. The most effective mayors tend to be strong public advocates of revitalization and the guardians of the redevelopment decision-making process, ensuring its staffing, financial resources, and smooth and effective functioning, while demanding real accomplishments from its participants. The following comments by Marvin Reed, the former mayor of Princeton, New Jersey, aptly describes his approach to such a role:

> In my experience, the mayor's role in redevelopment is critical. Not that the mayor has to think it up and design it, but the mayor is the key person that puts the pieces . . . and people . . . together and then can make it happen. The key is the mayor's ability to involve many other people. It can't just be "the mayor's plan." Advance it, but depersonalize it.

5. *Don't forget city council members.* In many municipalities, the city council will be making critical decisions about downtown redevelopment projects. Council members have to be willing to incur the political costs that supporting the redevelopment project might entail. They are more likely to withstand the political slings and arrows of redevelopment if they are brought into the redevelopment decision-making process earlier, rather than later. For example, Bob Benecke, the former city manager of Englewood, New Jersey, has held workshops on downtown revitalization for council members, and he frequently briefed them on potential projects in the confidentiality of caucus sessions to test and mobilize their support.

6. *Try to mobilize civic groups to support your project.* Neighborhood groups from areas not immediately adjacent to a redevelopment site sometimes may have good reasons to support a redevelopment project. A good illustration of this occurred in Garden City, New York, which is run politically by four residential property associations. A few years back, one property association—the one closest to the main commercial strip—objected to the implementation of long-planned parking improvements that were needed to ensure the financial health of some key office buildings. Their objections prevailed until the other property associations realized that this would result in more of the tax burden being shifted from downtown commercial rate payers to residential rate payers throughout the town. Such groups may be hard to find in your community, but the advantages of finding them and getting them to realize where their interests lie outweigh any costs incurred in mobilizing them.

A good starting point is networking with community groups and relevant decision makers early, even before you can talk about a project or perhaps even have a project to talk about. It's a lot easier to get people on your side when they already know and feel comfortable with you.

7. *Don't hold large public meetings.* In large public meetings in which the topic of discussion is a redevelopment project, the group dynamics will invariably encourage participants to be critical and vituperative. Rational discussions and civil exchanges of information are minimal. Project proponents never convert those on the fence or those opposed to the project. On the other hand, these meetings often galvanize, energize, network, and strengthen project opponents. A more effective approach for public outreach is to meet with small groups, especially with the leaders of significant neighborhood and civic associations. In these smaller meetings the conversation cannot be one-sided—be prepared to listen and negotiate. Also, look to establish common ground.

8. *Avoid long lists of development projects.* Downtown experts have long admonished downtown leaders to take a comprehensive approach to revitalization. Sometimes this advice impels downtown leaders to want to

publicly identify every possible downtown redevelopment project so they can show their constituencies just how thoroughly they are doing their job. For instance, one ambitious and nameless mayor insisted on presenting to his community a long and detailed list of recommended downtown redevelopment projects. If one project is going to stimulate public opposition, you can image how much agitation six or seven projects can ignite! A more prudent approach is to move project by project, using one project's success to garner support for additional redevelopment projects.

9. *Chose savvy and strong developers.* Look for developers who are willing to try to buy out property owners and who don't rely entirely on public takings (taking of property by government). Conversely, the municipality should try to minimize the number of properties on which it has to use its eminent domain powers.

Also, as Spencer Ferdinand of the Queens Overall EDC has observed: "There is an inherent secrecy that downtown developers surround their property acquisitions/negotiations in that sometimes blows up in their faces when their 'secret' plans hit the media and catch the 'pols' by surprise."

The need for redevelopment in many downtowns, be they large or small, is undeniable. Equally undeniable is the need for community support of these projects. Although redevelopment projects, by their very nature, engender conflicts, the key is not that such conflicts might occur, but the way that they are handled.

REFERENCES

Downtown Idea Exchange (2004). May 15.
Olson, Mancur (1965). *The Logic of Collective Action: Public Goods and the Theory of Groups.* First Edition. Boston: Harvard University Press.

Part VII:
International Perspectives

For many years, cities in North America have looked to other cities worldwide for design themes and inspiration. The broad avenues of Paris, the waterfront treatments in many European cities, and the pedestrian streets in Europe, Asia, and elsewhere have helped North Americans to better understand how business districts and town centers work. Now, these same business districts are looking to North America for management models—business improvement districts in particular. This section gives the reader a taste of how some other countries are approaching downtown management and leadership.

Chapter 32

Canada As an Urban Country

Douglas B. Clark

In many instances the urban examples of renewal and revitalization within the United States have become the models that downtown managers and urban advocates espouse as tried and true formulae. In Canada, we often view the activity south of the border and anticipate that within a two-year period, the momentum will slowly creep northward, and we too will feel the energy and enlightenment. How could things be that much different between the two countries sharing the North American continent?

Although clearly a less-populated landmass occupying climatic and vegetative zones that many would view as uninhabitable, Canada has a young, evolving urban context, linked by diverse demographic, language, and geographical zones. The issues of sustainability, housing, homelessness, and transportation are not necessarily unique, but the political framework and mechanisms available to deal with urban issues are significantly different.

The following overview attempts to illustrate the view that others have of Canada, as well as give some insights into the real challenges facing the future of Canadian cities and the magnitude of the problem confronting downtown managers and politicians.

INTRODUCTION

Canada is a country with a population of 31.6 million people spread throughout ten provinces and three territories, which encompass 9,985,210 hectares (2,467,311,803 acres) of land and water.

Currently, two-thirds of Canada's population, employment, and real output are located in twenty-seven census metropolitan areas (CMAs), which have a minimum of 100,000 inhabitants. Eighty percent of Canadians reside in urban areas with populations greater than 10,000 people (Statistics Canada, 2002). The recent growth rate in Canada has been calculated at 4.0 percent compared to 5.4 percent in the United States, 5.9 percent in

doi:10.1300/5137_33

Australia, and a world average of 7.0 percent. At present, 50 percent of Canada's growth is primarily attributed to a national urban policy on immigration (Statistics Canada, 2002).

The seven largest CMAs around Toronto, Montreal, Vancouver, Ottawa/Hull, Calgary, Edmonton, and Winnipeg account for 45 percent of the total Canadian population. Within these seven regions four significant growth centers are currently emerging, and they account for a large and growing proportion of the nation's population. These regions are:

1. Ontario Golden Horseshoe (6.7 million people in Oshawa, Toronto, Hamilton, and St. Catherine's-Niagara)
2. Montreal and region (3.7 million)
3. Lower Mainland and southern Vancouver Island (2.7 million)
4. Calgary—Edmonton corridor (2.2 million)

Twenty-five of the fastest growing municipalities in Canada, however, are those that surround the core of the CMAs. An increasing trend over the past decade suggests that suburban growth is substantially overtaking urban growth.

The United Nations consistently rates the quality of life in Canadian cities among the highest in the world. A recent survey also ranked Canadian cities as some of the least costly places to do business (KPMG Consulting, 2002; Boyd and Associates, 2002). A worldwide "quality of life survey" of 215 cities around the world ranked five Canadian cities at the following levels:

City	Rank
Vancouver	2
Toronto	18
Montreal	25
Ottawa	25
Calgary	31

However, the future is not necessarily as optimistic as it seems as Canadian cities struggle under the enormous pressure of eroding infrastructure (water, roads, and sewers), a lack of social housing, and public transit systems that all require massive reinvestment.

ECONOMIC DEVELOPMENT, TAX POLICY, AND THE NEW ECONOMY

Speculatively, the cost of operating a business will remain the single most important location criterion for new economy companies. Economic development is far more dependent on the availability of a highly trained and diversified workforce and competitive costs. Canadian cities are well positioned to compete globally for new economic investment. The ethnic diversity that has been encouraged and maintained in Canadian cities makes them attractive to foreign knowledge workers and to investors. In most Canadian cities these foreign investors and workers can readily find a community in which they feel at home. However, to be competitive, Canadian cities must come to grips with the immediate funding crisis that is limiting the ability to upgrade and enhance basic services.

The traditional political hierarchy and funding mechanisms in Canada are currently coming under stringent review by all levels of government, but most rigorously by the municipalities. Between 1995 and 2001 municipal revenues edged up only 14 percent compared to gains of 38 percent at the federal and 30 percent at the provincial level. In addition, Canadian cities have determined that their value to the overall provincial gross domestic product (GDP) is sharply increasing (TD Bank Financial Group, 2002):

1. Vancouver produces 53 percent of the GDP of British Columbia
2. Calgary and Edmonton produce 64 percent of the GDP of Alberta
3. Winnipeg produces 64 percent of the GDP of Manitoba
4. Montreal produces 50 percent of the GDP of Quebec
5. Halifax produces 48 percent of the GDP of Nova Scotia

In Canada, cities do not exist in the constitution—they are creations of the provinces, thus they have no independent status. They can raise and spend only what they are granted by the province. Even where Canadian cities do have some taxing authority—such as use of property taxes, development charges, and user fees—provincial governments have the right to impose restrictions on what goods and services can be taxed and at what rate. They can also, at any time, take away powers that had previously been granted. Thus, the only tool available, property tax, has become the primary revenue instrument for all Canadian municipalities. The time period, however, for maintaining fiscal responsibility through the use of property tax revenue has been reached in a number of Canadian centers.

The dilemma is further heightened by the fact that property tax is not a good mechanism for growth and sustainability because:

- it is not based on ability to pay;
- there is no guarantee that property values will continue to rise in accordance with city costs; and
- by increasing the taxes on commercial property, cities begin to affect their ability to be competitive.

Cities in Europe and the United States went through an unprecedented reinvestment of their infrastructure in the 1990s. In these areas, the senior levels of government, in partnership with the private sector, made substantial contributions. In addition, due to the local autonomy afforded to these cities, significant contributions were made toward renewal through a wide variety of financing options.

Twenty years ago many U.S. city cores were crumbling, and the air-photo image of many urban cores resembled a doughnut. Downtown shopping areas were boarded up, and urban municipalities were swept by an epidemic of crime and poverty. Eventually, governments could no longer ignore the deterioration. U.S. cities made a concerted effort to coax individuals back to the downtown area, investing in airports, roads, public transit, waterfronts, and social housing. Although many U.S. cities have received large sums from the federal government (for example, TEA-21, the Transportation Equity Act for the 21st Century, which was established 1999 and provided $217 billion over six years to solve traffic and associated environmental problems), they have also supported their source of revenue from sales taxes and user fees that rise in line with economic demand.

U.S. cities also have benefited from a variety of public/private partnerships:

- *Tax-exempt bonds:* This has proven to be a cheap source of financing for a municipality. Interest income is generally exempt from federal and/or state tax, thus allowing the city to charge a lower rate of interest.
- *Tax-increment financing (TIFs):* TIFs allow a city to designate an area for improvement and then earmark any future growth in property tax revenues to pay for initial and ongoing economic development. To fund the initial costs, cities can float debt backed by the expected flow of the tax increments as security.
- *Public private partnerships (PPP):* PPPs parcel out the risk and reward of a project between the private and public sectors and can be effective strategies for achieving objectives that the private sector alone might not be willing to pursue.
- *Other incentives:* U.S. cities make use of a wide variety of tax credits to encourage individuals and companies to locate in targeted areas close to downtown cores such as former industrial areas (brownfields) and low-income areas (enterprise zones).

In Europe, the mechanism for infrastructure funding came from the European Regional Development Fund (ERDF). Between 2000 and 2006, one-third of the entire budget ($175 billion US) will be redirected to infrastructure renewal. Within Europe, PPPs are used more and more to leverage investment (European Regional Development Fund, n.d.).

CANADIAN CITIES TODAY

Infrastructure

Up until recently, the perception was that since most Canadian cities were still relatively young, they did not require major investment by the federal government. However, realistically, maintenance is no longer enough. Replacement and modernization are now required. Estimates show that $44 billion will be required to meet the shortfall. An additional $2 billion plus will be required per year. Over the next five years the capital investment required in public transit will be at least $9.2 billion (TD Bank Financial Group, 2002).

Housing

To meet the needs of affordable housing, estimates show that 500,000 rental units will be required over the next ten years (TD Bank Financial Group, 2002).

Universities and Colleges

The Canadian education system is gradually getting research and operating grants restored, but they are still recovering from twenty years of cutbacks (TD Bank Financial Group, 2002). In the United States real government spending on education increased 20 percent in the past twenty years versus a 30 percent decline in Canada. Today it is estimated that fourteen times as much research is done in the United States as is done in Canada, and almost fifty times the revenue from patents and licensing goes to U.S. colleges and universities than goes to Canadian schools.

The economic sustainability of the Canadian city is of such concern that Prime Minister Jean Chretien established a Caucus Task Force on Urban Issues (Prime Minister's Caucus Task Force, 2002). The report was released in November 2002. The idea of a national urban policy is not new in Canada. It lies dormant and reemerges when there is a perceived crisis. (Past instances have involved the early 1900s and mass immigration, the 1930s Depression era, post–World War II, and the late 1960s when rapid growth was followed by spiraling interest rates, housing shortages, heritage conservation and environmental protection movements.) We are apparently now at a point of national concern.

The proposals of the task force recognize the necessity for cooperation and collaboration between all players on the urban scene, and the interrelatedness of all urban problems and their solutions. Within the report are some tangible and immediate recommendations:

I. That a federal minister responsible for urban regions be appointed to give a voice to urban interests in parliament

II. That an Institute of Urban Research, or university network, be established to organize the best practices from a national and international perspective

III. That an external Advisory Body composed of urban scholars, professional and business associations, and policy think tanks be established to advise the minister

IV. That a National Urban Summit be established consisting of provincial ministers and key urban partners

V. That the new Ministry concentrate on three priority programs:
  A. Affordable housing
    1. A review of the Canada Mortgage and Housing Corporation (CMHC) is proposed with a view of permitting it to be much more flexible with nonprofit groups
    2. More flexible financing initiatives to permit the construction of more rental housing
    3. The renewal of the Residential Rehabilitation Assistance Program (RRAP) and Supporting Communities Partnership Initiative (SCPI)
  B. Transit/transportation
    1. Improve regional transportation systems and local public transit in order to relieve congestion and reduce emissions
  C. Sustainable infrastructure
    1. Stable, long-term (fifteen-year) funding for upgrading
    2. Revamp existing programs: Strategic Highways Infrastructure Program, Local Transportation Infrastructure Program, and Infrastructure Canada—to coordinate strategies
    3. Transportation planning with a goal of reducing use of oil- and gasoline-burning vehicles, protecting the environment, using green technologies

Although the Prime Minister's Task Force report is a promising step toward a national solution, the financial pressures on the municipalities to deal with the day-to-day issues are reaching critical proportions. The need for an immediate "New Deal" to address funding options between the three levels of government is of paramount importance and is currently being tested at the local level by former Winnipeg Mayor, Glen Murray. The arguments for a "New Deal" are premised on the fact that current funding options other than multiyear federal and provincial programs need to be reviewed, as they still leave municipal governments at the mercy of shifting federal and provincial priorities. They also fail the accountability test in which funds are raised by one level of government and spent by another. It is proposed that any new agreement be based on the following criteria:

1. Reliability—is this revenue source likely to grow sufficiently to cover the rising costs of service delivery, and does it carry risk of interruption?
2. Accountability—is the same political entity responsible for administering both the spending and the associated funding?
3. Transparency—is there a good match between who society believes should bear the burden of a tax and who ultimately bears it?
4. Administrative simplicity—would the new revenue source be relatively easy and inexpensive to establish and administer?
5. Efficiency—does the tax present the most efficient allocation of resources?
6. Equity—is the revenue source fair, either by matching beneficiaries with those bearing the burden or by levying taxes based on the ability to pay?

All parties understand that Canadian cities need access to ongoing revenue sources, and that simply transferring federal/provincial revenues is not dependable—both governments can alter the agreements at will. The best alternative to ensure reliability and accountability—one that satisfies all imperatives—is for municipalities to piggyback off existing federal or provincial taxes. Some have suggested that this may involve a redistribution of the income tax. However, it may not be as desirable a source (as it is in the United States and Europe), because it would be difficult to tax locally and it would force companies to move. A better method for efficiency purposes would involve excise or sales taxes. These costs would then play into the cost of goods and consumer purchasing patterns.

Municipalities also need to realign the current tax structure so that the unfair advantage of overtaxation on commercial property versus residential, and downtown property versus suburban is corrected. Better use needs to be made of user fees. Cities need to be more flexible on labor contracts to facilitate contracting when stringent costs and standards criteria are met. Provincial governments need to loosen the shackles that impede municipalities from securing other sources of revenue and encourage public/private partnerships. As four-fifths of the current population live and derive economic activity from urban centers, it is apparent that the long-term performance of the Canadian economy and Canadian living standards will hinge on the fortunes of its cities.

HOUSING

Reports show approximately 11.6 million dwellings in Canada. Two-thirds of the housing is owner-occupied, and 58 percent is single-family/detached. Although housing aging is obviously increasing, only 25 percent of the housing stock is judged to require minor repairs and only 8 percent will require major repairs. No national housing strategy has been in place since the mid-1980s, and this has resulted in another area of immediate crisis: Approximately 96,000 families are waiting for assisted housing in the larger urban centers across the country (CMHC, 2003).

Canada Mortgage and Housing Corporation (CMHC), Canada's national housing agency, was originally created in 1946 with the mandate "to help Canadians gain access to a wide choice of quality, affordable homes." In 1993, however, funding was slashed for any new housing construction and new social housing programs were not restarted until 1999. Between 2001 and 2006 it is estimated that there will be an average of 185,000 new housing starts in Canada. Currently, programs are in place through CMHC that deal with housing renovation and repair ($384 million) and affordable housing ($1.0 billion over five years). Both plans have joint agreements with all provinces and territories. The four following trends will affect the future housing market in Canada:

1. Changing demographics—The 65+ age group will become 19.1 percent of the population, and the 75+ group will increase to over 1.0 million. (Statistics Canada, 2002)
2. Aboriginal housing issues (both on and off reserve)—Currently First Nations' residents occupy 89,000 housing units for 97,500 households. Only 57 percent of the housing stock is in good shape. Approximately 2,800 units per year are built for a demand that requires 4,400 units. (CMHC, 2003)
3. Urban issues—The Prime Minister's Task Force on Urban Issues has recommended a nationwide policy on all aspects of urban renewal of

which housing is a major component. (Skelton, 2003; Prime Minister's Caucus Task Force, 2002)
4. Incidence of low-income households—Approximately 7.9 percent of the population is below the poverty level. The housing programs for these people are currently inadequate. (Pohl, 2001)

In the United States, federal and state governments subsidize home ownership costs by allowing deductions on mortgage interest payments. This housing subsidy is a major factor contributing to the expansion of U.S. cities. Canadians, however, do not enjoy this tax break and, as a result, have consumed less land for housing, largely limiting development to established urban boundaries.

North American cities are undergoing a major transformation as many countries move from industrial to knowledge-based economies. In the United States competition for housing between old economy and new economy workers is elevating the cost of owning and renting a home in the cities beyond the affordability levels of many. However, Toronto is the exception. In Canadian cities, workers (e.g., teachers, firefighters, postal employees, police, and other urban workers) can still afford to find accommodation. In other parts of urban North America this growing crisis of providing "affordable" housing is rapidly becoming a pressing concern. The issue is perceived by many to be even greater than transportation congestion, greenhouse gas (GHG) emissions, and crime.

HOMELESSNESS

In Canada, the crisis in housing is a contributing factor to increased homelessness. This is yet another indicator suggesting that the quality of life in Canada's urban areas has begun to slip. Although the number of homeless is virtually impossible to measure accurately, increased traffic flows at homeless shelters and food banks point to a worsening problem. A recent survey, suggested that there are approximately 35,000 to 40,000 homeless people in Canada (Murphy, 2000). In the United States a similar survey reported an estimate of 350,000 homeless people, which is in line with the 10:1 ratio regarding most comparisons between the two countries. The homeless are generally distributed throughout the following Canadian cities in the following numbers (Pohl, 2001):

Montreal and Toronto—10,000 people each
Vancouver—5,000
Edmonton, Calgary, Ottawa, Winnipeg, Hamilton, Halifax, Saskatoon, Regina—between 1,000 and 2,000 each

In 1998, as a result of little or no action on homelessness, Canada received the strongest rebuke ever delivered by the United Nations for inactivity on this issue. Ironically, this rebuke was given despite the fact that Canada had been named for several years as the best country in the world in which to live (Murphy, 1999).

Although there was no national policy, city councils, in an effort to respond to the public pressure for action, created shelters and assembled task forces to look at the issue on a local basis. By 1998, Canada's ten largest cities passed resolutions to the federal and provincial governments declaring homelessness a national disaster. The rise in homelessness is directly linked to increased poverty, and over the past decade these levels have risen dramatically.

Poverty has had the greatest impact on the following five groups:

1. Single-parent families, whose poverty rate was 2.45 times higher than average
2. Aboriginal persons, whose poverty rate was 2.26 times higher than average
3. Recent immigrants, whose poverty rate was 2.17 times higher than average
4. Visible minorities, whose poverty rate was 1.53 times higher than average
5. Persons with disabilities, whose poverty rate was 1.47 times higher than average

In response to the pressure from the municipalities and social agencies, in 1999 the federal government announced a Federal Homelessness Plan. As part of a National Homelessness Initiative, funding has subsequently been approved in each of the past three federal budgets toward the Supporting Communities Partnership Initiative (SCPI) and the Residential Rehabilitation Assistance Program (RRAP). Additional funds have also been transferred to each of the federal/provincial affordable housing initiatives. Signed in 2001, this deal committed the spending of $1.36 billion over five years to create 27,000 new affordable houses across Canada.

TRANSPORTATION

The trend toward urban sprawl has led to burgeoning transit problems across all CMAs in Canada. As in all metropolitan areas, conventional transit is still uneconomical in the suburbs, and reliance on the private auto continues and grows. The trend is certainly evidenced by rising pollution and higher costs for road construction and repair.

Historically throughout Canada, the cities and provinces have exclusively funded the public transit system. To date, the federal government has not been an active participant. However, there is increasing pressure for the federal government to become a more active participant in the development, operation, and funding of public transit. The message coming from the leaders at the municipal and provincial levels is, "there is a strong case for a federal government role in urban transit; a multi-year, predictable funding program, preferably based in part on transportation user fees" (Zavergiu, 2003, p. 12).

On a per-capita basis, American cities have built four times the amount of freeway lanes than Canadian cities. This was in large part spawned by a significant presence by the U.S. federal government. In Canada during the 1950 to 1970 time period, the federal government concentrated on building the Trans-Canada Highway, the St. Lawrence Seaway, marine ports, and a national airport and air navigational system.

Compared to U.S. cities, Canadian cities are more environmentally sustainable and more affordable from a transportation perspective than the typical U.S. model. The average Canadian city emits less transportation-generated greenhouse gases than does the average American city (4,683 CO2 tonnes per capita [kg] versus 2,764 CO2 tonnes per capita [kg], respectively) (Zavergiu, 2003). In anticipation of meeting the stringent demands of the Kyoto Accord, both countries still have a long way to go to meet European emission standards, which average 1,887 CO2 tonnes per capita.

Canadian cities are more environmentally sustainable in providing intra-urban transportation. At the metropolitan level, Canadian cities are more densely populated with residents and workplaces. The United States averages 14.2 persons per hectare (5.8 persons per acre) and 8.1 jobs per hectare (3.3 persons per acre) compared to the Canadian average of 28.5 persons per hectare (11.5 persons per acre) and 14.4 jobs per hectare (5.8 persons per acre) (Zavergiu, 2003). This enables Canadian public transit systems to offer more effective alternatives to the automobile. Canadians relying on the automobile to travel within the metropolitan region, have shorter trip distances than in U.S. cities.

Unlike the 1960s, when Americans used public transit more than Canadians, trends now report that Canadian urban residents use public transit 2.7 times more than the average American.

REFERENCES

Boyd and Associates (2002). "Cities rated in tech survey." Canadian press, February 28.

CMHJC (2003). The state of Canada's housing: An overview: A portrait of Canada's housing stock. CMHC.

European Regional Development Fund (n.d.). Activities of the European Union, general provision on the structural funds. http://europa.eu.int/scadplus/leg/en/lvb/l160014.htm.

KPMG Consulting (2002). Competitive alternatives study comparing business costs in North America, Europe, and Japan. KPMG.

Murphy, B. (1999). *The rise and fall of a caring society.* J. Gordon Shillingford Publishing, Inc.

Murphy, B. (2000). *On the street: How we created homelessness.* J. Gordon Shillingford Publishing, Inc.

Pohl, R. (2001). Poverty in Canada. http://www.ottowainnercityministries.ca/homepage/homelessnessinCanada.

Prime Minister's Caucus Task Force on Urban Issues (2002). Canada's urban strategy: A visiion for the 21st century. Final report. Ottowa.

Skelton, I. (2003). Canadian planning and policy—Perspectives on a Canadian urban strategy. *Canadian Journal of Urban Research—Canadian Institute of Planners,* pp. 1-21.

Statistics Canada (2002). Census geography data: Highlights from the 2001 census of population. Ottowa, Ontario, Canada: Author.

TD Bank Financial Group (2002). A choice between investing in Canada's cities or disinvesting in Canada's future, TD Economics; Special report.

Zavergiu, R. (2003). Celebrating the Canadian city, (Bright lights, safe cities). *New Canadian Magazine,* (May/June), pp. 10-15.

Chapter 33

Case Studies from Around the World

Sarah Rose

BID management is far from a universal science in North America; downtown management organizations around the world, while working toward similar goals, can have varying structures, needs, and approaches. This chapter is a comparative study of BIDs and BID-like structures in South Africa, Serbia, the United Kingdom, and Ireland. South Africa, Ireland, and the United Kingdom have had downtown management organizations in place for fifteen to twenty years, but the BID structure is new in both Ireland and the United Kingdom. Serbia is also a newcomer to BIDs, having just recently developed a downtown management organization framework. South Africa and Serbia both have downtown management organizations working to promote urban redevelopment in the face of major political, economic, and social change. As public-private partnerships, all of these work within their specific political context creating local variations in BID structure.

SOUTH AFRICA

Of these four cases, South Africa has had the longest experience with BIDs (locally called city improvement districts, or CIDs). Having begun in Johannesburg in the mid-1990s, CIDs are now present in every major urban area in South Africa, as well as some secondary cities. As of the fall of 2003, in Johannesburg alone, there were seven CIDs, all of which are managed under the umbrella of the Central Johannesburg Partnership (CJP). The CJP has committed over ten years to the rejuvenation of Johannesburg's city center, working to make it clean, safe, and vibrant with economic and residential opportunities for its diverse community, all while preserving its distinct "Africanness." Though many cities struggle with crime, deteriorating or vacant buildings, and business recruitment, the CJP, working in close partnership with the Johannesburg Development Agency

doi:10.1300/5137_34

(JDA) and the Johannesburg City Council, has undertaken the task of addressing these issues in a context of political transition and reconciliation of racial and economic discrimination from the apartheid era.

In terms of the cycle of urban growth, degeneration, and revitalization, the history of central Johannesburg follows a pattern similar to U.S. cities. Established in 1886, Johannesburg experienced a period of fast growth, and the city center was the major center of business, manufacturing and retail up until the late 1960s and early 1970s. A dense cosmopolitan residential population resided in inner-city neighborhoods (although peripheral residential development was always prominent due to apartheid). The classical reasons of urban decay applied to Johannesburg. Congestion and lack of parking dissuaded people from coming into the city center; high property values and taxes led to high rental rates. Suburban locations attracted shopping centers which in turn enticed residential development and businesses. The exodus of people and business from the city created conditions for the growth of crime and grime, and the indifference of the local government (who were in those days expending their energy fighting apartheid battles, trying to preserve segregation) fostered an environment of decay which persisted until the 1990s. Since 2000, significant progress has been made.

Even though U.S. downtowns and central Johannesburg have followed similar time lines for regeneration, in South Africa there is the added context of a period of major political transition that creates a vastly different scenario. Under colonial and apartheid rule, blacks were not allowed to live nor trade in cities. They were restricted to black township areas in the south, separated by a buffer zone from the white cities and white suburbs in the north. As the country moved into its democratic phase after the November 1995 elections, this segregation was eliminated, producing an influx of urban poor into the already neglected cities. They came looking for jobs and housing nearby, since the city was still a major source of employment and a main transportation center. The city was not equipped for this influx though, and its design did not automatically accommodate 12,000 street vendors or 18,000 mini buses. The CJP, the CIDs, and the city had to find ways to incorporate these new elements, but in a way that preserved order, such as licensing vendors and providing alternatives to squatting in vacant buildings.

The CJP was established in 1992 as a trilateral partnership among businesses, communities, and the city council. After the country's first democratic elections in 1995 turned the city council into a legitimately elected local government, it was no longer necessary to preserve the trilateral structure of the CJP in the same way. The CJP restructured as a "section 21" (not-for-profit) company, representing solely the business community. As CJP's role in CID establishment and management increased, however, conflict grew with the business representatives who were more widely distributed. In January 1997, the CJP reorganized again, keeping its status as a not-for-profit organization, but focusing more on CID establishment and management. To maintain representation of business interests, the Johannesburg Inner City Business Coalition (JICBC) was formed, and, while still managed by the CJP, it is completely separate. Along with the city council and the community, the business community represented by JICBC is an important strategic partner to the work of the CJP in its role as CID manager.

Another reorganization took place beginning in 2000-2001 when the CJP entered discussions with the Kagiso Trust, one of the most successful black-owned companies in the country, which was formed before 1994 when it was set up as a reservoir for all foreign funds for the African National Congress. In early 2003, the CJP sold several of its development interests, including non-city BIDs, to Kagiso Urban Management (KUM), and now acts under its umbrella. KUM's mission is to establish and manage improvement districts, help businesses improve their markets and investments, and optimize municipal services and social welfare.

The benefit of having an umbrella organization such as CJP is that the CIDs work very compatibly and cooperatively with one another. In many cases, staff is shared among two or three CIDs keeping administrative costs lower, which is critical to CIDs established in areas where property values (and resulting property taxes) are low.

Funding is a major problem for the CJP and the Johannesburg CIDs. They do not have the widespread funding infrastructure that the United States has, nor are there federal, state, or local government tax incentives for urban renewal initiatives. In some cases, alternate funding mechanisms have to be used in addition to the CID levy. CIDs exist in a variety of areas in the city, including areas where businesses are marginal and cannot afford to pay for services, even though it is precisely these areas that have the greatest need. In these cases, the CJP has managed to negotiate funding schemes with the city council to redirect revenue into the CID that the council might otherwise have retained. Revenues from parking or outside advertising have been proven methods to increase CID budgets, and in one case, the city is looking into actually building a parking garage in one district and directing the revenue generated to the CID.

Many of the issues Johannesburg CIDs address are similar to those faced by U.S. BIDs. Clean and safe efforts were initially and remain the primary focus of CJP and the CIDs. Additional (unarmed) CID security officers have led to significantly reduced crime rates in the inner city. The CJP has also had great success installing closed-circuit television (CCTV) cameras throughout the city so that most areas are under surveillance. Although this has contributed enormously to crime reduction in Johannesburg, CCTV is not as widely used as a crime deterrent as it is in the United States. Many private companies use it in U.S. downtowns, and some BIDs (Downtown Visions in Wilmington, Delaware, for example) have successfully installed systems with broad coverage. Yet the spread of CCTV in the United States has drawn some protest by civil liberties groups concerned with the increasing "Big Brother-esque" monitoring of private lives in the name of increased safety. However, it has proven to be effective and accepted as a crime deterrent where it exists, especially in Johannesburg.

While maintaining cleanliness and security as priorities, the CJP is now shifting its focus toward economic issues, unemployment, business attraction and retention, and branding. Over 630 new residential units have been completed and major headquarters of banks and other businesses are expanding and upgrading their properties. The CJP was instrumental in convincing the provincial government to move from Pretoria to the city of Johannesburg. This move resulted in the reoccupation of over one million square feet of empty space, the refurbishment of several historic buildings, and the creation of thousands of job opportunities. This is viewed as one of CJP's major successes, not only because of the economic benefits, but also because Johannesburg has been redefined as a capital city, and the government now has a greater stake in showcasing it for all those who come to engage with them.

Human services, as they relate to social and economic development, are one of the top three priorities of the CJP. An endeavor specific to the particular social and political position of post-apartheid Johannesburg is the CJP's effort to find ways to turn its work into black empowerment and job creation. Its partnership with KUM gives the CJP the black representation at a managerial level they had previously lacked. Job creation for the homeless has been another success. The CJP and a partner organization, Partnerships for Urban Renewal, which focuses on urban issues outside the center city, have been responsible for directly creating between 200 and 300 jobs for homeless persons. This is in addition to indirect income production they created for 400 homeless.

The success of the CJP and the CIDs is evident in Johannesburg. They have addressed many of the same problems U.S. BIDs face in a context of political transition and a time of sensitive racial reconciliation.

SERBIA

Transitional societies bring their own set of challenges to downtown management. Serbia is another transitional society, having begun its shift to a market economy only since the 1990s. A BID pilot program, facilitated by USAID and the Serbian Local Government Reform program, is underway in four cities, Zrenjanin, Valjevo, Nis, and Krusevac. BIDs are a novel structure in Serbia; there was no prior model for any kind of downtown development organization. The very notion of a public/private partnership, especially at a local level, is foreign, since up until 1999, former Serbian leader Slobodon Milosevic had effectively dismantled local government. Almost all of the BIDs had difficulty forming partnerships with the new local governments, a common glitch in BID start-up proceedings, but especially when starting with a blank slate. However, despite a lack of precedence within the country, all parties involved worked hard to come to accord, and they gained widespread public support for the BIDs from businesses and government officials.

Cities in Serbia, as in much of Europe, have a historic position that is different from cities in either the United States or Johannesburg. The majority of the population lives in cities, and beyond urban boundaries, most communities are rural. The cities that are hosting the first BIDs vary in population size from 60,000 to 300,000. The current BIDs are mostly established in retail enclaves with office use interspersed. For the most part, the residential areas are not specifically incorporated within the district boundaries, except in the case of Valjevo which has significant second-story residential occupation.

The BIDs are funded by an assessment tax which is collected by the city. Taxes are collected in the beginning of the year, and since the BIDs did not form until mid-2003, their funding was not fully in place for their first several months of development. Properties are taxed according to building permit fees which generate good revenue assuming there is high growth. Although this was the condition in Serbia at the time of BID creation, there is no guarantee that growth will continue at high rates into the future. Because the government has a limited budget, it cannot provide additional funding in the form of incentives to BID efforts.

The four Serbian BIDs, at their outset, were mostly concerned with capital improvements. Serbian cities are dealing with much older infrastructure than U.S. cities or Johannesburg. Nis, for example, is home to structures from the time of Charlemagne. Therefore, there is a strong interest in historic preservation. In Valjevo, efforts by the BID have been made to talk with the business community to get permits to encourage businesses to reuse old buildings productively.

Because it's evolving from a state-run economy, Serbia still has a lot of state-owned buildings. Zrenjanin has the highest percentage. Almost all state-run property has experienced neglect, and due to its lower cost, has drawn undesirable tenants, which drags down the local economy. This is starting to change. With the transition, rents are going up and other capitalists are seeing the potential in the city center's economy and investing in it. The BID management in Zrenjanin should work closely with banks to transform the neglected state properties into productive retail use by providing incentives for desirable merchants to occupy these spaces.

Although both Serbia and South Africa experienced major governmental transitions, the social implications of each city's development are very different. While Johannesburg deals with racial integration and accommodating new populations of urban poor, Serbia, after the breakup of the former Yugoslavia, has been "re-Balkanized." The population is almost totally racially homogenous. Although there is some talk among BID managers about homelessness, there is relatively little evidence of it in the cities. This socialist state, before the transition, provided for citizens on a fairly universal level, so there was not a major lack of services, which would have led to the creation of a large homeless population.

Urban revitalization efforts are important, critical—in fact—in transitional areas. In countries experiencing change, it is important to have key players like BIDs to help direct change in a positive direction for economic development and improving quality of life.

UNITED KINGDOM

Urban revitalization strategies have been in place in the United Kingdom for years. The central government is actively involved in city issues, much more so than in the United States, South Africa, or Serbia. The national government created a National Urban Renewal Strategy within which local authorities work. One of the benefits of having such an involved central government is that they provide various financial aid to local governments in the form of incentives or matching funds in order to help them follow their strategies. However, some policies, like those designed to promote High Street retail zones, have proven detrimental to the development of independent, laissez-faire retail. The United Kingdom began looking into the possibility of BIDs in 1992-1993, and used several American models as resources, specifically Washington, DC, Baltimore, Philadelphia, Tampa, and Richmond, to name a few. The BID enabling legislation in the United Kingdom, Local Government Act 2003, was passed in 2004. Pilot BIDs started in twenty-two cities since January 2003. Currently, some have had ballots already, some are still working on it, while others have chosen not to go forward with BIDs.

Although starting a BID is an enormous task anywhere, BIDs in the United Kingdom are not starting with the same kind of blank slate that

Serbian BIDs are; Town centre management organizations have been active in the United Kingdom for over fifteen years. In fact, the Association of Town Centre Management, a national group, coordinated the pilot program and has had a lot of input in the BID legislation process, enabling the development of a useful law with a lot of research and experience as a foundation. The United Kingdom has the same advantage Serbia does in that many Europeans have a much more defined cultural mind-set about the role of cities. Whereas North Americans turned their backs on many of their center cities, town centers have always maintained a level of importance in the lifestyles of many Europeans.

Town centre management organizations work to deliver additional services and public improvements in cities and towns, but unlike BIDs, their funding comes from voluntary contributions. Although Town Centre Management has some notable successes, because of the voluntary nature of contributions, sustainable funding has proven to be a difficulty. With the secured funding BIDs provide, the budget for regeneration initiatives is already planned. The guaranteed revenue of BIDs offers a greater degree of leverage in obtaining grants and sponsorships. Each BID has a five-year sunset clause, so long-term planning, and funding for those plans, is guaranteed for at least five years, making financial donors more inclined to sign on to sponsor longer-range projects, rather than just short-term events. The existence of town center management organizations created a strong foundation upon which BIDs could build. Property owners, retailers, and the local authority have experience working together in a public-private partnership.

A fundamental difference between North American BIDs and British BIDs is that in the United Kingdom, the BID levy is imposed on the tenants rather than on the property owners. Local business taxes in the United Kingdom are currently paid by the occupiers, so the British Treasury concluded that adding the BID levy onto its current tax roles was more logical. It would not introduce an entirely new line of taxation that assessing the owners would create. Property owners are asked to voluntarily contribute, and tenants are expected to contribute. This has proven to be one of the more contentious points of the new BIDs. Many larger property owners have responded very positively, offering significant funds and even asking to find a way to add a compulsory charge into the legislation. However, the concern is that some owners, especially smaller landlords, may not contribute and will get a free ride from others' donations. Several retailers, among others, have pointed out that property owners are the main beneficiaries of revitalized areas, and feel they should pay into the effort to create enhancements.

The BID pilots are in twenty-two cities that range in size from tiny Suffolk, with a population of about 9,000, to the metropolises of Birmingham and Manchester. The average town in the program has a population between 100,000 and 150,000 people. The major issues the BIDs plan to tackle vary, of course, by the size of the town. Smaller towns are focusing more on marketing efforts, while the larger towns are expending more effort on clean and safe programs establishing warden programs, and installing CCTV. Tough, new, zero-tolerance laws were introduced in local British governments at the end of 2003 and at the beginning of 2004. The expectation is that they will be enforced against antisocial behavior in BID areas. The main component of the BIDs' agenda is promoting livability. They plan to start small and see where they can go from there, depending on size and the priorities of each area's businesses.

Liverpool, the fourth biggest city in the United Kingdom with a city population of 450,000 and a metropolitan region of over 2 million, is host to one of the BID pilots. Liverpool has international recognition (thanks in part to the Beatles), but it has followed a similar time frame of urban degeneration that North American and South African cities experienced. In 2003 it was coming off a thirty-year period of economic decline. The city's workforce of 85,000 is half of what might be expected in a metropolitan region of its size, although it is now on an upward swing. The 1960s zoning mentality of separating uses contributed, in part, to the economic stagnation and decline in vibrancy and importance of downtown Liverpool. Conglomerating business in office parks was viewed as a positive spatial development. Even within the city, areas were designated for certain uses. For example, Church Street had always been a hub for posh retail interspersed with niche retailers, cafes, and other businesses. However, with new zoning regulations it became exclusively retail oriented, and *all* retail in town was confined to the area. Because so many transportation systems were designed to bring people to Church Street for shopping, retailers that ventured out of the retail zone went out of business. Unique, small businesses were squeezed out, and the result was a retail destination populated by national chains. Even during the decline, the rents for these retail spaces were sky high, preventing small local businesses from coming in.

Historically, Liverpool had a large downtown population of bankers and businesspeople as well as lower-income people. In the past thirty years, the in-town population has decreased by fifty percent. It was mostly the wealthy and young families who moved out of the city beyond the tax boundary, leaving behind those that could not leave, including poorer and older residents. With the zoning mentality of "separation of uses," there was no logical space to build new housing; there is a growing commitment to turn this around. Several developers have indicated an interest in testing the market for constructing new family living space.

Liverpool has a strong and committed core of key public and private partners. Groups that are eager to see improvement in downtown are widespread, from residents and cultural organizations to the business community, entrepreneurs, and development groups. It also has a strong (and growing) community spirit related to the brand of downtown. The mind-set among local people is still in place from when Liverpool was an international city with culture and entertainment as a central part of its economy and business dealings. Loyalty plays a major role in maintaining downtown's retail and leisure economy, with suburban consumers using downtown for services, which in other cities are pushed out to the periphery. The city's population at large are for the recreation of a large-scale, vibrant city. Downtown Liverpool, an independent, nonprofit organization, has taken on the task of changing the mind-set of local officials, planners, and the general public, promoting the importance of the creation of a vibrant, livable, mixed-use downtown as a vehicle for economic development and an improved quality of life. This is integral to the success of the BID.

The main focus of the Liverpool BID at this point is providing increased street maintenance, security, and marketing activities in addition to those provided by the city council and its partners. Some groups express concern that the level of control the local authority is accustomed to having over urban policies may create a conflict for the partnership, but the commitment is there to improve the downtown in order to attract investment, visitors, and other catalysts for economic development to re-create the world-class city.

IRELAND

Just across Saint George's Channel, Ireland is also beginning the BID process. Legislation is currently being considered to allow for the creation of the first Irish BIDs in Dublin with several more throughout the country. The structures for a BID are already in place. The city is already divided into business districts, and like the United Kingdom, there is already a downtown development organization in place, upon which the BID can build. The Dublin City Business Association (DCBA) was formed in the 1970s as a network to enable businesses to talk to the government. It is a hybrid public-private association that forms a blueprint for the partnership of the BID. The DCBA is very active in local government. Its leadership sits on a variety of government committees, enabling them to represent business interests from the inside. The British Town Centre Management program was tried in Dublin, but it was found to be incompatible with the

Irish entrepreneurial and individualistic drive. The relatively cooperative and accessible nature of city governments is an asset to Dublin's city revitalization efforts.

Another asset is the European attitude and loyalty toward the city center as an important part of life. Although there is significant suburban development, the city still offers the best mix of coffee shops, culture, theaters, art, and quality shopping. The upmarket consumers always shop in the city center. The young, under-thirty crowds go to the city center for activity and socializing. So, throughout Europe, it is not in the same mind-set many North American cities find themselves in when they start up a BID.

Although many cities discussed in this chapter can claim significant growth at the beginning of the twenty-first century, Dublin has seen a veritable boom with growth levels at around 18 to 20 percent (having dropped down to a more manageable 2 to 5 percent in 2003), making it the fastest-growing European economy, with a 100 percent turnover in retail and a 100 percent increase in employment. In a metropolitan area of 1.2 million people, Dublin is a city of 500,000 and growing. By 2007, it is expected to grow by 60,000. Immigration has increased, with 35 percent of all new immigrants coming from Asian countries, making for a diverse population.

In the 1980s, the biggest urban issue was security, mainly because of the threat of terrorism and bombings from the period of conflict with Northern Ireland. Since the two warring groups entered negotiations though, security has not been as significant a concern. CCTV also became a prevalent crime prevention tool. Dublin, like many U.S. cities that use CCTV, dealt with civil liberties groups' protests, but these groups, along with business groups and the local government, signed a protocol ensuring that CCTV videos cannot be sold, distributed, or made public in any way. Incidents of bank robberies and armed robberies have significantly declined since the 1980s.

In the 1990s the focus for downtown redevelopment was infrastructure including building new bridges, roads, pedestrian bridges, plazas, and public art, including the Spire of Dublin, a towering structure in the middle of Main Street that is becoming part of Dublin's identity. The price tag for the infrastructure additions and improvements in a ten-year period was $5 billion, an impressive sum for a city of only 500,000.

In the twenty-first century, in addition to working on BID development, the DCBA is concentrating on globalization, making Dublin a force in the emerging industry of "knowledge management." Most new jobs created since the early 1990s have been in this industry. Ireland's close relationship with New York and Boston, and its proximity to the United Kingdom and continental Europe have helped it achieve that role.

Along with BID development, Dublin is looking into creating community courts along the lines of Times Square, New York. The courts fit in well with the Irish culture of citizen rule and referenda for making decisions.

A COMMON GOAL

BIDs are spreading across the globe. BIDs and downtown management organizations in many countries address many of the same problems, but historical and cultural nuances affect priorities and how those priorities are addressed. A common goal remains, however: to form a viable organization that will contribute to the creation of livable, dynamic communities in urban centers.

Chapter 34

Commercial Urbanism in Portugal: Evolution and Future Perspectives

Carlos J. L. Balsas

INTRODUCTION

The city centers in Portugal have changed dramatically during the past two decades. They experienced a cycle of decline and revitalization. The decline was caused by the appearance of new modern retail formats in peripheral areas of cities, such as shopping malls and hypermarkets, which captured a substantial market share of small and independent retailers located in the traditional city-center shopping precincts. This phenomenon started in the mid 1980s and achieved its peak during the mid- to late 1990s. To offset this cycle of decline, in 1994 the Portuguese government created a program of retail modernization and shopping district revitalization, known as commercial urbanism projects (CUPs).

The objective of this chapter is to analyze the evolution of commercial urbanism projects in Portugal. The main argument is that CUPs revitalized many city centers, but they lacked the implementation of management strategies capable of sustainably maintaining their urban livability. The research methods involved literature reviews, case study analyses, and semi-structured interviews with practitioners.

This chapter is divided into four parts. After this introduction, part one introduces the evolution of commercial urbanism in Portugal. Part two reviews the PROCOM and URBCOM Programs and discusses their weaknesses and positive contributions. Part three presents three case studies, the cities of Aveiro, Coimbra, and Porto. Finally, part four presents some concluding remarks and a list of recommendations.

Research presented at the First Conference Qualifying Places of Commerce, New Consumer Scenarios, Comparing Models and Case Studies, Turin (Italy), February 11-12, 2004.

doi:10.1300/5137_35

EVOLUTION OF COMMERCIAL URBANISM
IN PORTUGAL

What is called "commercial city center revitalization" in the United States is known in different countries by different names. In the United Kingdom it is know as retail planning and urban regeneration, in France it is designated as *urbanisme commercial,* and in Italy it is called *urbanistica commerciale.* In Portugal, there was some uncertainty about how to designate the planning and revitalization of commercial areas. The first use of the term commercial urbanism appeared in the early 1980s, when cities were conducting studies to characterize their retail offerings and supplies. The definition of commercial urbanism came to be known simply as the use of retail as an instrument of urban planning.

The first commercial urbanism developments started in the mid 1980s with the installation of the first hypermarkets and shopping centers. The first regional shopping center in the country, Amoreiras Shopping Center, opened in Lisbon in 1985. Since then, the shopping center industry has been very active and in 2003 the statistics showed that there is one shopping center for every 125,000 people in the country.

One of the consequences of this phenomenon was that traditional small- and medium-sized retail establishments lost market share and started going out of business. The statistics showed that during the beginning of the 1990s, there were five grocery stores closing down every day, mostly in city-center areas. This cycle of decline had not only socioeconomic implications in terms of job losses and decreases in economic activity, but also in terms of urban livability. Traditional shopping areas became less attractive, foot traffic decreased, and these areas became perceived as unsafe in the evening and during weekends. This is known as a "spiral of decline" that still characterizes many city centers in western countries.

To alleviate this decline, the Ministry of Economy created the PROCOM Program for the period 1994-1999 and the URBCOM Program for the period 2000-2006. These programs used European Union funds to modernize traditional retail establishments, from the point of view of their competitiveness in a more global economy, and to revitalize traditional shopping areas. Among the modernization activities funded by these programs were subsidies for human resources training, management skills, interior refurbishment, new furniture, window display skills, etc.

The second part of this program financed the revitalization of the public space in traditional shopping precincts, mainly in historic districts of cities. New pavements, streetscape improvements, creation of pedestrian streets, new urban furniture, aboveground parking spaces, and new lighting systems are among the main activities financed by these programs.

These programs also financed activities conducted by the local chambers of commerce aimed at promoting the city center to shoppers, tourists, and investors.

PROCOM AND URBCOM PROGRAMS

The PROCOM Program was created in 1994 and lasted until 1999. The central concept of the commercial urbanism projects was the creation of an "open air shopping center" in the city center. The main goal of the projects was to apply the same principles of a successful private and enclosed shopping center to the city center area. Among these principles were modernization of stores; personal treatment and professional management; adequate shopping environment; good car accessibility; pedestrian environment; high levels of comfort, cleanliness, attractiveness and safety; but above all, common management and promotion. Even though some of these principles were proposed and implemented by many projects, the common management of the intervention was very often overlooked. This led to the failure to create real city-center management schemes as they are implemented in other parts of the western world.

The PROCOM Program involved four types of partners: the central government, municipalities, chambers of commerce, and retailers. The central government coordinated the entire program, such as, the approval of the intervention areas, the evaluation of the projects, and the awarding of funding. The municipalities and the chambers of commerce constituted the main partnership responsible for conducting the preliminary and global studies, i.e., the city's main modernization and revitalization strategy. Since chambers of commerce in Portugal do not have many financial or technical resources, municipalities in most of the cases led the initiative. Retailers were asked to give input to the overall strategy during the global study phase and also had a critical role in the implementation of the commercial urbanism project. The project was financed only if at least 50 percent of the retailers in the intervention area declared to be interested in participating in the project by upgrading their retail establishments.

The program comprised three main phases, a preliminary evaluation and application, a global study, and the implementation phase. The preliminary application was the initiation of the commercial urbanism project. It was the first document to evaluate the strengths and weaknesses of the city center and how these could be maximized to bring back the shopping district to its past vitality. The global study, usually voluminous, comprised the market diagnosis from the points of view of supply and demand, analyses of consumer surveys, architectural diagnosis, public space evaluations, and an entire list of proposals and their respective time frames and responsible entities. The implementation phase corresponded to the execution of the proposals, i.e., the rehabilitation and modernization of retail establishments, the revitalization of public spaces, the implementation of retail training and skills development, and the promotion of the center as a whole.

The values of subsidies to be attributed to retailers ranged between 40 and 60 percent, depending on the quality of the project under consideration and its overall contribution to the entire modernization and revitalization strategy. Also, retailers had facilitated access to loans and mortgages at low interest rates. Even though many considered these benefits extraordinarily advantageous, participation rates by individual merchants were very low. The main reasons identified to explain this situation were that merchants in Portugal do not, generally, invest in high-risk ventures, they are not entrepreneurs, and they do not have investment funds because of decreasing profits due to increased competition. Nonetheless, according to the statistics provided by the Ministry of Economy, this program included about 3,500 projects in 129 municipalities, a total of 280 million Euros with 155 million Euros of public investment.

The URBCOM Program is the continuation of the PROCOM Program, but under a new European Union funding package (2000-2006). This program is similar to the PROCOM Program but with a small adjustment—the possibility to create coordination commissions. These commissions are the equivalent to town-center management schemes in the United Kingdom and in other European countries. However, these coordination commissions were proposed by law in 2000, but were never regulated. In a way, this is a lost opportunity for the creation of city-center management schemes. Nonetheless, as of January 2002, there were a total of forty-one commercial urbanism projects.

In summary, commercial urbanism projects have four major weaknesses.

1. They are sectorial programs: They do not integrate the rehabilitation of commercial establishments on the ground floor with housing on top floors. For instance, the store façade is renovated and the top floors are totally dilapidated. A better integration between funding programs at the central government level would have solved this situation.

2. They lack formal management structures: Commercial urbanism projects are based on partnerships between municipalities and chambers of commerce. However, in many cases, they do not work as one effective entity. Both entities are bound by joint proposals; however, they barely share decision-making procedures and resources. A formal management structure would be based on a real partnership, and

would include other partners with relevance to the revitalization and livability of the city center. These include police and firefighters, transportation and parking authorities, housing associations, leisure representatives, etc.

3. They lack professional city-center managers: Revitalization projects are separately evaluated by members of the chamber of commerce and the municipality. However, commercial urbanism projects normally do not include managers with specific training in city-center revitalization. (In many cases, mayors oppose the creation of the position due to fears of political protagonism by the new individual.)

4. They lack sustainable funding: Funds are given by the central government to retailers, chambers of commerce, and municipalities. These are very substantial amounts. Nonreturnable subsidies can be as high as 60 percent for an individual retailer project. The matching funds to be invested by retailers are relatively small compared to revitalization subsidies in other countries. Some believe that these projects can create a very high dependence on public subsidies that artificially boosts traditional retailing competitiveness and is not sustainable in the long term.

On the other hand, Portuguese commercial urbanism projects have had a positive contribution to the modernization and revitalization of city centers in three ways:

1. Urbanism projects have modernized more than 3,700 retail stores: This is a considerable number, though not as high as some would like to see it. However, considering that most of these stores are located in city centers, it seems that modernization has the potential to benefit local economies, strengthen jobs, and contribute to the livability of urban centers.

2. Urbanism projects have revitalized more than 180 city centers: This is also a considerable number. Revitalization projects give city centers a new face. Centers look more attractive, comfortable, and appealing not only to shopping, but also to leisure activities. New sidewalk pavements, more pedestrian areas, more appropriately designed public spaces, and new street furniture all increase community pride and vitality.

3. Urbanism projects create partnerships: Although embryonic, nonetheless, they were a first attempt to introduce a new philosophy in terms of participation and accountability in public projects. Partnerships require multidisciplinary teams of consultants to work together

and to integrate urban planning and economic development proposals into the revitalization of city centers.

CASE STUDIES: AVEIRO, COIMBRA, AND PORTO

Aveiro is a medium-sized city located in the coastal area of Portugal. Aveiro has about 40,000 inhabitants and it is considered the "Venice of Portugal" due to the numerous canals of the lagoon *Ria de Aveiro*. During the 1990s, Aveiro experienced some large-scale commercial development in its periphery. On the other hand, traditional retail stores in the city center were in need of modernization. The municipality had pedestrianized a few squares and streets, but these measures alone did not increase the vitality of the area.

In 1997 the city developed its commercial urbanism project under the PROCOM Program. This project included the renovation of more than sixty outlets, the pedestrianization of several streets, the installation of new "urban furniture," and the rehabilitation of a public market. In the meantime, the opening of a new shopping center (Forum Aveiro) in a vacant lot in the central area reinforced the centrality and viability of the city center.

Coimbra is also a medium-sized city in the central part of the country. Its population is 100,000. The city hosts the oldest university in the country and one of the oldest in Europe—Universidade de Coimbra. The university has been in existence for 700 years and it adds a distinct appeal to the city. The city is also linked to its merchant past. Commerce has been the main activity in the city center, called *"baixinha,"* for centuries. This area is in proximity to the medieval historic district, an area full of narrow streets, alleys, and courtyards. The main economic activity in the historic district is retail on the ground floor with housing on the top floors.

The revitalization of the city center was financed by housing and social programs, but there were no subsidies to modernize retail activities. In 1995, Coimbra was one of the first cities to apply to the PROCOM Program. Funds from this program contributed to the renovation of more than seventy-two establishments, the replacement of street pavement, and the installation of new street furniture. The program also helped the chamber of commerce to finance training and promotional activities. More recently, proposals have been made to create a semiprivate corporation to help revitalize the historic district and generate synergies with the commercial urbanism project.

Porto is the second largest city in Portugal. The city has 280,000 inhabitants, and the metropolitan area of Porto has 1.3 million people. The city is located on the northern margin of the river Douro. Its historic district is on a hillside by the riverfront. It has centuries-old narrow streets and courtyards. Although the historic district is comprised of mainly housing, the neighborhoods adjacent to *Rua das Flores* and *Rua Mouzinho da Silveira* have many commercial establishments. These two streets had a commercial urbanism project done in 1997, but due several delays and institutional programs, it was not totally implemented under the PROCOM Program.

In 2001, Porto hosted the European Capital of Culture, an annual rotating event among European cities that aims to celebrate different forms of culture in the host city. In addition, it offers an opportunity to host cities to undertake a series of urban regeneration projects. In the case of Porto, the city decided to focus mainly on the public space of the city center, which is north of the historic district. This included the renovation of public spaces, the installation of street furniture, the construction of several underground parking garages in the center, and the implementation of a new transportation system based on light rail and tram lines. The URBCOM Program is now in its third phase, and it is expected that most funds will be invested in the modernization of retail outlets. Even though the city center of Porto is not yet totally revitalized, the combination of different programs and interventions still underway should be critical to restore its livability.

CONCLUSION AND RECOMMENDATIONS

The objective of this chapter was to provide an analysis of the evolution of commercial urbanism in Portugal. Even though the commercial urbanism projects gave a very positive contribution to the revitalization of many city centers, they lacked management strategies capable of sustainably maintaining their urban livability. The URBCOM Program will come to an end in 2006, with no indication that a third commercial urbanism project will be created. Instead, new legislation has been discussed in Portugal on the licensing of new large retail formats that included an additional licensing fee. This fee would be used for the modernization of traditional retail stores. The key finding is that there is an urgent need to implement sustainable funding mechanisms and management strategies. Following is a list of recommendations based on international best practices that should be useful to the development of more integrated and effective city center management strategies in Portugal.

Recommendations at the Local Level

The recommendations at the local level include working principles for a city-center management office, the municipality, and for the chamber of commerce, and for economic activities.

City-Center Management Office

Create effective public-private partnerships. Foreign experiences show that public-private partnerships are a critical element in the success of city-center revitalization operations. The main characteristics of this partnership include joint decision making and responsibility sharing among the different partners to benefit the entire community. More recently, the private sector is taking on leadership in many partnerships, and not just the public sector, as is more common in Portugal. Even beyond the public and the private sector, many foreign partnerships include the participation of civic and voluntary associations.

Create the position of city-center manager. A city-center manager is critical for the implementation of the revitalization partnership and for the future management of the city center. The manager's main function is to help the board of directors to develop a strategy for the city center, including the implementation of the action plan, the program of activities, and the creation and coordination of the working groups. The manager is also the coordinator of the existing interests in the city center and the person responsible for gathering funds for the city center management office. The city-center manager must be on board from the start of the partnership or very soon thereafter.

Create a long-term strategic vision. The most successful revitalizations include a clear, strategic, proactive, and consensual vision for the city center in the future, for instance in the next five to ten years. All partners should contribute to the definition of this strategic vision and be responsible for it, and believe that it is realistic and capable of being achieved.

Holistically analyze the city center. Before defining the intervention strategy, it is necessary to holistically analyze the city center in its different dimensions, for instance: the commercial position in the regional hierarchy, strengths (e.g., diversified offerings), weaknesses (e.g., accessibility), opportunities (e.g., collaborative environment), and threats (e.g., peripheral retail areas). Many of these analyses can be done in studies of the municipality or of the chamber of commerce, however, it is important that the partnership produce a concise and clear document with the main diagnosis of the city center.

Have a coherent intervention strategy. The intervention strategies in the city center must contain action plans that allow the management office to successfully achieve the previously defined vision and capture the opportunities identified in the market study. This action plan results directly from the diagnosis and must be detailed to the point of identifying all the activities that need to be done, their beginning and end, who is responsible for them, how much money is allocated to each action, and where the money comes from. This action plan must be revised and updated annually.

Be selective and define priorities. With the exception of small cities, regular city centers can have considerable dimensions, which can make it difficult to solve multiple problems through only one program. On the other hand, there are always more skeptical partners who like to see immediate results. Due to these two limitations, the most successful city center programs are those that direct their (necessarily limited) resources to the target areas identified by the different partners. The concentration of resources in a certain geographical area makes it easy for the revitalization efforts to become more visible. Incremental action must be taken with realistic activities.

Have a city marketing plan. A city center partnership must have a city marketing plan that allows the management office to communicate effectively with the targeted consumers. This plan must give a positive image of the city center and of its activities. It must include promotional campaigns, tourist guides, maps, brochures, as well as events and public festivals. These festive events should portray the city center as an interesting and safe place to shop, reside, work, and be entertained. The results of these activities must be communicated to the elected officials and to the people at large, so that they can keep their interest in the activities being done by the management office.

Encourage and promote local leadership. In order to create successful partnerships, it is important that the leaders are from the local community and that they find resources within their own community. Auto-sustainability should be one of the main goals of the partnership. Local leadership involves establishing links with the most influential people in the community and between them and the merchants. This includes not only the ones located in the city center but those representing the entire community.

Promote sustainable funding. The management unit must have a mechanism that allows it to gather funds in adequate amounts so that the action plan can be implemented. The most successful partnerships abroad are the ones in which public government subsidies are minimal. Normally, public funding is used to create the management office and to keep it functioning for a certain period of time, during which the manager is supposed to gather funds from other sources in order to achieve autosustainability.

Recognize and value voluntary contributions. Voluntary contributions are very important to the functioning of the partnership. They can be monetary, goods, services, or even time participating in the working groups. Public funds are normally given to partnerships with the condition that they have to be matched with local funds. In these cases, city-center managers can be very useful in showing potential contributors what they can gain by contributing to the partnership.

Monitor and evaluate management activities regularly. The manager must conduct inspections of the city center as regularly as possible. In these inspections he or she should pay attention to cleanliness, safety, and attractiveness, services available in the center, parking, and conflicts between users, etc. The manager must regularly monitor a set of statistical indicators that can give the board of directors an idea of how the revitalization activity is evolving. These indicators include empty properties, number of pedestrians, crime, and the number of new jobs created, etc.

Municipality

Promote the revitalization of the center. The revitalization of the city center must be an economic development and political priority for the municipality. It is the municipality's responsibility to promote the identity and diversity of the city center through its active participation in the partnership. To have competitive economic activities in the city centers, municipalities have to review local ordinances and licensing processes to expedite investments in the center. These processes must be fast, but without the loss of quality or rigor in the interventions.

Create commercial development plans. These are being developed in the municipality of Lisbon, for example, and help all commercial interventions in the municipality. Even though it is still in an early stage, its operationalization with traditional planning documents (e.g., master plans, ordinances, and regulations) and processes (e.g., licensing and GIS analyses) can expedite the intervention process and help the work of the city-center manager.

Integrate retail activities in the municipal plans. Planning technicians working for the municipality are responsible for developing commercial activities in the municipal plans (e.g. strategic, master, urbanization, and site plans). Retail must be taken into consideration as would any other activity with profound implications in the organization of the territory, but also in terms of the socioeconomic dynamics of the localities.

Promote high standards of cleanliness, maintenance, and safety. Cleaning and maintenance of public spaces must have very high standards of quality and hygiene. These standards must apply to the mechanical and manual cleaning of streets and sidewalks, the emptying of litter and waste-baskets, and to the cleaning and removal of graffiti and other unwanted eyesores. The maintenance of trees, flower pots, and bushes, as well as the maintenance of street furniture, signals, and lights is very critical to the appearance of the city center as well as its safety.

Promote a compact and sustainable development. To promote mixed-use developments and to control suburbanization, reducing reliance on private cars in urban areas must be a critical objective of municipal planning. The implementation of this objective not only reinforces the livability of the center, but it also increases the quality of life to all city users.

Chamber of Commerce

Promote the creation of city-center management offices. The chambers of commerce have critical roles in the revitalization programs and in the creation of city-center management offices, since their direct activity involves the promotion of commercial activity in the community. In many foreign cities, the chamber of commerce temporarily houses the city-center management office and allows the manager to share its resources (e.g., installation, equipment, administrative support, etc.). This may help the city center revitalization initiative. However, the chamber of commerce normally has a territorial area broader than the city center, which can lead to long-term conflicts.

Mobilize retailers to become involved in the direction of the center. The chamber of commerce can have a critical role in inducing its members to be involved in the activities of the city-center management office. This involves the organization of events, the coordination of promotions and festivals, and the production of marketing materials.

Cooperate in the organization of events. The chamber of commerce can cooperate in the organization of events that aim to promote the activities in the center. Gathering sponsors, naming a coordinator, and the promotion of the event well ahead of time can make a real difference in terms of the number of participants.

Promote best practices of commercial management. The chamber of commerce must be ready to promote best practices of commercial management to its members. It can also organize and promote professional training sessions to increase the competitiveness of small businesses.

Develop alternative ways of doing business. In cooperation with the city-center management office and the municipality, the chamber of commerce can develop and promote alternative ways of doing business. For instance, it can promote business via the Internet such as e-commerce. It can even identify niche markets of traditional local products and sell them in cooperation with the tourism services of the municipality.

Economic Activities

Follow market principles. A market study is critical to knowing who customers are, which other customers can be attracted, what kinds of goods customers want, what their future preferences will be, and, finally, how to make loyal customers.

Target differences. In order to compete, the city-center retail area must be able to create and be known for a certain type(s) of product(s), also known as a niche market. The retailers in the city center cannot sell the exact same merchandise as the stores in the peripheral shopping malls. Instead, they can target certain themes and certain age groups. The idea is to coexist with the big shopping malls and not to compete directly with them. The difference should not be in price but in type of product.

Be unique. Even though there are now many new ways to buy the same product, city-center retailers can prosper by providing friendly, quality service to their customers. For instance, this might involve personalized service and an after-sale assistance program.

Participate in the resolution of common problems. The mission to create a livable center capable of attracting customers is not a responsibility of the municipality alone. Individual merchants must keep their establishments attractive, as well as participate in the resolution of the problems of the city center as a whole. The support of city-center management can go beyond money contributions; support can be offered with goods and services, time, equipment, and installations.

Recommendations at the National Level

Promote coherent public policies. Intersectorial public policies must be articulated to guarantee sustainable and compact urban development. Foreign experience shows that city center revitalization programs can only succeed if, at the different intervention levels, there are clear and coherent public policies that favor the city center and promote a compact and sustainable development.

Improve support information. Up-to-date information is imperative to implement city-center revitalization operations. This information must be uniform and can be compared across geographical jurisdictions. This can be done by developing a national set of indicators to aid city-center revitalization operations.

Recommendations at Other Levels

Coordinate the implementation of regional public policies. The coordination of public policies at the regional and metropolitan level is very important to proper planning and development of economic activities. It is important to distinguish between interventions to revitalize and interventions to increase economic dynamics.

Cooperate with international city-center management organizations. Portugal is not the only country to face revitalization of its city centers. Cooperation and sharing of good practices at the international level can be very positive.

FURTHER READING

Balsas, C. (1999). *Commercial Urbanism in Portugal—Implications for City Center Revitalization.* Lisbon: Ministry of Economy (in Portuguese).

Balsas, C. (2000). City center revitalization in Portugal, lessons from two medium size cities. *CITIES—The International Journal of Urban Policy and Planning,* 17(1): 19-31.

Balsas, C. (2002). *Commercial Urbanism and Public-Private Partnerships—Lessons Learned from Foreign Experiences.* Lisbon: Ministry of Economy (in Portuguese).

Fernandes, J. (1995). Commercial urbanism, the Portuguese experience. *Revista da Faculdade de Letras,* X/XI: 105-125 (in Portuguese).

Fernandes, J., Cachinho, H., and Ribeiro, C. (2000). *Traditional Urban Retail, Modernization and Public Policies.* Lisbon: Ministry of Economy (in Portuguese).

Salgueiro, T. (1995). Retail planning policy in Portugal. In Davies, R. (Ed.), *Retail Planning Policies in Western Europe* (pp.182-199). London: Routledge.

Teixeira, J. and Pereira, M. (1999). Les Projects Speciaux d'Urbanisme Commercial: un partenariat pour la qualification du commerce du centre-ville. In Salgueiro, T. (Ed.), *The Globalization of Consumption and Retail Places* (pp.193-214). Lisbon: GECIC.

Part VIII:
Case Studies

Theories and concepts can be useful, powerful tools in planning and decision making when it comes to managing downtowns and business districts. Yet what happens when a crisis occurs, as it did on the morning of September 11, 2001, in Lower Manhattan? Or, what can downtown organizations do when they are faced with an exploding social problem, as downtown Los Angeles has experienced with homelessness? How do theories and concepts play out over time, and how valid or useless do they become in light of changing circumstances, as was the case in the twenty-year development of Arcadia Creek in Kalamazoo, Michigan?

This section offers three case studies—two in the biggest cities in the United States, one in a smaller city—showing how downtown leaders acted with courage, resolve, and persistence to solve some of the most difficult problems a downtown manager might encounter.

Chapter 35

The Kalamazoo Prism: Downtown Michigan Metamorphosis

John E. Hopkins
Kenneth A. Nacci

AUTHORS' PERSPECTIVE

In 1980, the Kalamazoo Community Foundation made a $129,000 two-year grant from discretionary funds to the City of Kalamazoo for a project dubbed "Kalamazoo 2000," a citizen-based examination of the issues that would face the community over the next two decades with the intent of developing forward-looking solutions. This case study from the CEOs of two important community organizations, Downtown Kalamazoo, Inc. and the Kalamazoo Community Foundation looks back on the development of the central city over those two decades.

INTRODUCTION

The grand issues of downtown development and urban living play out on the largest of stages—New York, Los Angeles, Chicago, and the forty or so metropolitan areas with more than 1 million in population. Notably, however, the remaining 290 metropolitan centers in the United States have been faced with issues that are more than just small versions of those facing big cities. The challenges facing the small- to medium-sized cities over the past two decades include many of the same social dynamics, but also include these factors:

- The work, shopping, and entertainment patterns of individuals in smaller communities reflect less-distinct boundaries between urban, suburban, and rural living. The complexities of sprawl, land-use planning, and urban blight form unique challenges to medium-sized cities and "micropolitan" centers.[1]

- Income, age, and racial demographic changes have been more dramatic over the past two to three decades, exposing some smaller communities to urban issues they had never faced before.
- Out-migration patterns of young, single, college-educated people have had a disproportionate impact on smaller communities, particularly in the Midwest, as the destinations of choice[2] have been large cities and states in the West and South.
- Intrametropolitan property tax differential issues are pronounced in communities that place a large share of the social burden on the "core community," which typically contains the downtown, and tax relief can be as close as across the street.
- The abandonment of downtowns by manufacturing, retail, commercial, nonprofit, and religious entities has made it difficult for smaller communities to maintain a critical mass of activity in the central city, including activity that supports residential living.

As pointed out, the Midwest has been particularly vulnerable to out-migration due to weather and shifts in the national economic dynamics over the past several decades. None of America's fastest-growing cities is in the Midwest.

KALAMAZOO

The case of Kalamazoo, Michigan, is instructive. First, the social and economic challenges Kalamazoo has faced over the past two decades are representative of those faced by cities of similar size. Second, the community's leadership has dedicated significant resources to addressing those challenges. Moreover, this case study was written at a time (2004) when the central city faced yet another major challenge, namely that some 2,000 jobs—mostly research jobs—were moved out of downtown Kalamazoo and, in fact, out of the community. Like many states in the Midwest, Michigan is facing a state budget crisis and the effects of the recent recession of the late 1990s and early 2000s.

By way of background, Kalamazoo County is home to 238,000 residents, 6 percent more than in 1980, but the City of Kalamazoo has lost 4 percent of its population over the same span. The black population of the city has increased by 30 percent since 1980, and the Hispanic population has more than doubled in the city during that time. The city's black population is 21 percent while a large majority of the surrounding townships have black populations of less than 2 percent.

Kalamazoo has watched the paper industry evaporate and said good-bye to most of what grip it had on the auto industry, though some plastic suppliers to automakers remain. About 21 percent of the county's work-force is in manufacturing, and the decrease in numbers of men and women in organized labor has followed national trends. Many of the area's largest employers are now educational, governmental, and nonprofit, nontax-paying, entities.

Located halfway between Chicago and Detroit along Interstate 94, Kalamazoo is home to a large population of people of Dutch heritage, dat-ing back to waves of settlers in the mid-1800s, with more European trans-plants as industry developed.

Although the Glenn Miller tune "I've Got a Gal in Kalamazoo" is argu-ably the city's claim to fame, community-planning experts know Kalama-zoo for creating the nation's first pedestrian mall in 1959, resulting in Kalamazoo's nickname: "Mall City." For that reason, addressing the de-cline of the mall in the 1980s and 1990s was a matter of particular concern.

With voter approval, though, community leaders in 1997 did what many others were doing: they replaced two blocks of the pedestrian plaza with a street. Among the knotty planning issues facing Kalamazoo then, and now, is how to deal with traffic on the downtown's many one-way streets. That is-sue continues to burn.

The deterioration of the downtown, of course, was gradual. The diversi-fied economic base of the larger community helped Kalamazoo consis-tently outpace its Michigan neighbors through the 1960s and 1970s. The growing and prosperous Upjohn Company, which went public in 1962, fu-eled the economic fires of prosperity, and the paper companies were hold-ing their own at the end of the 1970s.

The first major "loss" in downtown Kalamazoo—the closing of the old Burdick Hotel in 1972—prompted a quick and creative response from com-munity leaders—a public-private partnership to build the Kalamazoo Cen-ter, a 280-room "convention hotel," which opened in 1975.

Interestingly, with the presence of a large department store and the con-tinued development of Upjohn research facilities in downtown Kalamazoo, it wasn't the deterioration of the urban core that had the community's leadership concerned.

As 1980 approached, issues such as the ownership of the airport, waste-water treatment, and education (following court-ordered busing in 1972) were on the front burner. Failure to annex Portage Township before it be-came a city in 1963 remained a source of community divisiveness in part because Upjohn's headquarters were built in Portage.

Portage, with its popular schools, and the addition of a large, regional shopping mall, had hit its stride. Portage, which had named itself "The City on the Grow," asked for and received a planning grant from The Upjohn Company to chart its future. Kalamazoo followed suit and, in 1980, under-took a more ambitious planning initiative—Kalamazoo 2000—and re-ceived a $129,000 grant from the Kalamazoo Community Foundation to engage literally hundreds of citizens to identify key community issues and develop solutions. Kalamazoo 2000 established an elaborate and energized team of task forces, which, in essence, created a community consciousness around its plight as a core city.

In the first two phases of the Kalamazoo 2000 process, little attention was given to downtown issues, per se. In the project's final phase, a fifty-person "blue ribbon" committee dedicated to economic development solu-tions addressed downtown issues. A self-appointed subcommittee devel-oped the "Arcadia Creek" plan that dovetailed with an unrelated charrette sponsored by regional architects and the City of Kalamazoo.

Arcadia Creek, a storm-water drainage system flowing from Kala-mazoo's West Side to the Kalamazoo River, was contained in a series of de-teriorating underground pipes flowing through the heart of downtown. The "creek" was seen as having aesthetic and development potential if opened—a la the San Antonio river walkway.

More important, the Arcadia downtown concept was one of the "link-ages" between the central city and surrounding neighborhoods and commu-nities. The creek to the West Side had counterparts linking to the north, east, and south, including Portage Creek, the Kalamazoo River, and Gull Road. The underlying philosophy was this: the downtown was being cut off from the other vital parts of the community. Traffic and development patterns should take into consideration the needs of people in the adjoining parts of the community.

A member of the Kalamazoo 2000 economic development committee was Dr. James Visser, the newly appointed director of Kalamazoo's Down-town Development Authority. Visser and his newly appointed board em-braced the concept in 1982. Over the next few years, as deterioration of properties became more pronounced on the downtown's near north side (through which Arcadia Creek flowed), the Kalamazoo City Commission became increasingly involved, as did other community leaders.

During the same time frame, a great deal of community attention became focused on a solution to consolidate railroad tracks and build a downtown overpass to relieve congestion caused by trains passing through the down-town.

The City of Kalamazoo managed to amass $21 million for that proposed solution, but voter approval was necessary for the final $7 million. When voters rejected the bond issue, attention turned to the concepts embodied in the Arcadia Creek Plan, namely the development of the Kalamazoo River and the improvement of Gull Road to the east and northeast.

Portions of the downtown were undergoing change at varying paces in the mid-1980s. The retail-dominated south end of the Kalamazoo Mall was holding its own—compared to deteriorating downtown shopping districts in nearby Battle Creek, Benton Harbor, and, at the time, Grand Rapids. On the east end, a new YWCA, the rehabilitation of some office buildings, and the promise of a rail overpass signaled new hope. It was the north end of the mall, closest to Kalamazoo's least-affluent neighborhoods that had continued to deteriorate. Issues of prostitution, crime, and loitering heightened the need to revitalize the blocks just north of the Kalamazoo Center. A hotel and shopping complex, itself less than ten years old, was showing serious signs of wear.

By 1986, the City of Kalamazoo's downtown efforts were again focused on Arcadia Creek, with plans for what it described as a massive public works and economic development project in Kalamazoo's north central business district.

As conceived at the time, the project called for ponds and gardens where historic structures stood. Coming off the rail-consolidation defeat, however, city leaders felt they couldn't convince city residents to support general obligation bonds.

In early 1988, three sets of community leaders began working independently of one another on issues facing the downtown. One formed the "Arcadia Creek Alliance" and began holding meetings with individuals and groups to develop the "Downtown Agenda for Progress." Spearheaded by The Upjohn Company, this was considered a one-year "do-or-die" process. A second group, formed by the Downtown Development Authority (DDA), examined the organizational structure of the DDA and the downtown retail merchants association (Downtown Kalamazoo Association). The third group worked behind the scenes to interest Kalamazoo Valley Community College, First of America Bank Corp., The Upjohn Company, Bronson Methodist Hospital, Borgess Hospital, and the Kalamazoo Public Museum to launch new projects in the Arcadia Creek district.

By the end of 1988, the efforts of the three groups coalesced. Leaders convinced the City Commission to put the Arcadia Creek plan, which was evolving into the "Arcadia Commons" project, in the Capital Improvement budget. A new umbrella organization, Downtown Kalamazoo Inc. (DKI) was formed to govern the activities of the downtown, and one of its affiliate organizations was the publicly funded DDA. All told, some $7.4 million was given to help fund Arcadia Commons.

In rolling out the new organizational structure in early 1989, leaders chose to employ the Tax Increment Financing (TIF) authority available to

DDAs for the first time. The city created a TIF district within the DDA boundaries. The district included the Upjohn Company's proposed research facility that would serve as the initial TIF generator. The TIF dollars were used to pay for debt service for the construction of Arcadia Creek channel and various parking structures. Prior to this action, city and business leaders compromised with school officials to protect special education millages from TIF capture. The DDA millage rate was increased from one to two mill to offset the loss of membership revenue from the dissolution of the Downtown Kalamazoo Association.

DKI continues today as a private, nonprofit organization that bridges the interests of the various stakeholders within the downtown, including the private sector. It is responsible for recruiting new business to downtown, planning public spaces, promoting downtown activities, such as a holiday parade and "Safe Halloween," and collective retail promotions, managing the parking system, providing grants to property owners to beautify their buildings, and providing financial incentives to businesses.

Kalamazoo has distinguished itself in creativity for downtown solutions through Downtown Tomorrow Incorporated (DTI), a private, nonprofit body that serves as the real estate development and fund-raising arm. It has owned and continues to own several properties in downtown Kalamazoo.

The final affiliate of DKI is DKA Charities, a private, nonprofit body that focuses on raising funds and putting on community events and promotions (such as Safe Halloween).

As it became clear that the Arcadia Commons project would involve extensive demolition, and with two Rose Street buildings on the National Register of Historic Places, historic-preservation interests heightened.

When the DDA's first director, Dr. Visser, decided to return to academia, DKI hired David Feehan as his successor. Feehan immediately capitalized on the historic issue as a positive, not a roadblock.

Based upon negative findings in an Environmental Impact Statement, Feehan formed—with the help of Kalamazoo Valley Community College (KVCC) and Upjohn—the Arcadia Commons "Project Enhancement Team" to merge the interests of developers, city officials, historic preservationists, and residents from the surrounding neighborhoods. The Project Enhancement Team worked on a design theme and set of guidelines that would make Kalamazoo eligible for a million-dollar Urban Development Action Grant (UDAG) utilizing the little-known 106 (historic preservation) process. With eight buildings destined for demolition and another eight to be rehabilitated, the guidelines were set for all future development in downtown Kalamazoo. Those guidelines called for "some uniformity of walkways, lighting, streetscape, signage, colors, railings, materials, pattern, etc., to unify the statement of the project."[3] Involving the private sector was important to the success of Arcadia Commons. The community's two largest private-sector employers, Upjohn and First of America Bank Corp., both stepped forward. Upjohn bought the failing Kalamazoo Center in 1990 and First of America agreed to move marketing operations into one of the historic buildings while adding a second new building for other corporate operations.

To help create critical mass in the new Arcadia Commons district, the community college (KVCC) committed to build a new, 58,000-square-foot campus in the proposed site. During the same time frame, Kalamazoo Public Schools transferred governance of the museum to KVCC. Voters approved a one-mill, county-wide operating tax, clearing the way for a $20 million fund drive for a museum of history, culture, science, and technology facility next to the downtown KVCC building. The Kalamazoo Valley Museum opened in 1996.

Bronson Methodist and Borgess Hospitals joined together to develop the West Michigan Cancer Center, a 35,000-square-foot facility in the district, and SDM&G investment advisory services moved their offices to the area.

Throughout the development of Arcadia Commons, leaders stressed the importance of that development to the vitality of the mall, but activity on the northern two blocks of the mall remained weak, and retail activity on the south end of the mall was softening as well. As early as 1991, DKI and the city commissioned a study of the Kalamazoo Mall. A number of studies followed, off and on, through 1994. In May of 1994, Kalamazoo invited a panel from the International Downtown Association (IDA), that included IDA President Richard Bradley, to weigh in on the future of the mall. Although they described the mall as "tired," the group stopped short of offering specific remedies. The city and DKI almost immediately went in search of a national consulting team for those remedies. The team ultimately was headed by LDR International Inc., of Columbia, Maryland. The team of consultants took a serious look at traffic, environmental reconnaissance, parking, and economic analysis. In addition, DKI hired Hyatt Palma to recommend retail recruitment strategies. Using the work of outside consultants and the energy of new DKI Director Kimberly Williamson, city and DKI leaders developed a Downtown Comprehensive Plan, which highlighted two major planning changes. The first proposed change was elimination of some of the downtown's one-way streets, an issue which has remained on the DKI's planning agenda ever since. The other change called for opening of two of the four blocks of the Kalamazoo Mall to vehicular traffic. The Downtown Comprehensive Plan stated: "The mall in the downtown has outlived its usefulness and should revert back to a street; the west side of the mall is a dead zone. The mall is dated and stale."[4]

Community leaders immediately embraced the mall portion of what was called the "Ten-Point Plan." The Kalamazoo Community Foundation provided a $1.7 million grant to advance the Downtown Project. As they had with the rail consolidation plan, voters showed resistance, but community leaders convinced residents to move ahead with the plan and a referendum to put the mall issue to a vote passed in 1996. Two years later, those two blocks were opened to one-way traffic.

KEY ELEMENTS OF PROJECT DOWNTOWN

The key elements and objectives of Project Downtown, which has remained the working agenda for the downtown for the past seven years, are as follows.

Gateways

Gateways create attractive entry points into downtown. One of the "knocks" urban settings often encounter is that they have become ugly because of old and abandoned manufacturing and commercial sites. Although shopping districts, such as the Kalamazoo Mall, can be maintained, the fringes of the downtown can look worn. Public utility dollars and financial incentives have been used to create attractive entry points to the downtown. Work on this issue is being done in concert with other elements of the plan, including linkages and land use.

Access, Traffic Patterns, and Transit

Another concern is improved mobility in and around downtown. The opening of the Kalamazoo Mall provided an extra dimension of increased mobility downtown, but the issue of two-way streets was not resolved in the twenty-year study period. However, it is a point of major deliberation (at the time of this writing), with various alternatives being floated publicly. A public bus system, operated by the City of Kalamazoo, remains vital and, in fact, has been strengthened in recent years with closer ties to Western Michigan University, where ridership has picked up significantly.

Pedestrian Environment

A third goal was to design attractive public spaces that meet the needs of multiple users. The mall was redesigned with aesthetic sensitivity and remains pedestrian friendly. An aspect of the mall redesign that has been difficult to achieve has been a linkage with what many consider to be the "town square," Bronson Park. Bronson Park was devastated in a tornado in 1980, but was quickly restored and later improved with city funds and with a band shell donated by the Rotary Club. An element of the original Arcadia Creek plan, a festival site, was developed on the near North Side and completed in May 2004.

Linkages

Linkages were required to foster greater synergy between downtown and its neighbors. Much of what was written in the original Arcadia Creek plan addressed this important need. Traffic improvements to the east and northeast, along with a $9 million revitalization of a city park—half of which was funded by private sources—have linked three challenged neighborhoods. A bikeway was built through the park area along the Kalamazoo River and is being extended, as of this writing, to Kalamazoo's West Side where it will meet a thirty-seven-mile rails-to-trail path that connects Kalamazoo to Lake Michigan. The city's largest public-private linkage plan, Edison Mainstreet, was in its fifth year of work on the Portage Street corridor.

Land Use and Development

To prepare a blueprint for successful mixed use, the DKI's private organization, Downtown Tomorrow Inc., has been instrumental in securing and protecting large portions of the downtown for coordinated development. In many ways, this could be the most distinguishing characteristic of the collaborative efforts to revitalize the downtown. Clearly, TIF and other incentives—closely coordinated between the DDA and City of Kalamazoo—have been important tools in redevelopment.

Attractions, Arts, and Entertainment

Attractions, arts, and entertainment are necessary to appeal to the leisure time of residents and visitors. On the heels of the $20 million fund drive to build the Kalamazoo Valley Museum came the passage of a successful millage to undertake a $16 million renovation of the Kalamazoo Public Library downtown. Shortly thereafter, the Civic Theatre and Kalamazoo Institute of Arts, conducted successful fund drives that totaled $20 million. With another $7.5 million raised for the Kalamazoo Symphony Orchestra, it was safe to say that Kalamazoo had invested in its "cultural infrastructure," much of it downtown. In addition, the Irving S. Gilmore International

Keyboard Festival and the existence of other homegrown musical and theater and dance groups, brought into focus the need for more cooperation in the arts. Out of that recognition came the Epic Center, a renovated, four-story department store that today houses two modern performance spaces, offices for eleven cultural organizations, a community box office, a restaurant, and a retail store. The restaurant proved popular and more restaurants in downtown Kalamazoo followed, some with nightly entertainment.

Residential Life

Housing opportunities also needed expansion. Downtown housing was seen as the "last phase" of the Arcadia Creek plan in 1980. Even when the Ten-Point Plan was finished in 1998, there were only a smattering of lofts and downtown residences. Activity picked up dramatically toward the end of the twentieth century, however, and has been an important force in the development of the downtown since 2000. Philosophically, planners knew the value of housing, but it wasn't something that community leaders could force. As of this writing, Kalamazoo has 1,000 downtown residents in 400 units, with a 1 percent vacancy rate.[5] When a large retail paint and home improvement store closed downtown, the building was quickly and successfully converted to condominiums. This property was acquired by DTI with resources from a program-related investment (PRI) or low-interest loan from the Kalamazoo Community Foundation. The low-interest loan was in turn passed along to the eventual developer, thus making the project viable.

Business Development

In order to encourage business retention and recruitment of new businesses to downtown Kalamazoo, Ken Nacci, former DKI vice president and downtown development consultant, was hired to develop a business recruitment strategy that would complement the efforts of the physical elements of Project Downtown. Nacci researched the efforts of several communities and developed a phased land acquisition plan and, with the Kalamazoo Community Foundation, created a fund-raising strategy for DTI. This provided for site control of key properties essential to the recruitment of new business.

Parking

Also required was a user-friendly parking experience. Although planners in major cities would scoff at the notion that Kalamazoo has a parking problem, one of the major hurdles in attracting shoppers and visitors in downtown Kalamazoo has been just this issue. The city has privatized the parking system and also has a validation program among retailers for parking in ramps. Although the parking issue is a perceived inconvenience, it also represents a $13 million debt to the city. Utilizing more free meters has helped short-term visitors.

STAKEHOLDERS AND THEIR ROLES

With Kimberly Williamson's departure to New Orleans, Kalamazoo looked to Nacci to assume the mantle of leadership for the downtown organizations. Visser created the organization structure; Feehan launched the Arcadia Commons project; Williamson revitalized the Mall; and Nacci spearheaded the business development efforts along with tackling the jobs in each of the above-stated areas.

Once downtown issues were brought into focus, twenty years after the famed Gruen Plan that created the Kalamazoo Mall, they were never far from the community's thoughts. The point was driven home by a series of politicians, public managers, and community leaders that Kalamazoo's downtown remained the heart of the metropolitan community.

A cadre of some 250 volunteers was assembled over two decades to execute fairly sophisticated, interrelated solutions to complex urban issues. During those two decades, there were changes and challenges facing virtually all of Kalamazoo's largest private-sector employers, from General Motors to what evolved (from Upjohn) into Pfizer. The educational, nonprofit, health care, and governmental sectors contributed to overall economic stability. Until community focus shifted in the late 1990s to an economic development strategy built on the development of the biosciences, much of the community's problem-solving energy and resources went into downtown issues. Over the past two decades, the key stakeholders in the downtown and their roles were as follows.

City Government

Kalamazoo has a strong city manager/commission form of government, with the top vote-getting commissioner serving as mayor. Elective politics were stable in the 1980s and 1990s, and each of the four city managers was committed to downtown improvement. On technical and financial issues, the Kalamazoo City Commission always had the final say, but chose not to meddle in the decision making and authority of the DDA and DKI.

DKI/DTI/DDA/DKA

This structure appears to have been an effective means of engaging a large numbers of volunteers and decision makers while holding administrative control in a single staff. The competing interests of property developers and retailers have been handled about as well as can be expected, with most disputes settled before they reached city hall. The structure also provides stability of leadership and representation as the City Commission is apt to change every two years.

Historic Preservationists

Creative and compromising, historic preservationists didn't win every battle, but by and large, they won the war to preserve the look and feel of a community they can live with and live in. Their major victories came from the design guidelines that remain in place today.

Kalamazoo Community Foundation

The Kalamazoo Community Foundation was in a unique position to play an active role in the development of the downtown during the two decades in question, beginning with its grant to the Kalamazoo 2000 planning process. The foundation made thirty-one grants in the downtown during the study period, totaling some $15 million. Most of those funds were leveraged with other contributions. One of the benefits of having a community foundation involved in downtown development is the foundation's understanding of the issues beyond development. Its president/CEO also is deeply involved in the community, serving on key community boards— including the board of DTI since its inception—and various economic development task forces. In addition to providing grant funding for conventional projects, the Kalamazoo Community Foundation also took part in creative projects, including a "hotel for the homeless," and a consolidated home for arts organizations.

Neighborhood Leaders

One of the challenges of a local, urban government is explaining to neighborhoods why limited city dollars are going to downtown development instead of neighborhood issues, particularly housing. The City of Kalamazoo has seven block-grant neighborhoods. Leaders in those neighborhoods formed a strong network during key times of downtown development and, more often than not, championed downtown issues.

Upjohn

Upjohn and its successors quietly provided much of the leadership needed for downtown development. From underwriting the original Arcadia Creek plan to allowing the expansion of the TIF district to include a new, major research building, Upjohn provided leadership at every level. Upjohn led the important fund drives that helped keep momentum in downtown Kalamazoo.

Educational Institutions

Kalamazoo Public Schools made tax sacrifices and relinquished control of the museum at a critical time. Kalamazoo Valley Community College's President, Marilyn Schlack, was a key figure in almost every decision influencing the success of Arcadia Commons. She also spearheaded the Kalamazoo Valley Museum fund drive and served as a liaison to other community leadership groups.

Cultural, Religious, and Nonprofit Organizations

Although some nonprofit organizations moved out of the central city between 1980 and 2000, more invested in their downtown facilities and programs. Kalamazoo was able to keep a strong base of churches in and around the downtown, along with charitable and cultural organizations, contributing to the occupancy of buildings and to much-needed human activity.

Retailers

Kalamazoo followed the national trend of losing the types of retail establishments that couldn't compete favorably with superstores and malls. During the study period, the Kalamazoo Mall lost its two department stores and a home-furnishing store. Specialty shops found their niche and as of this writing, downtown Kalamazoo has a retail vacancy rate of 14 percent.[6] An aggressive retail recruitment plan is in place.

Downtown Developers/Office Workers

Downtown Kalamazoo has the highest concentration of office space in the county, with 17,000 workers and some 200 offices. The vacancy rate is about 21 percent,[7] three to five times higher than rates in other parts of the county. There is an excess of Class B and C office space in downtown. DKI is working to upgrade space but as of this writing the demand for Class A office space was not high.

Private Business Interests

Noted area developers and businesspeople new to development increasingly have agreed to take risks on downtown properties and downtown businesses. Their work has been enhanced by government incentives and the work of the downtown organizations.

CUTTING-EDGE COLLABORATION

According to a survey of local governments,[8] the greatest barrier to economic development is the limited availability of land. In central cities, that problem is only exacerbated by environmental contamination. Over the twenty-year study period DTI was key in addressing land availability head-on. Land was assembled through DTI in part to provide coordinated incentives that dovetailed with planning and in part to head off small developments that could block larger efforts.

In a unique collaboration, the Kalamazoo Community Foundation made no less than thirteen low-interest, nonbankable loans—referred to in the foundation world as "program related investments" to DTI to assist with this property acquisition. Although the loans were executed shortly after the study period, they represent the work culminated in the 1990s and serve as evidence that downtown partnerships continue to evolve. Backed by mortgages, second mortgages, and holding costs, the loans have totaled some $5 million. The terms are 1.5 percent deferred interest annually at the time of principal payment, and have helped to continue the momentum of development in downtown Kalamazoo.

LESSONS LEARNED

Different individuals and organizations learned a number of lessons from the experiences of the past two decades.

Planning Works

As noted earlier, some issues such as the acceptance of downtown residential living, are hard to force. By and large, though, Kalamazoo benefited from broad-based involvement of its leaders, stakeholders, and citizens. At times, critics suggested that the community's problems were "studied to death," but ultimately, real solutions came from a mix of consultative and hands-on work.

The Downtown Is a Balancing Act

With the decline in downtown activity in the manufacturing, commercial, and retail sectors, some communities have looked for the "silver bullet," to reshape their destinies, but in medium-sized communities at least, resources don't exist for such strategies. Instead, communities need to look for an appropriate mix of aesthetics, historic detail, niche retail, limited housing, entertainment, public service, commercial, and cultural amenities—all within the context of making that mix unique. In that regard, preservation of green spaces and interesting architecture stand out.

Linkages Are Vital to Success

Downtown Kalamazoo's most significant successes may well have stemmed from community leaders' ability to understand the relationship between the downtown and the areas immediately surrounding it. Neighborhood linkages proved to be especially important to the success of development efforts.

Collaboration Is Key

One of Kalamazoo's first lessons in the study period was that a number of key players had to commit to the Arcadia Commons project before it had the critical mass to be successful. When they had banded together, they needed the help of historic preservationists, neighborhood leaders, and public officials. Throughout the study period, almost every advance resulted from harnessing human and financial resources from diverse interests. The community will continually be challenged to maintain the commitment of individuals and organizations over time and to sustain the momentum of its collaborations.

THE CHALLENGES THAT LIE AHEAD

The redistribution of economic activity within metropolitan areas continues to present a mismatch between low-skilled employees living in central cities and inner suburbs and potential employers located increasingly farther out in suburbia. Put another way, the survival of the urban core remains tantamount to those midsized, Midwest cities that still have downtowns.

Specifically in Kalamazoo, the ability to create and sustain linkages is where Kalamazoo appears to face its greatest remaining challenges. At the turn of the century, downtown leaders were attempting to forge a closer relationship with Western Michigan University (WMU), home to 27,000 students who have underutilized the downtown. City leaders and WMU officials had experienced success in bringing public transportation to students and building a business technology research park, but closing the gap with the downtown remains a challenge.

Moreover, Kalamazoo still needs to develop physical linkages with its largest suburban neighbor, Portage, but little progress was made in the twenty-year study period. If the philosophy holds that community linkages are important, relationships with Portage and other suburban communities will need to continue to improve. Similarly, intergovernmental cooperation with county government will be important, as the county—with its courts and administrative offices downtown—has been examining its own "development" future, particularly in law enforcement and the possible site selection of a new jail.

As of this writing, a large portion of the employee base that made up Pfizer's downtown workforce is being phased out or has moved out of downtown Kalamazoo. Pfizer purchased Upjohn's successor organization, Pharmacia, in 2002. Any community that relies on a large employer is vulnerable. Fortunately, Kalamazoo still has private individuals and development companies that are interested in investing in downtown. The once-threatened Kalamazoo Center, now an AAA four-diamond Radisson property, is receiving its third upgrade in fifteen years, the most recent being a $25 million expansion by a local, private developer and philanthropist.

Finally, a significant reality for downtown Kalamazoo is that challenges continue to evolve. Properties deteriorate. Businesses fail. Streets need repair. Parking continues to exasperate. Kalamazoo, like other cities its size, will need to continue to be vigilant, creative, and focused.

NOTES

1. OMB instructed Census Bureau to track "micropolitan" centers with populations between 10,000 and 50,000, starting in June 2003. Population Reference Bureau (www.prb.org).

2. U.S. Census Bureau (2000). The 2000 Census of net migration for the young, single, and college-educated for the United States, regions, states and metropolitan areas. http://www.census.gov/population/cen2000/phc-t34/tab02.pdf. U.S. Census Bureau (2003). Migration of the young, single, and college-educated: 1995-2000, Special report. http://www.census.gov/prod/2003pubs/censr-12pdf.

3. April 13, 1990 memo to DDA, Project Enhancement Team, Arcadia Commons Project Directors.

4. History Room, Kalamazoo Public Library, Subject File, Kalamazoo Mall Downtown Plan, City of Kalamazoo, Michigan, May 20, 1996.

5. Downtown Kalamazoo Inc. (DKI), 2003 annual report.

6. DKI.

7. DKI.

8. International City Managers Association, 1999.

Chapter 36

Incredible Crisis and Downtown Response: Alliance for Downtown New York

Carl Weisbrod
Jennifer Hensley

It started out as a normal and, in fact, beautiful day, which is something so many people have said. The skies above downtown New York City were the crisp, bright blue of an early fall day on the East coast. Things began right on schedule. At 6:30 a.m., the first shift of the Downtown Alliance public safety officers reported for duty at the Downtown Center, where select units of the New York City Police Department are also housed. The NYPD Downtown Center, located just a few blocks south of the World Trade Center at 104 Washington Street, was jointly created by the NYPD and the Downtown Alliance in 1999 and is, along with Philadelphia's Center City, one of the nation's first public/private partnerships between a police force and a private security staff. After their roll call on the morning of September 11, 2001, thirty-five Downtown Alliance public safety officers were deployed to their posts throughout their district. From City Hall down to the Battery, from the East River to West Street, they covered one square mile at the southernmost tip of Manhattan. Four of them were stationed at the World Trade Center.

By 7:00 a.m., most of the nearly 300,000 workers who commuted to Lower Manhattan each day had begun their journeys, making their way by car, bus, ferry, and train from throughout the tristate area. Set up for the fourth annual Dine Around Downtown—an event sponsored by the Downtown Alliance at which restaurants set up booths and offer small portions of their signature dishes during lunchtime—was well underway on the World Trade Center's huge plaza. The event, scheduled for the afternoon of the 12th, was expected to draw more than 10,000 workers, residents, and tourists to the World Trade Center. Early on the morning of the 11th, tents were being trucked in from New Jersey and the participating chefs were just beginning their prep work in nearby restaurants.

doi:10.1300/5137_37

Later, at 8:30 a.m., a handful of Downtown Alliance staff members had arrived for work at the main office on the 33rd floor of 120 Broadway, two blocks east of the World Trade Center. Coffee was brewing and I was checking my e-mail—the same morning ritual I had done for seven years, since I opened the Downtown Alliance in 1995. That morning, I was joined in the office by Mike O'Connor, a former NYPD transit chief and now senior vice president for operations at the Alliance, and Frank Addeo and Joe Timpone, also members of our operations department.

My first indication that this was not going to be a normal day was at about 8:50 a.m., when our office manager, Daisy DiGoia, came into the office ashen faced and shaking. She said she had just seen a plane crash into the World Trade Center. Like everyone else who first heard the news, I thought it must be a small plane that somehow lost its way, a confused pilot—surely, an accident.

Our public safety officers on the street who had seen the incident radioed to our base this mobilizing Safety Net, a radio system monitored and used by the Downtown Alliance and the NYPD's first precinct. This immediately got word out to forty-five security officers in commercial buildings throughout our district, informing them of the plane crash and providing instructions for building evacuations. Our office also got the call over the radio, and Mike ordered an evacuation.

We took the elevator downstairs and emerged from our building to see flames shooting out from the North Tower. Anxiously, we made our way to the Downtown Center, all the time looking at the fire burning inside the skyscraper. Just as we arrived at the Center, I watched—horrified—as the second plane roared overhead and slammed into the World Trade Center's South Tower, just two blocks from where I was standing.

From our vantage point, Mike and I watched as the fires burned, about two-thirds of the way up each Tower. We speculated, helplessly, about how many people could get out—from the floors above the fires as well as those below—and saw people wrapped in flames jumping out of windows to their certain deaths.

We wondered whether the buildings would survive. At about 10:30 a.m., approximately two hours after the first plane hit, we got our answer when we suddenly heard a great roar, a rumble, like an earthquake, and the sky overhead became pitch black. The first building was collapsing.

Being so close to the Towers, we saw the clouds of dust coming toward us so we rushed indoors, diving under desks for protection as we had practiced in grade school during countless drills meant to prepare us for nuclear attacks. The collapse of the second Tower, which once again forced us to shelter ourselves under desks, followed shortly thereafter.

At this point, land lines and cell phones were still operating episodically, and I was able to reach my son in college to assure him of my safety and to leave a message for my wife. Both knew that I frequently had breakfast at Windows on the World, the restaurant atop the World Trade Center. If I had been there on this morning, as so many others actually were, I certainly would not have survived.

After the Towers collapsed, Lower Manhattan—the nation's third-largest central business district—was eerily quiet. Thick dust filled the air and combined with the extensive power outages to create blackout conditions. Papers from the destroyed offices flittered about the streets and were strangely reminiscent of the hundreds of ticker tape parades that had ascended on downtown's Canyon of Heroes in celebrations of years past. There, as I stood on the barely recognizable corner of Washington and Carlisle Streets, the massive destruction, the magnitude of the loss, was almost incomprehensible.

Soon, we would get word of our friends and colleagues who didn't survive the attacks. Fortunately—and somewhat miraculously—we would learn that all thirty-nine Downtown Alliance employees and each of our sixty-eight public safety officers and fifty-six sanitation supervisors had survived the attacks. One of our sister organizations, Futures and Options, which places high school students in corporate internships, had offices in the North Tower. Though their space was destroyed, all their students and employees were safe. Still, at that moment, standing on that corner, we could not imagine the toll this disaster would take on Lower Manhattan and the world.

Back at the Downtown Center, just south of the Trade Center, our public safety directors had already secured generators from the NYPD and the Transit Authority. Once we had power, the Center quickly became a triage center providing emergency care to the injured. Area residents are familiar with our officers and with the facility we share with the NYPD, so when they had to flee their homes, several came to the Center for protection and comfort in the hours and days after the attacks. The Downtown Center remained open as a rest station for police and fire workers and other volunteers who were working on the Pile during the rescue and recovery. We took deliveries of food and water from the Red Cross and other groups to the emergency workers. Our staff operated a shuttle to transport senior citizens who couldn't be evacuated from their homes to area grocery stores for food and supplies. Our public safety officers provided the Downtown Alliance's maps to the rescue workers and security forces from the Office of Emergency Management, the Army, the National Guard, NYPD, FDNY (New York City Fire Department), and others who were unfamiliar with the winding streets of Lower Manhattan. Even those who were somewhat familiar with downtown needed maps because, covered with nearly two feet of debris, nothing was recognizable.

In the immediate aftermath of the attacks, downtown was virtually immobilized. The collapse of 7 World Trade Center later in the day on September 11th, and the consequent flooding of the area's power station and telecommunications hub, knocked out all power and land-line phone service to the area. Wireless service was spotty, at best, because so many repeater cells had been destroyed. Traffic was not allowed south of Canal Street and armed National Guardsmen patrolled all of downtown.

I'd been able to visit our office space at 120 Broadway, two blocks east of the Trade Center site, on September 13th and was surprised by how minimal the internal damage was. No windows were broken, there was just a bit of dust in the hallways, and, except for external communications, all our systems were operational. Con Edison and electrical generators had— amazingly—restored electric power to most parts of the area within forty-eight hours. However, with roads still closed and access heavily restricted, we would not be able to occupy the space for some time. Still, in the days that followed the attacks, every single member of the Downtown Alliance staff remained committed to the goals of our organization and determined to play an integral part in the recovery of our community.

Many of us volunteered at call centers set up by the city for businesses that needed to be relocated, or at intake/outreach stations putting displaced residents and families of victims in touch with direct service providers during those chaotic and emotional first days after the attacks. For many of us at the Downtown Alliance, it was a time of great sadness and grief as we mourned the loss of our friends and neighbors who died in the attacks and began to realize that the neighborhood we had worked so hard—and successfully—to revitalize in the 1990s was in a state of disrepair and despair that no other community in the United States had ever experienced.

On September 20, 2001, the city reopened the area east of Broadway in Lower Manhattan, and we resumed work at the Downtown Alliance's main office at 120 Broadway. Still without external communications systems, we relied on spotty cell phone service to get our jobs done. With the communications system being what it was, most of the staff spent a great deal of time out in our district, answering questions and providing hands-on assistance to the businesses, workers, and residents who had returned.

Immediately, the need for advocacy and assistance became clear. Our constituents faced seemingly insurmountable challenges and the Downtown Alliance, because of our preexisting relationship to the community and our broad resources, could help. We made our extensive databases available to public agencies seeking to reach businesses and residents. We directly distributed information regarding access restrictions including transportation changes, road closures, and emergency operating procedures for truck deliveries. In addition, we helped to put our constituents in touch with the direct services they needed, such as Federal Emergency Management Agency (FEMA), the Red Cross, and their insurance companies.

A week after the attacks, our public safety officers were back on assignment, stationed along the perimeter of our district, providing a sense of familiarity and comfort to the workers and residents coming back downtown. Access checkpoints had been set up throughout the area allowing only rescue workers and authorized personnel into Lower Manhattan. Our public safety officers coordinated with the Office of Emergency Management, the Army, and the NYPD to escort company representatives through the checkpoints to their office space to survey damage and collect essential materials. Our sanitation workers were back, too, making whatever dents they could in the piles of debris throughout our district. As the retailers came back to reopen their stores, our crews power washed storefronts and sidewalks thus helping to make our neighborhood a little bit more inviting. The Downtown Center continued to accept food deliveries and provided a rest station for the emergency workers and disaster volunteers. Throughout the September 11th attacks and during the aftermath, the Center never closed and continues to be a secure and inviting resource for the downtown community.

Soon it became clear that, besides the victims of the attacks and their families, Lower Manhattan's retailers had suffered the most immediate and worst economic hardship. Deli owners and pizza men could not work from home. Florists and dry cleaners could not pick up their inventories and temporarily move to New Jersey. Their businesses were based in Lower Manhattan and they were dependent on the foot traffic there for customers. Many of them operated with very small financial margins and didn't have the cash flow to immediately clean up their stores and get back to business, especially since it would be a long time before downtown retailers would see the client base they once had.

Just a few weeks after the attacks, Jack Rosenthal of the New York Times Foundation set up a meeting with Bill Grinker, CEO of Seedco, a preeminent nationwide economic development intermediary that provides financial and technical assistance and management support to nonprofits and small businesses throughout the nation, and me to discuss the need for quick and effective economic stimulation in Lower Manhattan. Our solution was to create the first privately funded loan, grant, and wage subsidy program for Lower Manhattan's small businesses.

The Lower Manhattan Small Business and Workforce Retention Project was designed to provide the cash businesses needed in order to reopen their doors as well as to minimize layoffs by subsidizing employees' wages as the retailers struggled to rebuild their client bases. To date, we have distributed

$7.8 million in grants, $17.8 in low-interest loans, and $3.8 million in wage subsidies to 888 small businesses. Perhaps most significantly, we were able to put this privately funded business assistance program in place by November of 2001, before the government could organize its own critically important response. It has proven to be one of the recovery's most successful small business assistance tools.

It was also clear from very early on that Lower Manhattan businesses would need the support of the local, state, and federal governments to make it through the tragedy. With support from the Manhattan Chamber of Commerce, we convened a group of fifty-seven small business owners and took them to Washington, DC, to lobby Congress for aid. We also participated in U.S. Congressman Jerrold Nadler's Ground Zero Task Force, a coalition of elected officials who represented downtown. Congressman Nadler, whose district includes Lower Manhattan and the World Trade Center site, asked us to participate because, though we are not part of an elected office, we had intimate and critical knowledge of the Lower Manhattan community. In an unprecedented show of cooperation among different levels and types of government, the task force was able to produce results. In the very early stages, we provided for deliveries of prescription medications to elderly citizens who were not able to leave their homes during the disaster. Later, the task force advocated for increased access to restricted areas for businesses and residents anxious to survey the damages, and for street openings to bring foot traffic back to the businesses who were able to reopen. By joining together, we were able to influence the city, state, and federal agencies and work on disaster relief to *really* respond to our community and to provide the information and services that were needed during this unprecedented disaster.

Lower Manhattan has always been a unique community, and since the area's first residential buildings were converted from decrepit commercial stock in the late 1970s, the residential and business communities have been largely united. In fact, more than a third of downtown's residents work for nearby businesses and choose to live here because they can walk to work. What has been good for Lower Manhattan businesses over the past several years—decreased commercial vacancy rates, development of new class A office space, conversion of old building stock for residential use—has also been good for residents. The September 11th attacks, in many ways, strengthened the relationship among the residents, businesses, and workers in Lower Manhattan. In tragedy, the downtown community became even more closely knit together. As access was restored, businesses and residents, both grateful to return, welcomed one another back.

Quickly, we realized that our community needed more than just access to information and direct technical assistance. As the streets reopened and businesses welcomed their employees back to the area, we needed to get the message out to people throughout the tri-state region that downtown was open for business. The impression that Lower Manhattan was closed was pervasive. In fact, for months, traffic signs throughout the city and on roads leading into the city read "Lower Manhattan Is Closed." Thus, it proved very difficult to attract visitors, shoppers, and tourists back to what many viewed as a "restricted area" or "war zone."

Our marketing department partnered with Kirshenbaum Bond & Partners, who provided their services pro bono, to develop a comprehensive advertising campaign aimed at bringing customers back downtown. The campaign, which we kicked off in late November 2001, included print ads placed in newspapers and magazines throughout the region, posters throughout the city's subway system, television commercials narrated by Robert DeNiro, and radio spots. In addition, we printed shopping bags that read "Fight Back—Fill This Bag Downtown," as well as posters, buttons, and postcards that reminded people to "Shop Downtown. Save Downtown."

Retailers weren't the only downtown businesses that suffered after the attacks. Downtown's cultural institutions had a hard time bringing back foot traffic. In addition, many of them saw significant drops in donations as people chose instead to make donations to 9/11-related charities. In late November, the Downtown Alliance convened a meeting of the cultural institutions in our district and, through those discussions, it became clear that we needed to create a tremendous and unprecedented joint effort to bring people back. Out of this emerged the concept for what would become the Downtown NYC River to River Festival.

Armed with the idea that we would create the largest free music and arts festival in the city's history to welcome the people of downtown back to their neighborhood in the summer of 2002, we, along with downtown's other major event producers—the Battery Park City Authority, the Lower Manhattan Cultural Council, the Port Authority of New York and New Jersey, the South Street Seaport, and the World Financial Center Arts & Events Program—approached Lower Manhattan's major corporations for sponsorship. In January of 2002, we signed a contract with American Express naming them the presenting partner and securing $1 million toward our $7.6 million festival. Once American Express was on board, other sponsors followed, including AT&T, Pace University, and almost all of downtown's major employers. The festival, then, was underway.

As people started coming back downtown, and as shops reopened and cultural institutions saw more visitors, we started to deal with the long-term process of rebuilding Lower Manhattan. In late November 2001, New York State Governor George Pataki and then New York City Mayor Rudolph Giuliani created the Lower Manhattan Development Corporation, a joint state/city agency charged with coordinating the rebuilding efforts. We have long recognized that the World Trade Center site should be the product of a good plan for the entire neighborhood, not the engine that drives planning for the surrounding area.

The Downtown Alliance remains heavily involved in the planning discussions for development on the World Trade Center site and throughout our district. We continue to weigh in on issues that affect our district including plans for allocating the remaining federal aid that has been appropriated to assist in Lower Manhattan's revitalization and planned capital improvements to downtown's transportation infrastructure. Yet we also have a responsibility to maintain a real and visible presence in the community during the short term. As the rebuilding of Lower Manhattan progresses, the needs of our constituents evolve. Because of the breadth of our resources, the Downtown Alliance's position as a non-profit entity, and our relationship to the Lower Manhattan community, we are able to respond quickly to the community's changing needs and create programs and tactics that better serve our neighborhood.

As part of our ongoing efforts to gauge and respond to these changes in our constituents' needs, we have convened a series of working groups to address specific issues in the rebuilding process.

The Transportation Users Group, comprised of representatives from the area's largest employers, discusses and advocates for transportation improvements for their employees who come to Lower Manhattan each day from throughout the tri-state region. The Transportation Users Group has done extensive analyses of the area's ferry services and has advocated for the expansion of regular Lower Manhattan ferry services to three main locations: LaGuardia Airport/Shea Stadium, the Upper East and West Sides of Manhattan, and Westchester/Connecticut. They also urge the establishment of a single regional agency to oversee ferry development, as well as increased public financial support of ferry transportation. Because this group represents downtown's largest employers and some of the city's biggest businesses, the weight of its recommendations is significant. The Port Authority of New York and New Jersey evaluated our suggestions and working toward implementation.

In conjunction with the Real Estate Board of New York, the Association for a Better New York, and the New York Building Congress, a Telecommunications Users Group has been developed. One of the main concerns of this group was the lack of telecommunications redundancy in Lower Manhattan. Though the New York Stock Exchange was up and running by the Monday after the September 11th attacks, many businesses had to wait months before their lines were restored. The Telecommunications Users Group, has been at the forefront of the effort to create downtown wireless redundancy systems. A proposal was developed that would provide the shared infrastructure in the form of five telecom hubs atop downtown's tallest buildings to which businesses could connect wirelessly creating both phone and computer redundancy.

The Human Resources Users Group provides another method to share information with downtown workers in a streamlined and efficient manner. In regular meetings with the human resource directors of downtown's biggest companies, rebuilding issues and development plans are discussed for the area. In return, employees' main concerns are discussed and addressed.

By convening these meetings and coordinating participation by the appropriate government agencies and private service providers, the Downtown Alliance plays a critical role in linking the stakeholders who are invested in our community and the groups charged with rebuilding it. It is a sensitive balance, but one that we have been able to manage because of our long history of providing quality services to a unique and world-class community.

Since the September 11th attacks, our operations department has increased its focus on training. The commanding office of the NYPD terrorism task force has provided our public safety officers a two-day training course focused on identifying and addressing terrorism risks. That training is now repeated monthly, with lessons that are up to date and relevant to our officers. The Downtown Alliance also provides assistance to area buildings during their evacuation drills, which are now much more frequent. In addition, in response to concerns of our constituents, the Downtown Alliance sends out an "alert" e-mail when out-of-the-ordinary events such as evacuation drills or a demolition/construction is planned. This keeps the workers and residents in the area from becoming alarmed when they suddenly see crowds of people evacuating a building or hear strange and loud noises. Our "alert" system has proven to be a very successful mechanism for distributing information in nonemergency situations and keeping our neighbors aware of what's going on in their community.

We also continue to help downtown's small businesses and retailers. The loan, grant, and wage subsidy program developed with Seedco is still going strong, and some of the first loan payments have come in. In an effort to attract more commercial businesses to the vacant downtown space, we developed a commercial attraction program and sent informational packets to more than 5,000 small companies in the New York metropolitan area, enticing them to move downtown.

We recently initiated a retail attraction program to fill Lower Manhattan's vacant storefronts. After completing extensive research on market conditions in our district, we identified prime retail spaces and have begun actively recruiting major retailers to the district. In an effort to diversify the uses of space downtown, we have also developed a similar program to attract art galleries. We believe that cultural uses beyond what will be developed on the World Trade Center site will be an integral part of the redevelopment of Lower Manhattan, particularly as residential development continues throughout the area and demand grows for after-hours and weekend services.

To this end, too, we have programmed open spaces throughout Lower Manhattan, improving the quality of life for workers, residents, and visitors. In the summer of 2003, the Downtown Alliance created WiFi networks in seven open spaces throughout Lower Manhattan, making downtown the most "wireless" central business district in the nation. We also worked with the NYC Department of Parks and Recreation to bring musical performances to Bowling Green Park every weekday at lunchtime during the summer. This has been a remarkable success and has furthered the goal of getting people out into the district and utilizing downtown's limited open space.

On Memorial Day, 2002, the first River to River Festival was held with a Sheryl Crow concert in Battery Park. More than 20,000 people came to Battery Park that day, and downtown was more bustling than it had been since before the September 11th attacks. In 2002, we drew more than 2 million people to more than 500 free River to River events. The Downtown NYC River to River Festival continued in 2003 to draw even larger crowds to Lower Manhattan. Planning for the third-annual festival is well underway, and as each year passes, the festival becomes a bigger and more important part of the downtown community. The Downtown NYC River to River Festival has become one of the most joyous parts of downtown's revitalization.

The September 11th attacks shocked the nation, but nowhere was the devastation greater than it was in Lower Manhattan. Even in those first days and months, though, when everything in sight was covered with ashen debris and the stench of the fires permeated the neighborhood, it seemed that we would get through this. Our residents, our businesses, and our workers never wavered in their commitment to rebuilding a better Lower Manhattan.

Now, more than four years since the attacks, we have come a long way toward reaching that goal. A master plan has been approved for development on the World Trade Center site and construction has already begun on a new office tower at 7 World Trade. Designs for the Freedom Tower have been evaluated and a winner has been chosen. Preattack transportation service has been restored and a free bus service has been added—the Downtown Connection. Already, Lower Manhattan is emerging from this tragedy stronger and more vibrant than it's ever been.

In almost every way, September 11th has changed the work that we do as a business improvement district (BID). But it has not changed our foundation—our roots in our community, our commitment to service, our dedication to the revitalization of the financial capital of the world. We remain a valuable resource, an innovative partner, and an enthusiastic supporter of the businesses we serve and the neighborhood we represent.

Our goal is nothing less than creating the first truly great urban center of the twenty-first century. I am sure that we will make it happen.

Chapter 37

The Homeless Situation in Los Angeles and the BID Response

Kent Smith

Perhaps nowhere in North America are homeless people so numerous and so concentrated than on the streets of downtown Los Angeles. In a county where an estimated 88,000 people are homeless on any given night, approximately 13,000 of those are in downtown.[1] City and county policies over the past thirty years sought to contain the homeless in Skid Row, a twelve-block radius that now includes fifty-five social service agencies. Until recently, the single-room occupancy (SROs) and Skid Row hotels made up over 50 percent of the downtown housing stock.

Although only 37 percent of Los Angeles County homeless are without a home for two years or more, many in the downtown population are chronically homeless.[2] Some are "housed" in downtown missions and in residential hotels that have become high-rise drug dens and major health hazards. Some 4,000 live on the streets in cardboard encampments in Central City East or Skid Row (Midnight Mission, 2004).[3]

According to the Downtown Mental Health Center, it is estimated that 50 to 75 percent of the downtown homeless have a substance abuse problem and over a third have a history of mental illness, with major depression being the most prevalent diagnosis.[4] A great many of these chronically homeless are also shelter-resistant, as shown in a 2000 study by Shelter Partnership.[5] The study found that the homeless using the cold and wet weather emergency shelters refused beds in missions and SROs because they require clients to be sober and to accept counseling.

Layered on top of substance abuse and mental illness is the propensity of the state and county prison systems to release parolees into Skid Row, which also houses the highest parolee population in California. In 2004, the Midnight Mission and Chrysalis conducted a survey of persons exiting the county jail. Of respondents, 21 percent indicated they had nowhere to sleep that very night.[6] With approximately 180,000 prisoners released in 2004,

doi:10.1300/5137_38

that means almost 38,000 homeless people are funneled into downtown by the Los Angeles County jail system annually.[7]

Until recently, the existence of Skid Row in downtown Los Angeles has been a major factor in deterring ground-floor retail activity and housing developments. As a consequence of the concentration of homeless in Skid Row, downtown was commonly perceived as an undesirable area. In fact, even office employment began to decline after the mid 1990s, and property owners watched property values plummet.

THE ROLE OF BUSINESS IMPROVEMENT DISTRICTS

This environment led to the establishment of business improvement districts (BIDs) in downtown Los Angeles. The LA Fashion District was first in 1996 followed by the Downtown Center BID (1998), Historic Core BID (1999), Toy District and Downtown Industrial BIDs (1999), Chinatown BID (2001), and Little Tokyo BID (2004).

The BIDs did not accept the premise that it was acceptable to allow chronically homeless people with self-destructive lifestyles to live on the streets of downtown. This led to street encampments in which the homeless are allowed to live in donated tents or cardboard boxes in downtown, often in front of businesses. Part of the problem was that shelters were open only in wet weather, with the unstated view that in good weather it was okay to live on the street. When shelters were closed, downtown businesses noticed a large influx of homeless encampments on the streets.

The "right" to live on the street became a death sentence for the chronically homeless, who suffer from all sorts of diseases. It also spawned public health issues as by their nature street encampments have no sanitation facilities. Although there is no statistical information regarding the health effects on the general population, the potential for spreading diseases is apparent. In 2005, several professionals working in Skid Row were diagnosed with MRSA "staph" infections. Common in the county jail, this life-threatening infection is now residing in the Skid Row homeless population and is spread through skin-to-skin contact.

Several of the BIDs responded to this situation with a zero-tolerance policy for encampments in their district. Leaflets were handed out to homeless listing shelters and service providers. BID Safe Team officers were accompanied by social workers who made direct contact with the homeless to advise them of these new strategies. The BIDs also sought to be part of the solution by employing homeless and formerly homeless individuals on their Clean Teams.

As BIDs were established, the pressures on the chronically homeless increased. Though BID Safe Teams did their best to encourage the shelter-resistant homeless to take advantage of the myriad social programs on their "doorstep," most remained on the street. Tensions increased as BID Safe Teams continued to make citizens' arrests for criminal actions witnessed in their presence.

THE CLASS ACTION LAWSUIT

In 1999, homeless advocates, who believe in the right to live on the street, convinced the American Civil Liberties Union (ACLU) to launch a class action lawsuit against four of the BIDs whose boundaries were immediately adjacent to Skid Row.

The advocates contacted the *Los Angeles Times* before the papers were served to the BIDs in order to try to influence public opinion. The tactic backfired when several BIDs responded by saying it was not their intention to violate the civil liberties of homeless individuals, only to control criminal behavior. The BIDs also expressed dismay that they were not even contacted beforehand to address the concerns raised in the lawsuit.

Led by the LA Fashion District, this strategy forced the ACLU and the homeless advocates into mediation, and over a several-month period a "code of conduct" was adopted for BID Safe Teams. The BIDs agreed not to search homeless people, not to photograph them, or ask them for identification. Most controversially, the BIDs agreed that they would not ask the homeless to "move along."

The code of conduct still allowed the BIDs to enforce a zero-tolerance policy for encampments. Most important, the LA Fashion District BID, which was first to settle the case, agreed to meet the ACLU and homeless advocates quarterly to discuss areas of concern before they evolved into lawsuits. This was helpful in diffusing situations and has led the ACLU and advocates to better understand the role of BID Safe Teams.

THE PERSONAL POSSESSION CHECK-IN FACILITY

The Toy District/Downtown Industrial (DI) BIDs decided not to settle with the ACLU. The focus of the case against the BIDs changed to address how the BID clean and safe teams were handling personal property left by the homeless on the sidewalk in front of businesses in the district.

The Toy District/DI BIDs were given a court order to establish a "check-in" facility for the homeless to store their possessions. Usually operated by the public sector in other cities, the Toy District/DI BID were compelled to establish the facility to address the large amount of personal property left by the homeless in their districts. A property owner donated 20,000 square feet in a warehouse building in which 150 donated containers were placed on shelves. Individuals could access their container on a daily basis. The facility is open seven days a week, from 8:00 a.m. to 8:00 p.m. and is used daily by over 250 people.

The effect of the Personal Possession Check-In Facility has been immediate. The sidewalks are now clear of possessions and shopping carts, and businesses have been able to function without interference.

Although this solution works well, it is costly. The Toy District/DI BIDs estimate that it costs $50,000 per year to staff the facility. Since the check-in facility was set up in response to a court injunction obtained by the ACLU, there is little flexibility to reduce costs.

OUTREACH TEAMS

The Downtown Center BID, in response to the lawsuit of the other BIDs (they were not a party), decided to set up a BID outreach team to address the mentally ill, shelter-resistant homeless, who are the most difficult to get into service programs.

The outreach team partnered with the psychiatric unit of one of the local hospitals and used the BID outreach teams as first contacts with these individuals. The teams are made up of one formerly homeless individual and a BID Safe Team member. The team members are given training in recognizing the signs of mental illness and are tutored in facilitating substantive yet compassionate interactions with homeless individuals. The BID Action Team is also linked with service providers who can address their various needs.

The LA Fashion District has also implemented a similar training model with its Safe Team, and both BIDs instituted quarterly update training to re-inforce this compassionate response to the most difficult-to-approach homeless individuals. The LA Fashion District has also partnered with the local missions to ensure that emergency shelter beds are available in the event BID Safe Team members encounter encampments in the district during their patrols.

California state law requires individuals who are mentally ill to voluntarily seek treatment unless they are found to be harmful to themselves or others.[8] This law has made it very difficult to get mentally ill individuals into services and the BID outreach has only been modestly successful in getting mentally ill homeless off the streets. However, the effort has shown that BIDs are committed to a healing model for the homeless as opposed to relying on traditional enforcement models to eliminate the encampment and substance abuse problems in Skid Row.

ADDRESSING DISORDERLY BEHAVIOR

One of the most challenging issues faced by BIDs and their constituents is the daily presence of homeless individuals living on the street. Property owners and their merchants constantly call complaining about the negative effects of the homeless loitering around their businesses with their possessions in shopping carts deterring customers from entering their stores. Worse, some mentally ill homeless individuals exhibit disruptive behavior that destroys the pedestrian activity that is so vital to commercial success. The drug addicted will often panhandle, tamper with parking meters, or, on occasion, break into motor vehicles. The presence of parolees (with an over 50 percent reoffending rate) adds to this criminal activity.

The BID Clean & Safe Teams must tackle these issues that even rank-and-file LAPD officers are reluctant to address. With no community court or penalties for these disruptive behaviors, BIDs are forced to rely on persuasion and firmness to eliminate disorderly behavior. Strategies include waking homeless up on an hourly basis with offers of a shelter bed to running sidewalk scrubbers constantly in areas where merchants find loitering to be a problem. Safe Team officers often flank panhandlers and encouraging the public to donate their change to social service agencies instead of individual panhandlers. As a last resort, Safe Team officers will exercise their rights as private citizens and detain individuals when they witness criminal activity such as meter tampering and drinking in public. As a result, everyone gets the message that civility codes are enforced within the boundaries of the BID.

THE POSITIVE EFFECT OF RESIDENTIAL DEVELOPMENT

A major ally in the effort to get the public sector to address the issue of homelessness is the growing downtown residential population. With a strong economy, increasing population, and the lack of NIMBYISM ("not in my back yard"), downtown is a focal point for a burgeoning housing conversion program. The first housing projects to open were in the Old Bank District at 4th and Main adjacent to Skid Row in the Historic Core BID. This brought new residents face to face with the problems of homelessness downtown. Since 1999, over 6,000 more units have recently opened with another 5,400 under construction. The new Downtown Neighborhood Council, has made addressing homelessness its number one priority.

STEPS TO ADDRESS THE SITUATION

In March 2003, the International Downtown Association's Technical Assistance Team visited Los Angeles to make a number of recommendations to the homeless situation in downtown. The team found a lack of coordination and leadership on homeless issues. The panel suggested the establishment of a coordinating council with a set of very specific goals and measurable objectives. Its specific recommendations included installing more shelter beds, establishing a community court, creating more supportive housing, and compiling more detailed information on the demographic profile of homeless individuals downtown.

By the end of 2003, many of the Technical Assistance Team's recommendations were being implemented. An effort to draft a plan to end homelessness in Los Angeles County is now well underway and is led by the mayors of Los Angeles, Santa Monica, Long Beach, and Pasadena. County supervisors, the sheriff, the LAPD police chief, many social service agencies, and several downtown BIDs are also represented.

As part of that effort, a new study was completed that profiles the homeless in terms of numbers, demographics, and most important, the nature of their problems. This has helped focus attention on the chronically homeless who are at the root of most of the problems in Skid Row.

In November 2003, the county and the city, with the help of private funds, agreed to open 2,000 "wet weather" beds all year long. In December 2005, Senator Gill Cedillo announced legislation to require county jail inmates to be released throughout the county instead of just Downtown.

Chief of Police Bill Bratton brought in George Kelling, co-author of *Fixing Broken Windows,* to formulate a strategy to eliminate encampments and drug use in Skid Row. He has made talking drug activity in Skid Row LAPD's number one priority in 2006. The city passed its first Urination and Defecation Ordinance in December 2003 to address the public health concerns of street living and installed permanent, self-cleaning toilets in Skid Row. A coalition of BIDs, businesses, and social service agencies worked together to ensure the ordinance was adopted.

The city attorney has tackled the drug and alcohol use problems in Skid Row hotels, and liquor stores closing some, and has enforced new codes of conduct on several of the largest hotels.

Finally, the state senate is formulating legislation to establish a community court in Skid Row.

All these efforts are beginning to be noticed in Washington, DC. The federal government's Interagency Council gave $5.7 million to a coalition of social services to develop supportive housing projects targeted to the service-resistant in Skid Row. The county's and city's homeless funding provider, Los Angeles Homeless Services Authority (LHASA), has recently recommended that funding be shifted to programs outside downtown Los Angeles to reduce the concentration of social service providers clustered in Skid Row. The LAHSA board approved this recommendation in February 2004.

AN OPTIMISTIC OUTLOOK

Many challenges remain before the problems of homelessness in downtown Los Angeles can be resolved. The county jail, hospitals, and other municipal police departments continue to dump people with no place to go into Skid Row. Many municipalities have no services for the homeless, making Skid Row one of the only places of welcome in the county. Still the homeless issue has the attention of political leaders like never before. This is a result of a poignant weekly column written by Steve Lopez in the *LA Times* chronicling the life of a former Julliard-schooled violinist who is struggling with mental illness and life on the street.

For property owners and businesses in the area there is a great deal of reason for optimism. The number of ground-floor retail businesses in the LA Fashion District has increased to over 2,500 stores with nearly 500 added between 2002 and 2004. The opening of major entertainment venues such as Disney Concert Hall, The Orpheum Theatre on Broadway, Staples Center, and innumerable restaurants have led to much more evening activity in downtown. Most important, new residents are providing the political constituency needed to ensure that downtown's quality of life measurably improves. Business Improvement Districts are committed to nothing less than a vibrant, pedestrian-friendly downtown that acts as a magnet to attract people from the region and beyond.

NOTES

1. Applied Survey Research, UCLA, January 2006, Los Angeles Homeless Services count—January 2005.

2. Ibid.

3. Officially called Central City East, Skid Row is usually defined as the area bounded by Third and Seventh to the north and south, and Main and Alameda Streets west and east.

4. According to Perry Johnson, assistant program director, Downtown Mental Health Center, 2000.

5. Study by Shelter Partnership 2000, quoted in the *Los Angeles Times,* July 8, 2000.

6. Unpublished survey conducted by Midnight Mission and Chrysalis, 2004.

7. Figures are based on a presentation by Chief Justice Chuck Jackson, head, Los Angeles Sheriff's Correctional Division at a Central City Association meeting, October 15, 2004.

8. Section 5150 of what is known as the Lanterman-Petris-Short Act that took effect January 1, 1969.

Part IX:
Reevaluating the Past and Anticipating Future Adventures

A wise person once said, "Life is an adventure to be lived, not a problem to be solved." Noted downtown leader and expert Paul Levy offers a perspective on this "adventure of a lifetime," taking the long-term view, and not only examining the history of downtowns and business districts but peering into the future as well. As the reader concludes this section and this book, we hope that he or she realizes what an adventure awaits the downtown practitioner.

Chapter 38

Looking Backward, Looking Forward: The Future of Downtowns and Business Districts

Paul Levy

LOOKING BACKWARD

In 1954 when the International Downtown Executives Association (IDEA) first formed, American downtowns were in decline but not many knew it. Department stores bustled with shoppers and sponsored huge holiday festivals. Historic "movie palaces" still appealed to broad audiences in an era before films and theaters were segmented to suit demographic niches. Commuters streamed in by trolley, bus, and train, choosing, in larger cities, from as many as four local newspapers. Nearby factories made clothes, hats, radios, locomotives, trucks, and cars, refined sugar, and processed steel. Longshoremen still lugged cargo from freighters on central waterfronts.

Yet beneath the surface, profound forces were at work. Since 1934, when the Federal Housing Administration first introduced the long-term, fixed-rate mortgage, vast portions of central cities had been denied credit through institutionalized redlining. Trucks and cars, which were mass-produced since the 1920s, freed industry from dependence on railroads and rivers, thus altering commuting patterns and the location of jobs. Still, in the 1930s, America's central cities held over 50 percent of their region's manufacturing jobs.

At the close of World War II, following fifteen years of the Depression and wartime scarcity, demand for consumer goods soared in a tidal wave of production and consumption. In the 1920s and 1930s home building was a small, family business. The average builder produced three and a half houses per year. In 1944, there were 114,000 housing starts in the United States. In 1946, this figure jumped to 937,000, and by 1950, it nearly doubled again to 1.7 million starts. At the same time, the housing business

doi:10.1300/5137_39

turned into mass production with 10 percent of all builders—led by giants such as Arthur Levitt—producing 70 percent of all units.[1] With redlining firmly entrenched, most building was in the suburbs. The pattern prevailed throughout the 1950s with an average of 1.5 million housing starts per year.[2]

Chicago provides a typical example: In 1927, 74 percent of new houses in the region were built in the city, 26 percent in the suburbs. By 1954, the proportions reversed: only 28 percent of private market units were built in the city, 72 percent in the suburbs.

In the mid 1950s department stores made their first tentative moves to follow the market to the suburban fringe, offering free parking and climate-controlled walkways. Between 1955 and 1977, 15,000 regional shopping centers were built in the United States, all in the suburbs. In 1945, central business districts (CBD) still accounted for 30 percent of regional retail sales. By 1975, CBD market share had plummeted to 11 percent. By 1984, the nation's 20,000 large shopping centers accounted for almost two-thirds of all retail trade.[3] Television replaced newspapers and movie theaters as a source for news and entertainment.

In 1956, the National Interstate and Defense Highways Act provided 80 percent federal funding for a freeway system that altered the demography of the United States. Giant ring roads around regions expanded the commuting zone and laid foundations for the "edge cities" of the 1970s. Cheap fuel and inexpensive air-conditioning opened up the South and the West to new development.

By the presidential election of 1960, candidates were actively courting a new generation of suburban voters as housing abandonment plagued a growing number of inner cities. African Americans were migrating in large numbers out of a still-segregated South to cities in the Northeast around the Great Lakes, and to California. Downtowns and older manufacturing neighborhoods were showing distinct signs of wear and tear and the federal government was promising help through urban renewal. By the late 1960s, years of discontent, declining opportunity, and racial animosity exploded into a wave of urban riots that accelerated middle class and business flight, reinforcing a negative image of cities.

Across the country, business leaders and major property owners had been forming downtown associations out of concern for the well-being of their central business districts. In September 1954, delegates from thirty cities came together in Chicago to form the International Downtown Executives Association. The following September, they held their first conference in Memphis.

By the 1970s, downtown business and political leaders were laying foundations for the current renaissance. New office towers, downtown shopping

centers, urban hospitals and universities, reclaimed waterfronts, and renovated historic neighborhoods were building blocks of the revival.

Demography, federal mortgage insurance, historic rehabilitation tax
credits, and rising energy costs helped as well. A significant portion of the
baby boom generation was trained in universities and hospitals whose expansion in cities was facilitated by urban renewal. When they bought their
first homes, many decided to stay in the city and benefited, after 1968, from
the end of mortgage red lining. The 1976 bicentennial celebrations prompted a new appreciation for urban history and architecture, and, at least until
1984, federal tax credits made it feasible to renovate heritage buildings. An
unintended consequence of the Oil Embargo of the early 1970s was the discovery by some that it was not only cheaper, but healthier to walk to work.

LOOKING AT TODAY

Fast-forward fifty years from the founding of IDEA and our downtowns
are clean and safe. New convention centers, multiplex theaters, concert
halls, sports arenas, and music and art museums are joining office buildings
and hotels as generators of downtown activity. Derelict waterfronts have
been converted into parks, boating marinas, housing complexes, and retail
pavilions. Vacant factories are being transformed into lofts and apartments.
High-rise towers and new, urbanist townhouses fill vacant industrial storage
and railroad yards. Hi-tech light rail systems carry commuters; restored
trolleys entertain tourists. Young people and empty nesters are flocking to
cities, valuing architecture, nightlife, and the pleasures of walking to work.
Like canaries in a mineshaft, the resurgence of sidewalk cafes have become
a sign of cities on the rebound. Even television, which still revels too much
in mayhem and operating-room gore, features hip and fashionable young
people living and loving in cool urban lofts, strolling without fear on
charming city streets.

LOOKING FORWARD

History can be humbling. Those running downtown organizations today
bask in the reflected glory of a decade of revival. To be sure, business improvement districts, downtown membership organizations, and transportation management associations deserve credit for nurturing the revival of life
on the street. Yet we are also heirs to decades of improvements not of our
making and of demographic and economic trends beyond our control. Just
as few pedestrians strolling on city sidewalks in 1954 saw the handwriting

on the wall, profound forces are working beneath the surface today to reshape cities and regions.

The Internet

False alarms do happen. Sometime in the 1990s, the Internet was supposed to make cities obsolete. Technology workers would camp with laptops under beach umbrellas or at new Walden Ponds. Downtowns would wither on the vine. Digital and cellular technology has blurred the boundaries between home, vacation, and work. You no longer need be in the office to review documents, or to make decisions or deals. As one tech-savvy CEO pompously declared, "Headquarters is wherever I am!"

As Moss and Townsend documented, miles of fiberoptic cable have only reinforced the centrality of certain markets with the vast majority of information ports being located in or nearby downtown central business districts.[4] In retrospect, the logic is obvious: the competing firms that wired most regions in the 1990s pursued economies of scale, seeking zones with very dense clusters of office customers. Old urban factories proved extraordinarily durable and adaptable as telecom hotels, just as abutting nineteenth-century rail lines offered unobstructed routes for fiber-optic cable. The Internet didn't turn regions inside out, making impoverished farm towns booming technology hubs. Rather, it reinforced market trends. "Telecommunications infrastructure," note the authors, "can make competitive places globally competitive, but can never make uncompetitive places competitive."

Office Sprawl

Nonetheless, jobs are decentralizing in the United States. A May 2001 Brookings Institution study notes that as late as 1950, "the typical city still had a high density core where most people worked," though a majority of Americans already lived in the suburbs and commuted by car.[5] By the mid 1990s, a study of 100 metropolitan areas found only twenty-two percent of employees still working within three miles of the city center.[6]

Another Brookings examination of thirteen of nation's largest metropolitan markets notes: "The suburbs, which began the post-war years as clear commercial subordinates to central cities, ended the century at near parity." As late as 1979, 74 percent of office space was still located in central cities and only 26 percent was in suburbs. By 1999, "the central city share of office space dropped to 58 percent while the suburban share grew to 42 percent." Office buildings were still being added downtown in the thirteen largest metropolitan markets. Although central city inventory grew by 112 percent between 1979 and 1999, suburban inventory leaped by 305 percent.[7]

These trends are likely to continue. "Two-thirds of the nation's current office stock in the largest office markets was built since 1980," notes Lang. "Almost four-fifths (79 percent) of the current suburban stock was added in the same period."[8] Quite simply, the suburbs have a greater supply of up-to-date inventory and as long as their occupancy costs are cheaper and their parking free, they will exercise a powerful draw on a growing number of publicly traded companies, governed not by loyalty to place, but by the bottom line.

Look ahead a few decades though, and possibilities abound. In this high-speed age, today's innovation becomes tomorrow's obsolescence. Many older office buildings in downtown markets have new life as apartments or hotels. Being in the midst of a vibrant downtown has enormous appeal to college graduates, empty nesters, and tourists. Exuberant 1920s office architecture and the high ceilings and large windows of industrial lofts have their own distinct charm. Will low-rise, spec-built, suburban office campuses find similar reuse when their buildings pass their prime? Will downtowns in the next decade put enough state-of-the-art inventory into the pipeline to regain office market share?

The Implications of 9/11

Given the disturbing trends following the terrorist attacks of September 11, 2001, downtowns may not regain office market share. The obvious signs are jersey or concrete barriers blocking buildings and monuments, new screening procedures for corporate office and sports facilities, fear of locating in tall, "signature" buildings, and the push to deconcentrate employees of professional services firms.[9] Yet beneath the surface, there may be a more profound shift in policing strategies, as counterterrorism concerns come to the fore.

The extraordinary growth of BIDs in the United States since the 1980s coincided with and stood on the shoulders of a significant shift in public policing strategies. In response to corruption and organized crime in the 1930s, American police departments after World War II downplayed the traditional cop on the beat. Seeking to professionalize, agencies placed officers into cars, rotated them frequently between sectors, and focused on the Federal Bureau of Investigation's (FBI) list of serious, *part one,* crimes (murder, rape, arson, and armed theft).

Urban disorders in the 1960s furthered these trends, as departments concentrated resources on highly mobile, tactical teams to be rapidly deployed to scenes of unrest. However, officers behind the windshield of air-conditioned cars, outfitted in riot gear, and rushing between 911 calls, became ever more insulated from communities they were meant to serve.

The countertrend began with a *community policing* experiment in Newark, New Jersey, in the 1970s. As James Q. Wilson and George L Kelling describe in their seminal article, "Broken Windows," when residents actually were asked what they wanted police to focus on, it was *not* the FBI's list of *part one* crimes.[10] No one wanted murderers and arsonists running loose, but they were far more concerned about teenagers drinking on corners, smashing bottles on walls, and intimidating residents walking home from work.

By the mid 1980s, commanding officers in police departments across the country understood that untended broken windows were an open invitation to more adventurous crimes. Moreover, as police made arrests for petty crimes, such as subway turnstile jumping, they caught in their net those wanted for more serious crimes. By paying attention to lower priority, *quality-of-life* infractions, police were able to decrease more serious crimes.

This trend dovetailed with the emergence of BIDs, similarly obsessed with signs of urban incivility: litter, graffiti, and dim lighting. In many cities in the 1990s, community policing and BIDs converged, sometimes, as in Philadelphia, sharing facilities; by working together to address little details, they dramatically altered the bigger picture.

> An epidemic can be reversed, can be tipped, by tinkering with the smallest details of the immediate environment . . . the streets we walk down, the people we encounter play a huge role in shaping who we are and how we act. It isn't just serious criminal behavior that is sensitive to environmental cues, it is all behavior.[11] (Malcolm Gladwell, *The Ti*
>
> pping Point)

Clean, safe, and friendly public spaces, the basics for downtown revival, don't happen automatically. It's a full-time job, funded by thousands of BIDs in North America. BIDs have done their job in concert with law enforcement professionals committed to community policing. Take away this support system, as city police departments focus instead on terrorist threats, and there is not a BID in the world with a budget big enough to fill this void.*

---

*Support for "community policing" has never been unanimous in urban police departments and September 11th may have given new license to those skeptical about the focus on quality-of-life crimes. Even departments focused on *quality-of-life* issues face major budget challenges in the absence of federal support for local counterterrorism efforts.

Fostering the Twenty-Four-Hour Downtown

What is the future of downtowns and central business districts? Once again, it helps to look backward. Travelers abroad understand that "downtown" is a uniquely American term. Outside the United States, *city centre, centre de ville,* or *el centro* are more common. The word "downtown," historian Robert Fogelson explains, emerged first in New York City to describe the extraordinary divergence from the European urban form that occurred in lower Manhattan.[12] After the Civil War, a dense concentration of commercial office and industrial loft buildings began to squeeze residential and other uses out of the business center. With height and land use loosely regulated in the United States, the pressure to cluster, concentrate, and—when steel frame buildings and mechanical elevators allowed—to go ever higher, enabled the creation of the signature American urban skyline.

Europeans sailing into New York harbors in the nineteenth century, were astounded by the "high sierra" of concrete and the "heaven storming audacity" of fifteen-story buildings.[13] "Downtown" gave birth to "uptown," as America's wealthy, unlike their European counterparts, moved away from the noise and crowding at the center of the city. The same process played out in successive decades across the continent as "downtown" evolved from a geographic to a functional term across North America.

Organized downtown groups first emerged in the 1890s. They were comprised of local owners of department stores, banks, utilities, insurance companies, and newspapers—those with a direct stake in the value of downtown real estate. They quickly pushed for public transit—first trolleys, then elevated railroads, then subways—which were powerful magnets to attract public infrastructure investment or to push for special transit assessment districts to meet demand for workers and shoppers.

For every action, there is a reaction. By the early twentieth century through the 1920s, concerns about congestion emerged, along with resentment from other areas of the city and resistance to more subways to serve downtown. In city after city, subways were derailed by antidowntown sentiment. Opposition to fifteen story "gigantic" towers turned into campaigns for height limits. Post–9/11 rhetoric about the perils of high-rises pales in comparison to descriptions, as early as the 1890s, about skyscrapers as "an outrage" creating crowded conditions "in which microbes flourish best . . . as a breeding ground for germs."[14]

By contrast, in the late nineteenth century, most European nations with stronger central governments imposed height limits—"downtowns" never formed. Even more consequential, most American transit systems assumed a "hub-and-spokes" form to serve towering downtowns during rush hours.

By contrast, low-rise European cities built underground transit webs that provided more uniform service both geographically and by time of day.

Fogelson notes the phrase "central business district" (CBD) is an American creation that is reactive in spirit. As the automobile enabled new commercial centers to emerge across metropolitan regions, downtown interests were quick to assert their primacy as *the central* business districts. In the 1920s, downtown groups pushed for parking and traffic regulations to deal with congestion; in the 1940s they lobbied for highways and garages to hold market share. Yet the decentralizing effects of the car were too strong and public funding for transit too scarce. By 1950, most CBDs were in decline.

Fifty years later, America's downtowns are rebounding, Fogelson suggests, because they have reverted from the monoculture of the skyscraper to a European mode in which arts and culture, sports and recreation, and living and working converge to animate a twenty-four-hour city center.[15]

Smart Growth

Downtown organizations should not lose sight of the importance of the commercial office sector. The decentralization of work is neither desirable nor inevitable. "The distribution of new office space," notes Lang, "can help determine the extent to which there is a jobs/housing mismatch in a region. It can also influence the spatial mismatch between economic opportunity and minority households."[16] A study of employment trends in Philadelphia's downtown, for example, finds that the commercial office sector accounts for $1.7 billion in annual wages paid to residents of Philadelphia's neighborhoods, as compared to $368 million generated by the arts, entertainment, and hospitality sectors. Residents of even the most impoverished city neighborhoods, who can rely on public transit to access downtown jobs, receive salaries in the office sector that are 1.4 times greater than the salaries paid to their neighbors who work in arts, entertainment, and hospitality sectors.[17] "If most new office space is constructed at the regional edge," Lang adds, "it may extend commuter sheds for many miles into undeveloped rural areas and thereby fuel sprawl."[18]

Thus, there is a prime imperative for downtown organizations to participate in regional growth, governance, and transportation debates. Some assert that low-density sprawl is inevitable in the automobile age.[19] Glaeser's analysis found "a significant relationship across metropolitan areas between political fragmentation and the degree of job decentralization." In politically fragmented regions, "firms may move to the suburbs to avoid the taxes or governments that are perceived as unfriendly to business in the central city."[20] City/suburban conflicts may play well in local elections, but in an era of global competition, only those regions that work together will succeed.

What the Future Holds

Downtowns in 2054 will not have the dominance they enjoyed in 1954. Even at the edges of London and Paris, American-style office districts have risen far from the historic core. On expressways to airports outside Amsterdam and Madrid, European developers are replicating North American sprawl. The greater use of automobiles is reshaping the topography in all developed nations.

However, North American downtowns can thrive as vital hubs in increasingly polycentric regions.[21] Arts, entertainment, and sporting venues flourish amidst the density that only city centers provide. The most successful convention centers are situated in successful downtowns. Diverse dining options, cultural offerings, historic architecture, hotels, and landmarks are critical components of the burgeoning tourism industry. However (with the exception of Las Vegas), downtowns are not likely to survive as theme parks alone. Visitors to Disney's ersatz Independence Hall in Orlando long ago surpassed those at the authentic one in Philadelphia.

Downtowns must continue to be vital places to work and live. They remain one of the few places in most regions where employees have the freedom to walk to work. When they are well served by public transit, they counter-balance sprawl, provide employers with unequalled access to a regional labor force, and provide public places in which diverse races and cultures interact.

Downtowns can play an increasing role as the setting for colleges and universities, particularly those that encourage internships and continuing education. To the extent that downtowns retain college graduates, young entrepreneurs, and artists, they will remain centers for creativity and innovation.

Challenges continue to plague downtown organizations: As more companies are publicly traded, or directed from headquarters outside the region, fewer captains of industry are willing or able to play the old-style civic role. Leadership thus devolves to a more diverse group, power becomes diffuse, and strategic alliances with other civic groups must be the norm. The CEOs of BIDs and downtown associations must engage at a regional scale, but remain both keepers of the vision of what downtown can be and implementers of initiatives to make it a reality. Working with elected officials, business, and nonprofit leaders requires creativity, a willingness to take risks, patience and persistence, diplomacy, and tact.

NOTES

1. Barry Checkoway, "Large Builders, Federal Housing Programs and Postwar Suburbanization" *International Journal of Urban and Regional Research,* IV, 1980.

2. The story of postwar suburbanization is told best in Kenneth Jackson, *Crabgrass Frontier: The Suburbanization of the United States,* (1985), Oxford University Press, New York.

3. Ibid, 259.

4. Mitchell L. Moss and Anthony Townsend, "Moving information in the twenty-first century city" in *Moving People, Goods, and Information in the Twenty-First Century City* (2004), Richard E. Hanley, Ed. (Routledge, New York).

5. Edward L. Glaeser, "Job Sprawl: Employment Location in U.S. Metropolitan Areas" Brookings Institution, May 2001, p. 1.

6. Robert E. Lang, "Office Sprawl: The Evolving Geography of Business" Brookings Institution, October 2000.

7. Ibid.

8. Ibid, p. 3.

9. A July 2003 survey of thirty-three big U.S. companies by the Conference Board notes however, that despite these highly visible signs, spending on security had increased only 4 percent—and most of this took the form of higher insurance premiums. Reported in *The Economist,* August 23, 2003.

10. James Q. Wilson and George L. Kelling, "Broken Windows: The Police and Neighborhood Safety" *The Atlantic,* March 1982, pp. 29-38.

11. Malcolm Gladwell, *The Tipping Point,* (2002), Back Bay Books, pp. 146, 168.

12. Robert Fogelson, *Downtown: Its Rise and Fall, 1880-1950,* (2003), Yale University Press, New Haven.

13. Ibid, pp. 137-138.

14. Ibid, p. 125.

15. Ibid, pp. 183-217.

16. Lang, p. 2.

17. *A Strategy for the Office Sector,* Center City District, 2003, available online at www.centercityphila.org.

18. Lang, p. 2.

19. Gerald A. Carlino, "From Centralization to Deconcentration: People and Jobs Spread Out," *Business Review,* November/December 2000, Federal Reserve Bank of Philadelphia.

20. Glaeser, p. 7.

21. Lang notes that by 1999 only New York and Chicago's central business districts held a majority of their region's commercial office space.

Index

Page numbers followed by the letter "e" indicate exhibits; those followed by the letter "f" indicate figures; and those followed by the letter "t" indicate tables.

Accessibility
    delivery and trash collection vehicle, 184
    urban design and, 174
Accountability
    parking management, 229-231
    safe and clean program, 170
Accounting systems
    explanation of, 65-66
    setting up, 72
Activity diversity, 173
Advocacy
    consensus and, 124-125
    downtown plan and, 125-126
    for homeless individuals, 253-254
    organizational structure and, 124
    overview of, 123-124
    transportation system, 203-204
Affiliate organizations, 85-86
Affordable housing, 287
Albany, New York, 29-30
Alcoholism, 52. *See also* Social behavior problems; Substance abuse
Allentown Downtown Improvement District Authority, 85
American Civil Liberties Union (ACLU), 405, 406
Americans with Disabilities Act (ADA), 87
Anchorage Downtown Partnership, 118, 119, 122
Ann Arbor Downtown Development Authority, 177-178
Annual programs, 85
Arcadia Creek Plan (Kalamazoo, Michigan), 376-378, 382, 385, 387

Association for Portland Progress (APP), 164, 165, 167
Association of Town Centre Management (United Kingdom), 351
Athens, Georgia, 188-189
Atlanta, Georgia, 15-16
Audits, 71
Aveiro, Portugal, 362

Baby boomers, 181-182
Back-office operations, 271
Baltimore, Maryland, 13, 118-119
Barnett, Johnathan, 174
Benchmarks
    for measuring human service partnerships, 256-257
    for parking programs, 231
Benecke, Bob, 329
Bicycles, 199
BIDs. *See* Business improvement districts (BIDs)
Bike lanes, 196
Birmingham, Great Britain, 352
Blackson, Howard M., III, 181
Blanchard, Ken, 28
Boards of directors
    changes affecting, 17
    conflicts of interest and, 46-47
    diversity initiatives and, 113-114
    overview of, 45
    reporting requirements and, 69, 72
    submission of work plans to, 98
Boise, Idaho, 241-242
Bonds, tax-exempt, 336
Bookkeeping systems, 72

Borgess Hospital (Kalamazoo), 377, 379
Boston, Massachusetts, 277
Bradley, Richard, 379
Brand, vision versus, 24-25
Bratton, Bill, 408
Bronson Methodist Hospital (Kalamazoo), 377, 379
Bryant Park Management Corporation (New York City), 173
Bryant Park Restoration Corporation (New York City), 173
Budgets
    preparation of, 67-68, 72
    for retail marketing plans, 144-146
Buildings
    appearance of, 171
    renovation of, 183
Bus systems, 195-196
Business districts
    change impacting, 7-8
    diversification of, 7-8
    transportation management and, 193-204
Business improvement districts (BIDs)
    assessments and, 66-67
    clean and safe programs and, 163-170
    creating vision for, 29-30
    economic development for, 269-282
    establishment of, 11-12, 116, 418
    homelessness and, 404-405
    human resource issues and, 57-62
    in Ireland, 353-355
    management of, 37, 58-59
    membership organizations and, 117-118
    programming and, 130
    in Serbia, 348-350
    in South Africa, 345-348
    statistics regarding, 62, 116
    in United Kingdom, 350-353
Business Improvement Districts (Urban Land Institute and International Downtown Association), 116
Business retention strategies, 278-279
Bypass roads, 195, 196

Calgary Downtown Association (Canada), 85
Canada
    economic development and tax policy in, 334-337
    homelessness in, 341-342
    housing in, 340-341
    profile of cities in, 337-340
    statistics related to, 333-334
    transportation in, 342-343
Canada Mortgage and Housing Corporation (CMHC), 340
Candy, Denys, 25
Carl Walker, Inc., 219
Cash flow management, 68
Caucus Task Force on Urban Issues (Canada), 337-338
Cause promotions, 85
CCTV. See Closed-circuit television (CCTV)
Cedillo, Gill, 408
Center-city neighborhoods, 19
Central Atlanta Progress, 12
Central Dallas Association, 38, 208, 212
Central Dallas/Transportation Management Association (CD/TMA), 210, 212
Central Houston, Inc., 251
Central Johannesburg Partnership (CJP) (South Africa), 345-348
Certified Administrator of Public Parking (CAPP), 224
Chambers of commerce
    relations with, 49-50
    revitalization programs and, 367-368
Change
    causes of, 15-16
    leadership to manage, 13
Charlotte Center City Partners, 84
Chicago, Illinois, 285, 286f, 414
Chief executive officers (CEOs)
    changes affecting, 17
    characteristics of, 76
    compensation for, 77, 78t
    survey data on, 75-76
Chretien, Jean, 337
Circulator bus systems, 196-197, 203
City councils, 329

Civic Ventures/Boettcher Permanent Endowment Fund (Downtown Denver Partnership), 86
Clean programs
  accountability and, 170
  explanation of, 163-165
  ordinances and, 169-170
  for parking areas, 232-233
Cleveland, Ohio, 249, 294
Cloar, James, 124
Closed-circuit television (CCTV)
  in Ireland, 354
  in South Africa, 347-348
Coimbra, Portugal, 362
Coleman, Cathy, 122, 124
Colleges. *See* Universities/colleges
Collins, Jim, 57
Colorado Housing Authority, 85
Communication
  human service partnerships and, 251-252
  membership benefits and, 120
  parking programs and, 227-228
Communities
  data collection on, 299
  involvement in parking programs, 221-222
Community courts, 167, 246-247
Community development corporations (CDCs), 86
Community Development Districts (CIDs) (Saint Louis), 38, 39
Commuter buses, 195, 196
Compensation, 77, 78t
Competition, 300
Conflicts of interest, 46-47
Consultants
  choosing, 264-265
  interviewing, 263-264
Costwold Project (Houston), 176-177
Crime prevention through environmental design (CPTED), 225-226
Cultural institutions, 133
Cunningham, Storm, 7
Custom transportation services, 202-203
Customer service, for parking systems, 237-238
Customers
  data collection in, 299
  downtown perceptions of, 313-314

Dallas, Texas, 208-213
Dallas Downtown Partnership, 208
Dallas Police Department, 208-209
Dana, Mo, 87
Data analysis, 303-304
Data collection
  methods for, 302-303
  for retail recruitment plan, 298-303
Dayton, Ohio, 275, 278, 280
DC BID (Washington, D.C.), 255
Decision making
  by consensus, 47-48
  strategies for, 48-49
Decision matrix, 48
Delray Beach, Florida, 185-186
Democracy in America (Tocqueville), 123
Denver, Colorado, 38, 39f, 86, 117-119, 121, 122
Denver Civic Ventures, 38
The Denver Partnership, 38, 39f
Des Moines Arts Festival, 87
Development, of business districts, 8
Development/redevelopment projects
  choosing consultants for, 264-265
  goal-setting for, 261-262
  interviewing consultants for, 263-264
  requests for proposals for, 262-263
  submissions for, 263
Diversity
  downtown organizations and, 110-111
  overview of, 109-110
Diversity initiatives
  board of director actions for, 113-114
  future management of, 114
  goals and objectives for, 112-113
  inclusion benefits and, 111-112
  strategies to promote, 112
Downtown: Its Rise and Fall, 1880-1950 (Fogelson), 283
Downtown Albany BID, 29-30
Downtown Alliance (New York City)
  community assistance and, 396-399
  retailers and, 395-396, 399-400
  September 11 attack and, 391-395, 400-401
  World Trade Center site development and, 398-399

Downtown Austin Alliance, 118
Downtown Billings, Montana,
    Association, 119
Downtown Cleveland Partnership, 249
Downtown Crossing Association
    (Boston), 277
Downtown Dayton Partnership (DDP),
    275, 278
Downtown DC Business Improvement
    District, 187-188, 255
Downtown Denver Partnership, 38, 85,
    86, 117-119, 121, 122
Downtown development authorities
    (DDAs), 36, 37
Downtown Havberhill, Massachusetts,
    Partnership, 279
Downtown Kalamazoo Inc. (DKI), 377,
    378
Downtown Lexington Corporation,
    118-119, 121-122, 251
Downtown management associations
    (DMAs)
    assessments and, 66-67
    audits and, 71
    budget preparation and, 67-68
    cash flow and, 68
    expenses and, 68-69
    financial reporting requirements
        and, 69
    internal controls and, 70-71
    overview of, 65-66
    reporting to board and, 72
    resource raising by, 81-92
    revenue and, 68
    staffing and, 72-73
Downtown membership programs
    benefits and services of, 118-120
    BIDs and, 117-118
    recruitment and retention for,
        120-121
    trends in, 121-122
Downtown Norfolk Council, 121, 122,
    124
Downtown organizations
    advocacy role of, 123-126
    changes in structure of, 18-19
    consensus decisions and, 47-49
    diversity and, 110-111
    future outlook for, 415-421

Downtown organizations *(continued)*
    historical background of, 35-37,
        115, 116, 414-415
    issue management and, 51-52
    management of, 45-47
    membership programs and, 117-122
    relationship issues facing, 49-51
    revenue sources for, 79
    smart growth and, 420-421
    staffing patterns for, 78-79
    transportation management and,
        198-204
    Web sites for, 119-120
Downtown Partnership of Baltimore,
    118-119
Downtown Phoenix Partnership, 249
Downtown programming
    areas of, 131
    background of, 129
    concierge, 137
    creating history and heritage, 134
    fundamentals of, 130
    new business, 136
    promoting cultural institutions as
        anchors, 133
    promoting merchants as celebrities,
        132
    special events, 135
    working toward a 24/7 downtown,
        135-136
Downtown redevelopment projects
    conflicts in, 326-327
    overview of, 325
    political problems associated with,
        327-330
Downtown retail committees,
    background of, 49-51
Downtown Saint Louis Partnership, 39,
    40f, 41, 42n
Downtown Seattle Association, 208,
    250
Downtown Services Center (DSC)
    (Washington, DC), 250, 255
Downtown Spokane Partnership, 117,
    118, 122
Downtown St. Louis, Inc., 38-41
Downtown Tomorrow Incorporated
    (DTI) (Kalamazoo), 378

Downtowns
    changes in, 15
    documenting drawing power of,
        314-315
    as historic transportation hubs,
        193-194
    office sprawl and, 416-417
    one-of-a-kind areas in, 321-323
    in small- and medium-sized cities,
        373-374
    strengths and weaknesses of, 312,
        419
    twenty-four hour, 419-420
    urban transportation and, 194-198
    usage and customer perceptions of,
        313-314
Dream Come True Downtown 500
    (Allentown Downtown
    Improvement District
    Authority), 85
Drop-in centers, 249-250
Dublin, Ireland, 353-355
Dublin City Business Association
    (DCBA) (Ireland), 353, 354

E-newsletters, 151-153, 152e
E-ZPass, 211
Economic activity centers, 15-16
Economic development
    BIDs and, 272-276, 280-282
    business retention strategies and,
        278-280
    in Canada, 334-337
    change and, 15
    data needs for, 273
    downtown programs and, 270-272
    explanation of, 269-270
    housing and, 271, 285
    start-up and expansion businesses
        and, 276-277
Economic development organizations,
    50, 51
Edwards, Michael, 120, 122
Egress, 199
Electronic brochures, 153-154
Electronic marketing
    active, 151-154
    guerilla marketing and, 158-159

Electronic marketing *(continued)*
    maximizing web site potential and,
        156-158
    passive, 154-156
Emergency shelters, 249
Employees. *See also* Staffing
    contracting for, 57-58
    disciplinary action for, 62
    evaluation of, 60-61
    with financial management
        responsibilities, 72-73
    motivation of, 61
    quality of, 58-60
    training for, 60
Employment
    industrial development and types of,
        271
    start-up and expansion businesses
        and, 276-277
Employment law, 61, 62
Endowments, 86
Europe, 336-337
European Regional Development Fund
    (ERDF), 336
Executive directors, 17
Expenses
    management of, 68-69
    monitoring of, 69-70
The Experience Economy (Pine &
    Filmore), 219
Expert opinion panels, 48

Facades, appearance of, 171
Facilities maintenance programs,
    232-235
Fair, Square and Legal (Weiss), 61
Faith community, 253
Fare box revenue, 198
FDNY, 393
Federal Historic Tax Incentives
    Program, 290
Federal National Mortgage
    Association, 202
Ferdinand, Spencer, 330
Fignole, M. C. Joelle, 111
Finance committees, 67
Financial management
    assessments and, 66-67
    audits and, 71
    budget preparation and, 67-68

Financial management *(continued)*
  for business districts, 8
  cash flow and, 68
  expenses and, 68-70
  internal controls and, 70-71
  parking programs and, 228-229
  reporting requirements and, 69
  reporting to board and, 72
  revenue and, 68
  staffing and, 72-73
  transportation and, 197-198
Financial records, 69
First of America Bank Corp., 377, 379
Fisher, Roger, 19
501(c)3 organizations, 86
Florida, 36, 37
Florida, Richard, 7
Fogelson, Robert, 283, 420
Fort Collins, Colorado, 242
Foundations, 86. *See also* Philanthropic
  organizations/foundations;
  Resource raising
From Good to Great (Collins), 57

GAAP (generally accepted accounting
  principles), 72
Gabler, Ted, 38
Garden City, New York, 329
Gehl, Jan, 172
Generation W, 182
Getting to Yes (Fisher), 19
Gilmore, J., 130, 219
Giuliani, Rudolph, 397
Goals
  staff analysis of, 97
  strategies to achieve, 100
  for work plans, 97-98
Governance
  achieving consensus and, 47-49
  conflicts of issues and, 46-47
  issue management and, 51-52
  leadership issues and, 53-55
  overview of, 45
  relations between organizations and,
    49-51
Government grants. *See also* Resource
  raising
  closing deals for, 89-90
  information sources on, 92
  resource raising with, 82, 83

Graffiti, 164-165, 168
Grand Junction, Colorado, 277
Grants, 82, 83, 91, 92. *See also*
  Resource raising
Grinker, Bill, 395
Ground Zero Task Force (New York),
  396
Guerilla marketing, 158-159

Haverhill Partnership, 279
Highways, 195, 196
Homeless Coalition of the Gulf Coast,
  248, 256
Homelessness. *See also* Social behavior
  problems
  availability of affordable housing
    and, 288
  behavioral problems related to, 163,
    245
  in Canada, 341-342
  communication issues and, 251-252
  human services partnership
    approach to, 247-248,
    252-259
  long-term assistance for, 250-251
  in Los Angeles, 403-409
  outreach and networking to address,
    248-249
  shelter and supportive services for,
    249-250
Hospitality management
  examples of, 185-189
  explanation of, 179, 180
  issues in, 182-185, 189-190
  trends in, 180-181
  2020 vision and, 181-182
Housing. *See also* Residential
  development
  affordable, 287
  in Canada, 337, 340-341
  design of, 289-290, 291f, 292
  economic development and, 271,
    285
  historical background of, 283-285,
    413-414
  rental, 287
  transitional and supportive, 250-251
Houston, Texas, 176-177

Human resources
    contracting for staff and, 57-58
    employee motivation and, 61
    employee quality and, 58-61
    employment law and, 61-62
    policy review of, 62-63
    role of, 57
Human service partnerships. *See*
    Partnerships

IDA. *See* International Downtown
    Association (IDA)
IDA Leadership Forum 2004, 38
Image, 140
Inclusion, 111-112
info.com, 88
Ingress, 199
Internal controls, 70-71
International Downtown Association
    (IDA)
    background of, 35-37
    BIDs and, 116
    function of, 109-110
    information available through, 73
    Kalamazoo Mall and, 379
    membership in, 117
    staffing structure survey, 75-79
    Technical Assistance Team, 408
    2003 Strategic Plan, 112
International Downtown Executives
    Association (IDEA), 35, 36,
    413. *See also* International
    Downtown Association (IDA)
International Events Group (IEG), 84,
    88
International Festival and Events
    Association (IFEA), 84
International Parking Institute (IPI),
    224
Internet, 416. *See also* Electronic
    marketing; Web sites
Ireland, 353-355
Issue management, 51-52
Ithaca, New York, 276, 277, 281
Ithaca, New York, Downtown
    Partnership (IDP), 276

Jacobs, Jane, 173
Job placement programs, 250
Job training programs, 250
Johannesburg City Council (South
    Africa), 346
Johannesburg Development Agency
    (JDA) (South Africa), 345-346

Kagiso Trust (South Africa), 347
Kagiso Urban Management (KUM),
    347, 348
Kalamazoo, Michigan
    downtown revitalization in, 376-380
    overview of, 374-376
Kalamazoo Community Foundation,
    384, 386
Kalamazoo Mall, 379, 380, 385
Kalamazoo Project Downtown
    challenges for, 388
    collaboration in, 386
    elements of, 380-383
    organizations involved in, 384-386
    results of, 387
    stakeholders in, 383-384
Kalamazoo Public Library, 377, 379, 381
Kalamazoo Valley Community
    College, 377
Kalamazoo Valley Museum, 379, 381
Kellar, Robert, 25
Kelling, George L., 418
Kirshenbaum Bond & Partners, 397
Krusevac, Serbia, 349

Lang, Robert E., 420
Leadership
    for business districts, 8
    challenges of, 15-17
    changes in political, 53-55, 55t
    changes in private sector, 53, 54t
    as collective and cooperative
        undertaking, 13
    demands for, 12
    historical background of, 12
    homegrown, 16
    importance of, 11-12
    to initiate and manage change, 13,
        17-21

Lexington, Kentucky, 118-119,
    121-122, 251
*The Life and Death of Great American
    Cities* (Jacobs), 173-174
Light rail, 52, 195, 196
LISTSERVs, 153-154, 252
Little Rock Downtown Partnership, 119
Liverpool, Great Britain, 352-353
Local development corporations
    (LDCs), 281
Local elected officials, 16
Local governments, 16
Location-efficient mortgages, 202
Lopez, Steve, 409
Los Angeles, California
    American Civil Liberties Union and,
        405, 406
    BIDs in, 404-405
    disorderly behavior in, 407
    homeless individuals in, 403-409
    outreach teams in, 406-407
    Personal Possession Check-In
        Facility in, 405-406
    residential development in, 407-408
Los Angeles Homeless Services
    Authority (LHASA), 409
Lower Manhattan. *See* Downtown
    Alliance (New York City)
Lower Manhattan Development
    Corporation, 397-398
Lower Manhattan Small Business and
    Workforce Retention Project,
    395
Lucas, Rose, 121

Macro marketing, 145
Mall Management District (Denver), 38
Management, 8. *See also* Financial
    management
Manchester, Great Britain, 352
Mariani, Rick, 328
Market rate rental housing, 287
Market segments, targeting, 142-144
Marketing
    developing calendar for, 146-148
    electronic, 151-159
    guerilla, 158-159
    macro versus micro, 145e
    parking system, 236
    retail, 139-149

Media
    homelessness and, 254
    relations with, 20
    resource raising using, 84
Mediators, 49
Memphis, Tennessee, 36
Memphis Center City Commission, 84,
    125
Mental health outreach, 169
Mental illness, 245, 403. *See also*
    Homelessness; Social
    behavior problems
Merchants, 132
MetroTech BID (Brooklyn, New
    York), 125
Miami, Florida, 37
Micro marketing, 145
Millennials, 182
Milosevic, Slobodon, 349
Mission, 50, 97
Mobile, Alabama, 256
Multnomah County, Oregon, 167
Municipal parking garages, 207
Murray, Glen, 339

Nacci, Ken, 382, 383
Nadler, Jerrold, 396
National Interstate and Defense
    Highways Act of 1956, 193,
    414
Neighborhood-based Prosecution
    Program (Portland, Oregon),
    167-168
Networking
    attracting members through, 121
    in human service partnerships,
        248-249
    redevelopment projects and, 329
New Orleans, Louisiana, Downtown
    Development District in, 36
New York, New York, 71, 167, 173,
    248, 250. *See also* Downtown
    Alliance (New York City)
Nis, Serbia, 349
Noise, 185
Nonprofit organizations, 253
Norfork State University (NSU) Social
    Research Center, 75
Norris, Donald M., 111

North Texas Council of Governments, 213
North Texas Tollway Authority (NTTA), 211, 213
NYPD, 391-393, 395, 399

Office sector, 271
Office sprawl, 416-417
One-of-a-kind facilities, 321-323
Open spaces, 172
Ordinances
  dealing with social behavior problems, 246
  invalidation of, 169-170
Organizational structure
  advocacy and, 124
  background of, 35-36
  changes in, 18-19
  considerations for development of, 41-43
  Downtown St. Louis and, 38-41, 40f, 42f
  evolving responses to, 36-37
  expanding missions and, 37-38
  models of complex, 38
  of parking organization, 222-224
  simple, 36
Osborne, David, 38
Outreach, 248-249
Owner market rate housing, 287

Panhandling, 168-169
Park-and-ride lots, 208
Parking meters, 207, 210
Parking/parking areas
  analysis of, 198
  business issues related to, 212-213
  design of, 174, 208
  example of improvement to, 210-214
  expansion opportunities for, 213
  on- and off-street, 195, 196
  proactive strategies for, 209-210
  proven options for, 207-208
  safety and security issues for, 183, 207-209, 225-227

Parking programs
  case examples of, 241-242
  communication for, 227-228
  community involvement in, 221-222
  competitive environment and, 240
  consolidated, 228
  customer service for, 237-238
  enforcement of, 239
  facilities maintenance for, 232-235
  financial planning for, 228-229
  management of, 224-225, 229-231, 243
  operational efficiency for, 231-232
  organization of, 222-224
  philosophy regarding, 218-220
  planning tenets for, 220-221
  policy decisions regarding, 215-217
  safety, security, and risk management for, 225-227
  special events, 238-239
  staff development and, 224-225
  technology use for, 235-236
  transportation demand management and, 240
  vision and mission for, 217-218
Parking system marketing, 236
Parking validation programs, 208
Partner organizations, 85-86
Partnerships
  advantages of, 258-259
  benchmarks for, 256-257
  communication tools for, 251-252
  explanation of, 247-248
  goals for, 254-255
  long-term assistance and, 250-251
  measurement standards for, 257
  organizations involved in, 252-254
  outreach and networking and, 248-249
  reporting outcomes for, 257-258
  resources for information on, 259-260
  shelter and supportive services and, 249-250
  structure of, 255-256
  U.S. cities benefiting from, 336
Pedestrian flow, 199
Pedestrian linkages, 175
Pedestrians, 184
Pegasus Parking, 210-214

Pfizer, 388
Philadelphia Center City District, 84
Philadelphia Technology Alliance, 84
Philanthropic organizations/
    foundations. *See also*
        Resource raising
    closing deals with, 89-90
    information sources on, 91
    revenue raising with, 82, 83
Phoenix, Arizona, 249
Pine, J., 130, 219
Pittsburgh Downtown Partnership, 118
Police departments, 252-253
Political leaders
    changes in, 53-55
    characteristics of, 53, 55t
    redevelopment projects and, 327-330
Portland, Oregon, 164-170, 209, 249
Portland Business Alliance, 164, 167,
        250
Porto, Portugal, 362-363
Portugal
    case studies of commercial urbanism
        in, 362-363
    commercial urbanism in, 358-359
    overview of, 357
    PROCOM and URBCOM programs
        in, 357-363
    urban management strategy
        recommendations for, 363-369
Poverty, in Canada, 342
Private security companies, 165-166
Private sponsorships, 82
PROCOM programs (Portugal), 357-363
Programming. *See* Downtown Albany
        BID
Project Respond (Portland), 249
Property tax, in Canada, 335
Public agencies, 252
Public meetings, 329
Public private partnerships (PPPs), 336,
        337
Public space
    management of, 199
    planning, design and management
        of, 200
Pushcart programs, 277

Quality-of-life ordinances, 246

Rail systems, 195, 196
Ramps, 195, 196
Redevelopment projects. *See*
        Downtown redevelopment
        projects
Reed, Marvin, 328
Regional Plan Association, 327
Reinventing Government (Osborne &
        Gabler), 38
Requests for proposals (RFPs)
    explanation of, 261-262
    method for issuing, 262-263
Residential development. *See also*
        Housing
    affordable housing and, 287-289,
        291f
    amenities to consider in, 289-290
    economic development and, 271,
        285
    historical background of, 283-285
    homelessness and, 407-408
    market rate incentives and, 290
    mixed use and mixed income issues
        and, 290, 292
    prerequisites for, 286-287
    by sector, 287-289
Residential Rehabilitation Assistance
        Program (RRAP) (Canada),
        342
Resource raising. *See also* Revenue
    categories of, 82-83
    explanation of, 81-82
    general examples of, 83-84
    guidelines for closing the deal when,
        89-90
    procedures for, 86-88
    resources for, 90-92
    specific examples of, 84-86
Restaurants, 318
The Restoration Economy
        (Cunningham), 7
Retail, views regarding, 129-130
Retail areas
    assessment of, 312-313, 315-316
    economic development and, 271
    overview of, 293-294, 311-312
Retail marketing plans
    downtown shopping image and, 140
    overview of, 139
    steps in, 140-149

Retail recruitment
    action-plan schedule for, 297-298
    data analysis in, 303-304
    data collection for, 298-303
    planning role for, 296-297
    steps in, 295-296
    strategies for, 304-309
Retail revitalization
    district options for, 305-306
    practical model for, 318-319
    steps in, 312-317
Revenue. *See also* Resource raising
    assessment, 68
    changes affecting, 18
    fare box, 198
    methods for raising, 68
    sources of, 79
Ridesharing, 202
The Rise of the Creative Class
    (Florida), 7
Roadways, 172
Roanoke Foundation for Downtown, 86
Rosenthal, Jack, 395

Safe programs. *See also* Security
    accountability and, 170
    explanation of, 165-166
    ordinances and, 169-170
    special programs enhancing, 166-169
Salaries, for chief executive officers,
    77, 78t
San Diego, California, 186-187
San Diego Homeless Outreach Team,
    248
San Diego Hospitality Resource Panel,
    187
San Jose Downtown Association, 177
Satellite parking lots, 208
Schlack, Marilyn, 385
Seattle, Washington, 170, 208
Security. *See also* Safe programs
    in dining and entertainment districts,
    184
    for parking areas, 183, 207-209,
    225-226
Security programs, 166-168
September 11 terrorist attacks
    events of, 391-395, 400-401
    implications of, 417-418

Serbia, BIDs in, 348-350
Shelters, 249, 250
Shuttle buses, 196-197
Sidewalks
    design of, 171, 174
    function of, 196
    management of, 197
Silicon Valley, California, 288
Smoking bans, 184-185
Social behavior problems. *See also*
    Homelessness
    agencies and organizations assisting
    with, 252-254
    building partnerships to address,
    254-256, 258-259
    collecting information on, 246
    communication tools for, 251-252
    community courts and, 246-247
    homelessness and, 163, 245, 407
    human services strategies and,
    247-248
    long-term assistance and, 250-251
    measuring success in reducing,
    256-258
    outreach and networking and,
    248-249
    overview of, 245
    shelter and supportive services and,
    249-250
South Africa, BIDs in, 345-348
Special events
    parking for, 238-239
    programming for, 135
Sponsors. *See also* Resource raising
    closing deals with, 89-90
    information sources on, 91
    resource raising with, 82, 83
St. James' Place, 251
St. Louis, 38, 39, 40f, 41, 42n
Staff meetings, weekly, 98
Staffing. *See also* Employees
    IDA survey on, 75-76, 78-79
Stamford Downtown Ambassador
    Program, 101e-102e, 103e
Stamford Downtown Special Services
    District (DSSD), 97, 98,
    101e-102e, 102-107, 103e
Stanford, Jeff, 125
Stoner, Jesse, 28

Strategic planning
    benefits of, 96
    explanation of, 96
    internal versus external, 175
    outcomes of, 102-103, 103e
    overview of, 95
    recommendations for, 190-191
    steps in, 96-98
    strategies for, 100
    SWOT analysis and, 100, 102
    work plan creation through, 98-99,
        101e-102e
Street vendor programs, 277
Student information, 84
Substance abuse, 245, 403. *See also*
        Homelessness; Social
        behavior problems
Subway systems, 195, 196
Supporting Communities Partnership
        Initiative (SCPI) (Canada),
        342
Supportive housing, 250-251
Surface streets, 195, 196
SWOT analysis
    explanation of, 98, 99, 99f
    function of, 102

Town Center Management program
        (United Kingdom), 351,
        353-354
Traffic, analysis of, 198
Transit passes, 202
Transit systems, management of, 200,
        202
Transitional housing, 250-251
Transportation
    basic elements of, 194-196
    in Canada, 342-343
    creating choice in, 204-205
    downtowns of future and, 194
    financial issues related to, 197-198
    management of, 196-204
    role of downtown organization in,
        198-204
Transportation demand management,
        240
Transportation Equity Act for the 21st
        Century (TEA-21), 197, 336
Transportation hubs, 193-194
Transportation management
        organizations (TMOs), 200,
        201e
Truman, Harry, 16

Tagging methods, 164
Target markets, 143-144
Tax incentives, 202, 290
Tax increment financing (TIF)
    explanation of, 208, 336
    Kalamazoo and, 377-378
Tax-exempt bonds, 336
Taylor, Terri, 122
Team building, 61
Technical assistance, 279-280
Technical Assistance Team
        (International Downtown
        Association), 408
Technology sector, 271
Tempe, Arizona, 241
Times Square BID, 167
Times Square Consortium, 248, 250
Tocqueville, Alexis de, 123
Tolltag system, 211-213
Tower City (Cleveland), 294

United Kingdom, 350-353
United Kingdom Local Government
        Act 2003, 250
Universities/colleges
    in Canada, 337-340
    downtowns as settings for, 421
The Upjohn Company, 376, 377, 379,
        385
Urban design
    to create sense of place, 176-178
    design and planning process for, 175
    guidelines for, 173-175
    importance of, 172-173
    public realm and, 171
Urban Development Action Grant
        (UDAG), 378
Urban Land Institute (ULI), 116
URBCOM programs (Portugal),
        357-363

Valjevo, Serbia, 349
Vanpool services, 195, 196
Vision
    brand versus, 24-25
    creating a unified, 26-27
    determining future, 27-30
    explanation of, 23
    staff analysis of, 97
Vision-driven downtown organizations
    creation of, 23-25
    past experience and, 27-30
    vision statement and, 25-27
Visitations, 278-279
Visser, James, 376, 378
Volunteer leaders, characteristics of,
    53, 54t

Washington, DC, 187-188
Web sites
    components of, 154-155
    marketing using, 154-155, 156e-157e
    maximizing potential of, 156-157
    obtaining feedback on, 157-158
    updating, 155-156
Weiss, Donald H., 61

Weiss, Michael, 125
West Palm Beach Downtown Business
    and Community Association,
    118, 119
Western Colorado Business
    Development Corporation,
    277
Western Michigan University (WMU),
    388
White, Otis, 18
Whyte, William H., 175
Williamson, Kimberly, 379
Wilson, James Q., 418
Winning with Diversity (Norris &
    Fignole), 111
Winnipeg, Canada, 166
Work plans, 98-99
World Trade Center (New York),
    391-395, 400. *See also*
    Downtown Alliance (New
    York City)
www.ePhiladelphiaInsider.com, 84

Zrenjanin, Serbia, 349, 350

Order a copy of this book with this form or online at:
http://www.haworthpress.com/store/product.asp?sku=5137

MAKING BUSINESS DISTRICTS WORK
Leadership and Management of Downtown, Main Street, Business District, and Community Development Organizations

_____ in hardbound at $54.95 (ISBN-13: 978-0-7890-2390-2; ISBN-10: 0-7890-2390-3)

_____ in softbound at $39.95 (ISBN-13: 978-0-7890-2391-9; ISBN-10: 0-7890-2391-1)

Or order online and use special offer code HEC25 in the shopping cart.

COST OF BOOKS_____

☐ **BILL ME LATER:** (Bill-me option is good on US/Canada/Mexico orders only; not good to jobbers, wholesalers, or subscription agencies.)

☐ Check here if billing address is different from shipping address and attach purchase order and billing address information.

POSTAGE & HANDLING_____
(US: $4.00 for first book & $1.50 for each additional book)
(Outside US: $5.00 for first book & $2.00 for each additional book)

Signature_____

SUBTOTAL_____

☐ **PAYMENT ENCLOSED: $**_____

IN CANADA: ADD 7% GST_____

☐ **PLEASE CHARGE TO MY CREDIT CARD.**

STATE TAX_____
(NJ, NY, OH, MN, CA, IL, IN, PA, & SD residents, add appropriate local sales tax)

☐ Visa ☐ MasterCard ☐ AmEx ☐ Discover
☐ Diner's Club ☐ Eurocard ☐ JCB

Account # _____

FINAL TOTAL_____
(If paying in Canadian funds, convert using the current exchange rate, UNESCO coupons welcome)

Exp. Date_____

Signature_____

Prices in US dollars and subject to change without notice.

NAME_____

INSTITUTION_____

ADDRESS_____

CITY_____

STATE/ZIP_____

COUNTRY_____ COUNTY (NY residents only)_____

TEL_____ FAX_____

E-MAIL_____

May we use your e-mail address for confirmations and other types of information? ☐ Yes ☐ No
We appreciate receiving your e-mail address and fax number. Haworth would like to e-mail or fax special discount offers to you, as a preferred customer. **We will never share, rent, or exchange your e-mail address or fax number.** We regard such actions as an invasion of your privacy.

Order From Your Local Bookstore or Directly From
The Haworth Press, Inc.
10 Alice Street, Binghamton, New York 13904-1580 • USA
TELEPHONE: 1-800-HAWORTH (1-800-429-6784) / Outside US/Canada: (607) 722-5857
FAX: 1-800-895-0582 / Outside US/Canada: (607) 771-0012
E-mail to: orders@haworthpress.com

For orders outside US and Canada, you may wish to order through your local
sales representative, distributor, or bookseller.
For information, see http://haworthpress.com/distributors

(Discounts are available for individual orders in US and Canada only, not booksellers/distributors.)

PLEASE PHOTOCOPY THIS FORM FOR YOUR PERSONAL USE.
http://www.HaworthPress.com

BOF06